Creating a New Reality
In Medicine and Manufacturing

The computer is more than just a number-crunching tool. In everything from animation to high-tech design, computers fuse art and science with super-human speed and accuracy.

Plate 3
CAD/CAM graphics systems have become essential tools in design and manufacturing firms. In a painstaking process similar to creating a physical prototype, designers construct three-dimensional models that can be manipulated and examined on screen. Here an engineer perfects the design on a new Chrysler automobile. (Andrew Sacks/Black Star)

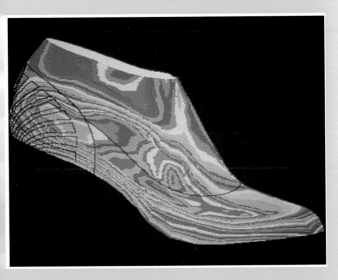

Plate 4
At left is a CAD/CAM image of a shoe design—a multicolored representation indicating stress points and use of a variety of materials. (Jerry Mason/Science Photo Library, Photo Researchers, Inc.)

The
Mystical
Machine
Issues and Ideas
in Computing

The Mystical Machine

Issues and Ideas in Computing

John E. Savage

Susan Magidson

Alex M. Stein

Brown University

⋏ ADDISON-WESLEY PUBLISHING COMPANY

Reading, Massachusetts ▪ Menlo Park, California
Don Mills, Ontario ▪ Wokingham, England ▪ Amsterdam
Sydney ▪ Singapore ▪ Tokyo ▪ Mexico City ▪ Bogotá
Santiago ▪ San Juan

Library of Congress Cataloging-in-Publication Data

Savage, John M.
    The mystical machine.

    Bibliography: p.
    Includes index.
    1. Computers.   2. Electronic data processing.
I. Magidson, Susan.   II. Stein, Alex M.
III. Title.
QA76.M247 1986   001.64   85-6096
ISBN 0-201-06462-6

BCDEFGHIJ-HA-89876

To our families and friends

Preface

This book tells the story of the computer, from its conception in the last century to its applications and implications in the present. It is a story told for those who want an understanding of computers and computing that has both breadth and depth.

Readers as diverse as high school and college students, professionals, and programmers will find that the book provides a wealth of information. It covers a range of topics with a depth that cannot be found in any single book on computers, whether written for novices or for experts. In addition, our treatment of each topic is built on an understanding of basic concepts and principles.

Relying on the forty-year contemporary history of computing, we have organized a book that contains topics fundamental to computer science. These include the history and architecture of the computer, operating systems, problem solving, programming languages, computer graphics, databases, and artificial intelligence. To this list we have added topics and issues that have contemporary practical value, including factory and office automation, the use of computers in education, privacy in the electronic age, electronic spreadsheets, and word processing.

Our book is designed to be read by anyone who wishes to know more about computers. In particular, the book is suitable for a one-semester introductory computer literacy course or as a way to add scope to an introductory programming course. Furthermore, it could be a valuable supplement for computer science and engineering students who may have considerable knowledge of the technical aspects of computing but inadequate exposure to applications and the larger social issues. Our book can also serve as a valuable guide for professionals and owners of personal computers who want a one-text introduction to computers and computing.

This book, in various stages of development, has been used at Brown University for the past two years. Several hundred students have read it as the primary text for a one-semester computer literacy course designed for nonscience majors. The book reflects our belief in the value of both basic knowledge and hands-on experience. Basic knowledge is well suited to a textual medium; hands-on experience is not. For this reason, instructors are urged to illustrate concepts from the text with hands-on exercises appropriate to the equipment they have available.

We have included programming chapters for both BASIC and Pascal to give instructors flexibility in their choice of language. Our treatment of these languages is not a replacement for a good programming manual; rather, it is meant to provide an introduction to programming concepts in these languages. However, these chapters, together with a limited amount of supplementary written material on the peculiarities of the local dialect of Pascal or BASIC and a set of lectures, have been sufficient for students in a computer literacy course at Brown to write four or five programs using concepts as sophisticated as procedures and arrays.

Acknowledgments

This book profited from the assistance of many people. Although we cannot mention all of them, we acknowledge those who were particularly helpful to us. Mark Dalton, Publisher, and Keith Wollman, Sponsoring Editor, of Addison-Wesley provided much encouragement and assistance throughout this project for which we are most grateful. Professors Philip W. Brashear, John A. Cross, Robert D. Cupper, David G. Kay, Kathleen Korb, Doris K. Lidtke, Edwin L. Marsden, Richard C. Maybury, Kevin McGivney, Chris L. Peters, Barbara Ryder, Syed Shababuddin, Karl A. Shump, Jr., Allen Tucker, and Stephen F. Weiss all provided valuable comments on early drafts of the manuscript. The book reflects the care they took on these drafts. Beverly Peavler deserves special mention for the careful editorial work that she has done

throughout the book. Her comments were invaluable in helping us refine the final draft of the manuscript.

We also thank the following individuals for their assistance: Billy
Abrams, Suzanne Andrews, Heidi Auerbach, Marc Brown, Eugene
Charniak, Brian Dalio, Debbi Dalio, Tom Doeppner, Julius Dorfman,
Hunter Dupree, Steve Feiner, John Forton, Ann Graham, Sharon
Grover-Renda, Barrett Hazeltine, Jim Hendler, Chuck Kenoian, Ed La-
magna, Charles de Lantsheere, Micki Magidson, John Maddox, Tom
McAuley, Elizabeth McKinley, Tony Medeiros, Barbara Meier, Norman
Meyrowitz, David Niguidula, David Peterson, Steve Reiss, Andee
Rubin, Leslie Rudnick, Robert Sedgewick, Gerald Shapiro, Robert
Shaw, Donald L. Shirer, Richard Staevely, Paul Tenczar, Stephen W.
Thompson, Valentine Urbanek, Andries van Dam, Peter Wegner, Eric
Wolf, Nicole Yankelovich, and David Zachei. Many others have con-
tributed to this book, reading portions of the manuscript, suggesting
sources for information, testing programs, or offering general support.

Finally, our deepest gratitude goes to our families and friends. Their
support and advice made this book possible.

Brown University   JES
                                                                                            SM
                                                                                            AMS

Contents

◼ Chapter 6   Solving Problems   127

◼ Chapter 7   Programming Concepts in BASIC   145

◼ Chapter 8   Programming Concepts in Pascal   179

The Mystical Machine

Issues and Ideas in Computing

Introduction

Any sufficiently advanced technology is
indistinguishable from magic.

ARTHUR C. CLARKE, "Technology and the
Future"

■ The Mystical Machine

For many people, the computer is a mystical machine. It can perform
in seconds calculations that would take humans years to do. It can store
file cabinets' worth of information in the space of a few file folders and
can find any piece of that information instantly. Yet all this power is
concentrated in a machine with few moving parts, a machine whose
small size and great speed make it all the more amazing. To some, the
computer seems to be nothing less than a piece of twentieth-century
magic.

The computer's mystique dates back to its introduction in the
1950s. Although the public was aware of the existence of early computers, initially computers were hidden away, the property of scientists,
governments, and large businesses. These machines required a small
army of specialists to keep them functioning and an environment containing elaborate temperature and humidity controls. They were also
difficult to use; it often took days to set up a simple problem for a computer to solve. And because detailed knowledge was required to use
these machines, a computer elite developed who could understand and

communicate with them. In addition, those who used the new computers developed an esoteric language with which to discuss them. Many members of the public, however, thought of computers in terms of the flashing lights, whirling tapes, and "electronic brains" of science fiction.

Today's computers are much smaller and less expensive than the early machines; they are also more powerful, more rugged, and easier to use (Fig. 1.1). The reduction in size and price has increased the role computers play in our society. They are less imposing and more prevalent—we find them in wristwatches, cash registers, telephones, automobiles, and banking equipment. They can hold entire dictionaries, encyclopedias, and card catalogs; plot graphs and charts; serve as an artistic medium; help us learn; and make it possible to type letter-perfect documents with minimal effort.

With these developments have come new problems. We must now come to grips with the rapid social change caused by the proliferation of computers. The amount of information about computers is constantly growing, and the terminology associated with them seems as incomprehensible as ever. With all of these changes it is no wonder that many people fear they will be lost without a knowledge of the computer.

Some would like to ignore these revolutionary developments. This is an understandable reaction, but it is impractical because computers are not likely to go away. The industrial revolution of the eighteenth century swept over a civilization without giving people a chance to anticipate the magnitude of change that would ensue. The computer revolution could do the same if we choose to ignore it. Computers have tremendous potential for benefit as well as for harm. To best employ this technology, we must all help decide how computers are and are not to be used. Our decisions will profoundly affect the future direction of society. For this reason, they must be informed decisions based on knowledge about computers and their uses.

The computer, after all, is not a mystical machine. It is only an artifact, a human creation resulting from more than a century of human labor. With a little effort and guidance, anyone can understand the computer's essential features and approach a computer with confidence.

In this book we present material with a minimum of technical jargon, drawing on such common tasks as preparing documents and balancing checkbooks to illustrate basic concepts. The early chapters establish a technical foundation. Later chapters explore computer applications and social issues. In the remainder of Chapter 1, we define the term *computer*, identify the different types of computers, discuss a common computer application, and introduce computer software.

(a)

(b)

Figure 1.1

(a) The 1946 ENIAC, the first general-purpose electronic calculator, contrasts sharply with (b) the modern personal computer. [(a) UPI/Bettmann Newsphotos; (b) courtesy of Apple Computer, Inc.]

■ What Is a Computer?

In its simplest form, a computer is an information processor. It takes in information, processes it in some way, and produces information in return. Simple computers exist around us without our being aware that they are computers. An example is the milk carton computer sometimes used in the early elementary grades. This simple machine can be built with a milk carton, a pair of scissors, and several index cards. As Fig. 1.2 shows, the milk carton has two slots, one at the top and one at the bottom. A card with a question on it—for example, "Is an apple a fruit or a vegetable?"—is shown to a child, who tries to predict the answer. The card is dropped into the computer and reappears at the bottom with the answer—"fruit"—displayed. The card has been flipped over inside the carton, exposing the answer printed on the other side.

The milk carton is a computer by the definition presented in the preceding paragraph: it takes in information, processes it, and returns information. However, it is missing one important element that we usually associate with computers—memory. Although the milk carton computer may perform its limited function adequately, more complex information processing requires that the computer be able to store information and retrieve it from storage for use in processing.

A modern computer has five parts: like the milk carton computer, it has a means of taking in information (input), a means of returning information (output), and a means of processing information (a central processing unit, or CPU). It also has a memory. In addition, it has something to control the whole process (a program).

Figure 1.2
The milk carton computer. (a) A card with a question is inserted in the top slot and appears through the bottom slot with the answer. (b) Side view shows how the card is flipped over inside the carton. (Adapted from *The Kids Arts and Crafts* by Patricia Petrich and Rosemary Dalton. Copyright.)

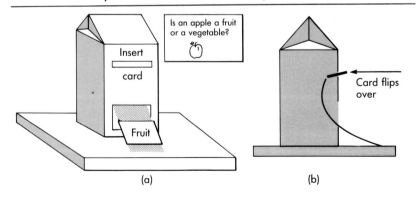

■ Types of Computers

Today when we speak of the computer we almost always refer to the digital computer as opposed to the analog computer. In an *analog* machine, data are measured or represented as a continuous entity; in a *digital* machine, data are measured or represented as exact small pieces or quanta. An hourglass can be thought of as an analog timepiece because sand moves constantly through the glass. Other analog timepieces include sundials and traditional clocks whose hands move continuously. A digital clock, on the other hand, measures time in small increments. For example, it remains at 05:35:23 for exactly one second and then makes a quantum leap to 05:35:24. Most modern computers are digital machines, although early calculators were analog devices. As late as the 1950s, it was believed that the analog computer would play a prominent role in certain applications, such as flight simulations. That is not the case today.

Computers can be either general-purpose or special-purpose machines. A *special-purpose* computer is built to serve one function or a few related functions. For example, the tiny computers in inexpensive digital wristwatches can do one thing—keep time. They cannot be used for word processing or video-game playing because their function has been directly wired into their circuitry. *General-purpose* computers can be instructed to do many different things. The user tells the computer what to do by means of a program, a series of instructions written in a language the computer can understand. Most of the machines we recognize as computers—from the large computers owned by big businesses to the smallest desk-top computers—are general-purpose machines.

■ A Simple Computer Application

New uses for computers seem to appear every day, and many of these applications affect the way we live and work. A commonplace example is provided by the automatic teller machine (ATM). We present a brief introduction to the ATM here to illustrate the various effects—both good and bad—that new technologies may create. Discussions of this sort dominate the latter portion of the book.

Figure 1.3 shows a typical ATM. ATMs were introduced at the end of the 1970s for a variety of reasons, most having to do with cost. Americans have always had a predilection for moving about and having ready cash when they do so. This trend accelerated during the 1970s, when

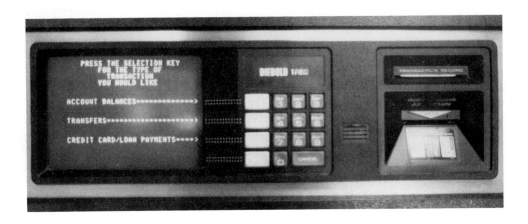

Figure 1.3
An automatic teller machine (ATM), simple to operate and usually available 24 hours a day, accommodates today's fast-paced lifestyles. (Photos by Darlene Bordwell)

bank transactions were being performed in record numbers. However, the amount of money on deposit in banks was not increasing relative to the number of banking transactions taking place. Thus, banks had to spend more money to hire additional tellers to process withdrawals and deposits without any increased income from consumer deposits.

Automatic teller machines appeared to solve many problems at once. Valuable employee time would not be wasted entering deposits and withdrawals as electronic pulses because these electronic pulses would be generated by the ATM itself. Since ATMs do not demand coffee breaks, salaries, or time off, they seemed to be more cost-effective than human tellers. Once a bank made an investment in ATMs, it would pay relatively little for maintenance. As for consumers, it was assumed that they would be drawn by one of the greatest advantages of this electronic banking system—the machines don't sleep. Consumers would no longer have to plan their days around banking hours; they could use the bank whenever they wanted.

In spite of their convenience, however, ATMs have met with a mixed reaction from the public. Some people are delighted to have access to cash at a moment's notice, even at night or on weekends. Others prefer not to deal with machines; they enjoy contact with human tellers. Still others are afraid to use an ATM at night or in a deserted area for fear of being robbed by someone witnessing the transaction. Finally, tellers who have lost their jobs to the machines are certainly not happy with the effects of this new technology. These are all immediate reactions to ATMs. Long-term effects, such as differences in the way we spend or think about money, have yet to become clear.

■ Putting Computers to Work

Computers as special-purpose machines are designed to perform a specific task; as general-purpose machines they can do anything they are instructed to do. The instructions given to general-purpose computers are called computer *programs*, also referred to as *software* to distinguish them from *hardware*, the actual physical components that make up a computer. Software, then, consists of the instructions that tell computers how to carry out various tasks.

Computer programs are written in special languages the computer can understand. Computer languages consist of a relatively small number of commands that the programmer combines to direct the computer's activities. Writing computer programs can be a complex task, requiring careful planning and logical thinking. With a little practice, however, anyone can acquire the skills necessary to do some simple computer programming. Those who choose not to write their own programs can still put computers to good use. A wide variety of commercial software programs exists, ready to be loaded into a computer and run.

The computer revolution has begun. Where it will end is hard to predict. The information in this book should help you reach your own conclusions about the future. For now, let us begin with an examination of the past.

ISSUES AND IDEAS

1. What is the distinction between a pocket calculator and a computer?
2. Identify a common device not normally thought of as a computer and argue that it is a computer, using the definition given in this chapter. What are the limitations of your justification?
3. An hourglass can be described as either an analog or a digital timepiece. How could an hourglass be described as an analog device? How could it be thought of as a digital device?
4. Give an example of a general-purpose computer and an example of a special-purpose computer other than the examples given in the chapter.
5. Select a common computer application other than the ATM and discuss the impact of this new technology on society.

The History of the Computer

Scientific "progress" does not move
along some path determined by nature
itself, but it mirrors human interests
and concerns.

JOSEPH WEIZENBAUM, *Computer Power
and Human Reason*

■ Introduction

The history of the computer is long and rich. It began with the first
attempts to develop mechanical aids to calculation several millennia ago
and extends through the current microminiaturization of general-purpose computers. It is a history of many individuals, their ideas, and their
inventions. The history of the computer is important for two reasons.
First, we can better understand the complex modern computer by realizing that it is the result of several centuries of evolution. Second, the
history serves to introduce many important concepts about computers
in a nontechnical setting.

Our treatment of the computer's history begins when humans
counted on their fingers. We show how a long succession of ideas and
inventions, from the abacus to the microchip, has contributed to the
development of the modern computer. We describe the role that scientists' needs have played in motivating the development of mechanical aids to computation and the role that nonscientific technology has
played in providing ideas and means to implement them. We also discuss some difficulties that were encountered in putting these ideas into

practice. The history of the computer is intertwined with the history of humanity. Major historical events have provided powerful stimuli to the development of the computer, and at certain critical junctures computer technology has had a major impact on the direction of history.

Early Aids to Calculation

The Abacus

The *abacus,* one of the first mechanical calculating devices, was used as early as 500 B.C. and perhaps much earlier. Despite its simplicity, the abacus has proved to be so useful that it is still widely used today, particularly in China and Japan.

Most abacuses consist of a wooden frame with beads strung on vertical wires or rods. The Japanese abacus, known as the *soroban,* is illustrated in Figs. 2.1–2.4. The beads are strung in columns of five. The dividing rod separating the uppermost bead from the other four in each column was said to separate the "heaven" bead from the "earth" beads. The Chinese abacus is similar, but it has two beads above the rod and

Figure 2.1
Counting with a Japanese abacus. From left to right, the digits from 9 to 3 are represented.

Figure 2.2
From left to right, the digits from 6 to 0 are represented.

Figure 2.3
The number 73 on an abacus.

Figure 2.4
Adding with an abacus.

five below. In the soroban the topmost bead represents five units, and the other beads represent one unit each. The positions of the beads represent numbers. Using these five beads, we can represent any digit from 0 to 9. The abacus in Fig. 2.1 shows the digits from 9 to 3, and the abacus in Fig. 2.2 shows the digits from 6 to 0. Each column of the abacus represents a power of ten, just as each column in our Arabic numbering system does. On an abacus, then, the number 73 is represented as shown in Fig. 2.3.

Additions and subtractions are carried out by raising or lowering beads. Multiplications are performed by repeated additions, and divisions by repeated subtractions. To add 22 to 73, we move two beads in each column and obtain 95, as shown in Fig. 2.4. This simple process was invaluable for adding or subtracting many numbers.

Although the abacus is a simple device, it is powerful. As late as 1941, a skilled user could calculate faster with an abacus than with a mechanical adding machine. Even today, many Japanese can add multidigit numbers more quickly and accurately with an abacus than with a pocket calculator. For more complex calculation such as multiplication and division, however, the abacus is clumsy to use. Another early mechanical invention, the slide rule, made reasonably accurate multiplications a fairly simple task by its use of logarithms.

Logarithms and the Slide Rule

John Napier (1550–1617) invented the logarithm in 1614. A *logarithm* (or *log*) is the power to which a fixed number (called the *base*) must be raised to produce another number. Logarithms are useful because they reduce the task of multiplying two numbers to a simple addition. This is possible because the logarithm of the product of any two numbers is equal to the sum of their logarithms. Napier constructed *log tables* to translate numbers to their logarithms and *antilog tables* to translate logarithms back to numbers. To multiply two numbers, one need only find their logs in the log table, add the logs together to find the product's log, and look up that log in the antilog table to find the product itself. A similar process transforms division into a simple subtraction.

The invention of the slide rule mechanized the use of logarithms for multiplication and division. Edmund Gunter (1581–1626) plotted a logarithmic table on a two-foot-long ruler in 1620. In 1621, William Oughtred (1575–1660) demonstrated that logarithms could be added mechanically by sliding one such ruler alongside another. This principle is illustrated by the two rulers in Fig. 2.5. To multiply 2 by 3 using these rulers, (1) find 2 on the lower ruler and align the number 1 on the upper ruler with it; (2) find 3 on the upper ruler, and read the corresponding number, 6, on the lower ruler. This number is the product because it represents the sum of the two logarithms. The accuracy of the slide

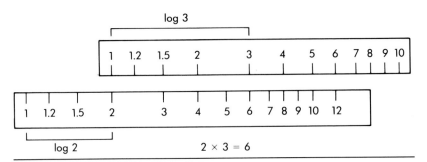

Figure 2.5
The principle behind the slide rule.

rule depends on the size of the logarithmic scale plotted on its component rulers and on the exactness with which the user aligns the rulers. Thus, it gives an estimate of results and is not accurate beyond several decimal places.

Amedee Manheim, a French army officer, is credited with the modern form of the slide rule (see Fig. 2.6). With it, one can multiply; divide; find powers, roots, reciprocals, and logs; and perform trigonometric functions. Paradoxically, the slide rule cannot be used to perform simple addition and subtraction.

Figure 2.6
The modern slide rule.

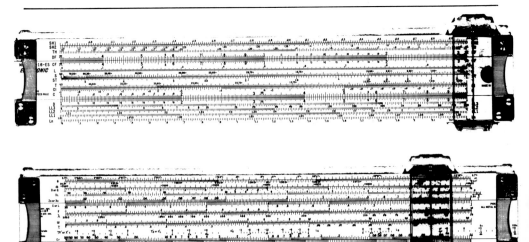

Schickard's and Pascal's Adding Machines

The first person to build an automatic adding machine was Wilhelm Schickard (1592–1635), a German astronomer. Unfortunately, Schickard's machine was destroyed in a fire and we have no pictures or copies of it. We know how it operated only through his correspondence with friends.

The machine, completed in 1623, used a series of gears for adding. Each gear had ten spokes, one for each digit. To add 1, a gear was advanced one-tenth of a revolution, or one notch, as in an automobile odometer. Schickard's machine added by counting, just as humans count on their fingers—by starting with one number and counting out by ones the number to be added. A major drawback of counting on fingers is that we have only ten fingers, so we must mentally store any number greater than 10. Schickard solved the storage problem by using several gears, one for each decimal place. As a gear completed a full revolution (that is, counted to 10), the gear to its left was advanced one notch, thus mechanically recording a "carry," as shown in Fig. 2.7.

The result of an addition is the number represented by the position of the gear wheels. Such a series of wheels can be thought of as an *accumulator* because it accumulates the result of an addition. Accumulators are integral parts of modern computers.

Later, Blaise Pascal (1623–1662), the French philosopher and scientist, built a similar machine, known as the Pascaline. Pascal's father, a customs official, spent long hours bookkeeping. At age 19, Pascal invented an adding and subtracting machine to help with this tedious work. Although Pascal had no knowledge of Schickard's machine, the

Figure 2.7
The principle behind Schickard's calculating machine.

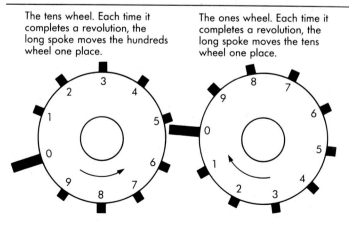

The tens wheel. Each time it completes a revolution, the long spoke moves the hundreds wheel one place.

The ones wheel. Each time it completes a revolution, the long spoke moves the tens wheel one place.

Pascaline operated according to the same principles. Several were built, and working models still exist. Because of the unreliability of their mechanical gears, however, the machines were more admired than used.

Leibniz and the Multiplying Wheel

In the seventeenth century, "computers" were people who spent their lives performing calculations by hand. Our modern meaning for computer derives from this occupation. Gottfried Leibniz (1646–1716), a philosopher and mathematician, was one of the first to recognize that talented individuals were wasting their valuable time doing repetitious hand calculations. He wrote, "It is unworthy of excellent men [scientists] to lose hours like slaves in the labour of calculation which could safely be relegated to anyone else if machines were used."

Leibniz expanded on the ideas of Pascal to create the Leibniz wheel, a device that performed multiplications automatically. The Pascaline performed multiplications by repeated additions (to multiply 7 by 8, for example, one added 7 to the accumulated sum eight times). The Leibniz wheel also multiplied by repeated additions. However, it would store the multiplier (7 in our example) and when the handle was turned automatically add the multiplier to the accumulated sum. For example, to multiply 7 by 8, one set the wheel at 7 and turned the handle eight times. While the wheel did not alter the way multiplications were done, it made the process much easier. Its advantage over the slide rule was that it could provide exact rather than approximate results.

Leibniz's and Pascal's machines were unreliable because they had many moving parts that had to work in close synchronization. In the seventeenth century, cutting and shaping metals was a difficult and inaccurate process. This problem continued to thwart attempts to build more advanced calculating machines and was not solved until the twentieth century.

Leibniz is also interesting for his early thinking about how to represent numbers. He considered building a calculating machine to work in base 2 instead of base 10. Although Leibniz never built such a calculator, it is significant that he thought of doing so, since all modern computers work in base 2.

Binary Arithmetic

Counting in base 10—that is, in a number system based on ten digits— is natural for us because we have ten fingers to serve as place holders. Undoubtedly, Schickard used wheels with ten spokes and counted in base 10 in his mechanical adding machine without giving the system of arithmetic much thought. However, counting can be done in other number systems as well. For example, time is measured in seconds, minutes, and hours, a system that uses base 60. In general, arithmetic can use any integer base. The *binary number system,* which uses *base 2,* is particularly important to computers.

The binary number system is far easier to represent electrically than the *decimal,* or *base 10,* system. The decimal system has ten different states, so ten different electrical signals would have to be used to represent these states. The difference between two adjacent signals (say, the representations for 5 and 6) would be small, and it would be difficult to differentiate between the states they represented. The binary system has only two states: switches are either open or closed; a current is either absent or present. The difference between the signals can therefore be greater, making it easier to tell which state is intended. Base 2 is far easier to use for people working with mechanical as well as electronic representations of numbers. Just think how much trouble Pascal must have had trying to create gears with ten grooves and how much easier it would have been to use switches with only two positions—on and off.

To understand the logic of numbers notated in base 2, it is useful to reexamine base 10 notation. In base 10, digits from the set {0, 1, 2, 3, 4, 5, 6, 7, 8, 9} are used in positions representing powers of 10. The rightmost digit in a number is said to be the units digit, a multiple of 1 (10^0); the next is the tens digit, a multiple of 10 (10^1); the third is the hundreds digit, a multiple of 100 (10^2); the fourth is a multiple of 1000 (or 10^3), and so on. Thus, the number 3,278 has 3 thousands, 2 hundreds, 7 tens, and 8 units.

We read binary numbers in the same way, except that we use powers of 2 rather than powers of 10. There are only two possible digits, 0 and 1. The rightmost digit represents the 2^0 or units place. The next position holds the 2^1 or twos place. The next position is the 2^2 or fours place, followed by the 2^3 or eights place. The decimal number 13 is represented in base 2 as 1101: it is made up of 1 eight, 1 four, 0 twos, and 1 one ($8 + 4 + 0 + 1 = 13$). The decimal number 33 is represented as 100001, 1 thirty-two and 1 one.

Counting in base 2 is similar to counting in base 10, as illustrated in Fig. 2.8. In both systems, we add 1 to the rightmost digit. If the result exceeds the largest digit that can be represented in that place (1 in binary; 9 in decimal), then a 1 is carried to the next position. Thus, in base 2, if the sum in the rightmost place is 2, a 1 is carried to the twos position and a 0 is placed in the ones position. If necessary, carries are also made to higher positions.

Addition in base 2 also follows the same rules as addition in base 10. To add two base 10 numbers, we add the columns of digits one at a time starting with the rightmost column and carry a 1 when the sum

```
   0 =  0
   1 =  1
  10 =  2
  11 =  3
 100 =  4
 101 =  5
 110 =  6
 111 =  7
1000 =  8
1001 =  9
1010 = 10
1011 = 11
1100 = 12
1101 = 13
1110 = 14
1111 = 15
```

Figure 2.8
Counting in base 2 compared with counting in base 10.

of a column is greater than 9. The same rule applies in base 2, except that a 1 is carried when the sum is greater than 1 because 1 is the largest single digit that base 2 can represent. For example, to add 101 and 110, we complete the sequence of steps shown in Figure 2.9. Since 101 is the equivalent of 5 in decimal notation and 110 is the equivalent of 6, the answer, 1011, is the equivalent of 11. Although binary addition may seem cumbersome to humans, it is far easier to perform mechanically or electronically.

Nineteenth-Century Developments

Babbage, Lovelace, and the Analytical Engine

Charles Babbage (1791–1871) holds a distinguished place in the history of computing. The many accomplishments of this eccentric genius include the design for a machine that incorporated most of the principles

Figure 2.9
Adding in base 2.

101	101	^{1}101	101
110	110	110	110
1	11	011	1011

rles Babbage
1–1871)

behind the modern computer. This was no small accomplishment: not only were there no means of building this computer, there were no other machines that even approximated it. Because Babbage had no concrete way to demonstrate his ideas, they were underestimated and misunderstood by many of his contemporaries. His work was forgotten shortly after his death and only came to be fully appreciated more than half a century later.

Babbage's fascination with computing machines is said to have grown out of an interest in astronomy shared with his friend Sir John Herschel. According to one account, the two found a large number of errors while examining mathematical tables. Clerks had made mistakes when they calculated the numbers in the tables, and still more errors had been introduced by the printers who had hand-set the tables into type. In exasperation, Babbage exclaimed, "I wish to God these calculations had been executed by steam." Herschel replied, "It is quite possible."

Herschel's words haunted Babbage. In 1822, Babbage proposed the construction of a *difference engine* to compute and print mathematical tables. Unlike early machines, which required human control and intervention after every step in the calculation process, the difference engine could automatically calculate an entire table once it was instructed in the pattern on which the table was based—a pattern of differences between numbers.

For his groundbreaking work, Babbage was awarded the first gold medal ever given by the Astronomical Society. After listing some applications in which the government could use the difference engine (chiefly navigation and astronomy), Babbage received government support to build a working model of his machine. At a time when scientific research was still considered a gentleman's hobby, this represented a major achievement.

Babbage never completed a working model of the difference engine. His passion for tinkering led him to redesign its parts constantly, slowing construction. In addition, his insistence on using the highest-quality materials and labor exhausted his funds. After four years the government withdrew its financial support.

In 1834, George Scheutz (1785–1873), a wealthy Stockholm printer, read of Babbage's ideas for a computing machine and decided to build a difference engine of his own. With some financial support from the Swedish government and the Swedish Academy, Scheutz and his son were able to complete a less ambitious model of the difference engine in 1854. It was bought and used by an American businessman, and a duplicate model in London produced the life expectancy tables used for many years by British insurance companies.

Meanwhile, Babbage had started on an ambitious new project to

rge Scheutz
5–1873)

build a more powerful and more versatile machine. While the difference engine was meant as a special-purpose computer, designed specifically for generating mathematical tables, the *analytical engine* was conceived as a general-purpose computer, capable of carrying out any mathematical operation.

The analytical engine was partially inspired by an earlier invention, the Jacquard loom (shown in Fig. 2.10). Invented at the beginning of the nineteenth century by Joseph Jacquard (1752–1834), the Jacquard loom was the first successful fully automatic loom. It was used to weave elaborate patterns in silk, a tedious process when performed manually. Jacquard attached rods to the threads that would be lifted together to form the pattern, and he used cards with holes punched in them to control the positions of the rods. The pattern designed by the artist was transferred to the cards as a series of holes. Wherever there was a hole

Figure 2.10
(a) The Jacquard loom, invented in 1746, was the first successful automated loom. (b) Loom cards controlled the positions of the threading rods. (Photos courtesy of IBM Archives)

(a)   (b)

in the card, a rod would pass through the hole and would not be lifted up. The cards made it possible to store large quantities of information that could be "read" by the machine, which would weave the intended pattern.

Designed to be as versatile as the Jacquard loom, the analytical engine was capable of calculating any equation. Like Jacquard, Babbage used cards, such as the one shown in Fig. 2.11, to communicate with his machine. He used two sets of cards. The first set specified the operations to be performed—the equations, or the program, that the machine would follow. The second set supplied the numbers to operate on. Babbage conceived of his analytical engine as having two essential parts: the *store*, which held the values to be operated on and the results from earlier calculations, and the *mill*, where all the operations took place.

Babbage was assisted in his work by Ada Augusta, Countess of Lovelace (1815–1852), a brilliant mathematician and the daughter of poet Lord Byron. She was perhaps the only one of Babbage's contemporaries who thoroughly understood and appreciated the analytical engine, and her careful documentation provides us with the understanding of the analytical engine that we have today. She also painted a vivid picture of it when she wrote, "The Analytical Engine weaves algebraical patterns just as the Jacquard Loom weaves flowers and leaves."

Unfortunately, it was not possible to build a working model of the analytical engine with nineteenth-century technology. Even if it had been possible, Babbage might not have been the person for the job. He was known for ideas, not for his patience in carrying them through to

da Augusta,
ountess of Lovelace
815–1852)

Figure 2.11
Babbage's punched card, which he used to communicate with his difference engine. (Photo courtesy of IBM Archives)

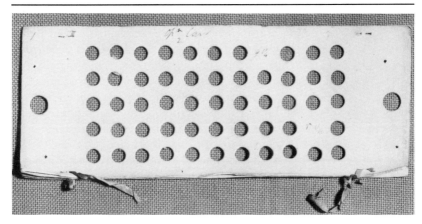

completion—his mind jumped quickly from one project to the next. It was not until 1944 that modern technology would realize Babbage's farsighted ideas.

George Boole and Mathematical Logic

George Boole
(1815–1864)

Another Victorian whose ideas contributed significantly to the development of the computer was George Boole (1815–1864), an Irish mathematician. Boole's writing laid the foundation for the modern subject of symbolic logic, now referred to as *Boolean algebra*, a system in which logical statements can be stated symbolically and proved in the same way as algebraic statements. For example, each of the statements "It is the weekend," "It is hot," and "I am baking bread" is either true or false. We can use the symbol W to represent "It is the weekend," H to represent "It is hot," and B to represent "I am baking bread." The symbols can be linked by such words as AND and OR to form compound statements. Thus the compound statement H AND W is true only if "It is hot" is true and "It is the weekend" is true. If either H or W is false, then H AND W is false. Similarly, the statement H AND (NOT B) is true only if "It is hot" is true and "I am baking bread" is not true.

In 1938, Claude Shannon (b. 1916) demonstrated that Boolean algebra could be used to study relay circuits. This discovery was important in the design and analysis of computers, as you will see in Chapter 3.

Claude E. Shannon
(b. 1916)

Hollerith, the Electric Tabulator, and the 1890 Census

According to constitutional mandate, the United States must take a census every ten years. By the 1880s, the task of tabulating the census had grown to such proportions that the old means of tabulation were inadequate. The U.S. population was growing rapidly, and increasing amounts of information were being sought about its members. In addition to vital statistics such as age and sex, the census collected information on a person's immigration status, health, race, degree of literacy, and employment. As a result, the 1880 census required more than seven years to complete. The 1890 census was expected to take even longer. To avoid starting a new census before completing the last one, the U.S. Census Bureau held a competition to find an efficient way to tabulate the enormous amount of data collected.

Three finalists emerged from the contest. William C. Hunt used colored cards and Charles F. Pidgin used color-coded paper chips in innovative systems of manual tabulation. Herman Hollerith (1860–1929) introduced the first electric tabulating machine. Census data from St.

Herman Hollerith
(1860–1929)

Louis provided a test for the three systems. With Hunt's system of cards, 55 hours were required to tabulate the data; with Pidgin's tokens, 44 hours; and with Hollerith's tabulating machine only 5½ hours. A journalist wrote of Hollerith's machine: "This apparatus works unerringly as the mills of the gods, but beats them hollow as to speed."

Hollerith borrowed his idea from Jacquard's loom and Babbage's analytical engine. He used punched cards to record the census data; each card was the size of a dollar bill and contained 288 locations where holes might be punched. One corner of the card was clipped so that the bottom could be easily distinguished from the top. Hollerith developed a system to minimize the number of holes required to represent each possible answer, a system similar to that used on many modern forms. He also created a keypunch machine to punch holes in the cards. As shown in Fig. 2.12(a), Hollerith's tabulating machine had a grid of iron rods, one for each hole position, that were placed against the card. The rods were mounted on springs so that wherever there was a hole, a rod would pass through it and make contact with a small container of mercury. This contact between rod and mercury completed an electrical circuit that caused a counter to advance one unit. Complicated tabulations could be performed if a counter was rigged to advance only when a certain group of rods made contact with the mercury. For example, if census takers wished to determine the number of Protestant mail carriers in the United States, a circuit could be built that would be completed only if a person's census card indicated that he was both Protestant and a mail carrier.

Although Hollerith's machine was not a general-purpose computer, it is significant because of its use of punched-card input and electricity. Hollerith patented his machine, shown in Fig. 2.12(b), and established the Tabulating Machine Company, which later became part of the International Business Machines Corporation (IBM).

■ Twentieth-Century Developments

The use of tabulating equipment was not restricted to census compilation. Soon after the 1890 census, large industries such as railroads, insurance companies, and public utilities began using tabulating machines to handle their large volumes of data. Hollerith incorporated an electronic adding mechanism in his tabulating machine, thus making it possible to combine cost and sales analysis with accounting. This greatly increased the usefulness of tabulating machines and led to their widespread application.

Interest in tabulating machines spread from government and busi-

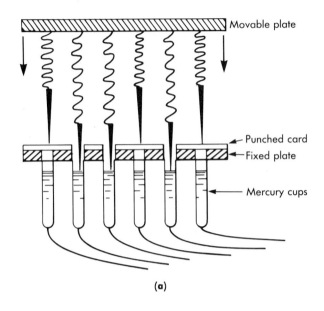

Movable plate

Punched card

Fixed plate

Mercury cups

(a)

(b)

Figure 2.12
(a) The principle behind Hollerith's tabulating machine; (b) the machine itself. [(b) Photo courtesy of IBM Archives]

ness to science. As people saw how these machines could be used to organize and analyze data, demand for powerful computing equipment grew. This demand fueled further advances in computing equipment. It was another turn of events, however, that provided the major stimulus for development.

World War II was a turning point in the development of the computer. The war intensified a need for computers, and the machines that were developed affected the war's outcome. Computing devices were needed to decipher cryptographic messages, compile tables of ballistics data, train air crews, and process radar signals. The war showed that scientific research was no longer merely a hobby, but a serious pursuit. Governments were now prepared to fund large research and development projects, including the design and construction of large electronic computers.

Zuse and "Home" Computers

On the eve of World War II, a German student, Konrad Zuse (b. 1910), began work on a series of machines to perform automatically the "big and awful calculations" that occupied so much of his time as a civil engineering student. Using an erector set, he built his first machine, the Z1, in the living room of his parents' apartment in Berlin in 1936. (See Fig. 2.13.) Shortly thereafter, he constructed a second model, the Z2, from second-hand telephone relays. These machines served as test models for Zuse's Z3, built in 1941. The Z3 was the world's first working general-purpose program-controlled computer.

onrad Zuse
b. 1910)

Zuse's calculating machines were distinctive for several reasons. First, all other calculating machines in use in the 1930s did arithmetic in base 10 and multiplied either by successively adding the numbers to simulate multiplication or by using an internally stored multiplication table. These methods were thought to be the only possible means of mechanical multiplication. Instead, Zuse converted decimal numbers to their binary equivalents, then added and multiplied in base 2. Addition and multiplication, scientists have found, are much easier to automate in base 2.

Second, where Schickard, Pascal, Leibniz, Babbage, and others used spoked wheels to record and operate on numbers, Zuse used electromagnetic relays. An *electromagnetic relay,* shown in Fig. 2.14, is a mechanical switch controlled by an electromagnet. An *electromagnet* is made up of a coil of wire wrapped around an iron bar; it acts as a magnet when electrical current is sent through the wire. When the magnet is not activated, the switch is held in an open position by a spring. When the magnet is activated, a magnetic field attracts the switch, closing it and completing a path through which electricity can flow. A closed path

Figure 2.13
The Z1, Konrad Zuse's 1936 relay calculator, shown in his family's living room. (Photo courtesy of Konrad Zuse, Hünfeld, Germany)

Figure 2.14
An electromagnetic relay.

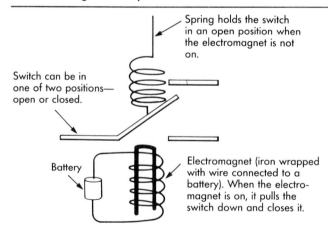

Spring holds the switch in an open position when the electromagnet is not on.

Switch can be in one of two positions— open or closed.

Battery

Electromagnet (iron wrapped with wire connected to a battery). When the electro-magnet is on, it pulls the switch down and closes it.

of this sort is called a *circuit*. Electromagnetic relays can be combined to form a *flip-flop*, a device that can store one of two values—for instance, a 0 or a 1. When flip-flops are used to store digits, it is fairly easy to perform binary arithmetic automatically. Because Zuse's computer used both electricity and mechanical parts, it was an *electromechanical* machine.

The Z3 had several other significant features common to today's computers. It had input and output devices: information was entered with a keyboard (similar to a typewriter keyboard), and output was displayed by lights representing answers in binary notation. Numbers, but not instructions, could be stored inside the machine. Instructions were recorded on punched tape and read into the computer using a method similar to that used for punched cards.

While employed in an aircraft factory, Zuse worked on two special-purpose computers commissioned by the German air ministry. They were used to calculate the position of the wings on a remote-controlled guided missile. The S1 and S2, as they were called, were in use 24 hours a day for two years during the war. Zuse, however, was denied the opportunity to continue his work on a machine to automate the calculations needed to design aircraft. "The German aircraft is the best in the world," an officer commented. "I don't see what to calculate further on." If the Germans had been less confident of their military superiority and had given more money to the development of computing machines, they might have won the war. The significance computers played in this war is illustrated by the success of the British machines for deciphering codes.

British War Efforts: The Colossus and Bletchley Park

While the Germans were convinced of their military superiority, the English, weaker in military force, were trying desperately to outwit the Germans by cracking encoded messages. If the English knew what the German military planned to do, they could better prepare for it. Some of England's brightest mathematicians and engineers were spirited away in 1939 to a mansion in Bletchley Park, England. The cryptology unit they formed—under the code name ULTRA—would eventually employ 10,000 men and women. Between 1940 and 1944, they successfully decoded hundreds of German messages.

The ULTRA story began in 1938 when a young Polish engineer named Richard Lewinski offered his service to the British. He had worked in a German factory that secretly manufactured enciphering machines but had been fired because he was Jewish. His offer to sell his knowledge to the British turned out to be invaluable. Lewinski had an extraordinary memory and managed to reconstruct a model of the German machine. Although this information was not sufficient to allow the British to unscramble German codes automatically, it gave them a clear idea of how messages were being scrambled in the first place.

The enciphering machine that was used by the German High Command was called the Enigma. It was inexpensive, easy to use, lightweight, and about the size of a small typewriter. Used both to encode and to decode messages, the Enigma used a set of rotors for scrambling the alphabet. Each rotor consisted of two disks joined together. Each disk had 26 electrical contacts equally spaced around its outside face. Each contact on one disk was connected to a single contact on the other disk by a wire, as shown in Fig. 2.15. If a person typed the letter A into a one-rotor encoder, the machine would print out the letter associated with A, perhaps a P. Such an encoder would perform only one *permutation* of the alphabet, providing very little security. A permutation is a one-to-one translation from one set to another set. Here is a simple alphabetical permutation:

A B C D E F G H I J K L M N O P Q R S T U V W X Y Z
D E F G H I J K L M N O P Q R S T U V W X Y Z A B C

By noting the frequencies of letters, a decoder could quickly determine the wiring within the rotor and break the code.

The Enigma used not one rotor but a set of three rotors placed

Figure 2.15
A single rotor of the Enigma.

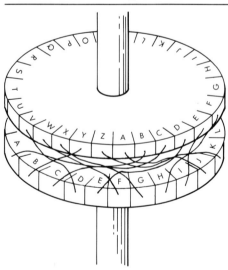

next to each other. After passing through the three rotors, the signal was reflected and sent back through the rotors again, as shown in Fig. 2.16. As a result, each letter went through six permutations. After a letter had been enciphered, the rotors turned, each by a different amount; thus, an A typed twice in a row would be assigned a different letter each time. On the three-rotor Enigma machine, 9×10^{20} permutations were possible. Discovering which permutation was in use on any given day was potentially a herculean task. The problem was solved with the aid of special-purpose computers that ran through sets of permutations at high speed until a permutation was found that made sense.

Because of the great secrecy surrounding the ULTRA project, its activities were rigidly compartmentalized, and few individuals were privy to all aspects of it. Consequently our current knowledge of many of the technical aspects of the project, including the nature of the special-purpose computers used, remains fragmentary. However, we do know that these computers were the first large-scale computers to use *vacuum tubes,* electronic components that had been developed for radio communication. (In the United States, an American named John Atanasoff had used vacuum tubes on a small scale in a special-purpose computer designed to solve simultaneous equations, but the Bletchley Park scientists had no knowledge of his work.) Vacuum tubes can perform the same functions as relays but are faster because they have no moving parts. On the other hand, they have a shorter life span and are less reliable. Overall, the use of vacuum tubes in computers represented a major technological advance. Computers using electronic components, such as vacuum tubes, are called *electronic computers.*

Figure 2.16
The encryption of a letter with the Enigma. (Adapted from *Alan Turing: The Enigma.* Copyright © 1983 by Andrew Hodges. Reprinted by permission of Simon & Schuster, Inc.)

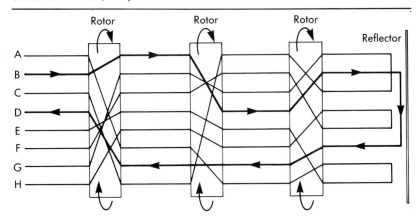

The first of several types of machines that played vital roles in the ULTRA project was the Robinson series, named for Heath Robinson, the British counterpart of the American cartoonist Rube Goldberg. Both men are famous for their drawings of fantastic machines that accomplish simple tasks in unbelievably complex ways. The Robinson series was used at Bletchley Park to scan through many rotor combinations until a sensible translation was uncovered. The Robinson series was significant primarily because it led to the more successful Colossus computer.

Built in eleven months and put to work in 1943, the *Colossus* had 1,500 vacuum tubes, compared with 30 to 80 in the Robinson machines, and was externally programmed with switches. Like Zuse's machines, Colossus used binary arithmetic. Colossus was the first electronic special-purpose computer to be put into full-time operation. Many feel that the vital information provided by Colossus's code-breaking shifted the balance of the war and enabled the Allies to emerge victorious.

Alan Turing and the Theory of Computation

Alan Turing
(1912–1954)

One of the individuals who played a substantial role in the development of Colossus was Alan Turing (1912–1954). In addition to his work on Colossus during World War II, Turing is known for his theoretical conception of the modern computer, published in 1936, and his work on defining artificial intelligence through the Turing test (described in detail in Chapter 12).

Turing developed a simple mathematical model of a computer, illustrated in Fig. 2.17, which became known as a Turing machine. The model consists of an infinitely long tape divided into squares and a control unit that could read a symbol from a square, write a new symbol over the old one, and move from one square to the next. This model embodies the general principles of any computer that has ever been constructed, principles that originated with Babbage, whom Turing ad-

Figure 2.17
A Turing machine.

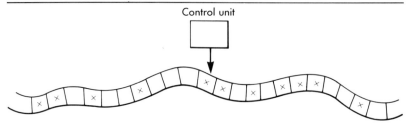

Control unit

mired. Turing demonstrated two important concepts of computing: (1) that there are some theoretical problems that cannot be solved by any computer and (2) that a general-purpose computer can be built to solve any problem that can be solved by a special-purpose computer. Turing's work provided the theoretical basis for the development of the modern computer.

Howard Aiken and the Mark I

Howard Aiken
(1900–1973)

While computers were being developed in Europe before and during World War II, a parallel development was occurring in the United States. By the early 1930s the IBM Corporation had become the major supplier of tabulating machines. Consequently it was with the support of IBM that a nonprofit institution was created in 1933 to investigate the applications of tabulating machines to scientific computations. Named for the president of IBM, the nonprofit institution was called the Thomas J. Watson Astronomical Computing Bureau.

Howard Aiken (1900–1973), one of the researchers supported by the Watson Bureau, spelled out the changes needed to transform ordinary tabulating machines into machines suitable for scientific computation. He declared that these machines should have the ability to handle positive and negative numbers, perform various mathematical functions, operate automatically (without human intervention during calculation), and carry out calculations in a natural mathematical sequence. Aiken himself had been working on a series of special-purpose calculating machines that had some of these characteristics. Realizing that they were all essentially identical in their logical construction and that a general-purpose machine could be built to solve any of his problems, he began in 1939 a collaborative project with four IBM engineers to build the IBM Automatic Sequence Controlled Calculator, commonly known as the Mark I.

Aiken was aware of the significance of Babbage's work and commented to a friend: "If Babbage had lived seventy-five years later, I would have been out of a job." Completed in 1944, the Mark I was a realization of Babbage's dream with the benefit of twentieth-century technology. In fact, the British magazine *Nature* described the Mark I as "Babbage's Dream Comes True."

The Mark I performed computations by automatically following a program fed into it on punched tape. The numbers on which the program operated were stored inside the computer, eliminating the need for human intervention. It was an electromagnetic machine, the last large computer to use primarily electromagnetic relays. Indeed, compared with the Bletchley Park machines, which used vacuum tubes, it

Grace Murray
Hopper (b. 1906)

was already technologically out of date. However, unlike the Colossus, the Mark I was a general-purpose computer built to solve an infinite variety of problems. As we see today, general-purpose computers are far more powerful than special-purpose computers.

The Mark I project has left at least one lasting imprint on the computing field—the term *bug*, commonly used to describe an error in a program or computer circuit. The origin of the term is described by Grace Murray Hopper (b. 1906), a mathematics professor at Vassar, supervisor of the project that created the first computer language translator, or *compiler*, and third programmer of the Mark I: "Things were going badly. There was something wrong in one of the circuits of the long glass-enclosed computer. Finally, someone located the trouble spot and, using ordinary tweezers, removed the problem, a two-inch moth. From then on, whenever anything went wrong with a computer, we said it had bugs in it" (*New York Times*, 7 August 1981).

J. Presper Eckert, Jr.
(b. 1902) and
John W. Mauchly
(1907–1980)

The First General-Purpose Electronic Digital Computer

There is a great deal of controversy over who should be credited with the invention of the first general-purpose electronic digital computer. For many years, full credit and patent rights were awarded to J. Presper Eckert, Jr. (b. 1902) and John W. Mauchly (1907–1980) for their construction of ENIAC (Electronic Numerical Integrator and Computer), completed in 1946 at the University of Pennsylvania's Moore School of Electrical Engineering. In 1973, however, a court case brought by Honeywell invalidated Eckert and Mauchly's patent. The judge ruled that "Eckert and Mauchly did not themselves invent the automatic electronic digital computer, but instead derived the subject matter from one Dr. John V. Atanasoff." This decision is misleading because the computer invented by Atanasoff (b. 1903) was a special-purpose computer, whereas Eckert and Mauchly's was general-purpose.

John V. Atanasoff
(b. 1903)

At the time of his invention, Atanasoff was a physicist at Iowa State College. Although building a computer was not his primary goal, he found that there were no machines or systems to solve complex problems in a variety of scientific areas. Therefore, early in 1940, Atanasoff built a special-purpose computer to solve simultaneous linear equations. This machine used binary representations of numbers and had an internal memory. It was also the first computer to use vacuum tubes. Although Atanasoff's work preceded that of the Bletchley Park scientists by several years, they were not aware of his work. Because Atanasoff's budget was modest, he built a small prototype computer that was far less sophisticated than ENIAC. Atanasoff's computer contained 800 vacuum tubes—less than one-twentieth the number ENIAC had.

ENIAC, on the other hand, was an enormous machine that weighed more than 30 tons and contained more than 18,000 vacuum tubes. It could do nearly 5,000 additions or subtractions per second. It used so much electricity that a popular legend claimed that lights in West Philadelphia dimmed slightly whenever ENIAC was in use. Scientists programmed ENIAC by manually connecting cables and setting 6,000 switches.

Conceived in 1943, ENIAC was designed and built for military applications—specifically to produce firing and bombing tables for the U.S. Army Ballistic Research Laboratory. Since it was designed as a general-purpose computer, ENIAC was eventually used for nonmilitary purposes, such as weather prediction, atomic energy calculations, cosmic ray studies, thermal ignition, random number studies, and wind tunnel design.

Vacuum tubes provided ENIAC with great speed. As mentioned earlier, vacuum tubes have no moving parts, so they respond almost instantaneously. Unfortunately, they tend to be unreliable and have a short life span. To solve these problems, Eckert followed the example of large, electric theater organs that used tubes at less than their full current and voltage capacities. Used in such a way, vacuum tubes proved far more reliable than had previously been thought possible. Calculations could be carried out three times faster using vacuum tubes than using relays. This speed was evident in ENIAC's fulfillment of its original purpose: it would have taken a skilled person with a desk calculator 20 hours to compute the trajectory of a missile; it took the ENIAC 30 seconds.

Although the technology needed to complete ENIAC was available long before the machine was completed, it took a combination of factors to bring ENIAC to fruition. Without World War II and the foresight of Eckert and Mauchly, ENIAC might not have been built until even later.

Von Neumann, Eckert, Mauchly, and the Stored-Program Concept

While the electronic computer was evolving, the stored-program concept was also being developed. The *stored-program concept* is essential to the functioning of the modern digital computer. It permits the storage of both programs and data in the computer's memory and eliminates the necessity of reading a program from some external storage medium, such as punched tape, or of manually programming the com-

John von Neumann
(1903–1957)

puter by setting switches or making external plug connections. The credit for the idea is usually given to John von Neumann, although it too has an uncertain history.

John von Neumann (1903–1957) was born in Hungary and came to the United States in 1930 as a visiting professor of mathematical physics at Princeton University. He became interested in electronic computers through a chance meeting at a train station with Herman Goldstine, who was involved in the ENIAC project. Von Neumann worked with Eckert and Mauchly in extending ENIAC's capabilities.

Programming ENIAC was a tedious task that involved manually setting switches and connecting cables. Setting up a problem sometimes took several individuals several days. Many people sought a solution to this problem. Turing's theoretical model of a computer could read programs and data from the same memory, and Eckert and Mauchly proposed storing both programs and data inside the machine. They discussed their idea with von Neumann, who was very receptive. It was von Neumann, however, who wrote up a formal discussion of the stored-program concept. Because his name was the only one on the document, he is usually credited with the conception of the idea.

EDVAC (Electronic Discrete Variable Automatic Computer) was one of the first computers to utilize the stored-program concept. It was built by the ENIAC team in response to an army request for a computer more powerful than ENIAC. EDVAC programs were not entered on punched tape or by moving cables or setting switches; instead, they could be stored as a series of binary numbers inside the computer. Once inside, a program could be run over and over again. For the first time, logical choices of program sequence could be made inside the machine—instructions could be modified by the computer as the program was executed. This meant that different computer programs could be used in rapid succession, that programs could be designed to be more flexible, and that programs could utilize other programs. This last advantage is integral to today's emphasis on structured programming, a concept discussed in detail in Chapters 7 and 8. Once again, it was von Neumann who wrote up a comprehensive report synthesizing the early thought on EDVAC, and he was mistakenly given complete credit for it.

Eckert and Mauchly took a break during their work on EDVAC to run a conference on computers in the summer of 1946. Attending that conference was Maurice Wilkes of Cambridge University. On returning home, Wilkes set about building a computer based on the EDVAC concept of the stored program and succeeded in completing his machine before EDVAC became operational. His computer, called EDSAC (Electronic Delay Storage Automatic Calculator), was completed only a few months before EDVAC in 1949.

MIT and the Whirlwind Computer

The Whirlwind was a very different kind of computer from ENIAC and EDVAC, although it too emerged from wartime research and development. The Whirlwind project was conceived in 1943 and begun in 1944, when an MIT alumnus and naval engineer asked MIT to build a machine to train naval bomber flight crews. The machine was to train pilots and test new airplane designs by simulating the motions of a wind tunnel test and observing the pilots' response. To be useful, such machines required the ability to do *real-time computation*—that is, to simulate the execution of many tasks quickly enough to keep up with events as they occurred. For example, when simulating the flight of an aircraft, a real-time computer had to be able to solve simultaneously many equations dealing with aircraft position, gravity, wind speed, momentum, acceleration, and other factors and to solve them quickly enough to give a pilot the illusion of flying a plane. Whirlwind evolved into a project to build a general-purpose digital computer and resulted in the first digital computer that could be put to uses such as controlling manufacturing processes or directing airplane traffic. This was significantly different from the earlier computers, which were designed primarily for large-scale numerical computation.

Several other features made the Whirlwind computer unique. Its speed and reliability surpassed those of its ancestors—necessary improvements if the goal of real-time control was to be reached. To create authentic simulations, for example, Whirlwind not only had to calculate as quickly as events occurred in real time, but it also had to be able to run continuously for several hours without breaking down. The Whirlwind team created a vacuum tube computer that was much more reliable than its predecessors by building checking equipment to test for deteriorating components. This was an important innovation in computing. By discovering potential problems before they occurred, the Whirlwind scientists were able to make their machine far more reliable than others of its size (13,000 vacuum tubes) and capability.

Whirlwind also pioneered the use of magnetic core storage, which afterward was used for many years as the primary memory on all computers. Magnetic core storage provides rapid access to data in a so-called random access fashion, a concept described in detail in Chapter 3. With magnetic core memory, it was possible to get at any piece of data with equal speed; when data was stored on tape, it was necessary to advance or rewind the tape to find the needed piece of data.

The Whirlwind used a *cathode ray tube* (CRT) to display output graphically and dynamically, quite a change from the printed paper tables used in earlier computers. The user could communicate with the computer by touching the screen of the CRT with a *lightpen*. These were two truly innovative developments. Another was the use of *synchronous parallel logic*, that is, circuits that permit several operations to be performed simultaneously rather than sequentially. This led to a great increase in the speed of problem solving because different parts of the same problem could be worked on at once.

One of Whirlwind's creators, Robert Everett, describes Whirlwind as the first *minicomputer*. Paradoxically, it was one of the largest computers ever built; but in its architecture, intent, design, structure, and use, it more closely resembles a minicomputer than any of the other early machines. He wrote, "So if you will be quiet and listen, you will hear a faint rustle, and that is the millions of Whirlwind's children coming along in the form of chips to invade our houses and our automobiles and, just like the Whirlwind, they are going to be smart and reliable and fun to be with."

New Technologies

Computers became more powerful, reliable, and versatile after World War II. In addition to military and scientific users, businesses began to buy computers. The UNIVAC (Universal Automatic Computer) was the first commercial electronic digital computer. It was built by Eckert and Mauchly for Sperry Rand and completed in 1951. Programming became less tedious with the stored-program concept and easier-to-use computer languages (discussed in Chapter 9). Computers were still being built with vacuum tubes, however, and consequently they were large machines that demanded special cooling machinery and constant maintenance. They were certainly not intended for use by the general public.

In 1947 a technological development occurred that would eventually render vacuum tubes obsolete. The *transistor* was invented. The transistor served the same purpose as the vacuum tube but used far less energy and was much smaller, more reliable, and longer-lived. Suddenly it was possible to produce computers that were smaller, cheaper, and more dependable.

In the late 1950s, a technique called *photolithography* made it possible to place one circuit consisting of thousands of miniature transistors on a small piece of silicon called a *chip*. A circuit that once took up the space of thousands of vacuum tubes could now fit on a chip far smaller than one vacuum tube.

M. E. Hoff, Jr., an engineer for Intel Corporation, built an entire *central processing unit* (CPU) on a single chip in 1969. A CPU is the part of the computer that performs the actual calculations and controls the sequence in which instructions are executed. A miniaturized CPU on a chip is called a *microprocessor*. Hoff's chip, the Intel 4004, was a piece of silicon less than $\frac{1}{16}$ inch long and $\frac{1}{2}$ inch wide; yet it matched the computing power of ENIAC (see Fig. 2.18). By adding two more chips—one to move data in and out of the CPU and another to direct the actions of the CPU—Hoff built a three-chip general-purpose computer. By the end of 1973, the 8080, a microprocessor 20 times faster than the 4004, had been built.

As a result of this technology, computers have become more compact, cheaper, faster, more powerful, more reliable, and more widely used. Computer memory has likewise become more compact and cheaper, making it possible to store vast quantities of information in a very small space. After a period in which the computer was the domain solely of experts with years of technical training, it has begun to find

Figure 2.18
A microprocessor chip is so tiny it can easily pass through the eye of a needle. (© 1984 Joel Gordon)

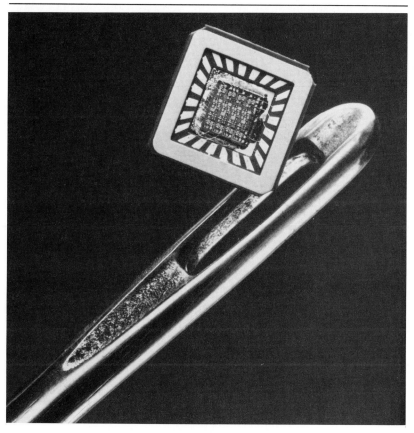

its way into everyday functions. Like its predecessor the abacus, the computer is helping millions of people make daily tasks easier.

SUMMARY

The computer's history dates back to the beginning of calculation, when human beings developed number systems and arithmetic operations. By using physical objects such as beads and gears to represent numbers, they developed mechanical ways and devices such as the abacus to add, subtract, multiply, and divide. Blaise Pascal and Wilhelm Schickard invented adding machines, Gottfried Leibniz invented an adding and multiplying machine, and Edmund Gunter, William Oughtred, and Amedee Manheim used John Napier's invention of the logarithm to derive the slide rule.

In the mid-nineteenth century, Charles Babbage designed a machine, called the difference engine, to compute tables of calculations automatically. A working version of this machine was built by George Scheutz. The difference engine led to a more sophisticated idea, that of the analytical engine, a machine that anticipated the essential ideas behind the modern general-purpose computer. Babbage's ideas were carefully documented by Ada Augusta, Countess of Lovelace. Also in the mid-nineteenth century, George Boole invented a system of logic now known as Boolean algebra, a system that plays a large role in computer programming.

Around the turn of the century, the first electric computer was built and used. This was Herman Hollerith's electric tabulator, a special-purpose computer used to tabulate the 1890 U.S. census. It was later sold commercially and used for a variety of tabulating purposes.

World War II marked a turning point in the development of the computer. The war provided scientists with new motivation to develop calculating machines. Konrad Zuse in Germany constructed an electric general-purpose program-controlled computer, a machine that the Germans might have found useful if they had taken Zuse's work more seriously. At about the same time, British scientists built special-purpose electronic computers to break the encoded messages of the German High Command. Their success contributed significantly to the outcome of the war.

In the United States, John V. Atanasoff built a special-purpose electronic computer to demonstrate the potential of calculating machines. Howard Aiken built the Mark I, a relay-based general-purpose computer. Technologically out of date by the time it was completed, the Mark I was nevertheless significant because it realized Babbage's dream for a general-purpose computer. In 1946, J. Presper Eckert, Jr., and John Mauchly built ENIAC, considered by many to be the first electronic general-purpose computer. EDVAC, built by the ENIAC team, was the first computer designed to use the stored-program concept, a concept integral to all modern computers. Another computer that resulted from wartime research was the Whirlwind, a computer that could simulate events in real time.

Since World War II, computers have become progressively smaller, faster, more powerful, and less expensive. This is largely due to the invention of the transistor, an electronic device that has been shrinking in size since the 1950s. Currently, it is possible to place many thousands of transistors on a silicon chip the size of a fingernail.

FURTHER READING

Charles Babbage, *Passages from the Life of a Philosopher* (London: Longman, Green, Longman, Roberts, & Green, 1864).

Jeremy Bernstein, *The Analytical Engine: Computers—Past, Present and Future* (New York: William Morrow and Company, 1981).

B. V. Bowden, ed., *Faster Than Thought* (London: Sir Isaac Pitman & Sons, 1953).

Christopher Evans, *The Micro Millennium* (New York: Washington Square Press, 1981).

Robert R. Everett, "Whirlwind," in Metropolis, Howlett, and Rota, pp. 365–384.

Herman H. Goldstine, *The Computer from Pascal to von Neumann* (Princeton: Princeton University Press, 1972).

Andrew Hodges, *Alan Turing: The Enigma* (New York: Simon and Schuster, 1983).

N. Metropolis, J. Howlett, and Gian-Carlo Rota, *A History of Computing in the Twentieth Century* (New York: Academic Press, 1980).

Doris Langley Moore, *Ada: Countess of Lovelace* (New York: Harper & Row, 1977).

Brian Randell, ed., *The Origins of Digital Computers: Selected Papers* (New York: Springer-Verlag, 1973).

Joel Shurkin, *Engines of the Mind: A History of the Computer* (New York: W. W. Norton and Company, 1984).

Nancy Stern, *From ENIAC to UNIVAC: An Appraisal of the Eckert-Mauchly Computers* (Bedford, Mass.: Digital Press, 1981).

ISSUES AND IDEAS

1. Many Japanese prefer to use the abacus for routine addition and subtraction despite the availability of pocket calculators. What might be the advantages and disadvantages of using an abacus rather than a calculator?

2. Mechanical calculators were used for many years. Give several reasons why they have been replaced by electronic calculators.

3. Humans prefer to count and calculate using decimal numbers, while computers are better suited to binary notation. Why is this so? Why would we not want to count in binary numbers? Why would it be difficult to make computers that used decimal numbers?

4. How was the development of the analytical engine influenced by the technology available at the time?

5. How did Charles Babbage's analytical engine affect the development of computing?

6. Trace the conception and use of the punched card in the development of computing machines.

7. What effect did World War II have on the development of computing?

8. What effect did the development of computing have on World War II?

9. Who do you think deserves the credit for the invention of the first general-purpose computer? Justify your answer.

Photo credits: Charles Babbage: The Mansell Collection, London; George Scheutz: Science Museum, London; Ada Augusta, Countess of Lovelace: Historical Pictures Service, Chicago; George Boole: IBM Archives; Claude E. Shannon: AT&T Bell Laboratories; Herman Hollerith: Columbiana Collection, Rare Book and Manuscript Library, Columbia University; Konrad Zuse: Konrad Zuse, Hünfeld, Germany; Alan Turing: Bassano Studios, London; Howard Aiken: Cruft Photo Lab, Harvard University/Paul Donaldson; Grace Murray Hopper: The Bettmann Archive; J. Presper Eckert, Jr., and John W. Mauchly: UPI/Bettmann Newsphotos; John V. Atanasoff: Iowa State University; John von Neumann: Princeton University

The Architecture of Computers

When a man has to cut down trees,
drag them out of the forest, dress and
fit the logs by hand, and raise them
with brute force to build his log cabin,
he does not give great consideration to
the niceties of architecture. It is
enough to have four walls and a roof
which doesn't leak. But when the local
lumber yard stocks two-by-fours,
sheets of plywood, prehung doors, and
preassembled window units, he can
begin to pay attention to the aesthetics
of living as well as to the imperatives.
He may even consider hiring an archi-
tect trained in the arts of designing
buildings for graceful living.

CAXTON C. FOSTER, "A View of Computer Architecture"

Introduction

The computer is a marvelous product of human imagination and in-
genuity. In its simplest form, a computer accepts input; stores, retrieves,
and processes information; and generates output. The computer is not
special in these respects; humans also perform these functions. However, the computer is distinguished by the speed and reliability of its
calculations, the amount of data it can store, and the precision and
predictability of its responses. This chapter provides a conceptual introduction to the internal structure of the modern electronic computer.
It also describes the internal activity of a computer and explains how
this activity is controlled.

A computer performs several simple steps repeatedly and at high
speed. They consist of reading input from external devices, supplying
output to such devices, storing and retrieving information, and carrying
out operations such as adding and subtracting numbers, comparing
quantities, and selecting computation sequences. In this chapter, we
begin by illustrating these basic steps using a fictitious machine we call
the pocket calculator computer (PCC). Then we identify the parts of

the modern computer, emphasizing its "control center," the central processing unit. The central processing unit itself is constructed of many very small units called logic gates. These are basic building blocks built of transistors that are combined to produce all of the components of the central processing unit. We explain how they can be combined into logic circuits to perform many tasks.

The modern computer represents all information as *binary digits* or *bits*. We discuss ways in which computers store such information in various kinds of memories. We also examine the integrated circuit that makes today's computers so small and powerful. Next, we define the broad categories into which computers are divided and highlight the personal workstation, the modern personal computer. Finally, we discuss computer networks.

■ The Pocket Calculator Computer

The pocket calculator computer (PCC) shown in Fig. 3.1 is a fictitious machine that illustrates many of the important features of the modern digital computer. We use it to solve an everyday problem, balancing a checkbook. In so doing we illustrate how such a machine can be "programmed," that is, told how to solve a problem.

Although the PCC is a very simple machine, it conforms to the definition of a computer given in Chapter 1. It accepts one piece of input at a time through its IN BOX, generates output one piece at a time through its OUT BOX, stores information in its memory, and performs computations with the aid of a pocket calculator. The PCC is not a modern general-purpose computer because its activities are directed by a human being rather than a computer program stored in its memory.

The PCC's memory can be thought of as a series of file drawers, each of which can hold only one piece of paper. To store information in memory is analogous to opening a drawer and placing a piece of paper inside or replacing the piece of paper already there with a new one. Similarly, retrieving information from memory is like opening a drawer and reading the information stored or recorded there. Information is entered into the PCC through the IN BOX. From there it can be transferred into one of the file drawers. The drawers have names beginning with MEM (MEM1, MEM2, and so on) to remind us that they represent memory.

Now that we have introduced the PCC, we can use it to balance a checkbook. Suppose that over the monthly statement period you have written three checks and also deposited money into your account. What information do you need to know to calculate the new balance?

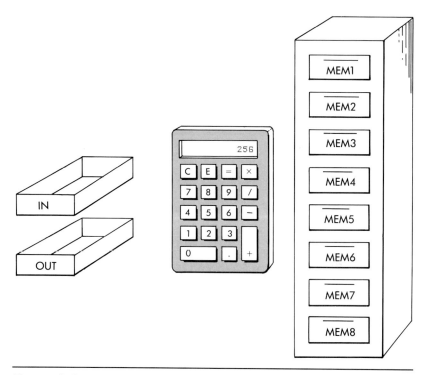

Figure 3.1
The pocket calculator computer (PCC).

- The initial balance of the account (BAL)
- The amount deposited (DEP)
- The number of checks written (NCK)
- The value of each check (CK1, CK2, CK3)
- The service charge per check (COST_CK)

Notice that we have used labels (such as BAL) to identify the information. Such labels are called *variables*.

We will now enter each piece of information through the IN BOX, sending it to the appropriate file drawer for later use. If the initial balance is $50, we enter that number into the IN BOX and transfer it to MEM1. Figure 3.2 illustrates the steps needed to place the data into the PCC's memory. These steps are stated as commands that suggest instructions that might be given to an actual computer.

Let's now consider the problem of balancing the checkbook. This task amounts to adding the deposit (DEP) to the old balance (BAL), subtracting each check (three in this example, CK1, CK2, CK3) to obtain a

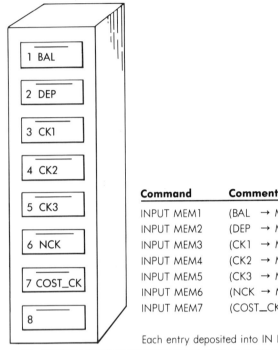

Command	Comment	Explanation
INPUT MEM1	(BAL → MEM1)	Balance to MEM1
INPUT MEM2	(DEP → MEM2)	Deposit to MEM2
INPUT MEM3	(CK1 → MEM3)	Check #1 to MEM3
INPUT MEM4	(CK2 → MEM4)	Check #2 to MEM4
INPUT MEM5	(CK3 → MEM5)	Check #3 to MEM5
INPUT MEM6	(NCK → MEM6)	Number of checks to MEM6
INPUT MEM7	(COST_CK → MEM7)	Cost/check to MEM7

Each entry deposited into IN BOX is moved to memory.

Figure 3.2
Memory and commands to read data into memory.

temporary balance (TEMP_BAL), and then subtracting the service charge (SERV_CHARGE). The temporary balance can be computed from the following formula:

$$TEMP\_BAL = BAL + DEP - CK1 - CK2 - CK3$$

To calculate the service charge, we multiply the number of checks (NCK) by the service charge per check (COST_CK):

$$SERV\_CHARGE = NCK \times COST\_CK$$

We compute the final balance (FIN_BAL) by subtracting the service charge from the temporary balance:

$$FIN\_BAL = TEMP\_BAL - SERV\_CHARGE$$

Now that we understand this problem, let's see how to instruct the PCC to perform the calculations.

Figure 3.3 shows a sequence of steps that the PCC can use to balance the checkbook. The left-hand column displays the commands the PCC must execute, and the right-hand column explains them. The

Command	Comment
LOAD MEM1	(BAL → CALC)
SUM	(+)
LOAD MEM2	(DEP → CALC)
SUBTRACT	(−)
LOAD MEM3	(CK1 → CALC)
SUBTRACT	(−)
LOAD MEM4	(CK2 → CALC)
SUBTRACT	(−)
LOAD MEM5	(CK3 → CALC)
EQUALS	(= TEMP_BAL)
STORE MEM1	(TEMP_BAL → MEM1)
LOAD MEM6	(NCK → CALC)
MULTIPLY	(×)
LOAD MEM7	(COST_CK → CALC)
EQUALS	(=SERV_CHARGE)
STORE MEM2	(SERV_CHARGE → M2)
LOAD MEM1	(TEMP_BAL → CALC)
SUBTRACT	(−)
LOAD MEM2	(SERV_CHARGE → CALC)
EQUALS	(= FIN_BAL)
OUT	(FIN_BAL → OUTPUT)

Figure 3.3
A program to balance a checkbook.

commands LOAD and STORE transfer information: to LOAD a value is to enter it into the calculator; to STORE it is to place it in memory. Thus, LOAD MEM1 means that the contents of MEM1 are moved into the calculator display, while STORE MEM1 means that the current value in the display is placed into MEM1. When a value is stored in a memory location that already contains a value, the new value will replace the old value. The commands SUM, EQUALS, SUBTRACT, and MULTIPLY are equivalent to striking the keys +, =, −, and × on the pocket calculator.

To balance the checkbook following the program of Fig. 3.3, we would enter the previous balance into the calculator, add the amount of the deposit, and subtract the value of each check to obtain the temporary balance, TEMP_BAL. This figure is stored in MEM1. By storing the temporary balance in MEM1, we lose the information that previously was stored there (the original balance). We no longer need to know the original balance because we have already used it, so this is perfectly acceptable. We then multiply the number of checks by the cost per check to obtain the service charge, which we store in MEM2, losing the value it previously held (the amount of the deposit). Finally, the temporary balance is retrieved from MEM1, the service charge is subtracted from it, and the final balance is put in the OUT BOX as output.

The steps depicted in Fig. 3.3 are similar to the instructions followed by an actual computer. Most computer programs are more powerful than this one, however; their vocabulary of commands is not limited by the functions of a pocket calculator. Computers can compare the contents of two variables, for example, and follow one set of instructions if the result is positive and another if it is negative. They can repeat sequences of statements and can jump from one part of the program to another and back again. These ideas are discussed in detail in Chapters 6, 7, and 8.

■ The Components of a Modern Computer

Understanding how the pocket calculator computer uses input, output, memory, and calculation should make it easier to understand how more complex computers work. We begin our examination of the modern general-purpose computer by briefly surveying its main components—central processing unit, memory, and input and output devices.

The most important part of a computer is its *central processing unit* or *CPU*, which performs operations on data and follows the sequences of instructions that make up computer programs. As you can see in Fig. 3.4, the CPU has several parts: *registers* for temporarily storing small

Figure 3.4
A block diagram of a central processing unit (CPU).

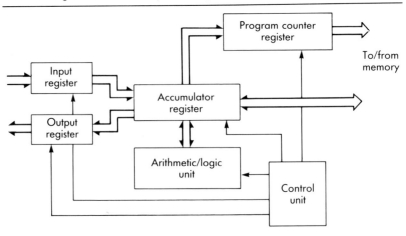

amounts of data or instructions, a *control unit* to direct and coordinate the computer's activities, and an *arithmetic/logic unit* or ALU to perform arithmetic and logic operations. (Some of these operations are described later in the chapter.) The CPU almost seems to be a computer in itself. Without the other components of a modern computer, however, the CPU's usefulness would be limited.

In modern computers, memory stores both data and instructions. Recall from Chapter 2 that before computers could store programs (before the *stored-program concept* was developed), computer operators had to use switches or other external means to give the computer its instructions, just as we had to "program" the pocket calculator computer by pressing the calculator's keys. In the modern computer, the CPU retrieves, or *reads*, data and instructions from memory and stores, or *writes*, data into memory. Memory, for the moment, can be thought of as a series of electronic file drawers, something like the file drawers the pocket calculator computer used to store data. The CPU interacts most frequently with *primary memory*, a form of fast memory in which the time to read or store information from or into a memory location is the same for all locations. *Secondary* or *peripheral memory* generally is slower but holds much more information than primary memory. Both types of memory are discussed in more detail later in the chapter.

Input and output devices make it easy for people and computers to communicate with each other. Figure 3.5 shows a typical input/output configuration: a *keyboard* to generate input and a *cathode*

Figure 3.5
Input/output: a keyboard and CRT.

ray tube or CRT to generate output. A keyboard is simply a set of labeled switches; when a key is depressed, a switch is closed, sending an electronic message to the computer. A CRT is nothing more than a television screen. A popular communication device that combines the keyboard and the CRT is the *terminal*. Many other devices can be used to communicate with computers; some of them are discussed later in the chapter.

■ Data Representation

Before going into greater detail about the parts of the computer and how they work, we should look more closely at how they represent data. As we saw in Chapter 2, modern digital computers use binary representations for data. A binary quantity can have one of two values, usually represented by 1 and 0 and sometimes by True and False. These values can be represented inside the computer by switches, which can be on or off, or by the output voltage of electronic devices such as transistors, which can be high (say, 5 volts) or low (say, 0 volts). Computers represent not only numbers but also letters and special characters as groupings, or strings, of binary digits. The phrase *binary digit* is used so frequently that it has been shortened to *bit*. A group of eight bits is called a *byte*.

The bit strings used to stand for letters and numbers must be fairly long so that enough characters can be represented. Two-bit strings, for example, allow only four characters to be represented—by 00, 01, 10, and 11. When seven bits are used, up to 128 characters can be represented.* A computer that can represent 128 different characters can represent the decimal numbers, all the letters of the alphabet in both uppercase and lowercase, the punctuation marks, and a number of special characters. Therefore, computers typically use seven-bit codes. An eighth bit is often added as a check for errors that might be made in recording the first seven bits. Table 3.1 shows some of the bit strings and corresponding characters in the American Standard Code for Information Interchange (ASCII), a standard for much of the U.S. computer industry. Other standards for representing characters as bits exist as well.

---

*There are two possible choices for the first digit (0 or 1), two possibilities for the second digit, two for the third and so on, or $2 \times 2 \times 2 \times 2 \times 2 \times 2 \times 2 = 2^7 = 128$ possible strings.

Table 3.1 □ ASCII Code for Characters

Character	Binary Code	Character	Binary Code
A	100 0001	0	011 0000
B	100 0010	1	011 0001
C	100 0011	2	011 0010
D	100 0100	3	011 0011
E	100 0101	4	011 0100
F	100 0110	5	011 0101
G	100 0111	6	011 0110
H	100 1000	7	011 0111
I	100 1001	8	011 1000
J	100 1010	9	011 1001
K	100 1011		
L	100 1100		
M	100 1101	blank	010 0000
N	100 1110	$	010 0100
O	100 1111	(	010 1000
P	101 0000	)	010 1001
Q	101 0001	*	010 1010
R	101 0010	+	010 1011
S	101 0011	,	010 1100
T	101 0100	-	010 1101
U	101 0101	.	010 1110
V	101 0110	/	010 1111
W	101 0111	=	011 1101
X	101 1000		
Y	101 1001		
Z	101 1010		

■ Logic Gates

Just as ones and zeros can be combined to form a complete system of data representation, basic electrical circuits called *logic gates* can be combined to build the complicated and powerful circuits that allow computers to solve problems. These circuits, called *logic circuits*, perform arithmetic and logic operations. We will examine two such operations after we look more closely at logic gates.

The logic gate typically has two inputs and one output. Each input or output has a value of either 1 or 0. Here 1 is normally associated with True and 0 with False; 1 and True are associated with the presence of electrical voltage, and 0 and False are associated with the absence of voltage. A logic gate examines each input and then produces an output. The three most common logic gates are AND, OR, and NOT. Schematic representations for them are given in Fig. 3.6.

The AND and OR gates each have two binary input digits and one binary output digit. The NOT gate is different; it has one binary input and one binary output. Each gate follows a rule to decide whether the output bit should register 1 or 0 (True or False). The AND gate produces a 1 only if both inputs are 1, while the OR gate produces a 1 if either or both inputs is 1. The NOT gate produces a 1 if the input is 0 and a 0 if the input is 1. These rules are often pictured in *truth tables,* as shown in Fig. 3.7.

In Fig. 3.8, a few wires, switches, batteries, and light bulbs are combined to show how AND, OR, and NOT gates can be built. Electrical current passes from the battery through the wires, but it can flow only if there is a complete path of wires and closed switches from one side of the battery to the other. The light bulb is either on or off depending on whether a closed circuit has been created so that current can flow. As you can see from the drawing, the AND gate conducts current only when both switches are closed. Thus, when both switches are closed— when both are in the True position—current flows and the bulb is lit, that is, the output is 1 or True. The OR gate permits current to flow if either of the switches is closed. The NOT gate opens a second switch if the first is closed and closes that switch if the first is open, thereby reversing the meaning of the first switch.

The binary inputs given to logic gates can have many meanings. They can represent digits of binary numbers. They can represent pieces of words. Or they can represent the truth or falsity of particular statements. In mathematical logic, or Boolean algebra, statements are either True or False, as you may recall from Chapter 2. For example, the statement *It is Monday* can be either True or False, as can the statement *My alarm clock is ringing.* It is customary to represent statements of this kind with letters so that they can easily be joined to form compound statements. We will use the letter M to represent the statement *It is Monday* and the letter R to represent the statement *My alarm clock is ringing.*

Figure 3.6
A schematic representation of AND, OR, and NOT gates.

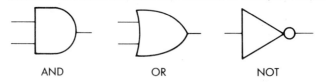

AND   OR   NOT

A	B		A AND B		A	B		A OR B		A		NOT A
False	False		False		False	False		False		False		True
False	True		False		False	True		True		True		False
True	False		False		True	False		True				
True	True		True		True	True		True				

Figure 3.7
Truth tables for three gates.

Such statements can be combined with the logical connectives AND, OR, and NOT to form more complex statements. For example, the compound statement M AND R represents the statement *It is Monday* AND *My alarm clock is ringing.* We might use the truth of this statement to determine some other action—for example, whether to get up in the morning.

Statements can be combined in other ways when the OR and NOT operations are used. Consider the compound statement M OR R. This statement is True if M is True, if R is True, or if both are True. Only if both conditions are False will the compound statement be False. Finally, we can use the NOT operation to negate a statement. For example, the statement NOT M is True when M is False, and it is False when M is True.

These examples illustrate how AND, OR, and NOT are used to form simple *Boolean equations.* We will see later that Boolean equations are very useful in writing computer programs as well as in describing computer circuits. They permit us to state the conditions on which choices of future actions can be based.

It is interesting to note that the simple operations of AND, OR, and NOT can be combined to build the CPU of any computer, no matter how complex. We cannot show that here, but we can illustrate how these operations can be used to solve certain simple problems. In the next section we build a circuit that can determine whether two binary strings are equal and a circuit that can add two binary numbers. Logic

Figure 3.8
Logic gates constructed from batteries, bulbs, and switches.

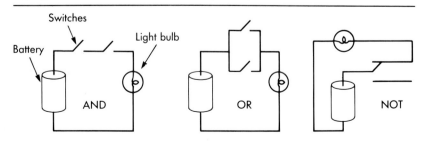

gates can also be used to construct memory cells, so they are used not only for computation but for storage as well.

Operations in the Arithmetic/Logic Unit

The arithmetic/logic unit (ALU) is the part of the CPU that performs arithmetic and logic operations. Arithmetic operations include addition, subtraction, multiplication, and division. Logic operations include AND, OR, and NOT, as well as others. The ALU also can test to determine whether a number is positive, negative, or zero or whether two characters are the same. Each of these operations requires logic circuits. This section describes the construction of such circuits to solve two problems—testing two binary strings for equality and adding two binary numbers.

Equality Testing

Often the computer must compare two strings of binary digits to determine whether they are equal. Such strings might represent binary numbers or text in which characters have been translated into binary digits. The result of a comparison may determine what the computer will do next. For example, a program may instruct the computer to perform one operation if the result of a comparison turns out to be positive and another operation if the result is negative. For humans, testing two strings for equality is straightforward; we simply look at them and check to see that they contain the same values in corresponding positions. The situation is completely different for computers. They must be given a detailed, logical description of a method for comparing strings.

The first step in comparing strings of digits is to compare individual digits. A logic circuit to compare individual digits has two inputs, a variable A to denote the value of one digit and a variable B to denote the value of the second digit. A circuit that compares A and B for equality must be able to respond to four patterns of values for A and B: $A = 0$ and $B = 0$, $A = 0$ and $B = 1$, $A = 1$ and $B = 0$, and $A = 1$ and $B = 1$. Here again, 1 is associated with True and 0 with False. The two digits are equal only when $A = 0$ and $B = 0$ or when $A = 1$ and $B = 1$. Therefore, we need to build a circuit that will give a response of True (or 1) in these cases and a response of False (or 0) in the other two cases. We will call this circuit $A \ominus B$.

To construct the circuit, we first find a Boolean equation for $A \ominus B$ by building the truth table shown in Fig. 3.9. This table has three columns, labeled A, B, and $A \ominus B$, and four rows, which correspond to the

A	B	A ⊖ B
0	0	1
0	1	0
1	0	0
1	1	1

Figure 3.9
A truth table for equality testing of bits.

values for A, B, and A ⊖ B. There is one row for each of the four patterns of values for A and B mentioned in the previous paragraph. The third column lists the values that A ⊖ B has for each of these patterns. Our equation must reflect the fact that A ⊖ B is 1 only when A is 0 and B is 0 or when A is 1 and B is 1. In other words, the equation must contain a statement that is True when A is True and B is True ($A = 1$ and $B = 1$) and a statement that is True when A is False and B is False ($A = 0$ and $B = 0$). As noted earlier, if either of these statements is True, then A ⊖ B is True. Thus, the statements should be joined by OR.

First, we write a statement that is true when $A = 1$ and $B = 1$. That statement is A AND B because A AND B is True only when A is True and B is True. Next, we need a statement that is True when $A = 0$ and $B = 0$. This statement is a bit less straightforward, because it involves changing 0 (False) to 1 (True). You may remember that the NOT statement reverses the meaning of an input. Thus, when $A = 0$, NOT $A = 1$ and when $B = 0$, NOT $B = 1$. In that case, (NOT A) AND (NOT B) is a true statement.

Now we can use OR to link the two statements we have written. The result is a Boolean equation for A ⊖ B.

A ⊖ B = (A AND B) OR ((NOT A) AND (NOT B))

Furthermore, we can draw a circuit corresponding to this equation, as shown in Fig. 3.10.

Now that we have constructed a circuit for the equality-testing gate, we can use it to compare two binary strings. Suppose that the two strings of letters $a_1a_2a_3a_4$ and $b_1b_2b_3b_4$ represent strings of binary digits. For example, if $a_1a_2a_3a_4 = 1011$ and $b_1b_2b_3b_4 = 0010$, then $a_1 = 1$, $a_2 = 0$, $a_3 = 1$, $a_4 = 1$, and $b_1 = 0$, $b_2 = 0$, $b_3 = 1$, $b_4 = 0$. For the two strings to be equal, all of the corresponding digits must be equal: a_1 must equal b_1, and so on.

To construct a logic circuit to test the equality of two four-bit strings, we use the circuit we built above to construct four gates, EQ_1, EQ_2, EQ_3, and EQ_4, each of which tests the equality of a pair of corresponding bits. EQ_1 is equal to the value of $a_1 \ominus b_1$. Thus, $EQ_1 = 1$ means a_1 equals b_1, or $a_1 \ominus b_1 = 1$. $EQ_1 = 0$ means that a_1 does not equal b_1. $EQ_2 = 1$ means

Inputs

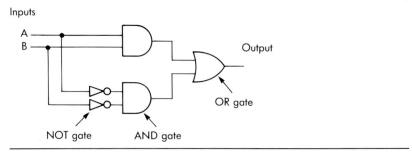

Figure 3.10
A logic circuit to realize the function A ⊖ B.

that a_2 equals b_2, or $a_2 \ominus b_2 = 1$, and so on. We must link EQ_1, EQ_2, EQ_3, and EQ_4 together to form a larger circuit that compares two four-digit strings. (We'll call this larger circuit EQ.) Since all digits must correspond for the strings to be equal, we will use AND to link the terms:

$$EQ = (EQ_1 \text{ AND } EQ_2) \text{ AND } (EQ_3 \text{ AND } EQ_4)$$

This statement is true only when the four-digit strings are equal at every position; so it correctly describes the circuit we want to build. The circuit that corresponds to this equation is shown in Fig. 3.11.

Binary Addition

Addition is a basic operation that must be performed by every CPU. Chapter 2 introduced binary addition. This section describes in more detail how a circuit can be designed to add two binary numbers.

Adding binary numbers is much like adding decimal numbers, as you can see in Fig. 3.12. In both cases, we start by adding the numbers in the rightmost column to produce a sum digit. When the sum exceeds the largest single digit that can be represented in one column (9 in the decimal system, 1 in the binary system), we produce a carry digit, which is added to the next column to the left. For example, in the decimal addition example in Fig. 3.12(a), the sum of the rightmost column is 10. We place a 0 in the unit's place and carry a 1 (representing one 10) to the tens place. Similarly, in the binary addition example in Fig. 3.12(b), the sum of the rightmost column is 2 in decimal and 10 in binary. We place a 0 in the units place and carry a 1 (representing one 2) to the twos place. The carry bit is the number of 2s in the sum. For example, if the two binary numbers to be added are 1011 and 0101, then the sum of the least significant digits (those in the ones column: 1 + 1) is 2 in

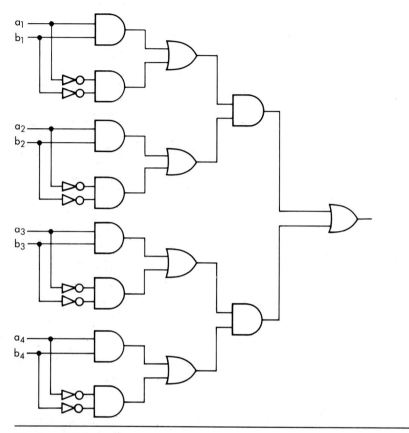

Figure 3.11
A circuit to test for equality of strings of digits.

Figure 3.12
Examples of (a) decimal and (b) binary addition.

$$2\ 0^1 3\ 6$$
$$4\ 9\ 8\ 2$$
$$\overline{7\ 0\ 1\ 8}$$

$$0^1 1^1 1^1 1^1 1$$
$$0\ 1\ 0\ 1\ 1$$
$$\overline{1\ 1\ 0\ 1\ 0}$$

(a)   (b)

decimal or 10 in binary. The leftmost digit in this pair is the number of 2s in the sum, which is 1 in this case. A carry from the first position is added to the numbers in the twos column to produce a second sum and a carry. The carry from this position is the number of 4s in the second sum. This process is repeated with the other digits in the two numbers.

Let's now construct a logic circuit for the addition of two four-digit binary numbers. We represent the two binary numbers as $a_4a_3a_2a_1$ and $b_4b_3b_2b_1$. We add a_1 and b_1 and produce a sum digit (or *sum bit*) s_1 and a carry digit (or *carry bit*) c_2. The carry c_2 is added to the twos column, represented by a_2 and b_2, to produce a second sum bit s_2 and a second carry bit c_3. This process is repeated for the entire number.

We begin by devising a logic circuit that produces a sum bit and a carry bit. We call the sum bit S and the carry bit C_O (for carry out, since this carry bit is carried out of the addition). $C_O S$ must represent the sum of the two inputs (call them A and B) plus the carry bit from previous stages of the addition. We'll call this second carry bit C_I (for carry in, since it is carried into the addition). The circuit we build can be repeated for each step of our four-digit addition. The rightmost column will have no C_I bit, of course, since there will be nothing to carry into this column, but we can allow for that by setting C_I to 0 for the rightmost column.

To design our circuit, we first set up a truth table and write Boolean equations based on the table. Figure 3.13 shows a truth table for computing C_O and S from A, B, and C_I. The last two columns represent the sum of the three bits A, B, and C_I, whose values appear in the first three columns. We seek Boolean equations for the sum and carry bits.

Let's consider first the carry bit C_O. Notice in the table that it can have the value 1 in four situations—when two or more of the three input bits have values of 1. In these four situations, a 1 will be carried out of the addition. We will not go into detail here about how these

Figure 3.13
The truth table for a sum and a carry.

A	B	C_I	C_O	S	Terms	
0	0	0	0	0		
0	0	1	0	1		V_1
0	1	0	0	1		V_2
0	1	1	1	0	U_1	
1	0	0	0	1		V_3
1	0	1	1	0	U_2	
1	1	0	1	0	U_3	
1	1	1	1	1	U_4	V_4

expressions are derived. However, you should be able to determine this yourself by referring to the truth table and to the equality-testing example. The four expressions, which we will call U_1, U_2, U_3, U_4, are as follows:

$$U_1 = ((NOT\ A)\ AND\ B\ AND\ C_I)$$
$$U_2 = (A\ AND\ (NOT\ B)\ AND\ C_I)$$
$$U_3 = (A\ AND\ B\ AND\ (NOT\ C_I))$$
$$U_4 = (A\ AND\ B\ AND\ C_I)$$

Remember, $C_O = 1$ when any of these four expressions is True. Therefore, we can link the expressions with OR to describe C_O:

$$C_O = (U_1\ OR\ U_2)\ OR\ (U_3\ OR\ U_4)$$

We can build a circuit directly from this equation, as shown in Fig. 3.14. Now let's find an equation for the sum bit S. In the truth table, the

Figure 3.14
A circuit for the carry bit C_O.

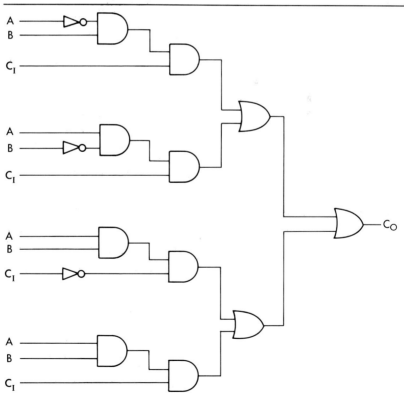

column marked S has four entries with values of 1. We create four expressions, called V_1, V_2, V_3, and V_4, to correspond with these entries:

$$V_1 = ((NOT\ A)\ AND\ (NOT\ B)\ AND\ C_I)$$
$$V_2 = ((NOT\ A)\ AND\ B\ AND\ (NOT\ C_I))$$
$$V_3 = (A\ AND\ (NOT\ B)\ AND\ (NOT\ C_I))$$
$$V_4 = (A\ AND\ B\ AND\ C_I)$$

Again, the desired expression is formed by linking those four expressions with OR:

$$S = (V_1\ OR\ V_2)\ OR\ (V_3\ OR\ V_4)$$

This equation can also be translated into a circuit, as shown in Fig. 3.15.

The two circuits of Figs. 3.14 and 3.15 can be combined into one circuit called a *full adder*. The full adder is shown schematically as a

Figure 3.15
A circuit for the sum bit S.

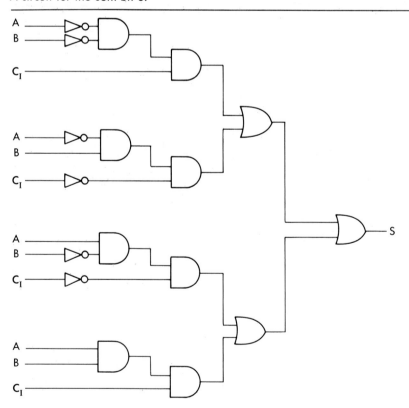

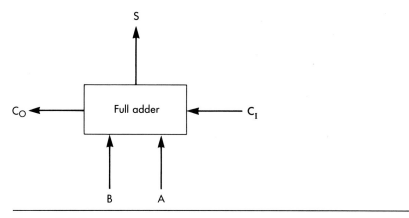

Figure 3.16
A "black box" representation of a full adder.

single "black box" in Fig. 3.16. Only its inputs and outputs are shown explicitly; we will not describe its operation here. We can combine four such adders to add our two four-digit numbers $a_4a_3a_2a_1$ and $b_4b_3b_2b_1$. Figure 3.17 shows such a circuit.

Many other important CPU circuits can be designed in the same manner. This exercise demonstrates that one basic method underlies the design of many complex circuits. However, this method poses serious difficulties when problems involve many numbers of variables because writing one expression for each 1 in a large truth table can involve an enormous number of expressions. Fortunately, there are ways around these difficulties, but a discussion of such methods is beyond the scope of this book.

Figure 3.17
A full adder chain to add two four-bit binary numbers.

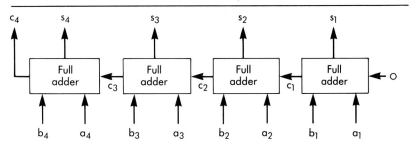

Computer Memory

We now turn to another important part of the modern computer—its memory. Convention divides computer memory into two broad categories, primary and secondary memory.

Primary Memory

Primary.memory is memory space inside the computer that allows for immediate access. Information currently being used by the computer is stored in primary memory. The file cabinet in the PCC is a form of primary memory because information stored in the drawers can be retrieved quickly and easily. Primary memory is fast to keep up with the high computation speeds of typical CPUs, but it is also fairly expensive, so most computers have a relatively small amount of it. Primary memory in today's digital computers is divided into three categories: registers, random access memory, and read-only memory.

Primary memories are constructed from *binary memory cells*, simple devices that store one of two values. Today binary memory cells are assembled from small numbers of logic gates, such as AND, OR, and NOT. Such cells are called *flip-flops* because they flip from one state to another.

The *register* is a collection of flip-flops that stores a collection of bits. Registers hold the results of computations or other important data, such as the name of the location of the next instruction that is to be executed.

Random access memory or *RAM* is a physical realization of the file cabinet memory described earlier. It is called random access memory because each of its memory locations can be *accessed*, or located, in the same amount of time. The time to retrieve the first item stored in memory is the same as the time to retrieve the last or to retrieve any one in between. In many other types of storage devices, the time required to retrieve a piece of information depends on where it is stored. This is particularly true of most types of secondary memory, as we describe later.

A random access memory can be viewed as a set (or *array*) of registers, each playing the role of one of the file drawers in the file cabinet memory. (See Fig. 3.18.) To use a RAM, a CPU must supply the name (or *address*) of the memory location from which to retrieve information or in which to store it. A *memory address register* or *MAR* holds these addresses. If information is to be stored, the *memory data register* or *MDR* holds the information temporarily until it can be moved inside the RAM. Data to be retrieved from the RAM will appear temporarily in the MDR as well.

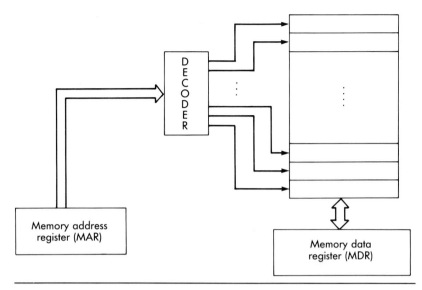

Figure 3.18
A random access memory.

Inside a RAM is a special circuit called a *decoder* that translates the address in the MAR into a command to the RAM to select the appropriate register. Each register is represented by one line in the decoder. If the address in the MAR is that for the 17th register in RAM, for example, then the line for the 17th register will carry 1 while all the other lines will carry 0. Each line causes a register to be prepared to change its values or to read out its contents.

The amount of information a RAM can store depends on several factors. Each register in a RAM can hold what is called a *word* of information. The number of bits per word is fixed for each RAM, but it varies from RAM to RAM. The number of bits per word is called the *word length*. The number of registers and thus the number of words in a RAM is determined by the size of the MAR. If the MAR has n bits, then its bits can take on 2^n different values. This is the maximum number of memory locations that the RAM can have. For example, if $n = 8$, then the RAM can hold up to $2^8 = 256$ words. If w is the length of each word in the registers, then the total storage capacity of the RAM in bits is the product of the number of words of memory (2^n) and the length of each word (w), for a capacity of $w2^n$ bits. If the capacity is measured in bytes, this number is divided by 8 because there are 8 bits per byte.

A memory device similar to RAM is *read-only memory* or *ROM*. As implied by the name, read-only memory can only be read from but cannot be written into. In other words, a program can use information stored in ROM but cannot change it or store new information there. Otherwise, ROM is similar in operation to RAM. Typically, ROM contains information crucial to the operation of a computer, information that should not change over its lifetime. Both RAMs and ROMs can store both programs and data.

■ The Stored-Program Concept

Let us take a moment to look at how information is transmitted between the primary memory and the CPU. One important aspect of these interactions involves the ability of memory to store both data and program instructions. When the CPU reads from its primary memory it must be able to distinguish between data and program instructions. If it attempted to interpret a piece of data as a program statement, or vice versa, it would do something totally unexpected and would probably *crash*, or stop working. Fortunately, a device called the *program counter* prevents this from happening. The program counter lets the computer determine where in memory to find the next instruction. (Often the next instruction is found at the memory location directly following the one just used, but from time to time it is necessary for the program to jump to a distant location.)

What a CPU actually does is to read an instruction from memory, interpret it, and then execute it. A special circuit called a *control unit* interprets and executes each instruction. For example, when two numbers are to be added, one number must be fetched from memory and put into a special register called the *accumulator* and then the second must be retrieved and added to the first. The ALU performs the addition. The control unit oversees the moving of information from registers to the ALU. This cycle of getting instructions and executing them is called the *fetch-and-execute cycle*. It is interrupted from time to time— say, if the user needs to supply a program with the value of a variable while the program is running.

The program instructions actually read and executed by the CPU are written in the *machine language* of the computer. Machine language instructions are strings of zeros and ones and can be directly executed by the CPU. Instructions usually consist of two parts, an operation code or OP_CODE and an ADDRESS. The OP_CODE is the instruction to be executed, and the ADDRESS indicates where to fetch or store relevant information. For example, if the OP_CODE indicated that an addition was to be performed, then the control unit would use the ADDRESS to find the number that was to be added to the number currently in the accumulator. Chapter 9 establishes the connection between machine languages and the so-called high-level languages, in which most programs are written.

Figure 3.19 shows a diagram of a typical small computer. It has a program counter, an accumulator, two registers for input from and output to the external world, an ALU, and a control unit. It also has a RAM with a memory address register and a memory data register. *Data paths* between various registers and the ALU are shown, as are *control paths* between the control unit and the other components of the computer. Control paths are used by the control unit to direct the transfer of data and instructions.

Figure 3.19
A block diagram of a small computer.

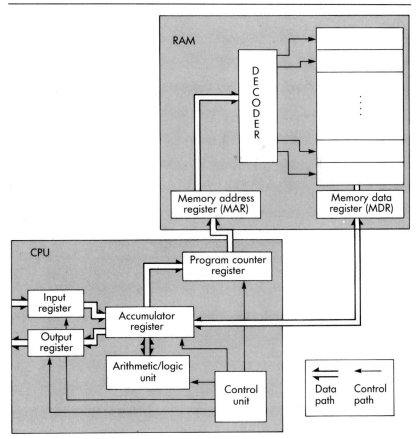

■ Secondary Memory

Secondary (or *peripheral*) *memory* is a place for long-term storage of information. Secondary memory typically provides large amounts of storage at a much smaller cost than random access memory or read-only memory. However, it also takes much more time to retrieve the information. Examples of secondary memory include magnetic disks, magnetic tapes, punched cards, and paper tapes. Some of these are described later.

Magnetic media, such as tapes and disks, are popular for secondary storage. The surfaces of these media carry a thin film of magnetizable material. In this film small magnetizable regions called *magnetic domains* can be created. Each domain can be magnetized in one of two directions. A domain magnetized in one direction can represent a 1, and a domain magnetized in the other direction can represent a 0. The direction of magnetism is sensed or read by a *head,* a device analogous to a compass in its ability to detect the direction of magnetism.

A computer tape is made of plastic with a thin magnetizable coating. Tapes can be hundreds of feet long with several thousand bits per inch. For this reason, it can take a long time to retrieve a piece of information located at the far end of a tape.

A disk resembles a phonograph record in shape, but it has a magnetizable coating rather than grooves. It is divided into concentric circles, called *tracks,* and into pie-shaped regions, called *sectors* (see Fig. 3.20). The tracks and sectors facilitate the placement and location of information.

There are two kinds of disks, hard disks and floppy disks (see Fig. 3.21). *Hard disks* are inflexible; they are usually stacked as phonograph records can be stacked, but with space between them for reading and writing heads. Hard disks usually spin at the rate of 3600 revolutions per second and may have a capacity ranging from several million bytes (*megabytes**) to several billion bytes (*gigabytes*). *Floppy disks* are made of inexpensive plastic. They are cheaper than hard disks but are also smaller and slower. They spin at hundreds of revolutions per minute and have capacities of tens to hundreds of *kilobytes* (thousands of bytes). The time required to retrieve a piece of information from a disk consists of the time to find the information plus the time to read it. The sum of these times is called the *latency* of the disk. The average latency of hard disks is typically 5 to 40 milliseconds, and the latency of floppy

---

*One megabyte is enough storage capacity to hold about 650 double-spaced typed pages, assuming 300 words per page, 5 characters per word, and 1 byte per character.

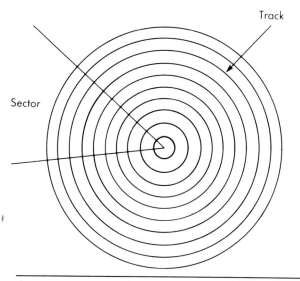

Figure 3.20
Organization of a disk.

disks is typically hundreds of milliseconds. Floppy disks are cheaper, smaller, and slower than hard disks.

Tapes and disks are generally used to store information that is not in constant demand. Because the time required to retrieve information stored on tapes and disks is much greater than the time required to retrieve information stored in random access memory, tapes and disks are not used as primary memory. However, since tape and disk storage costs much less per bit than RAM storage, tapes and disks are often used for bulk and longer-term storage.

Figure 3.21
(a) A hard disk unit; (b) a floppy disk.

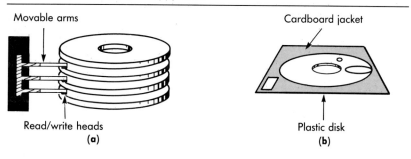

Magnetically stored information cannot fade with time, but it is not impervious to harm. It can be damaged when a magnet or electromagnet is passed over it. Since a CRT uses large electromagnets to operate, placing a disk on top of a CRT can erase information. In addition, a tape or disk can be damaged if it is dropped; the jolt can cause the magnetic domains to loosen, and the small magnetic field of the earth can then displace them, giving them a new orientation and changing the information that has been recorded.

■ Integrated Circuit Technology

Much of the computer architecture we have described depends on integrated circuit technology, which in turn is based on *semiconductors,* materials whose conductivity lies between that of insulators and good conductors. Transistors are made of semiconductor materials, and all the gates and nonmagnetic memories described in this chapter can be built from transistors. The decreasing size of transistors has brought about decreases in the size of computers.

The first transistors were about the size of a thimble and yet were considerably smaller than the vacuum tubes they replaced. Their size has decreased with time; today up to one million transistors can be placed on one *chip,* a piece of silicon so small that it can sit comfortably on a fingernail. The complex circuits imprinted on such chips are called *integrated circuits.* The cost of chips currently runs from fractions to hundreds of dollars, and the decreases in cost and size of chips show no sign of abating.

The technology used to imprint circuits on chips is called *photo-lithography.* A circuit is designed by engineers from logic elements and flip-flops, and then the circuit elements are arranged to fit within the physical dimensions of a chip. Individual wires, transistors, and gates are constructed from metal or semiconductor materials such as poly-silicon. At the level of the chip, these transistors and gates are represented as a set of rectangles.

A chip is created by using guides called *masks* to deposit the correct material at the correct place on the chip. The chip itself is a thin slice of pure crystalline silicon. To deposit a material such as polysilicon, for example, technicians place a light-sensitive substance on the chip and expose it to light through a mask that corresponds to parts to be made of polysilicon. The portion exposed to light—the regions on which polysilicon is to be deposited—has its chemical composition changed so that with a special solvent the exposed regions can be washed away and the deposit made. Another type of chemical can remove the excess light-sensitive material later. A kind of sandwich is eventually created because one layer contains polysilicon while another contains metal. An insulating material is deposited between layers.

The chip-making process has many steps of the general kind described here. The size of wires and transistors on chips is determined by the precision with which masks can be made and chemicals deposited. At the present time, most chips are manufactured with a process that permits wires to be created whose widths are as small as several micrometers (millionths of a meter).

Families of Computers

We have now examined the parts of a computer. These parts can be assembled to form a simple computer or a machine of great speed and complexity. In this section, we describe some characteristics of the major classes of computers—namely, microcomputers, minicomputers, mainframes, and supercomputers. We then turn our attention to a new class of computers that has great potential for future use—the personal workstation.

In the early days of the computer era, one could learn much about a computer from its size. Larger computers were obviously more powerful because they had more memory space and more processing equipment. General classifications were made according to size, and a knowledgeable person could tell approximately how powerful a computer was by looking at it. Today it is no longer possible to make such deductions; smaller computers are often more powerful than larger ones. Furthermore, the dividing line between classes is no longer well defined. Nevertheless, some distinctions can be made.

The microminiaturization of computer circuits on chips has led to the development of the *microcomputer*, or *micro*. This small computer typically has some tens of kilobytes (thousands of bytes) of primary memory and uses floppy disks for secondary storage. Micros are widely used in homes and small businesses.

The distinction between the *minicomputer*, or *mini*, and the *mainframe* is hard to draw. Both are multi-user machines designed to be accessed by tens or hundreds of users simultaneously through terminals. Both may contain many megabytes (thousands of kilobytes) of primary memory and use many hundreds of megabytes of secondary storage. One technical distinction that can be made between them is that mainframes usually have a small auxiliary CPU dedicated to handling communications with terminals and secondary storage, while minis typically do not have such processors.

Supercomputers are among the fastest computers in existence. They are fast in serial computation (performing one action at a time) and also, typically, in parallel computation (performing several actions simulta-neously)—some can do a computation every few nanoseconds.* Su-percomputers are very expensive and as a consequence are used most frequently for problems requiring very large amounts of computation, such as weather prediction and nuclear weapons research.

A new member of the computer family is the *personal workstation,* shown in Fig. 3.22. This type of machine combines the compact size of the home computer with the power, storage capacity, and graphics capability of much larger machines (graphics are discussed further in Chapter 10). Although the personal workstation sits comfortably on a desk top, it can generally execute a million or more instructions per second, a rate several times that of the average home computer. In ad-dition, it typically operates on 32-bit words, whereas most home com-puters operate on 8-bit or 16-bit words. This longer word length means faster computation since fewer memory accesses are required per op-eration. As a rule, workstations contain between one-half and a few megabytes of primary memory; most home computers do not contain more than several tens of kilobytes of primary memory. For secondary memory, personal workstations typically employ hard disks that can hold tens of megabytes of information. In comparison, an average floppy disk may contain up to 300 kilobytes of storage. When compared with the size and speed of most home computers, the workstation's capabilities are impressive. Furthermore, workstations can connect to other work-stations to form networks, allowing users to share programs and other information. Networks are discussed in more detail later in this chapter.

Workstations have graphical capabilities far greater than those of home computers. While home computers display disjointed, low-reso-lution pictures where curves look like uneven staircases, a workstation can display fine lines and smooth curves. This is due to the high res-olution of its bitmapped display. Before we explain the bitmapped dis-play, we provide some background on traditional terminals.

Some CRTs are designed specifically for computer terminals and can display only characters (letters, numbers, and special characters, such as punctuation marks). The screens of these terminals are divided into a series of small blocks, one for each character. The characters themselves consist of groupings of dots. Since each character has a pre-determined configuration of dots, the computer must store only the 7-bit identification of each character; the encoding of the character is automatically translated into its graphical equivalent. These bits must

---

*A nanosecond, one billionth of a second, is approximately the time it takes for light to travel 12 inches.

Figure 3.22
A personal workstation is a powerful computer system that is popular with executives and entrepreneurs. (Photo courtesy of Apollo Computer Inc., Chelmsford, Mass.)

be stored in the local memory of the terminal. Thus, a home computer, which typically has 24 lines and 40 columns, has 960 blocks on its screen and requires about 960 bytes of memory to store a full screen.

By contrast, a *bitmap* is a complete bit-by-bit representation of the display in memory. The screen is divided into a two-dimensional array of picture elements, or *pixels*. Each pixel is like one square cell in a piece of graph paper: the finer the graph paper, the more detailed a picture that can be drawn by blackening squares. The fineness of the graph, or in this case of the array of pixels, is called the *resolution* of the screen. High-resolution screens use a very fine grid and allow detailed drawings, while low-resolution screens have a coarse grid and permit only crude graphics. Why, then, aren't all computer screens high-resolution screens?

The answer lies in the extra precision required of the electron gun at the back of the CRT and the amount of memory required to record the many pixels in the display; each pixel requires at least one bit of memory to describe it. If the display is a two-tone display (black and

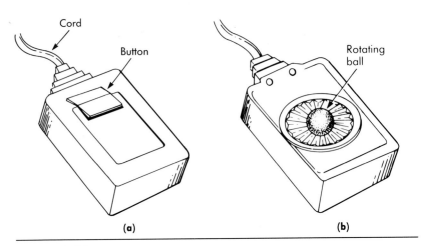

Cord

Button

Rotating ball

(a)   (b)

Figure 3.23
The mouse: (a) top view; (b) bottom view.

white or black and green), then one bit is needed per pixel to record whether the pixel is on or off. (It is white or green when on.) If the display is in color or permits shading, then more bits are required to describe color and brightness. The memory required by high-resolution screens is beyond the reach of most home computers, as is illustrated by a simple calculation. A large high-resolution screen typically has 1,024 rows and 1,024 columns. If there is one bit per pixel, then 1,048,576 bits must be stored to record the contents of such a screen. This amounts to 131,072 bytes (dividing the number of bits by 8), which should be compared to the 960 bytes needed to record the low-resolution screen found on many home computers.

For input, workstations typically use *pointing devices* in addition to keyboards. Pointing devices permit the user to point to places on the display, and perhaps to select actions, providing faster and easier communication than typing.

A *mouse*, such as the one shown in Fig. 3.23, is a typical pointing device. It is a small object that fits in the palm of a hand and connects to the computer with a wire. It typically has one or more buttons on top and a ball underneath that rolls as it moves across a surface. The movement of the ball is communicated to the computer, which causes the cursor to follow the motion of the mouse.* The mouse makes it

---

*A cursor, a flashing line or box, highlights on the screen the space after the last character that was entered. The cursor provides a means to determine the user's current position on the screen. Without a cursor, there would be no way of knowing where the next character would appear.

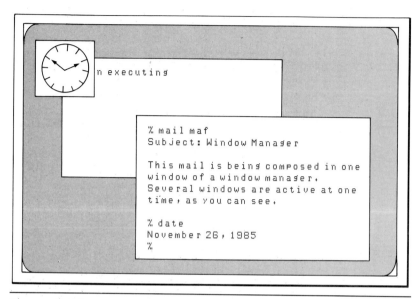

Figure 3.24
A typical window manager display.

easy to position the cursor on the screen and to request an action by pressing one of the buttons.

Another feature found in some workstations is the *window manager,* a program that permits work to be done on several different projects at once with all of them visible on the screen. Each project can be viewed through a computer *window.* Several windows may appear on the screen at the same time, as in Fig. 3.24. For example, a user might run a program in one window, read electronic mail in another, and play a game in a third. These windows may overlap to permit more information to appear on the screen; they can be brought to the foreground or moved to the background with a click of a mouse button.

Computer Networks

A single computer can be very useful. Its value, however, is greatly enhanced if it can communicate with other computers. A user can then obtain access to many sources of information that would otherwise be unavailable. She can, for example, communicate with other computer users through electronic mail, share programs with colleagues, or access databanks all over the country.

Computers usually communicate over telephone lines. As you know, information is encoded in the computer in digital form, that is, as zeros and ones. Since the telephone lines available to most users send analog, not digital, information, some means must be found to translate digital information into analog information and back again. Two devices are used—one to send data and another to receive it. A *modulator* is the device used to send data; it translates the digital signals produced by a computer into analog signals. For example, a modulator might convert zeros and ones into tones of two different frequencies. A *demodulator* can then receive the tones and convert them back into digital form. A *modem* is a modulator and demodulator combined into one unit.

Telephone lines are not the only means of sending data. Data can also be sent via satellites and microwave transmission or through cable for communication within a small area such as a single building or a university campus.

There are two kinds of data transmission—synchronous and asynchronous. *Synchronous communication* involves a continuous transmission of data, while *asynchronous communication* involves transmission of data in spurts. Synchronous communication is faster but requires careful timing—synchronization—between sending and receiving devices and is therefore more expensive. Most inexpensive modems transmit data asynchronously. Figure 3.25 graphically describes these two methods of communication.

Electronic transmission can be disrupted by *noise*, any disturbance that interferes with accurate data transmission. It can be caused by power interruptions, electrical storms, electric motors, automobiles, switches in telephone switching centers, and many kinds of electronic equipment. To combat this problem, special codes are used for error detection and correction. One way to detect potential errors is to encode data redundantly. The simplest form of *redundancy* involves repeating a message several times. If a message is repeated three times, for example, the receiver is more likely to detect errors. Even if noise changes the value of a bit in one transmission, the bit will likely be represented correctly in the other two transmissions. Thus, when the number of errors is small, they often can be detected and corrected.

Computer networks exist to facilitate communication between computers. Messages are typically sent over networks in packets, groups of perhaps a thousand bits of information. Packets contain information about their destination, which is used to ensure that a path is found on which to route them. As illustrated in Fig. 3.26, there are a variety of ways to form a network.

A *ring net* places all the users in a ring and allows them to pass information to each other around the ring. Typically only one user can transmit information at a time. To ensure that only one user is transmitting, one "token" is circulated and must be held by the sending

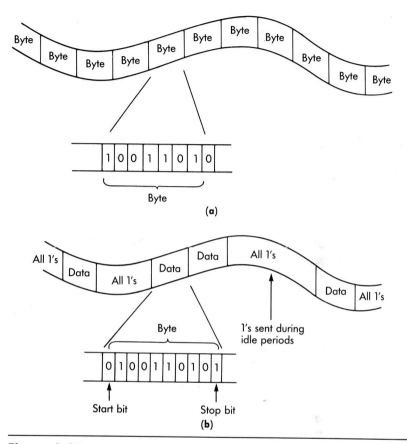

Figure 3.25
(a) Synchronous communication; (b) asynchronous communication.
[Adapted from H. Dominic Covvey and Neil Harding McAlister, *Computer Consciousness*, © 1980, Addison-Wesley, Reading, Mass. Pg. 83, Fig. 6.2 and pg. 85, Fig. 6.3 (adapted material). Reprinted with permission.]

Figure 3.26
Some common network configurations.

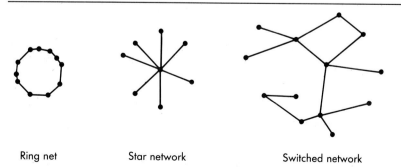

station at the time of transmission. Ethernet is an example of a *collision-based* network. In Ethernet every user is connected with every other user by a continuous cable, and messages may be sent by any station when no other user is transmitting. Occasionally, two users may begin to transmit simultaneously, and their messages may collide. In that case, the users simply delay transmission until the network is open.

In a *star network,* each station is directly connected to a central node. A message to be sent to another station is first sent to the central station and then back out to the designated recipient. A *switched network* transmits information in the same way as a telephone company does: a connection is created by making many local connections to form a path between the caller and the receiver.

SUMMARY

Computer architecture is a collection of methods that has been developed over the past 150 years to build computers. Certain basic ideas are common to all modern computers. Computers store and retrieve information and perform arithmetic and logical operations on it. Since they run programs that are stored in the same physical memory as are the data on which they operate, they must be able to discern program instructions from data.

All modern computers are constructed from logic gates, which can be combined to make circuits for basic operations such as equality testing and binary addition. They can also be used to form memory cells. Random access memory, or RAM, is a type of primary memory that provides rapid access to information. Secondary memory, used for long-term, bulk storage, typically uses devices such as magnetic tapes and disks. Secondary memory provides slower access to information than primary memory does.

Several types of computers have been developed, including microcomputers, minicomputers, and mainframes. The newest member of the computer family is the personal workstation, which has the potential to bring high-quality computing power to large numbers of people. Computers can be integrated into networks for sharing of information. Such networks, which combine communication with computing, are likely to have a major impact on the way we work, live, and obtain information.

FURTHER READING

John P. Hayes, *Computer Architecture and Organization* (New York: McGraw-Hill, 1978).

M. Morris Mano, *Computer System Architecture* (Englewood Cliffs, N.J.: Prentice-Hall, 1976).

Carver Mead and Lynn Conway, *Introduction to VLSI Systems* (Reading, Mass.: Addison-Wesley, 1980).

ISSUES AND IDEAS

1. Use the PCC to balance a checkbook with the following transactions. Using Figs. 3.2 and 3.3 as a guide, write out the instructions and explanations required to balance the checkbook. Give the generic steps and the specific numbers that would be used.

Initial balance:	$ 225
Deposit:	$ 30
Check:	$ 55
Check:	$ 15
Deposit:	$ 50
Check:	$ 22
Cost per check:	$ 0.30

2. Does every computer contain a CPU? Can a single computer contain more than one CPU? Explain your answers.

3. Are the following statements True or False under the given conditions?

A = F	B = T	[A AND (NOT B)] OR (A AND B)
A = T	B = F	[A OR (NOT A)] AND [B OR (NOT B)]

4. Write a Boolean expression using the statements A, B, and C that is true when both A and B are true or when C is false. Construct a truth table for your equation.

5. Find an equation to compare two digits A and B whose output is 1 (True) only when the two digits are not equal. Then use this circuit to draw a larger circuit that will compare two four-digit binary numbers and produce an output of 1 (True) only when all of the corresponding digits in the two numbers are unequal. [For example, the circuit would return a value of 1 (True) if given the two numbers 1011 and 0100. It would return a value of 0 (False) if given the numbers 1011 and 0101.]

6. Add the two binary numbers 101101 and 110001.

7. What is the purpose of an ALU? What is the relation between an ALU and a CPU?

8. We have described several types of memory, including RAM, hard and floppy disks, and magnetic tape. Which of these are used for primary memory and which for secondary memory? Why do we use them in this manner?

9. The stored-program concept is mentioned in this chapter and in Chapter 2. Show how this concept influenced the development of computers and explain how it is actually implemented.

10. What distinguishes a workstation from a microcomputer?

11. Many schools and businesses have currently moved from mainframe computer systems to microcomputer systems. Few of these institutions, however, have entirely given up their mainframe system. Describe several advantages of each system, and postulate why it might be most desirable to have a system that combines the two types of computers.

Word Processing

I use my [word] processor to write, to
store notes, to create, to edit, to organize. . . . It's the most important tool
writers have been given since Guten-
berg created moveable type.

CHRISTOPHER CERF, consultant to "Sesame
Street"

■ Introduction

One of the simplest and most direct ways to make contact with a computer is through the use of a word processor. Word processors are
special-purpose computers or computer programs for creating and modifying documents. Word processors have become popular because they
greatly simplify the preparation of letters, résumés, papers, and manu-
scripts, once a laborious process for even the most experienced typists.

With a typewriter, correcting mistakes can be a messy, time-consuming task involving erasers, correction fluids, ribbons, or cartridges.
After a page has been removed from the typewriter, correcting it becomes particularly difficult because the paper must be reinserted in
exactly its former position. Even when a document is error-free, the
formatting—aligning text on the page, properly arranging footnotes, including information at the top and bottom of each page, and numbering pages—can be painstaking.

With a word processor, the typist can correct typographical errors
where they occur without retyping the correct portions of the document. Writers can insert or delete words, sentences, or entire para-

graphs without disturbing the rest of the text. If reorganization is desired, small or large sections of text can be moved. The word processor can automatically set left, right, top, and bottom margins and can automatically print page numbers as well as headings and footings. Many word processors automatically provide footnoting (ensuring that the note stays on the same page as the corresponding text), indexing, spelling, and bibliographic aids.

In this chapter, we begin by describing word processors and formatting. To illustrate the spectrum of word processing capabilities, we examine three popular systems—Bank Street Writer, WordStar, and MacWrite. We then introduce document preprocessors, special programs to enhance the power of word processors. Finally, we examine trends likely to influence future word processors.

■ Components of Word Processing Systems

A *word processor*, whether a special-purpose computer or a program for a general-purpose computer, is used to create, modify, format, and print textual documents. *Textual documents* include any pieces of text entered from a keyboard, such as personal letters, memos, outlines, papers, résumés, or books. A word processor consists of two parts: an editor and a formatter. The *editor* is a computer program used to create and manipulate documents. The *formatter* is another computer program that puts documents into proper form for printing or display.

As with most software, users communicate with editors and formatters by using input and output devices. Most users create documents with a terminal, which consists of a keyboard and a CRT. Many editors now permit the editing of an entire screenful of text at once; these are called *full-screen editors*. (Older programs, called *line editors*, permit the editing of only one line at a time, making revision of large documents considerably more difficult.)

A blinking solid rectangle or line called a *cursor* is displayed on the CRT screen to mark the user's current position in the document. Users can position the cursor anywhere on the screen with *cursor movement keys*, special keys often labeled with arrows to indicate their direction, or with a *pointing device*, such as a mouse, a joystick, or a data tablet (see Fig. 4.1). Recall that a *mouse* is a small device with a ball underneath and one or more buttons on top. Moving the mouse on a flat surface rotates the ball, whose movement is then translated into movement of the cursor. A *joystick* can be moved forward, backward, right, or left to maneuver the cursor on the screen. A stylus on a *data tablet*

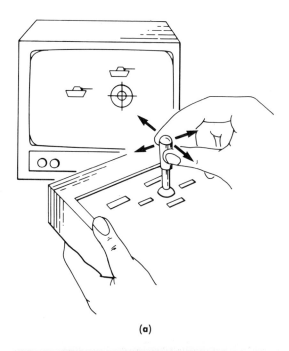

(a)

(b)

Figure 4.1
Besides the mouse, (a) the joystick and (b) the data tablet are other common pointing devices. [(b) Photo courtesy of Houston Instrument]

can also control the cursor. The tablet contains sensors that electronically determine the position of the stylus, which is then represented by the cursor position on the screen.

We can see output from word processors displayed on a CRT screen or printed on a variety of printers. Output displayed on a screen is called *soft copy,* and printed output is called *hard copy.* Most users of personal computers have dot-matrix or daisy wheel printers. Dot-matrix printers use pins, hammers, or jets of ink to print patterns that form characters. Daisy wheel printers, like typewriters, use preformed characters; each character is located at the end of a spokelike projection that radiates from the daisy wheel's center as a petal radiates from the center of a daisy. As you can see from the enlargements of printed characters in Fig. 4.2, daisy wheel output is clearer than dot-matrix output. Professional work often requires other types of printers, such as laser printers or phototypesetters.

Editors

This chapter focuses on *text editors,* programs that process text. Other types of editors also exist: *program editors* simplify the creation of computer programs; and *graphical* or *layout editors* aid in the creation of pictures. All of these editors perform similar basic functions. We will mention program editors and graphical editors again in later chapters.

Types of editors

Editors can be classified according to the type of editing they permit, which in turn reflects the conceptual models on which they are based. The types of editors discussed here are line editors and stream editors.

Computers store each document internally in a *file,* a storage area that can hold a collection of alphabetic, numeric, and special characters. In the early days of computing, programmers had to record files on 80-column punched cards that contained one character per column. Each card corresponded to one line in a file. If any character on a card was changed, the entire card had to be manually repunched. Editing a program consisted of punching new cards or rearranging old ones.

Figure 4.2
(a) Dot-matrix and (b) daisy wheel output.

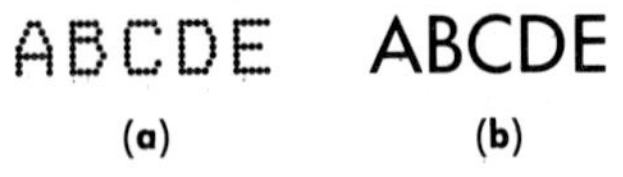

ABCDE   ABCDE

(a)   (b)

The introduction of terminals allowed the display of a file on a CRT screen. At this point, it also became possible for users to type programs directly into the computer via the terminal keyboard and to correct mistakes on the screen with an editor. The first editor programs, called *line editors*, attempted to reproduce the punched-card model by treating a file as a disconnected series of lines, like cards. Since only one line at a time could be seen or edited, this model made many tasks difficult. Although line editors are no longer in widespread use, they are still used as program editors for home computers.

Stream editors provide a much more flexible model of a document. Such editors record a document as a continuous stream of characters, something like a rope (see Fig. 4.3). Special characters can be likened to knots in the rope; they mark the ends of lines, the ends of files, and special formatting commands. In the stream model, lines may be of any length.

A *full-screen editor* is a type of stream editor that permits the viewing and editing of an entire screen of text at one time—a big improvement over line editors. Since most documents are too long to fit entirely on one screen, a portion of the file is visible through a *viewing window*. As Fig. 4.4 illustrates, a user can shift the viewing window from top to bottom and sometimes from left to right. For example, if the file is wider than the screen width, it is possible to view the portion of text to the right of the window by moving the window to the right.

Many editors allow a user to insert special formatting commands at the same time as they enter the text itself. *Formatting commands* control the final appearance of the document, specifying division of paragraphs, size of margins and headings, typeface, typesize, and spacing. Editors that also format text to give some semblance of the printed document are called *editor/formatters*. Editors used with high-resolution displays may show the document as it will appear on paper by immediately executing each formatting command and displaying the result on the screen. These editor/formatters are called WYSIWYG (pronounced "wizzywig") editor/formatters because "what you see is what you get."

Figure 4.3
The rope metaphor for streams, in which formatting commands are knots in a string of text.

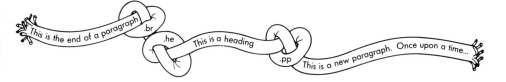

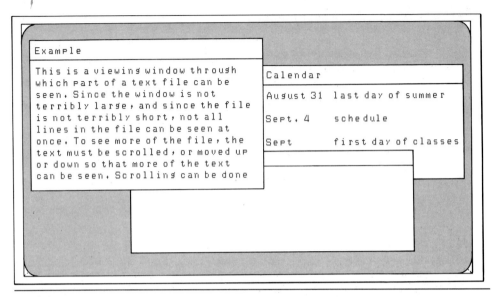

Figure 4.4
A document examined through the viewing window of a display editor.

Functions of editors

The functional capabilities of an editor include the ability to travel through a document, to mark regions of text, and to insert, copy, delete, and locate material. Some editors also permit users to insert the contents of another file into the edited file.

One important function of an editor is to allow the user to enter new text. As the user types text into a file, the cursor moves to the right. When it reaches the right-hand edge of the viewing window, the editor may stop the cursor and wait for the user to hit the RETURN key or it may wordwrap. *Wordwrapping* causes the cursor to move to the next line and display there the entire word that overlapped the viewing window (see Fig. 4.5). On some systems, when the cursor reaches the right-hand edge of the window, the window may be automatically moved to the right, making room for more text. Text may also be entered into a file by use of overstriking or insertion. In using *overstriking,* the user types new text directly over old text, replacing the old text with the new. In *insertion,* the user moves the cursor to the place at which new text is to be entered and types in the new text. The cursor moves to the right, pushing the old text ahead of it. Thus, no old text is destroyed.

To edit a document, the user must be able to move around in it

```
<<
<<
This is the first line of text. <<
<<
This line of text will demonstrate wordwrappi_
                    (a)

<<
<<
This is the first line of text. <<
<<
This line of text will demonstrate
wordwrapping._
                    (b)
```

Figure 4.5
A text file (a) just before and (b) after wordwrapping.

quickly and easily. Most editors provide a series of traveling commands to facilitate such movement. These commands typically permit the user to move to the top or bottom of the file as well as to advance or backtrack by several lines or an entire screenful at once. Other commands allow the user to move the cursor one space at a time in any of the four directions (up, down, left, and right). Many editors also allow the cursor to jump from word to word or from line to line. Finally, editors include travel commands to locate a specific piece of text in the file. For example, a user wishing to change a date somewhere in a ten-page document might call upon a locate command to find the date. Once located, the information could be updated easily.

Full-screen editors typically permit the user to mark portions of text so that they can be moved, copied, or deleted. In the stream model, a special *mark character* indicates the beginning of marked text and the current cursor position denotes the end of the marked text. Many editors highlight the marked region, as shown in Fig. 4.6(a). In copying and deleting marked regions, a display editor saves the selected region in a *buffer*, a special area of storage separate from the edited file. The buffer in Fig. 4.6(b) is called the "Clipboard." Buffers temporarily store material for later retrieval and insertion into the body of the file. Some modern editors use the analogy of cutting and pasting paper documents. To *cut* a piece of text is to remove it from the file and store it temporarily in a buffer. To *paste* text is to move it from the buffer back into the body of the file, as shown in Fig. 4.6(c).

There are many opportunities to make mistakes when using editors. Some errors, such as deletions of large amounts of text, can be disastrous. For this reason, many editors feature an *undo facility* that allows users to reverse the effects of previous commands. Some editors

🍎 File Edit Search Format Font Style

c4.1

A *full-screen editor* is a type of stream editor that permits the viewing and editing of an entire screen of text at one time -- a big improvement over line editors. Since most documents are too long to fit entirely on one screen, a portion of the file is visible through a *viewing window.* As Figure 4.4 illustrates, a user can shift the viewing window from top to bottom, and sometimes from left to right. For example, if the file is wider than the screen width, it is possible to view the portion of text to the right of the window by moving the window to the right.

Many editors allow a user to insert special formatting commands at the same time they enter the text itself. *Formatting commands* control the final appearance of the document, specifying division of paragraphs, size of margins and headings, typeface and typesize, and spacing. Editors that also format text to give some semblance of the printed document are called *editor/formatters.*

Editors used with high-resolution displays may show the document as it will appear on paper by immediately executing each formatting command and displaying the result on screen. These editor/formatters are called WYSIWYG (pronounced "wizzywig") editor/formatters because

(a)

🍎 File Edit Search Format Font Style

c4.1

A *full-screen editor* is a type of stream editor that permits the viewing and editing of an entire screen of text at one time -- a big improvement over line editors. Since most documents are too long to fit entirely on one screen, a portion of the file is visible through a *viewing window.* As Figure 4.4 illustrates, a user can shift the viewing window from top to bottom, and sometimes from left to right. For example, if the file is wider than the screen width, it is possible to view the portion of text to the right of the window by moving the window to the right.

Editors used with high-resolution displays may show the document as

Clipboard

Many editors allow a user to insert special formatting commands at the same time they enter the text itself. *Formatting commands* control the final appearance of the document, specifying division of paragraphs, size of margins and headings, typeface and typesize, and spacing. Editors that also format text to give some semblance of the printed document are called *editor/formatters.*

(b)

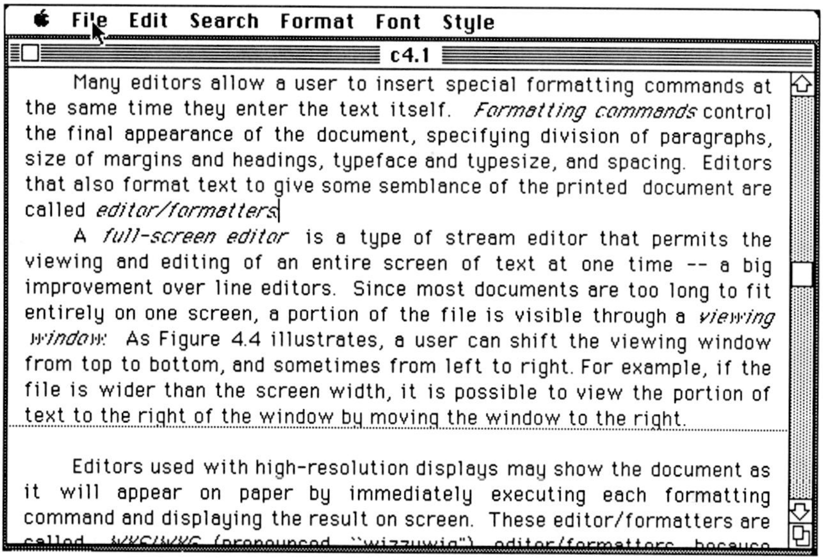

```
 File   Edit   Search   Format   Font   Style
```

```
                              c4.1
```

Many editors allow a user to insert special formatting commands at the same time they enter the text itself. *Formatting commands* control the final appearance of the document, specifying division of paragraphs, size of margins and headings, typeface and typesize, and spacing. Editors that also format text to give some semblance of the printed document are called *editor/formatters*

A *full-screen editor* is a type of stream editor that permits the viewing and editing of an entire screen of text at one time -- a big improvement over line editors. Since most documents are too long to fit entirely on one screen, a portion of the file is visible through a *viewing window*. As Figure 4.4 illustrates, a user can shift the viewing window from top to bottom, and sometimes from left to right. For example, if the file is wider than the screen width, it is possible to view the portion of text to the right of the window by moving the window to the right.

Editors used with high-resolution displays may show the document as it will appear on paper by immediately executing each formatting command and displaying the result on screen. These editor/formatters are called *WYSIWYG* (pronounced "wizzywig") editor/formatters because

(c)

Figure 4.6
Marking and moving text. (a) The text is marked; (b) the marked text is cut and stored on the clipboard; (c) the marked text is pasted elsewhere in the text.

permit undoing only the last operation, others allow undoing only certain operations, while still others allow unlimited "undos."

Some editors are more difficult to use than others, especially for new users. Some editors require users to memorize commands, while others display on-screen *menus* that list various command choices. In some editors, users must type in commands; in others, users can activate a command by moving the cursor over a menu item and hitting a special key, such as a button on a mouse. Some editors even employ *touch-sensitive screens* whereby users can execute a command simply by touching a place on the screen with a finger or special pen.

The menus that list commands can take several forms. Menus that remain continuously visible on the screen are known as *sticky menus*. They reduce the amount of screen space available for viewing a document; however, the extra help provided may more than offset this disadvantage for novice users. In contrast, *pop-up menus* are visible only when requested. (The menu labeled Edit in Fig. 4.7 is a pop-up menu.) Pop-up menus save screen space but can increase the time required to

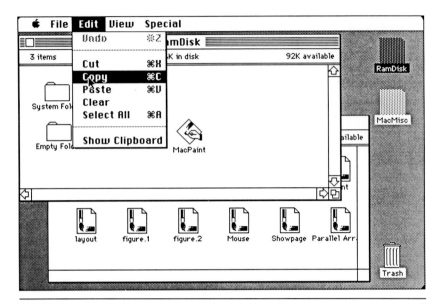

Figure 4.7
Apple Macintosh menus and icons.

execute a command, since the menu may have to be popped up before the user can select the desired command. Some editors have sticky menus containing *icons,* small labeled figures that pictorially represent a command. For example, an icon shaped like a file folder might represent a file. Placing the cursor over the folder and clicking a mouse button might cause the contents of the file to appear on the screen. Similarly, selecting an icon representing a particular file and moving it to another icon shaped like a garbage can might tell the editor to erase that file.

■ Document Formatting

Document formatters are the elements of word processors that determine how the printed document appears. Formatters control basic formatting such as centering, indentation, margins, spacing, and tab setting. Many of them can automatically print headings, footings, and page numbers. In addition, many can place footnotes at the bottom of a page. Some formatters can even generate indexes, glossaries, and tables of contents automatically.

There are two principal types of document formatting systems:

batch formatters and interactive formatters. *Batch formatters* format a
document all at once after the user has inserted formatting commands
to specify the way the document should look. *Interactive formatters* format the document as it is created or edited. They continually produce
on the screen a rendition of the document as it will look when printed.
(This is called a *soft-copy facsimile*). WYSIWYG editor/formatters are
interactive.

Formatting can be specified in a variety of ways. In some modern
systems, users select both editing and formatting commands from
menus. These systems blur the distinction between editing and formatting. The distinction is further blurred with WYSIWYG edi-
tor/formatters, since the formatting is done along with the editing rather
than later. In older systems, a clear division exists between editing and
formatting. The editor is used to enter and edit lines in a file, lines that
contain both text and formatting commands. The file is then run
through a program that formats the text according to the formatting
commands in the file.

These systems require placing formatting commands in a file, usually in the form of *dot commands*. Dot commands, placed at the beginning of a line and starting with a period, indicate a special command
for the formatter. For example, .pp might denote the beginning of an
indented paragraph, and .b followed by a word might print that word
in boldface. See Fig. 4.8 for an example of text interspersed with formatting dot commands.

Some editors, both batch and interactive, specify formatting with
control characters. A *control character* is a character typed by holding
down the CONTROL (or CTRL) key and typing some other key. In
this book we mark such special keys with a caret (^) preceding the character. Thus, ^P specifies the control character pronounced "control P."

Figure 4.8
Text containing batch formatting commands .pp and .b.

Batch formatting commands, placed at the beginning of a line and starting
with a period, indicate a special command for the formatter.
For example,
.pp
might denote the beginning of an indented paragraph and
.b
followed by a word might print that word in boldface. These sentences
show text interspersed with formatting commands.
.pp
Some editors specify formatting with control characters.

It might denote the start of an indented paragraph. Users type these commands directly into documents as needed.

Document formatting can be very sophisticated. Some formatters provide facilities for formatting equations, tables, footnotes, and simple pictures. Describing exactly how these elements should look may require complex sequences of formatting specifications. To save the user time and effort, dot commands called *macros* are used to stand for sets of formatting specifications. Special programs called *macro preprocessors* then translate the macros back into series of formatting commands. We discuss preprocessors in more detail at the end of the chapter.

■ Examples of Word Processing Systems

Users must often consider the trade-off between the power of a word processor and the time necessary to learn and use it. Usually, the easier one is to learn to use, the more limited its capabilities. We now introduce three systems with differing editing and formatting capabilities: Bank Street Writer, WordStar, and MacWrite.

Bank Street Writer

The Bank Street Writer is a simple full-screen word processor developed by the Bank Street College of Education in New York. It was designed to teach writing to grade-school children, but its ease of use has made it a popular word processor for adults as well. We discuss the Bank Street Writer to illustrate how easy using a simple word processing system can be as well as to introduce concrete examples of word processing commands.

Bank Street Writer has three modes of operation: the write mode, the edit mode, and the transfer mode. As might be expected, the write mode is for writing (entering text), and the edit mode is for altering entered text. The transfer mode is used to leave the editor, to clear away the current file, and to transfer files—from floppy disk to primary memory, and from primary memory to the printer. All users start in the write mode but can move from any mode to any other. For each mode, the editor displays a sticky menu listing all available commands.

Only two actions are possible in write mode: entering text using insertion (the text at the cursor shifts to the right to make space for the new text, as described earlier) and deleting characters to the left or right of the cursor by advancing the cursor with arrow keys (or their equivalent). These actions permit text to be entered initially. The user may not otherwise move the cursor in write mode; to move the cursor, the user must first enter edit mode.

Figure 4.9 shows the menu for the edit mode. As the figure shows, edit mode offers a wider choice of options than write mode. The user can select options from the menu by moving the cursor over the item and hitting the RETURN key. For example, positioning the cursor on the item TRANSFER MENU and pressing RETURN causes the transfer menu to appear. To move around in the text, the user can position the cursor with arrow keys or their equivalent or can use the D, U, B, and E keys (for down, up, beginning, and end) to "jump" down ten lines, up ten lines, to the beginning or to the end of the file.

In the edit mode the user can perform actions in one of three categories: erasing, moving, and searching. She can ERASE a block of text and then UNERASE it if she wants. Similarly, the user can MOVE a block of text from one place to another and MOVEBACK the text if she doesn't like the change. Finally, the user can FIND a word in the text and RE-

Figure 4.9
The edit mode menu for Bank Street Writer. (Courtesy of Broderbund and Bank Street College)

PLACE the old word with a new one. The UNERASE and the MOVEBACK operations will undo only the last ERASE or MOVE action performed in edit mode. When the user selects ERASE, the editor allows the user to highlight the text to be erased by moving the cursor over it. Hitting RETURN causes the editor to prompt with the question Are you sure you want to erase highlighted text (Y/N)? This gives the user a chance to change her mind. The notation ESC to WRITE in the upper right-hand corner means that pressing the ESC key will return the user to the write mode.

Users of the Bank Street Writer may use only two formatting commands when creating a document. ^I at the beginning of a line indents the subsequent text, while ^C at the start of a line centers that line. Users can also set general specifications such as spacing, margins, line length, and page length that are used when the document is batch formatted. The PRINT command causes the program to ask the user for this information.

The WordStar Editor

The Bank Street Writer is a simple word processor, readily understood with little training. When compared with other word processors, however, it grants users very little control over the editing process or the appearance of the final document. The next editor we examine is WordStar, a product of MicroPro International, Inc. WordStar is much more powerful than the Bank Street Writer, but along with the advantage of increased power comes the disadvantage of increased difficulty.

WordStar is a full-screen editor based on the stream model; it can handle two types of files, which its developers call documents and non-documents. The distinction between the two is that WordStar will right-justify a document (adjust the lines of text so that they have an even right margin as well as an even left margin) but will not justify a non-document. Instead, it will print the non-document just as it appears on the screen. Non-documents include lists, poetry, programs, drawings, and the like.

WordStar provides help and feedback to the user with a variety of sticky menus. These menus function only as memory aids; all commands must be typed in from the keyboard. Users who have memorized many of the commands can elect to have menus appear only when requested. Figure 4.10 shows the opening menu that appears when WordStar is started up. This menu offers many basic options. The user can choose to change the current disk (on a personal computer), obtain a list of the contents of the current disk, run programs, leave the editor, or print, copy, or delete files.

When a user begins editing a file, the main menu will appear (unless

```
                  not editing
                    < < <  O P E N I N G   M E N U  > > >
     ---Preliminary Commands---  | --File Commands-- | -System Commands-
  L  Change logged disk drive    |                   |  R  Run a program
  F  File directory     now ON   |  P  PRINT a file  |  X  EXIT to system
  H  Set help level               |                   | -WordStar Options-
     ---Commands to open a file---|  E  RENAME a file |  T  Run TelMerge
     D  Open a document file      |  O  COPY   a file |  M  Run MailMerge
     N  Open a non-document file  |  Y  DELETE a file |  S  Run CorrectStar

 partial directory of disk C:  ^Z=scroll down
   INSTALL.COM   MP.KEY        SALES.DST    CODE         INS-1.BAT    INS-2.BAT
   AUTO2.BAT     EZ.BOM        WS2.BAT      WS2FLPY.BAT  TUTORS.BAT   WS2INS.EXE
   WS2INS.MSG    PRINTERS.DB   MONITOR.DB   AUTO3.BAT    CONFIG.BAT   DRIVERN.OVR
   DRIVERB.OVR   MEMO.SPL      TABLE.SPL    OUTLINE.SPL  NORMAL.BAK   PROPOSAL.SPL
   LETTER2.SPL   LETTER3.SPL   SALES        META.$$$     NORMAL.FRM   INSCONF.EXE
   SPELL.SPL     SGCHMOD.EXE   JUSTIFY.FRM  WS2000.EXE   WS2.OVR      WS2MSG.OVR
   WS2.KEY       LICENSE.NET   MEMOFORM.FRM MSCRIPT.FRM  RAGGED.FRM   UNFORM.FRM
   STD.SAV       WS2LIST.FRM   INTERNAL.DTY MAIN.DTY     WS2LIST.COM  NOTE
   STD.LOG       LICENSE.2     LABEL.LST    LABEL3.LST   LABELXL.LST  PHONE.LST
   PROOF.LST     WS2INDEX.EXE  MACHINES.SPL OUTLINE.STY  SIMPLE.STY   NONUMBER.STY
   3ACROSS.LST   MSCRIPT.STY   TELMERGE.EXE TELMERGE.SYS WS2HARD.BAT  FONTS.DB
   MCI           OAG           ONT          RCA          SOU          STD
   SAMPLE        SAMPLEH       README       PRINT.SPL    WSCONVRT.EXE WS2CD.WS2
 1HELP    2INDENT 3SET LM 4SET RM 5UNDLIN 6BLDFCE 7BEGBLK 8ENDBLK 9BEGFIL 10ENDFIL
```

Figure 4.10
WordStar opening menu. (Courtesy of MicroPro International Corporation)

she has elected not to see menus). The main menu lists control keys
for cursor movement; for movement of the viewing window; for selection of insertion or overwrite typing; for deletion of characters, words,
and lines; for selection among five other menus; and for other miscellaneous actions (see Fig. 4.11). The main menu also displays a ruler
showing tab stops.

Figure 4.12 lists all WordStar commands, grouped by control prefix,
such as ^J and ^K. Although space does not permit a detailed description

Figure 4.11
WordStar main menu. (Courtesy of MicroPro International Corporation)

```
        C:EXAMPLE   PAGE 1 LINE 1 COL 19              INSERT ON
                   < < <      M A I N   M E N U    > > >
     --Cursor Movement--  | -Delete- |  -Miscellaneous-  |  -Other  Menus-
  ^S char left ^D char right |^G  char | ^I Tab   ^B Reform | (from Main only)
  ^A word left ^F word right |DEL chr lf| ^V INSERT ON/OFF  |^J Help  ^K Block
  ^E line  up  ^X line down  |^T word rt|^L Find/Replce again|^Q Quick ^P Print
     --Scrolling--           |^Y  line  |RETURN End paragraph|^O Onscreen
  ^Z line down ^W line up    |          |  ^N Insert a RETURN |
  ^C screen up ^R screen down|          |  ^U Stop a command  |
L----!----!----!----!----!----!----!----!----!----!----!--------R
Example of screen*
```

```
 1HELP    2INDENT 3SET LM 4SET RM 5UNDLIN 6BLDFCE 7BEGBLK 8ENDBLK 9BEGFIL 10ENDFIL
```

^A	Cursor word left	^KF	Directory ON/OFF
^B	Paragraph REFORM	^KH	Hide/Display Block
^C	Scroll up screen	^KJ	Delete file
^D	Cursor character right	^KK	Mark Block end
^E	Cursor up line	^KL	Switch Logged drive
^F	Cursor word right	^KO	COPY file
^G	Delete character right	^KP	PRINT
^H	Cursor character left	^KQ	Edit abandon
^I	TAB advance	^KR	Read a file
^J	Prefix HELP	^KS	Save file re-edit
^K	Prefix Editing	^KV	Block move
^L	FIND/REPLACE AGAIN	^KW	Write Block to file
^M	RETURN	^KX	Save file Exit
^N	Insert carriage return	^KY	Block Delete
^O	Prefix Formatting	^OC	Center cursor line
^P	Enter control character	^OD	Display DOT commands
^Q	Prefix cursor editing	^OE	Soft hyphen entry
^R	Scroll down screen	^OF	Set margins, tabs as exist
^S	Cursor character left	^OG	Paragraph tab
^T	Delete word right	^OH	Hyphen Help ON/OFF
^U	INTERRUPT commands	^OI	Set tab stop
^V	INSERT On/Off	^OJ	Justification ON/OFF
^W	Scroll down line	^OL	Set left margin
^X	Cursor down line	^ON	Clear tab stops
^Y	Delete line	^OP	Display page break ON/OFF
^Z	Scroll up line	^OR	Set right margin
^JB	Defines REFORM	^OS	Set line spacing
^JD	Print directives	^OT	Display Ruler
^JF	Defines FLAG characters	^OV	Variable tabs ON/OFF
^JH	Set HELP level	^OW	Word Wrap OFF/ON
^JI	Command Index	^OX	Release margins
^JM	Defines Tabs, Margins	^PM	Overprint next line
^JP	Defines Place Markers	^PO	Enter non-break space
^JR	Defines Ruler Line	^Q0-9	Cursor to Marker
^JS	Defines Status Line	^QA	REPLACE
^JV	Defines text moving	^QB	Cursor Block beginning
^K0-9	Set/Hide Place Markers	^QC	Cursor file end
^KB	Mark/Hide Block begin	^QD	Cursor right end of line
^KC	Block COPY	^QE	Cursor top screen
^KD	Save file		
^KE	RENAME file		(continued)

Figure 4.12
WordStar commands. (Courtesy of MicroPro International Corporation)

^QF	FIND	TAB	tab
^QK	Cursor Block end	NO FILE	(When no file is being
^QP	Cursor previous position	MENU-	created or edited)
^QQ	REPEAT next command	D	Create or edit document file
^QR	Cursor file beginning	E	Rename file
^QS	Cursor screen left	F	File Directory OFF/ON
^QV	Cursor source (Block, Find)	H	Set Help level
^QW	Downward scroll	L	Change Logged drive
^QX	Cursor screen bottom	M	Merge-Print
^QY	Delete to end of line	N	Create, edit non-document file
^QZ	Upward Scroll	O	Copy file
^Q←	Deletes to front of line	P	PRINT, stop print, start print
←	Deletes character left	R	Run program
ESC	Error release	X	Exit to system
RETURN	Hard carriage return	Y	Delete file

Figure 4.12 (continued)

of each of these commands, we should note that several give users access to menus. The command ^J gives access to the help menu, which allows users to set help levels based on their level of experience. The quick menu (^Q) controls actions performed on large blocks of text. The onscreen menu (^O) controls many common formatting features. The print menu (^P) controls printing effects, such as boldface, underscoring, subscripts, and superscripts. The block menu (^K) defines blocks of text on which to perform operations. Each of these menus contains other features as well. Unfortunately, WordStar does not provide an undo facility. With no undo facility, the user can negate an undesired editing command either by manually correcting the change or by canceling the entire editing session, thus losing all changes and additions made during the session.

Figure 4.13 shows a typical text screen for a WordStar page. The first line displays the name of the disk (A), the file (FILE1), the type of file (DOC), and the numbers of the page, line, and column containing the current position of the cursor. It also shows the ruler with tab stops. The < character in the right-hand margin denotes insertion of a carriage return in the file. The < reminds the user that the printer will go to the next line at that point.

For formatting, WordStar provides a number of dot commands. For example, the dot commands .LH 6, .PL 66, .MT 5, and .MB 60 set the line height at 6 lines per inch, the paper length at 66 lines, and the top and bottom margins at 5 and 60 lines, respectively. Page numbers, page breaks, and page headings and footings can also be controlled. For ex-

```
          C:SAMPLE.96  PAGE 1 LINE 1 COL 16              INSERT ON
                      < < <     M A I N    M E N U     > > >
      --Cursor Movement--      ¦ -Delete- ¦  -Miscellaneous-  ¦ -Other  Menus-
  ^S char left ^D char right   ¦^G  char  ¦ ^I Tab   ^B Reform ¦ (from Main only)
  ^A word left ^F word right   ¦DEL chr lf¦ ^V INSERT ON/OFF   ¦^J Help  ^K Block
  ^E line  up   ^X line down    ¦^T word rt¦^L Find/Replce again¦^Q Quick ^P Print
      --Scrolling--            ¦^Y  line  ¦RETURN End paragraph¦^O Onscreen
  ^Z line down ^W line up      ¦          ¦ ^N Insert a RETURN  ¦
  ^C screen up ^R screen down  ¦          ¦ ^U Stop a command   ¦
 L----!----!----!----!----!----!----!----!----!----!----!--------R
 September, 1985                                                          <
                                                                         <
 John A. Hanley                                                          <
 1435 West 16th Street                                                   <
 West Colorado, CO 99999                                                 <
                                                                         <
 Dear Mr. Hanley:                                                        <
                                                                         <
 We appreciate your response to our inquiry on September 4,  1985.
 There is some additional information we require.                        <
                                                                         <
 How  many parcels do you expect to ship within a regular business
 month?   Is there a peak season in your business,  and if so when
 does it begin and end?   Does your company use UPS Blue or  Brown
 1HELP     2INDENT 3SET LM 4SET RM 5UNDLIN 6BLDFCE 7BEGBLK 8ENDBLK 9BEGFIL 10ENDFIL
```

Figure 4.13

WordStar's text as it appears on the screen. (Courtesy of MicroPro International Corporation)

ample, the dot command .HE January 15 will set January 15 as the heading on the first line of every page.

WordStar also uses control characters for formatting. Underlining of text begins at the first instance of ^PS and ends at the next instance. Similarly, a pair of ^PB commands delimits boldface text, and pairs of ^PT and ^PV commands set superscripts and subscripts, respectively. Personal computers running WordStar generally cannot display on their screens underlining, boldface, superscripts, or subscripts. Because of this, WordStar is not a true WYSIWYG word processor. To display a completely formatted WordStar document requires printing a copy of it.

The MacWrite Word Processor

MacWrite is a word processor developed for Apple's Macintosh personal computer. In contrast to WordStar, which requires the use of numerous control sequences, MacWrite permits editing in various intuitive ways. The Macintosh screen is analogous to a desk top containing any number of documents and work tools. Icons are used to identify files and commands, and menus are used to select commands. MacWrite can be combined with a drawing system, MacPaint, to produce documents containing both pictures and text. Every detail of the formatted documents, including underscores, boldface, italics, and font size and shape, appears on the screen exactly as it will on the printed page. Thus, MacWrite is a true WYSIWYG editor/formatter.

MacWrite's user-friendly interface relies heavily on a mouse to specify movement within a document. The user can type text at any point in a file by moving the mouse to the desired point and clicking the mouse button. This positions the cursor; MacWrite subsequently inserts typed text there, moving existing text to the right and word-wrapping as required. The mouse makes moving within a MacWrite document easier than moving within a WordStar or Bank Street Writer document. To move the cursor anywhere within the viewing window, the user simply repositions the cursor with the mouse.

Scrolling, or moving the viewing window, is accomplished by maneuvering the mouse to the scroll bar on the side of the screen (see Fig. 4.14). The *scroll bar* is a rectangular region containing a solid white box that shows the position of the viewing window within the document. By clicking the mouse button on the arrows at the top or bottom of the scroll bar, the user can move the viewing window up or down a few lines; the white box within the scroll bar moves up or down to correspond with the window's movements. The user can also move the window forward or backward a full screen and can make even larger jumps by clicking on the white box, holding the button down, and dragging the image of the box to another place in the scroll bar. This method of editing is novel in moderately priced personal computers, although it appeared earlier in the Xerox Star workstation, a much more expensive machine.

Figure 4.14
Document traveling with a scroll bar.

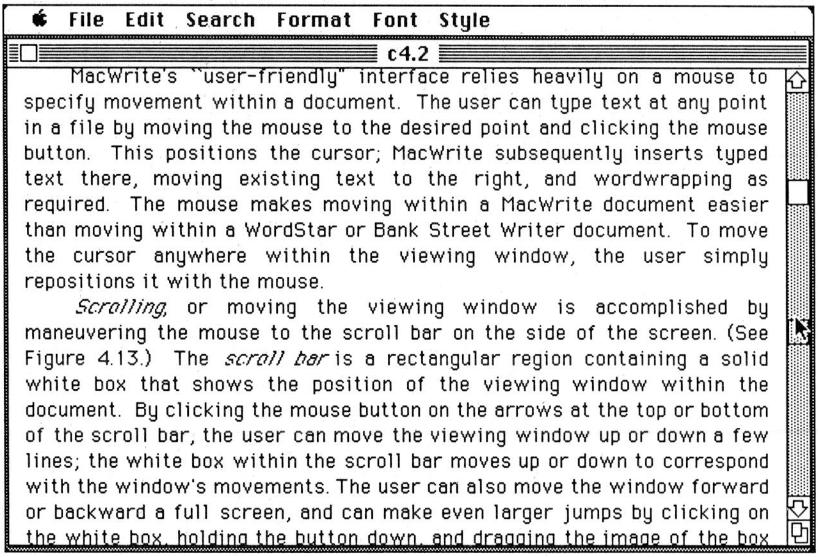

```
 ✎  File  Edit  Search  Format  Font  Style
▤☐▥▥▥▥▥▥▥▥▥▥▥▥ c4.2 ▥▥▥▥▥▥▥▥▥▥▥▥
     MacWrite's "user-friendly" interface relies heavily on a mouse to  ⬆
specify movement within a document. The user can type text at any point
in a file by moving the mouse to the desired point and clicking the mouse
button.  This positions the cursor; MacWrite subsequently inserts typed
text there, moving existing text to the right, and wordwrapping as
required.  The mouse makes moving within a MacWrite document easier
than moving within a WordStar or Bank Street Writer document.  To move
the cursor anywhere within the viewing window, the user simply
repositions it with the mouse.
     Scrolling, or moving the viewing window is accomplished by
maneuvering the mouse to the scroll bar on the side of the screen. (See
Figure 4.13.)  The scroll bar is a rectangular region containing a solid
white box that shows the position of the viewing window within the
document. By clicking the mouse button on the arrows at the top or bottom
of the scroll bar, the user can move the viewing window up or down a few
lines; the white box within the scroll bar moves up or down to correspond
with the window's movements. The user can also move the window forward
or backward a full screen, and can make even larger jumps by clicking on
the white box, holding the button down, and dragging the image of the box  ⬇
```

MacWrite provides menus for selection of editing and formatting commands. Format choices include page layout and style and size of type fonts. A menu allows users to search for words and replace them with other words. Menus also contain options for cutting, copying, pasting, undoing, or redoing.

On the top of the screen is a horizontal sticky menu known as the menu bar. To select a menu item, the user places the cursor over an item on the menu bar and presses the mouse button. While the button remains depressed, a menu associated with the item on the menu bar pops up, as shown in Fig. 4.15. To select an action in this pop-up menu, the user holds the mouse button down while moving the cursor to the desired option. MacWrite highlights the menu option underneath the cursor. Releasing the button will cause the command associated with the highlighted action to be executed. This simple method of selecting actions reduces the need to remember available commands; it also allows users to select commands without typing. (Many of these actions can also be taken using control key combinations.)

Among the options shown on the pop-up menu in Fig. 4.15 is Save as ... . Executing this command causes a dialog box to appear, as shown in Fig. 4.16. The dialog box permits MacWrite to ask questions about the chosen command (Save as ... in this example). The user can change the name of the file, if desired, as well as the disk on which it is to be saved.

Figure 4.15
A MacWrite page with the file pull-down menu.

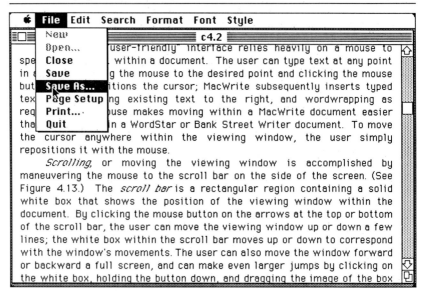

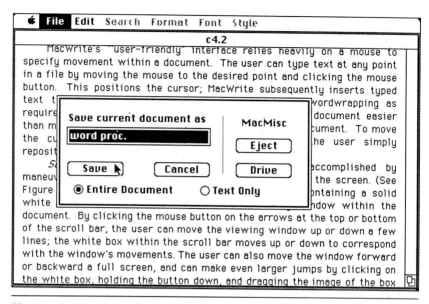

Figure 4.16
The Save as ... dialog box.

Figure 4.17
Some of the available MacWrite fonts.

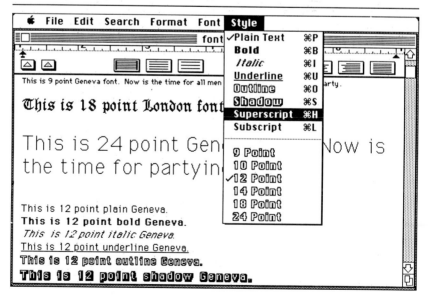

The Style menu allows the user to choose from a wide variety of font sizes and types. Figure 4.17 shows some of these options. When the font type or size is changed, all new text will appear in the new type and size. To change the font of existing text, the user must mark the region and use the font and style menus shown in Figure 4.17.

The edit menu allows a large variety of options, including cutting, copying, and pasting. In addition, it allows viewing of the contents of a buffer (called the "Clipboard") that temporarily stores cut or copied text. The search menu opens another dialog box that allows the user to search for words and replace them if necessary.

MacWrite is an example of a new generation of word processors. An editor/formatter with an attractive user interface, MacWrite is easy to learn yet adequate for basic editing and formatting. Unlike earlier editor/formatters, MacWrite uses graphical methods to format and edit documents.

Formatting Preprocessors

The document formatting available with the three word processors described above is primitive compared with that of professional document formatters. Very high quality typesetting requires that the person or program setting type have fine control over the position and size of each element placed on the page. An example of a high-quality formatter is nroff (or troff for phototypesetters) that is available with the UNIX operating system (described in the next chapter). Such document formatting systems have a rich repertoire of low-level commands, commands understood by the printing or typesetting machine.

It is too much to expect even experienced users to master all the commands of a complex document formatter unless their profession is typesetting. For example, it should not be necessary for them to know how much vertical and horizontal displacement is needed to put characters into a superscript. Similarly, users should not need to know the dimensions of individual letters to be able to compute the height and width of a box to put around a block of text. The solution, touched on earlier, is *macro preprocessors*. These are programs that take as input a document with high-level formatting commands, such as dot commands, and replace each high-level formatting command with a set of low-level commands understood by the formatter. Preprocessors expand brief high-level commands into their component low-level parts. The high-level command is often called a *macro*. A *macro language* is a collection of macro statements. Macro languages provide much control over the formatting of text, tables, equations, and simple pictures.

The standard UNIX operating system has the macro packages tbl to create tables and eqn to set equations. Figure 4.18 shows a sample set of macro commands for tbl and the formatted result. As you can see, .TS denotes the start of the table and .TE denotes its end. The second line in this example contains general formatting information: center to center the table and tab(:) to designate the colon as a tab marker. The next lines provide specific formatting information. In this case the table will have four columns, with each entry centered in each column. The remaining lines contain the actual entries separated by the tab marker : (colon).

Figure 4.19 shows a sample of eqn text and the resultant equation. The equation definition starts with .EQ and ends with .EN. The keywords sqrt, sup, and over indicate square root sign, superscript, and placement of some text over other text. Braces ({ }) delimit portions of the text for the formatter so that it will know how long to make the upper bar in the square root sign and what text to place above what other text.

Refer is another macro preprocessor available with some nroff and troff systems. When it encounters a keyword in a document, refer accesses a set of bibliography files and selects references that match the keyword. For example, the commands

```
.[ [
     furuta scofield shaw formatting
.]].
```

will cause refer to search the bibliography for a single entry that can be identified with the keywords furuta scofield shaw formatting (these key-

Figure 4.18
(a) Sample tbl commands and (b) the formatted result.

```
.TS
center tab(:);
c c c c.
BOL:EOL:BOF:EOF
+SLIDE:-SLIDE:+PAGES:-PAGES
+LINES:-LINES:+WORD:-WORD
+FIND:-FIND:+FIND/RPLC:-FIND/RPLC
.TE
```
(a)

BOL	EOL	BOF	EOF
+SLIDE	-SLIDE	+PAGES	-PAGES
+LINES	-LINES	+WORD	-WORD
+FIND	-FIND	+FIND/RPLC	-FIND/RPLC

(b)

```
.EQ
x = {-b +- sqrt {b sup 2 -4ac}} over 2a
.EN
```
(a)

$$x = \frac{-b \pm \sqrt{b^2 - 4ac}}{2a}$$

(b)

Figure 4.19
(a) Sample eqn commands and (b) the formatted result.

words identify a reference for this chapter). In the body of the document, refer replaces the keywords with a number in brackets, such as [2], or some other identifier and puts the full entry at the end of the document or in a footnote at the bottom of a page. You can see the full reference for furuta scofield shaw formatting at the end of this chapter. Refer automatically numbers or alphabetizes citations. It is a very useful tool because citations need only be typed in their entirety once, when they are entered into a bibliography file.

Several preprocessors may be applied in sequence to a file to result in a formatted document that contains text, tables, equations, and pictures. We have edited and formatted drafts of this book on the UNIX operating system using the macro preprocessors we have described here.

Advantages and Disadvantages of Modern Word Processors

The technology for formatting documents and for providing immediate feedback to the user is advancing rapidly. While WYSIWYG editor/formatters have sacrificed some speed and capability to provide continuous feedback, what they do offer is appealing. As we have seen, the Macintosh with MacWrite offers a fine user interface. With another package, MacPaint, it can also format text, equations, tables, charts, and pictures, although these have to be entered and formatted by hand, since no macro preprocessors exist for MacWrite.

WYSIWYG editor/formatters have the obvious advantage of allowing users to see the formatted document on the screen before committing anything to paper. In addition, WYSIWYG editors typically provide a pointing device and pop-up menus or icons for easy user interaction. A user can prepare and edit documents that contain a mixture of many different types of materials, including graphs, equations, and drawings.

Some of these appealing features are also weaknesses, however. Word processors that use a mouse often require that users move one hand from the keyboard to reach for the mouse. This takes time. Simple operations, such as moving the cursor back one character, can be performed more easily on a conventional keyboard than with a mouse. However, in fairness to modern word processors, control keys are often available as alternatives to mouse-and-menu combinations.

A basic limitation of WYSIWYG, however, is that (in the words of Brian Kernighan, one of the developers of UNIX) "what you see is all that you get." If a WYSIWYG editor/formatter does not provide enough document control, the user probably cannot obtain more control without rewriting the editor program—and that is usually a difficult or impossible task. In contrast, it is relatively easy to extend the capability of non-WYSIWYG formatters since programmers can combine low-level commands in new and powerful ways.

SUMMARY

This chapter provides an overview of word processing, one of the most practical computer applications. Traditionally, word processors have consisted of editors and formatters. The editor allows the user to create and modify text. The formatter prints the document on paper or displays it on a CRT screen. Batch formatters run after the document is completely prepared; interactive formatters, on the other hand, display a soft-copy facsimile of the document on the screen. Modern word processors, called editor/formatters, combine the two functions.

Bank Street Writer is a simple word processor that can be used by anyone. It does not provide very much control over the way a document looks, however. WordStar provides great flexibility in determining how a document will look when printed. The disadvantage to WordStar is that it can be difficult to learn to use. MacWrite combines some of the best features of Bank Street Writer and WordStar. As a WYSIWYG editor/formatter, it allows nearly total control over the appearance of a document. Because of its user-friendly qualities, MacWrite does not require much time or effort to use effectively.

Some word processors allow the use of macros to perform specialized formatting commands. Formatting preprocessors go through files before they are formatted to convert the macros into low-level commands. Refer, tbl, and eqn are three such formatting preprocessors.

REFERENCES

N. K. Meyrowitz and A. van Dam, "Interactive Editing Systems: Part I," *ACM Surveys* 14(3): 321–352 (September 1982).

N. K. Meyrowitz and A. van Dam, "Interactive Editing Systems: Part II," *ACM Surveys* 14(3): 353–416 (September 1982).

R. Furuta, J. Scofield, and A. Shaw, "Document Formatting Systems: Survey, Concepts, and Issues," *ACM Surveys* 14(3): 417–472 (September 1982).

ISSUES AND IDEAS

1. Many people are giving up their typewriters in favor of word processors. Typewriters, however, have not become obsolete. What are the advantages of using a word processor instead of a typewriter? What are the advantages of using a typewriter instead of a word processor?

2. Suppose you were preparing an advertisement for a magazine. Describe the features of an editor/formatter that would be needed for this application.

3. Consider the preparation of a lengthy document, such as a paper or report, and list the various technical steps involved, from the first draft to the final copy. Explain how the Bank Street Writer could be used to perform these tasks.

4. Repeat question 3 for WordStar and MacWrite. Explain the important differences between these two WYSIWYG editor/formatters, using this problem as an example.

5. Debate the advantages and disadvantages of using a mouse or other pointing device with a word processor.

Operating Systems

An operating system is probably the
most important part of the body of
software which goes with any modern
computer system. Its importance is reflected in the large amount of [time
and effort] usually invested in its construction, and in the mystique by which
it is often surrounded.

A. M. LISTER, *Fundamentals of
Operating Systems*

■ Introduction

General-purpose computers are capable of performing a large variety
of tasks. However, they need to be told what to do and when and how
to do it. Although programs provide directions, these directions are not
sufficient to control the computer. The computer must know how to
start and stop programs, where in memory to find various programs,
and how to communicate with users of the machine. This level of control is the responsibility of the operating system.

Specifically, an *operating system* is the set of programs that controls
a computer. A computer can be run without an operating system, but
then the user must manually perform many tasks usually performed
automatically. For example, in a computer without an operating system,
the user must manually load programs into memory, delete them from
memory, and determine where programs should reside in memory and
how much memory they will use. An operating system provides a convenient and ready-made set of programs for these purposes.

On multi-user computers, the operating system also supervises the way in which users share the computer. The operating system decides how much time and what percentage of primary memory to allocate to each user. In this way, the limited resources of the CPU and the memory are divided, giving each user a fair share. In addition, the operating system supervises the storing and retrieving of information, ensuring that no program interferes with the running of another. Thus an operating system is an important mediating agent between person and machine.

In this chapter we provide an introduction to operating systems in general and to three operating systems in particular. In the first two sections, we summarize the evolution of operating systems and describe their components. Then we describe two popular operating systems for single-user microcomputers, CP/M and MS-DOS, and one popular multi-user system for minicomputers and small mainframes, UNIX. We examine these three systems primarily from the user's point of view. CP/M is the simplest of the three, followed by MS-DOS and UNIX. MS-DOS and UNIX have many features in common, especially the way they treat files and handle commands typed at the keyboard. Differences among the three systems are greater than they may appear to be from the user's point of view.

The Evolution of Operating Systems

The first computers were used by a single person at a time to perform a single task at a time. A user programmed an early machine by setting switches or plugging in cables. The programmed machine then ran uninterrupted until the job was finished. Later, programs were stored in the computer's memory and run from there. Computer users would typically write programs in a computer programming language, such as FORTRAN, that bore some resemblance to human language. Another program would translate this program into the machine language understood by the computer. (We discuss this process in greater detail in Chapter 9.) The translator program would first have to be loaded into memory. Next it would take the user's program as input and produce machine language as output. The computer would then run this machine-language version of the user's program. Figure 5.1 shows a user's program and a translator in the memory of a computer.

Each of the preceding steps required manual intervention by the operator of the computer. The user controlled the computer by depositing punched cards into a reader or mounting tapes on a tape drive. Such a method of operation demanded constant attention and required

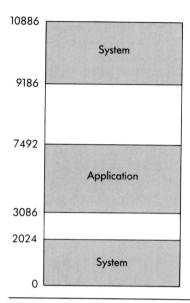

Figure 5.1
An application program and a system program in computer memory. The system program is stored in two pieces although the computer treats it all as one program.

humans to perform many of the tasks now handled by operating systems.

Early computers were very expensive, and manual operation was not the most cost-efficient method of harnessing their power. For example, each user who needed a particular language translator had to load it manually into memory. Computer resources could be more efficiently used when all jobs requiring a particular language translator were run at the same time. The translator could be loaded into memory and could translate and run the entire "batch" of jobs awaiting it. A full-time operator could coordinate this *batch processing* of jobs for the computer.

Eventually a program called a *system monitor* was developed to perform most of the work of the human computer operator. The system monitor, like its human predecessor, supervised the use of the computer's resources. Users specified which system programs, such as language translators, were necessary to run their programs. *Job control languages* were introduced to help users make such specifications and to signify the start and end of programs and data. A user typically prepared a series of punched cards to submit to the computer through a card reader. The cards contained not only the application program and data but also the job control cards indicating which programs and translators would be needed to successfully run the program.

The automatic batch processing of users' programs demonstrated the need to protect one job from another. If, for example, a user forgot to include a job control card marking the end of a program, the system monitor might continue reading cards from the card reader and try to execute their instructions as part of that program. If the cards it read were part of another user's program, then neither program would run correctly. Similarly, a user might have written a program that would run endlessly unless stopped by the monitor.

Another problem arose because the monitor program resided in the same physical memory as other programs. What was to prevent a user's program from changing the portion of memory that contained the monitor program? Such a change could destroy the way the computer separated jobs, accessed tapes, or allocated its memory resources. A user with knowledge of the operating system could, for example, change the monitor so that it would always run his programs before anyone else's. This problem was solved by the introduction of special hardware to create a "fence" between the system monitor and the user's programs (see Fig. 5.2). The monitor would stop running any program that attempted to access an address on the wrong side of the fence (such an

Figure 5.2
A fence between the monitor and the application programs.

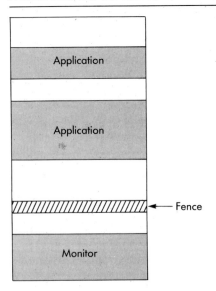

action is colorfully referred to as "killing" the job) and would notify a human operator of what had transpired.

Other operational problems presented themselves. Users needed to be able to read and write data to and from cards, tapes, and other external storage devices. (This reading and writing is often referred to as *input/output* or *I/O*.) It is wasteful for every user to have to write personal routines for this purpose. Thus, from the earliest days, requests for I/O were made to and performed by the system monitor.

Other developments were introduced to make operating systems more efficient. The speed with which a CPU can execute program instructions is much higher than the speed with which it can communicate with users or with external storage devices such as disks and tapes. In fact, a CPU can typically execute more than 10,000 instructions during the time it takes to find a single piece of information on a disk. Thus, if a program that is running must stop to fetch information from secondary storage, the CPU will remain idle for a relatively long time. Multiprogramming was developed so that this idle time could be used. *Multiprogramming* is simply the capability to keep more than one program active simultaneously—that is, to have several programs ready to run so that when one program must wait for input, another can be progressing. These programs do not necessarily receive equal shares of CPU time. Rather, when one program must wait, another can begin. If a running program does not need to stop for input, however, then other programs that are ready to run must wait. Multiprogramming can be combined with batch processing to provide more efficient use of a computer.

An innovation that extended multiprogramming is time sharing. *Time sharing* entails dividing the CPU's operation time into segments, giving each user a small slice of time. This requires creating some sort of schedule whereby one user after another receives a *time slice*. The first does not receive another slice until all have had their turn. However, time slices are so small that users of time-sharing systems are not often aware of their temporary loss of the CPU to other users. In effect, each has the impression of being the sole user of the system.

Unlike batch processing, time sharing allows many people to use the computer at the same time. These users get instantaneous feedback from the computer instead of submitting a job and waiting for the printed result. We refer to such an environment as *interactive* because users can interact directly with the computer, editing, debugging, and running programs without batch processing. Interactive computing makes programming easier by reducing the time needed to see the effect of changes in a program. Interactive computing also makes some tasks feasible that were previously very difficult, such as word processing.

The next development in operating systems was multiprocessing. A *multiprocessor* is a computer that has several cooperating CPUs. A simple example of a multiprocessor is a computer in which one large CPU handles computation, while another, less powerful CPU called an *I/O processor* communicates with slow I/O devices such as disks, tapes, terminals, and printers. An I/O processor relieves the CPU from some tasks so that the entire system can work at maximum efficiency.

The most recent step in the evolution of operating systems was the development of programs to manage interactions among several powerful computers arranged in a network. Such networks typically ship programs and data at the rate of many millions of bits per second, and these data typically pass through several dozen computers. Networks offer several advantages. For example, with time sharing on a single computer, the failure of one piece of hardware or software can prevent hundreds of individuals from performing important tasks. A computer network can continue to operate even when one or more of the computers in the network has failed.

This discussion would not be complete without a few words about the set of programs supplied with an operating system. Usually included are one or more translators for languages such as Assembler, BASIC, or FORTRAN (discussed in later chapters) and an editor to create or modify files. The operating system may also come with other programs that simplify the use of the computer.

Features of Operating Systems

A typical operating system provides commands and programs to control the operation of a computer, to access devices attached to it, to schedule jobs, to make good use of the resources of the computer, and to translate programs. The sophistication and number of such commands and programs depend on the operating system. Operating systems designed for large time-sharing machines are much richer than small operating systems designed for personal computers.

Some vital distinctions separate operating systems for small machines from operating systems for large machines. The most important of these is the way the operating system treats files. Most personal computers store files on floppy disks, whereas large time-sharing machines generally use hard disks. Owners of personal computers must always be aware of which disk holds the file they need, whereas users of the larger machines are usually oblivious to the physical location of their files. Furthermore, the creation of *backup* (or duplicate) copies of files is the responsibility of the individuals who use small machines; most large machines create backup copies of files automatically. (Backup copies are important because files are sometimes destroyed by malfunctioning computers or inadvertently erased by users.) In the following discussion, we highlight some important features of operating systems that deal with files.

File Systems

A *file system* is a set of commands and programs to manage files on a computer. Files, as mentioned earlier, contain alphabetic, numeric, and special characters. They can represent text, programs, and images. File systems have several capabilities. They can store files on or retrieve them from external storage devices such as disks and tapes. Programs to access these external devices are very complex. The file system enables users to treat all storage devices in the same way, although these devices may have different designs.

The file system also allows users to perform many common filing functions. Files can be created and deleted, named and renamed, copied and moved. Files are created in a variety of ways. Individuals can use editors to create them. System or application programs can also create files. For example, a language translator creates a file that is interpreted by the computer as a machine-language program to be executed. Some other file functions are described later in this section.

In addition, the file system associates with each file information on the date of creation or last modification, the type of file, and the owner of the file. The file system can organize the files and sort them by date, type, and owner. A date on a file can be a useful way to identify it, especially if there are many files with similar names. For systems with more than one user, the name of the owner can be recorded in each file. In this way, each user's files are protected from intentional or unintentional access by others. Once the file system records the name of the owner of a file, the owner usually designates the type of access other users should have to the file. For example, the owner may declare that the file is read-only (it can be viewed but not changed) or read/write (it can be viewed and modified). In addition, files can be declared executable, indicating that they contain programs for the computer to run.

To explain two other operations, the movement and organization of files, we must first describe file *directories*. A directory is a list of file names. File directories can be either flat or hierarchical. A *flat directory* lists all file names under one heading and a *hierarchical directory* may contain files, *subdirectories* (a directory within a directory), and sometimes subdirectories of the subdirectories, and so on; each subdirectory may contain files and more subdirectories. Thus, hierarchical directories organize files into a treelike structure, as shown in Fig. 5.3.

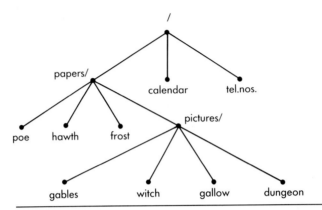

Figure 5.3
A hierarchical file directory showing subdirectories and files.

A hierarchical file system encourages users to store related files together in their own directory, resulting in a better organized system of
storage. Figure 5.3 illustrates a root directory and its subdirectories. The
root directory contains all other files and subdirectories. In this example,
the root directory is called slash, /. It has one subdirectory, called papers,
and two files, one called calendar, which contains the user's calendar of
events, and one called tel.nos, which contains telephone numbers. The
subdirectory papers contains three files—poe, hawth, and frost—which
store papers on Poe, Hawthorne, and Frost. It also contains a subdirectory pictures, which contains pictures to illustrate the paper on Hawthorne. Organizing files in this way makes it easier to locate a particular
file, especially if a user has many files in storage.

To identify files and directories in a hierarchical file system, we use
pathnames. The *pathname* of a file or subdirectory is a name that specifies the path to it from the root directory. It consists of the set of subdirectory names that must be entered successively to reach it. The two
operating systems described later in the chapter that support hierarchical file directories, MS-DOS and UNIX, separate subdirectory names
in a pathname with slashes (/). For example, in Fig. 5.3 the pathname
of the file gables is /papers/pictures/gables. Pathnames can usually be
abbreviated. If the current subdirectory is /papers, then to address the
gables file it is sufficient to use the *relative pathname* /pictures/
gables.

On most operating systems it is possible to specify names with wildcards. A *wildcard* allows the user to address a file or subdirectory by
specifying only a portion of its name, thus reducing the amount of typing required. Most operating systems use the special characters ? and
* as wildcards; ? refers to any single character and * to any string of
characters. For example, intro.? refers to any file whose name begins

with intro. and contains one additional character. Thus, intro.? could refer to intro.1, intro.2, or intro.Q. Similarly, intro.* refers to any file whose name begins with intro. and contains any number of additional permissible characters. Thus, intro.* could refer to intro.1, intro.2, or intro.Q as well as to intro.me, intro.ASM, or intro.old_1984. Commands given to file names that contain wildcards perform the specified function for each file whose name is consistent with the wildcard. For example, if rm means remove, then rm intro.? will remove any file whose name begins with intro. and contains one additional character, such as intro.1, intro.2, and intro.Q.

Some operating systems also use and recognize filename extensions. A *filename extension* is a short string of letters that follow a period in a filename to indicate what type of information the file contains. For example, ASM, BAS, and COM might be filename extensions indicating assembly language programs, BASIC programs, and executable commands. A language translator will typically check the filename extension before attempting to translate a file to be sure it is translating the correct type of file.

Every hierarchical file directory system includes a set of commands to create and delete subdirectories, to move files from one subdirectory to another, to list the files, and to determine which subdirectory the user is currently in. In MS-DOS and UNIX, the command pwd (which stands for "print working directory") performs the latter operation. The command mkdir directory_name creates (makes) a new directory called directory_name, and the command rmdir directory_name removes the empty directory called directory_name. Similarly, the command rm file_name deletes (removes) the file called file_name, and the command mv file_name1 path_name moves the file called file_name1 to the directory or file identified with the pathname path_name. If the pathname is that of a directory, the file is moved to the directory without changing its name. CP/M and MS-DOS employ the REN (for rename) command. For example, the command REN QUERY.BAS = TEST.BAS would cause the file TEST.BAS to be renamed QUERY.BAS. The file name extension BAS indicates that the file contains a program written in BASIC. To change from one directory to another, UNIX and MS-DOS use a command such as cd new_directory. These mnemonic commands are designed to resemble the words they represent.

File systems also provide commands to list all files in the current directory or all files and subdirectories under the root directory. In MS-DOS and UNIX the command ls lists all files in a directory. If the current or "working" subdirectory were /papers/pictures, for example, the ls command would show the files gables, witch, gallow, and dungeon, The CP/M command DIR fulfills a similar function for that system's flat directory.

In addition to the already described commands, systems that have user-operated disk drives must provide commands to control them. These commands include the command to *format* a disk, which involves coding certain information onto a blank disk so that the operating system can subsequently store files on it.

Command Processing

A *command processor* is a program that accepts user commands and interprets them. The filing commands described in the preceding section are examples of the commands this processor interprets. The command processor executes proper commands, informs users of illegal commands, and permits minor corrections of commands. Each operating system gives its command processor a different name. In CP/M it is called the console command processor, or CCP. In UNIX it is called the shell. Regardless of the name, the command processor is the actual interface between user and machine. It provides the means for users to control the computer.

The most visible feature of a command processor is the *prompt,* the symbol that appears on the terminal screen when the operating system is ready to process another command. In some operating systems, users can personalize their prompt, changing it to whatever message or character they desire.

A vital feature of command processors in operating systems such as UNIX and MS-DOS is redirection. To understand redirection, we must explore the concept of standard input and standard output. *Standard input* is input received in "the usual method," from a keyboard or mouse. Unless told otherwise, the computer expects all input to be standard input. *Standard output* is output displayed in "the usual method," on a terminal screen. Unless told otherwise, the computer will send all messages and output to the terminal. *Redirection,* then, is taking input from a nonstandard source or sending output to a nonstandard destination. These nonstandard inputs and outputs are usually files. Redirection allows information to be stored in a file and that file to be supplied as input to an application program. Redirection also allows the results of running a program to be stored in a special file rather than printed immediately on the screen.

UNIX and MS-DOS use special symbols to redirect input and output. Normally, a command such as sort sorts lines in a file and expects to receive information from the standard input and then send sorted data to the standard output. Typing the command

```
sort < filein_name
```

will cause input to be taken from the file called filein_name instead. The result will be sent to the standard output medium (the screen). When the command

    sort > fileout_name

is used, input will be received from the standard input. However, the result will be directed to the file called fileout_name instead of the screen. We can combine the two commands to produce

    sort < filein_name > fileout_name

Here input is received from filein_name and output is sent to fileout _name. The character > followed by a filename will either create a new file with that name and redirect output to it or, if the named file already exists, replace what was in the file with the output. Sometimes it is convenient to add output to the end of a file. To do this, we replace > with >>.

We can use redirection to channel results through several commands or programs. For example, the sequence of commands

    sort < filein_name > work_file
    format < work_file > fileout_name
    rm work_file

applies sort to a file called filein_name, creates a temporary file work_file, and then passes its contents through the program format, stores the output in the file called fileout_name, and removes work_file. Some operating systems simplify this series of steps by the use of a pipeline. The *pipeline* allows the output of one operation to be used as input to another operation without the creation of intermediate storage files. For example, the notation

    sort | format

creates a new command that takes its input from the standard input, sorts the result, and then sends the sorted result to the program format, which in turn sends it to the standard output. The symbol | separates programs in a pipeline. The pipeline actually creates an internal storage area (a *buffer*) to store intermediate results. The operating system automatically removes this buffer when pipeline operations are complete.

Some operating systems simplify usage even more by enabling a single command to represent a series of steps for the computer to perform. Such compound commands, called *batch commands* or *scripts*, are stored in executable files. A user can execute the commands in the file in sequence simply by typing the name of the file. Scripts are very useful to represent a series of commands that are usually executed together in the same order.

Password Protection

Many operating systems protect files with *passwords*. When a user enters the system, a process called *logging in* or *logging on*, the system
prompts him for an ID (usually a set of initials, a name, or an account number) and a password. Below is an example of such a sequence
for a computer that uses UNIX:

```
login:jes
Password:
```

As a security measure, the password will not appear on the screen after
the user has typed it in. If the password is typed incorrectly, the system
denies access.

Password verification ensures that the person using a particular ID
gives the correct password. There are several ways to verify passwords.
An old and rather undesirable method is to maintain a file containing
login IDs and corresponding passwords. Such a file is called a *password
file*. Systems that employ password files simply check that each password typed in corresponds to the appropriate password in the password
file. This method provides little security: a person who gains access to
the password file can also gain access to all accounts on the system.
This file, then, must be carefully guarded.

To combat the problem of password security, some operating systems, such as UNIX, verify passwords using a *one-way* or *trap-door function* that encodes a password. A formula is applied to a password and
a new word is produced that looks like a random sequence of letters.
When this method is used, the password file contains the encoded passwords along with associated IDs and other user information. Even if
this file is made public, which it is on many computers, it is difficult
for a person to figure out what someone else's password is because it
is very difficult to invert the one-way encoding function. Chapter 14
contains a further discussion of password protections and violation.

Utilities

An operating system usually provides a number of basic application programs, called *utilities*, along with the commands and system programs
mentioned in the preceding sections. The application programs typically include editors (discussed in Chapter 4) and translators for various
programming languages. The editor programs may be quite primitive,
so most users eventually acquire one that is more sophisticated. Many
operating systems come equipped with a mail program to send electronic messages to other users. Some operating systems also provide

programs to locate spelling errors, to format text, to analyze and plot data, and to perform other tasks.

Translators for programming languages translate programs from higher-level languages, such as FORTRAN, BASIC, and Pascal, into machine language. (This procedure is discussed in Chapter 9.) Translators fall into two categories. *Compilers* translate a program in its entirety in one step. *Interpreters* translate each statement individually. Operating systems usually provide other language support tools such as *debugger* programs to help locate programming errors.

Mail systems allow users to send messages to other users and receive and respond to messages from other users. They are among the most useful application programs available. A close relative of a mail system is a system to send immediate messages—that is, to *write* to another user who is currently active at a terminal. The message appears immediately on the other user's screen, and a beep usually signals its arrival. The receiver of the message can then respond in the same way. The discussion of UNIX describes in greater detail these two methods of communicating.

Of the other utility programs mentioned, we will describe only one type—the spelling programs. Spelling programs help detect spelling mistakes in electronic documents. A spelling program takes a text file and produces a new file that contains the words from the original file, sorted in alphabetical order. The program then compares each word with a list (an electronic dictionary) of properly spelled words. Words in the sorted file that do not appear in the dictionary are shown to the user. Some spelling programs merely provide the user with a list of words not in the dictionary. Others highlight occurrences of these words in the original file, making it easier for the writer to locate them. An example of the latter type is the SpellStar program run from within WordStar. Many spelling programs allow users to supplement electronic dictionaries by adding names, places, acronyms, and other legitimate words not already contained in the dictionary.

■ Three Operating Systems

We now describe from the user's point of view the three operating systems CP/M, MS-DOS, and UNIX. Both CP/M and MS-DOS were designed as single-user systems for personal computers. UNIX was originally developed for a small computer that contained less memory than many of today's personal computers. However, it evolved into a system that now supports multiple users in a fairly complex computer environment.

The CP/M Operating System

Of the three operating systems described in this chapter, CP/M (Control Program for Microcomputers) is the least sophisticated. It has, however, provided a uniform set of user and system commands for a family of microprocessors. It is designed to be used on computers with floppy or hard disk storage.

CP/M has a small set of commands to manage files. They are shown in Table 5.1 along with their purposes. The acronym for each command suggests its purpose. PIP, for example, stands for peripheral interchange program.

You may remember that CP/M uses a flat file directory; that is, all files on a given disk are in the same directory. Each filename consists of two parts, the primary name and the secondary name. *Primary names* are strings of up to eight characters consisting of any printable characters except the following:

   < > , . ; : = ? * [ ]

Secondary names, or filename extensions, are separated from the primary names by a period (.) and consist of up to three letters. Secondary names indicate the type of the file. Table 5.2 shows some of the sec-

Table 5.1 ▫ File Manipulation Commands in CP/M

Command	Purpose
DIR	List files on a disk
ERA	Erase a file
REN	Rename a file
SAVE	Save a file onto a disk
PIP	Move and copy files
STAT	Show the status of files
TYPE	Display the contents of a file
ED	Call a simple text editor
LOAD	Load a file from disk
DUMP	Print the contents of an executable file
DDT	Call the program debugger
ASM	Assemble a program file
FORMAT	Format a new disk
SYSGEN	Generate a new copy of the operating system
SUBMIT	Execute a file containing operating system commands
XSUB	Same as SUBMIT

Table 5.2 □ Secondary Filenames

Extension	Type
ASM	Assembly language program
BAS	BASIC Program
C	C program
COM	Executable command
FOR	FORTRAN program
PAS	Pascal program

ondary names used by CP/M to indicate different types of files. CP/M permits the use of wildcards, as described earlier.

Because CP/M is most often used with personal computers and floppy disks, that is the use we will describe. When the user first turns the computer on (sometimes referred to as *booting the system*), one of its disk drives must contain a disk that holds the operating system. *Disk drives* are devices to read from and write onto disks. They are commonly labeled by the letters of the alphabet; usually, drive A contains the operating system. When the computer begins to operate, the prompt contains the name of the drive that holds the operating system. Thus, an operating system booted from drive A will give as a prompt

    A>

The prompt indicates that the console command processor is waiting for a command to be typed in. In addition, the A> indicates that, unless specifically told where to search for a command, the command processor will look to the disk in drive A. Drive A, then, is referred to as the *default drive*. If the computer contains a second disk drive, the operating system will label it B. We can change the default drive from A to B with the following command:

    A > B:

This command includes the name of the new default drive followed by a colon. To refer to a file on drive B when drive A is the default, we type:

    A > B:file_name

Here file_name is the name of the file we wish to access.

Before we elaborate on the commands provided by CP/M we should note that a set of *control characters* can control CP/M itself. As you may remember, the user obtains a control character by typing a character while holding down the key labeled CONTROL or CTRL. We denote the control character with the symbol ^. Table 5.3 shows

Table 5.3 ☐ Some Control Characters in CP/M

^C	Reboot
^P	Printer on/off
^S	Stop display
^Z	End of string

some available control characters and their meanings. ^C terminates the command being executed and reboots the operating system. ^P causes an attached printer to begin printing any output displayed on the screen. Pressing ^P again stops the printer. The command ^S causes the program that is running to pause until the user types any character other than ^C. This is most useful when a user wishes to stop a rapid flow of information in order to read it. The command ^Z is used to terminate a string that is being typed in.

Now we will discuss operating system commands in more detail. Of all these commands, DIR is perhaps the most important. DIR displays the names of all files on the default disk. The following is a representative listing.

```
A>DIR
A:MBASIC    COM   :STAT       COM
A:SORT      BAS   :PIP        COM
A:DDT       COM   :WS         COM
A:FILTER    BAS   :SORT       BAS
A:GO        COM   :TESTSORT   DAT
```

Each line displays the name of the disk drive followed by the names and types of two files. As you recall, the filename extension, which appears separated from the primary filename, indicates the type of each file.

We can also follow DIR with a filename or a name containing wildcards. The name of a disk drive (followed by a colon) may precede any such filename. For example, DIR B:*.BAS lists all BASIC programs on disk B.

The command ERA file_name erases a file (file_name represents the file's actual name). The REN command renames files. For example, the command

```
REN SORT.BAS = TEST.BAS
```

changes the name of the file from TEST.BAS to SORT.BAS. The REN command cannot be used with wildcards.

The command TYPE file_name displays on the terminal the contents of a file (again, file_name represents the name of the file). For example,

TYPE LETTER.TEXT

will display the text file called LETTER.

The commands just described are said to be built-in commands because they reside in the primary memory of the computer at all times. Another set of commands, the transient commands, reside on a disk and are called into primary memory only when requested. These commands appear as part of the directory listing generated by DIR. They include the commands ASM to call up the assembler program, DDT to debug programs, DUMP to print (or dump) the contents of an executable file, and LOAD to convert an assembly language program into an executable command.

The command STAT, another executable command, prints the status of the disk in the default drive. A response to the command

A > STAT

might be

A: R/W, Space: 92k

This response indicates that drive A is the default drive, that it can be both read from and written to, and that it has a storage capacity of 92 kilobytes. STAT used with the name of a disk drive prints the same information about the disk in that drive. Thus the command STAT B: will elicit information about the disk in drive B. STAT used with the name of a file prints statistical information about the file as well as the protections on it. STAT can also designate the devices from which input is to be received and to which output is to be sent.

The last command that we describe here permits batches of operating system commands to be submitted through one command name. The transient command SUBMIT followed by the name of a file containing operating system commands causes each command to be executed as if the user had typed it in separately. Thus, if the file OPEN_FIL.SUB contains the commands DIR and ED TESTP.BAS on separate lines, then SUBMIT OPEN_FIL.SUB will first list the files in the current disk and then edit the file TESTP.BAS. The SUBMIT command has many more features, but discussing them is beyond the scope of this book.

The MS-DOS Operating System

MS-DOS (Microsoft Disk Operating System) lies somewhere between CP/M and UNIX in terms of features and capabilities. Designed primarily to be used in 16-bit computers (small personal and business computers) with floppy or hard disk storage, MS-DOS uses a hierarchical file system for each disk drive and allows pipelines as well as redirection of standard input and output.

MS-DOS has more than 50 commands, some of which are available only in later versions of the operating system. The commands fall into roughly five categories: file manipulation commands, disk commands, assembly programming commands, programming language commands, and miscellaneous commands. We will discuss the first category in some detail later.

The second category of commands, disk commands, change the default disk, format a new disk, and copy a disk in its entirety. Also included is a command called DISKCOMP to compare the contents of two disks for exact match and one called CHKDSK to check a disk to determine if errors occurred while files were being recorded and to correct errors if requested. One command checks the contents of individual files for errors and rebuilds directories (RECOVER), and another command verifies by comparison that disks contain the information sent from primary memory (VERIFY). There are also commands to transfer hidden operating system files to a disk (SYS) that cannot be copied with the normal copy command and to determine what label will be put on a formatted disk (VOL).

The third category of commands supports the writing of assembly language programs, and the fourth category contains a set of programming language statements understood by the command processor, called the shell. These programming language statements permit a user to write new commands. Since both categories of commands are used primarily by experienced programmers, we will not discuss them here.

The fifth and last category contains miscellaneous commands, some of which are utilities, programs used in many different applications. These commands include VER to determine what version of the operating system is being used, DATE and TIME to read or reset the date and time, and SORT to sort lines from a file. Another useful command, CLS, clears the terminal screen.

As in CP/M, a small set of control characters controls the command processor in MS-DOS. MS-DOS uses the same control characters as CP/M except that ^N rather than ^P stops the printer from printing all the information shown on the terminal.

As explained earlier, MS-DOS uses a hierarchical file system. Filenames within a directory follow the same conventions as CP/M filenames, although there are slight variations in the types of special characters allowed. As in CP/M, each name in a directory has a primary name and a secondary name, or filename extension. The use of wildcards is identical in the two systems.

Since the file system in MS-DOS is hierarchical, we must specify a pathname to find a file, as described earlier in the chapter. We can specify an *absolute path,* which is traced from the root directory, or a *relative path,* which starts at the current subdirectory and continues downward. As explained earlier, a slash (/) separates the name of the root and the names of the subdirectories. Thus, from the working directory /mnt/as, the relative pathname to a subdirectory called chapt3 might be /book/chapt3. The absolute pathname for this same directory is /mnt/as/book/chapt3.

Disks are identified in the same way as in CP/M, and the operating system prompt indicates which is the current default disk. When a command is given to move or copy files, MS-DOS assumes that the pathname for the files exist on the default drive unless the pathname explicitly specifies another disk. For example, B:/mnt/as/book/chapt3/references refers to the file references in the subdirectory chapt3 on disk B. Note that when specifying a file not on the default disk, MS-DOS requires the absolute pathname.

We will now discuss the first category of MS-DOS commands, the commands to manage files. DIR displays the name of each file in the working directory, its size, and the time it was last modified. DIR can also be followed by a filename or a name with wildcards in it. The filename can include the name of a disk drive and the path to the file on that drive, as in the preceding example. Although the file system in MS-DOS is hierarchical and the file system in CP/M is not, the use of DIR is similar in both systems. DIR combines features of CP/M's DIR and STAT. It will display the filename and its extension, size, and date.

The command PWD prints the name of the path to the current or working directory. The command CHDIR, often abbreviated CD, changes the working directory to the directory whose name follows the command. The name of the new directory can be relative or absolute. The command MKDIR creates a new directory as a subdirectory of the working one. The command RMDIR removes a specified empty directory. To protect users from inadvertently destroying files, MS-DOS will not remove a directory that contains files or subdirectories. Thus, to remove a directory that is not empty, the user must first remove all of its files and subdirectories. The command TREE lists the tree of all the files and subdirectories listed under the working directory or under any directory named.

The command ERASE, or its equivalent DEL, functions similarly to CP/M's ERA. The rename command REN is also similar to that found in CP/M except that its syntax is a bit different. It does not use an equal sign, and it places the old name last, reversing the order used in CP/M. For example, the command

REN *.YYY *.ZZZ

changes the file extension of all files ending in .YYY to .ZZZ. The command COPY copies files. Two filenames follow COPY; the first is the name of the original file and the second is the name of the new copy of the file. The command TYPE displays the contents of a specified file. The command PRINT sends any printable file to a printer, allowing other useful work to be performed during printing. In contrast, some simple operating systems do not allow other work to be done while the printer is working. The command EDLIN edits files. MORE displays a single page of output on a screen and will not continue until signaled to show the next page; FIND discards all lines except those containing certain key-words.

The DATE command produces the following display:

```
Current date is Wed 07-24-1985
Enter new date:
```

and waits for the user to type in a new date or to hit the RETURN key, which leaves the date unchanged. The command TIME produces similar output. The command SORT sorts lines in the standard input (which can be redirected) into alphabetical order, starting with the first char-acter on each line, and displays them on the standard output (which also can be redirected).

The UNIX Operating System

The UNIX operating system, developed in the late 1960s and early 1970s and modified continuously since then, has been widely used, tested, and improved over the years and has become the operating system of choice on many multi-user machines. UNIX has been used by many universities around the world and has in recent years been adopted by many manufacturers for a variety of applications on a variety of ma-chines.

The UNIX file system is hierarchical, as described earlier. UNIX supports the concepts of standard input and output, redirection, and the pipeline. Disks are of no importance to most UNIX users since UNIX runs on large machines that give users no control over their disks (usually hard disks). As UNIX becomes available for smaller machines that use floppy disks, control over disks will obviously receive greater attention.

UNIX allows file and directory names to consist of any sequence of letters and characters. It is identical to MS-DOS in its use of wild-cards, its hierarchical structure, and the name of its root (/). On most UNIX systems a subdirectory of the root contains the home directories of all users. A *home directory* is the directory from which a user operates;

it contains all of a user's files and subdirectories. The name of a home directory is typically the same as the user's login ID. Thus, /mnt/as would be the home directory of the person with login ID as. When a user logs in, her current working directory is set to her home directory.

The UNIX commands pwd, chdir or cd, mkdir, rmdir, and cp (for copy) have the same meaning as the parallel commands in capital letters in MS-DOS. Note, however, that the commands in UNIX must be typed in lowercase letters.

The command rm followed by a filename that may include wild-cards deletes the named file or files. The command mv path_name1 path_name2 moves the file whose location is given by path_name1 to the location given by path_name2. The command ls lists the contents of the working directory, as follows:

```
% ls
budget      house      library     policy
catalog     liaison    planning    tenure
fellows
%
```

(The % in this example is UNIX's standard prompt; users can change and personalize this prompt if they wish.) Like many UNIX commands, ls includes variations that cause it to perform related but different tasks. For example, the command ls -l gives the following long listing:

```
% ls -l
total 174
-rw-rw----   1   jes      847 Jul   28   20:08 budget
-rwxrw----   1   jes     1796 Jun    1   10:42 catalog
drwxrwxr-x   2   jes      128 Jan   17   19:83 fellows
-rw-rw----   1   jes    10247 Jul   28   20:08 house
drwxrwx--x   2   jes      368 May   20   09:41 liaison
-rw-rw----   1   jes     1536 Apr   27   08:28 library
-rw-rw----   1   jes     3786 Apr    8   07:34 planning
-rw-------   1   jes    13424 Apr   12   17:38 policy
drwxrwx--x   2   jes      496 Apr   18   10:29 tenure
%
```

This listing illustrates some of the file protection features offered by the UNIX system. The first character in each line is either - or d, identifying the entry as either a file or a directory. In the example, the working directory contains three subdirectories and six files. The nine characters that follow each initial character (d or -) are rwxrwxrwx, some of which have been dashed out. The first group of three characters indicates the privileges given to the owner of the files, the next three the privileges given to a group of people designated by the owner, and the last three the privileges given to anyone else on the system. Here r, w, and x are mnemonics for "read," "write," and "execute." Thus the file catalog can be read, written, and executed by the owner and read or written by any member of the owner's group, but it cannot be read, written, or executed by anyone else. Owners can change such privileges on their files. The column following the privileges is a complex UNIX notation that we will not discuss here. The login ID of the owner follows this special UNIX notation. Following the owner's ID are the number of bytes contained in each file or directory and the date and time of its last modification. The last piece of information on each line is, of course, the name of the file or directory.

Once a file has been found, its contents can be displayed with the cat (short for concatenate) command. This command types the filename on the standard output. Like most UNIX commands, cat can redirect output or accept filenames that contain wildcards. Used without a filename, cat will take the standard input from the terminal and deliver it to the standard output (also the terminal) until the user terminates input with the control character ^D.

Like FIND in MS-DOS, the UNIX command grep searches a file for all lines that contain a given pattern and sends these lines to the standard output. For example, the command grep pattern file_name will print on the terminal screen all lines from the file called file_name that contain the string of characters pattern. Users can combine grep with other UNIX commands to perform various powerful functions.

In addition to the preceding commands, most UNIX systems offer many utilities. Typical utilities include those that display the current date and time (date), print a calendar for any month or year (cal), provide facilities for electronic mail (mail), transmit messages immediately to other users logged on to the system (write), list users logged on to the system (who), and check spelling (spell). UNIX systems may provide editors, formatters (such as nroff and troff), and preprocessors (such as eqn and tbl), all described in Chapter 4. Most UNIX systems provide translators for several programming languages.

Let's look at some of these utilities more closely. The command date prints out the current date and time as follows:

```
% date
Tue Aug 2 14:52:19 EST 1985
%
```

The time appears in 24-hour notation in this example; EST stands for eastern standard time. The command cal followed by the month and year prints the calendar for that month. For example, the command cal 6 1985 yields the following result:

```
                 June 1985
    S    M    Tu    W    Th    F    S
                                    1
    2    3    4     5    6     7    8
    9    10   11    12   13    14   15
    16   17   18    19   20    21   22
    23   24   25    26   27    28   29
    30
```

If we specify a year alone (such as cal 1986), the standard output is the calendar for the entire year.

Calendar systems permit users to store a list of their daily commitments in a special file. Every day the system automatically generates a list of the day's events. These systems typically operate by periodically searching files called calendar in a user's home directory. A user's calendar file contains a list of the dates and times of important events, updated by the user. Most systems search this file early every morning to find each line with that day's date, perhaps using a grep command. These lines are grouped together in a file and the file mailed electronically to the user by the operating system.

As mentioned, the command who lists each user on the system, showing his login ID, what terminal he is working on, and the date and time when he logged in:

```
% who
as          ttyu0     Aug 2     16:08
sm          ttyn4     Aug 2     09:20
jes         ttyf4     Aug 2     10:09
%
```

Login information can facilitate communication among users. A user can write or send an immediate message to another user by typing in the other user's login ID. For example, one might type write jes, hit the RETURN key, type a message on one or more lines, and terminate the message with ^D. If jes was logged on, he would receive the message; if not, the sender would be so informed. This is a useful way for two users at different locations to communicate simultaneously.

For users not logged on at the same time, a mail system can send delayed messages. Users can send mail to any person known to the computer by specifying that person's login ID. Most mail systems also allow the sender to use an editor to correct mail messages before transmitting them and to send electronic carbon copies to other interested users. Mail systems typically allow receivers to scan a list of senders and subjects of mail to decide which messages to read, respond to, save, and discard. Computer networks for the transmission of electronic mail are available for many small and large computers. The following UNIX mail message was sent to jes from sm with an electronic "carbon" copy sent to as.

```
From sm Mon Aug 5 13:47:30 1985 remote from brunix
Date:          5 Aug 85 (Monday) 13:47 EDT
From:          Sue Magidson <sm@brunix.UUCP>
To:            jes
Cc:            as
Subject:       Babbage
```

Could you send me the copyright date on the Babbage autobiography? (I need it for the references for the history chapter.)

Like many sophisticated operating systems, UNIX provides electronic help to users. UNIX has an on-line systems manual that explains UNIX commands in detail. The man (short for manual) command displays information about UNIX commands. For example, the command man cal produces the following output:

```
CAL(1)          UNIX Programmer's Manual          CAL(1)

NAME
     cal - print calendar

SYNOPSIS
     cal [month] year

DESCRIPTION
     Cal prints a calendar for the specified year. If a month is
     also specified, a calendar just for that month is printed.
     The year can be between 1 and 9999. The month is a
     number between 1 and 12. The calendar produced is that for England
     and her colonies.

     Try September 1752.

BUGS
     The year is always considered to start in January even
     though this is historically naive.
     Beware that 'cal 78' refers to the early Christian era, not
     the 20th century.
```

SUMMARY

An operating system provides the user with control over a computer. Operating systems on the earliest machines were primitive, requiring the user to carry out many steps manually to get programs to run. To increase the use of these expensive machines, more sophisticated operating systems were developed. Features were added to simplify the handling of input and output, protect one user from another, run several programs in sequence (multiprogramming), and give users the appearance of having a dedicated computer at their disposal (time sharing). The most recent development in operating systems is their extension to networks of computers.

Operating systems typically provide users with a file system, command processing, password protection, and utilities. Many of them also provide unseen assistance by scheduling the activities that take place in a computer. In particular, operating systems give each user equal access to the resources of the computer.

A file system is a set of commands to manage files on a computer. Commands typically permit users to create, delete, name, rename, copy, and move files. They also allow users to arrange files in either a flat or hierarchical fashion. In the latter case, directories and subdirectories are used. A file system also provides commands to obtain data about files, such as size and time of creation or modification. On personal computers, file systems permit users to tell a computer which disk drive should be the default drive.

A command processor is a program that responds to input typed at a keyboard. It identifies incorrect commands and passes on correct commands for execution. In many operating systems, a command processor permits the user to redirect input and output, that is, to receive input from or send output to nonstandard sources and destinations.

Password protection is a feature of operating systems used to authenticate users with IDs and corresponding passwords. If a password system is good, an unauthorized user will have great difficulty in determining the correct password for a known user ID. Operating systems may permit users to control the rights that others have to read or modify their files.

The three operating systems examined in this chapter are CP/M, MS-DOS, and UNIX, in order of increasing complexity and power. CP/M has a flat file system, and MS-DOS and UNIX have hierarchical file systems. The latter two have commands to move within the file systems. UNIX has the largest set of utility programs, including a mail system, a message system, a calendar system, and an on-line reference manual.

FURTHER READING

S. R. Bourne, *The UNIX System* (Reading, Mass.: Addison-Wesley, 1982).

David E. Cortesi, *Inside CP/M: A Guide for Users and Programmers* (New York: Holt, Rinehart and Winston, 1982).

Thomas A. Dwyer and Margot Critchfield, *CP/M and the Personal Computer* (Reading, Mass.: Addison-Wesley, 1983).

Thomas A. Dwyer and Margot Critchfield, *Pocket Guide to CP/M* (Reading, Mass.: Addison-Wesley, 1983).

Peter Norton, *MS-DOS and PC-DOS: User's Guide* (Bowie, Md.: Robert J. Brady Co., 1984).

James L. Peterson and Abraham Silberschatz, *Operating System Concepts* (Reading, Mass.: Addison-Wesley, 1983).

ISSUES AND IDEAS

1. Compare and contrast the evolution of the automobile and the evolution of an operating system.

2. A file system is an integral part of an operating system. Explain in your own words the hierarchical file system and describe features not mentioned in this chapter that you think it should have.

3. Examine the sets of commands of the three operating systems described in this chapter. Compare their capabilities and ease of use.

4. Suppose you have collected 350 files. Compare CP/M and UNIX from the point of view of naming and retrieving these files. Now suppose that each file contains 2,000 bytes of information and that CP/M is available only on a microcomputer, while UNIX is available on a large minicomputer. How does this change your point of view?

5. Analyze the problem of maintaining sales and inventory records for a small company. Would you prefer to use MS-DOS running on a microcomputer or UNIX running on a large minicomputer to carry out this task? Why?

Solving Problems

Just as freewheeling westerners developed a characteristic pride in their frontiersmanship and a corresponding conservatism, so many programmers of the freewheeling 1950s began to regard themselves as members of a priesthood guarding skill and mysteries far too complex for ordinary mortals.

JOHN BACKUS, *A History of Computing in the Twentieth Century*

■ Introduction

Problem solving, far from being a rare skill, is so basic to our daily lives that we hardly think about it. We solve simple problems almost automatically. Some problems, however, are so complex that they require a formal approach. To help us acquire the skills we need to solve such problems, education often includes formal training in methods of organizing papers, doing library research, and solving problems in mathematics and the sciences.

In computer science, problem solving plays a visible and significant role. The problems are often complex, and formal methods are needed to guard against errors in programs; such errors can result in catastrophe if they are not discovered and rectified in time. Computer scientists develop plans of approach called *algorithms* (after the ninth-century mathematician Al-Khowarizmi) to help them solve abstract or complex problems.

We begin this chapter by demonstrating how methods used to solve ordinary problems can be recast as methods for developing algorithms. Step by step, we build a framework that can be used to solve virtually any problem. We then discuss how to refine these methods for use in computer programming. Although some of the methods may at first seem elementary, understanding them thoroughly is necessary to the development of the complex skills required for problem solving in computer science.

■ Why Structured Design?

Why bother with a step-by-step, detailed plan of approach for solving what may be a very simple problem? Why not just jump into the problem and solve it by dealing with each successive step as it arises? For simple tasks, it does not make sense to work out structured designs in advance. We can silence a noisy alarm clock by reaching for the button and thrashing around a bit, if necessary, to find the clock. It is not necessary to plan a strategy or to recall that strategy when half-awake. This unstructured approach to problem solving is popularly known as the *brute force method* because it approaches the problem in a spontaneous fashion, without a carefully formulated strategy. It is suitable for very small and simple problems but is completely inadequate for large and complex problems. As the complexity of a task increases, structured design becomes desirable and eventually indispensable.

An essential aspect of structured design is meticulous attention to detail. Only through attention to detail can structured designs prove practical in solving problems. The old Dutch recipe for jugged hare, "One taketh a hare and prepareth jugged hare from it," is not specific enough to be of any use to novice cooks. On the other hand, solutions to specific problems must contain details organized in a logical way. In fact, the difference between a structured algorithm and a brute force method often lies in how and when details are dealt with. Following is a description of an unstructured (brute force) approach to backing a car out of a driveway:

Reach out to grab handle of car door.
Pull handle toward body to open door.
Release door handle.
Standing on left foot, move right foot into car.
Lower head and move body into car and sit.
Sitting, move left foot into car.
Reach out and grab interior door handle.
Pull door toward body until it closes.
Release interior handle.

Remove car keys from pocket.
Select car key and insert into ignition switch.
Place transmission in neutral position.
Start engine by turning auto ignition key.
Place transmission in reverse.
Twist body in seat to observe driveway as car moves.
Release clutch gently while applying throttle.
Adjust clutch and throttle to control speed of auto.
Drive out of driveway until reaching the curb.
Stop by applying brakes.
Examine traffic in both directions on street until safe to proceed.
Resume driving in reverse.
Select a direction for car to travel, left or right.
Turn wheel to effect such a turn and back car up until parallel with sidewalk.
Stop car by applying brakes.
Place transmission in first gear and resume driving.

This description would probably not be very helpful to a beginning driver, who would likely find the level of detail confusing. A more useful description for the same process might look like this:

Open door.
Enter car.
Close door.
Find correct key.
Start engine.
Put car into reverse.
Check for careless cats, kids, or bicycles.
Move car in reverse through driveway.
Check for other cars.
Pull out onto street.

In less than half the number of steps, the second description has completed the job. The lower level of detail makes the description less confusing. Because the second description takes an organized approach, we can think of it as an algorithm. The method of problem solving used in this algorithm is commonly known as *divide and conquer* because the original problem is broken down into smaller problems that can subsequently be broken down into more easily manageable subproblems. Although it is very important to divide the problem into smaller subproblems, it is equally important to divide it in a sensible way that accounts for all relevant details. Failure to do so could lead to a design that is inefficient, incomplete, or dangerous.

For problems less familiar than backing a car out of a driveway, proper division is vital. An overlooked step or an incompletely specified problem can invalidate an entire solution. For example, a moon launch that does not provide for a backup oxygen supply or a rocket control system could result in the loss of a mission and the death of astronauts.

Elements of Structured Design

Describing the Problem

On approaching any problem, we must ask several important questions: What is the goal? What materials or information are provided? What additional materials or information are needed? To illustrate such an approach to a problem we consider three examples: peeling potatoes, baking a quiche, and traveling abroad. We do not devote the same amount of space to each. Instead, we invite you to complete those details not fully presented here.

Edsger Dijkstra, an early champion of the structured approach to computer programming, describes the problem of peeling potatoes. He divides the problem into four subproblems:

Fetch the basket from the cellar.
Fetch the pan from the cupboard.
Peel the potatoes.
Return the basket to the cellar.

This illustrates the simplest method used in structured design. Rather than using brute force to attack the whole problem at once, Dijkstra divides it into four more manageable subproblems. This is the divide and conquer method. Subordinates (such as children) could even be used to perform some of the less demanding tasks (such as fetching and returning the basket). The more demanding and challenging part of the problem (peeling the potatoes) needs to be further subdivided. One solution would be to produce a method for peeling one potato and then apply it repeatedly until all potatoes have been peeled.

Here is one method to peel a potato:

Hold peeler at top of potato.
Turning potato in hand, slice circularly until potato is completely peeled.

We now turn our attention to a different example, baking a quiche, which we develop in much greater detail.

Pâte à Croûstade*
(Pastry Dough for Upside-down Tart Shells,
Pastry Cases, and Turnovers)
For a 10-inch shell

2 cups granular "instant-blending" flour
1 stick (4 ounces) chilled butter
3 Tb chilled white vegetable shortening
⅓ cup ice water
1 egg
1 tsp salt
⅛ tsp sugar

Place flour in the large bowl of your electric mixer. Cut the chilled butter and shortening into ¼-inch pieces, and add to the flour. Run machine at moderate speed, pushing fat and flour into the blades with a rubber spatula, until mixture looks like very coarse meal.

Beat the ice water, egg, sugar, and salt in your measuring cup to blend. Pour into the flour and butter, and mix at moderate speed for a few seconds until dough clogs in the blender.

Turn out onto a board and press dough into a rough mass. By 2-tablespoon bits, push the dough out and away from you with the heel of your hand in quick, rough 6-inch smears. This constitutes final blending of fat and flour, and incorporates any too-large bits of fat. Scrape dough into a ball, dust lightly with flour, and wrap in waxed paper. Refrigerate for 2 hours or overnight: flour needs rehydrating and butter needs chilling before dough can be rolled easily. (Dough may be frozen.)

Upside-down Pastry Shells

(Preheat oven to 425 degrees.)

You can mold and bake pastry shells of almost any size and shape by forming the dough on almost any upside-down fireproof object, such as a cake or pie pan, a bread tin, a baking dish, a ring mold, or muffin cups. To do so, butter the outside of the mold lightly, roll the dough between ⅛ and 3⁄16 inch thick, and press snugly onto the bottom of the mold. Even off edges with a ravioli wheel or knife to make the shell about 1 inch deep. To prevent dough from puffing in oven, prick all over at ¼-inch intervals with a sharp-pronged table fork. To minimize shrinkage during baking, refrigerate for an hour: this will relax the gluten in the dough.

---

* From *The French Chef Cookbook*, by Julia Child, pp. 239–241. Copyright © 1968 by Julia Child. Reprinted by permission of Alfred A. Knopf, Inc.

To bake, place dough-covered mold, still upside down, on a baking sheet and set in middle level of oven for 6 to 8 minutes, until shell has just started to color and to separate slightly from the mold. Remove, let cool 5 minutes, and unmold on a rack. Baked shells may be frozen.
. . .

Quiche Lorraine
(Cream and Bacon Quiche)
For 4 to 6 servings

6 to 8 pieces thick-sliced bacon
An 8-inch partially cooked pastry shell placed
on a buttered baking sheet
3 eggs (U.S. graded "large")
1¼ to 1½ cups heavy cream
¼ tsp salt
Pinch of pepper and nutmeg
1 to 2 Tb butter

(Preheat oven to 375 degrees.)
Slice bacon into ¼-inch pieces and brown lightly in a frying pan; drain and spread in bottom of pastry shell. Beat eggs, cream, and seasonings in a bowl to blend. Just before baking, pour cream mixture into the shell, filling to within ⅛ inch of the top. Cut butter into bits and distribute over the cream. Bake in upper third of oven for 25 to 30 minutes, until quiche has puffed and browned, and a small knife, plunged into custard, comes out clean. Serve hot, warm, or cold; quiche will sink slightly as it cools.

To look at quiche-baking from the point of view of structured design, it is important to determine precisely what we want when the "problem" has been solved, what items we need for the solution, and what method we use to combine these items. In the case of quiche-baking, our final goal is fairly simple: we wish to produce an appetizing food. The items needed for preparation of quiche are spelled out quite explicitly, although not completely, in the recipe; the description of the method of preparation, however, leaves something to be desired for the beginner.

Recipes, although structured, often have unstructured elements. This recipe is more structured than most; it has already been broken down into two sections (or subproblems): the preparation of the crust and the preparation of the quiche itself. The recipe provides a set of ingredients—the items needed to complete the recipe. However, the

Figure 6.1
Algorithm for baking quiche.

list of ingredients does not contain everything necessary to make the quiche. Note that the preparation of the dough requires use of an electric mixer and a large bowl, neither of which has been explicitly mentioned as material required for the task.

In cooking, we don't ordinarily think of large bowls as being ingredients in the same way butter and flour are; rather, we think of mixers, bowls, and other utensils as tools that help us cook. But structured design demands that we begin with a list of everything we need to solve the problem. If we tried to make the quiche without the mixing bowl, we'd run into trouble just as we would if we tried to make the quiche without the butter. Similarly, we must be aware of our need for a frying pan in the second part of the problem.

Having noted these shortcomings in the ingredients lists, let's look at the major components of the quiche-baking procedure. Figure 6.1 shows the items needed in the first box, the process to follow in the second box, and the end result in the third box. However, the figure has not divided the problem into sufficiently small pieces for us to solve each piece easily. Each piece needs to be divided further before we attempt to conquer the problem. We know, for example, that the Cooking box can be easily divided into two additional boxes, as shown in Fig. 6.2—one for the preparation of the dough and another for the preparation of the quiche. These boxes represent subproblems, and the methods used to solve them are known as *procedures*. Note that the Prepare Dough procedure must be completed before the Prepare Quiche procedure begins, since the end result of the first procedure (prepared dough) is an ingredient in the second procedure.

Figure 6.2
The Cooking procedure divided into subproblems.

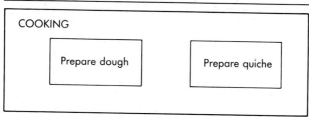

Solving the Problem

Now that we have formulated the problem, we will solve it using the methods of structured design. Recall from our discussion of the divide and conquer method that the easiest way to solve a complex problem is to break it down into smaller subproblems that can be solved individually. As with the main problem, questions must be asked about the goals and necessary ingredients for solving the subproblems. We have already broken down the quiche-baking problem into the subproblems Prepare Dough and Prepare Quiche. We next examine an approach to the Prepare Quiche subproblem. Note that solving the Prepare Quiche problem assumes that the Prepare Dough problem has been solved. We will leave this task to the gastronomically inclined reader.

It is important that each problem not be broken down into too many subproblems, lest the task of coordinating the subproblems become too difficult. Psychological research indicates that the number of different items most people can keep track of at one time is seven, plus or minus two. We can break down the Prepare Quiche problem into five subproblems: Prepare Bacon, Beat Other Ingredients, Place Ingredients in Shell, Bake Quiche, and Test Readiness of Quiche. Our Prepare Quiche box now has been subdivided into five boxes, as shown in Fig. 6.3.

Notice that the Prepare Bacon box is positioned above the Beat Other Ingredients box. This indicates that either of these tasks may be performed first; they have no effect or interaction with each other until they have been completed. Both, however, must be solved before we can move on to the subproblem to its right.

The process of continuing to break each subproblem down into sub-subproblems is known as *stepwise refinement,* an important characteristic of good structured design techniques. A *top-down approach* starts with the main problem and breaks it into smaller problems, as we have done in the quiche example. A *bottom-up approach* starts with the

Figure 6.3
Prepare Quiche procedure divided into subproblems.

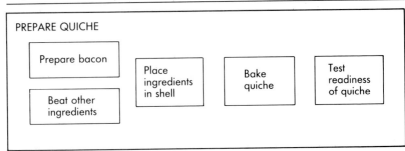

solution to a subproblem and moves toward a solution of the larger problem. Usually the best way to approach a problem is through a combination of top-down and bottom-up approaches using stepwise refinement.

Algorithmic Procedures

We must elaborate still further the procedures into which the quiche-baking problem has been divided before we can actually bake the quiche. Let's first focus our attention on the Prepare Bacon subproblem. To tackle this problem, we must know the ingredients needed (in this case bacon, a sharp knife, a stove, a frying pan, a utensil to remove the cooked bacon, and a surface on which to drain the bacon) and the goals of the subproblem. The goal here is to transform the raw bacon into browned strips. As shown in Fig. 6.4, we accomplish the goal by dividing the task into two subproblems: slicing the bacon into ¼-inch pieces (Slice Bacon) and browning the pieces in a frying pan (Brown Bacon). The Slice Bacon subproblem will serve to introduce a simple yet powerful concept in problem solving: the loop.

A *loop* is a set of commands to be repeated again and again. If we were writing a structured design of the Slice Bacon subproblem we wouldn't want to write out "slice off a ¼-inch piece of bacon" each time another slice was needed. To avoid doing so, we could write a loop that expressed the same thing. The loop

LOOP 24 times: slice off ¼-inch piece of bacon

would tell us to slice twenty-four ¼-inch slices of bacon. Although writing this loop statement is easier than writing out the instruction twenty-four times, such a statement requires an exact knowledge of how many times the instruction should be repeated (in this case, how many ¼-inch slices of bacon there will be). It would be more convenient to have a way of looping that didn't require a predetermined number of loops so that we could account for inaccuracy in our measurement of slices.

Figure 6.4
Prepare Bacon procedure divided into subproblems.

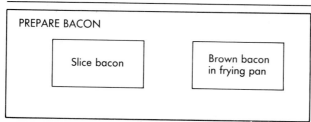

Fortunately, we can formally distinguish between two basic types of loops. A *definite loop*, like the preceding one, specifies in advance the number of times it will be used. An *indefinite loop* includes some other method to determine how many times it should be used. What we'd really like to do is allow the bacon-slicing loop to be executed until the supply of bacon is gone. A loop that would allow us to do this would include a way to evaluate a simple statement, such as < there is bacon left > to determine whether execution would continue. We call this type of loop a while loop since execution continues *while* a certain condition is true. Figure 6.5 shows a while loop for the Slice Bacon subprocedure.

Another somewhat similar problem-solving method is the IF-THEN-ELSE construct. This specifies that IF a condition is true, THEN an action is taken ELSE another action is taken. The importance for cooking quiche should be fairly clear. You may suddenly discover that you have no more butter in your refrigerator. Since the recipe calls for butter, you would prefer to use butter, but you recognize that the recipe will still work if you have to use margarine. To solve the quiche preparation problem, then, you need to evaluate the condition < there is butter in the refrigerator >. IF this condition is true, THEN you will use the butter ELSE you will use margarine. Such statements are known as *conditional branching* statements, since the path taken depends on the truth of a given statement. There are also more complex methods of conditional branching that divide the path into more than two possible routes.

You may have noticed that the box that represents mixing the eggs, cream, and spices in Fig. 6.3 is labeled Beat Other Ingredients, and not Mix Eggs, Cream, and Spices. It contains a general method of solving the subproblem of beating things. When we solve the beating problem, we don't care what we are beating—it could be cream, eggs, and spices or milk, honey, and raisins. The important point is to have a general procedure that we can adapt and use in many different situations. Once we have established the general beating procedure, we can insert the *parameters* of the particular task we wish to perform into the procedure.

Figure 6.5
Cut Bacon procedure with while loop.

```
SLICE BACON

    WHILE ⟨there is at least one strip of bacon
    larger than 1/4 inch⟩:
        Slice another 1/4-inch piece of bacon.
```

For example, in quiche-making, we supply the parameters cream, eggs, and spices. If another recipe called for milk and honey to be beaten, we would not have to find a separate procedure to beat them; instead, we would simply use the procedure we had already developed and insert the new parameters. Like many of the problem-solving methods presented in this chapter, this is something that most of us have learned to do without reflection.

Let's stop and assess our progress. Each time we divide a problem, we say we have made a *pass* through the problem. So far, we've made several passes through the quiche-baking problem. First, we identified three components of the problem—items needed, procedure to follow, and result (Fig. 6.1). Then we divided the procedure component into two subproblems—Prepare Dough and Prepare Quiche (Fig. 6.2). Next we broke Prepare Quiche into five subproblems (Fig. 6.3) and divided one of them, Prepare Bacon, still further (Figs. 6.4 and 6.5). When should we stop subdividing the problem?

Although we could refine the quiche-baking procedure still further, we can stop here with a clear conscience. We have reached the point at which each subproblem can be easily accomplished without any other external information or assistance. Note, though, that some subproblems may require more passes than others. This is perfectly acceptable; some parts of problems are simply easier to solve than others.

In developing subgoals and subprocedures, it is important to be aware of how each procedure interacts with other procedures. The relationship between subprocedures is known as *coupling*. Closely coupled procedures depend very much on each other, perhaps sharing some of the same utilities. Conversely, procedures that operate independently are known as uncoupled procedures. As noted earlier, the Beat Other Ingredients procedure and the Prepare Bacon procedure in Fig. 6.3 are two uncoupled procedures. Another type of coupling is known as *input/output coupling* because the output of one procedure is used as the input of another. The coupling between the Prepare Dough procedure and the Prepare Quiche procedure is an example of an input/output coupling since the dough from the Prepare Dough procedure is used in the Prepare Quiche procedure.

Getting Back to Computers

You might be wondering what the method of problem solving we have described has to do with computers. In computer programming, the problems tend to be large and complicated, and their solutions tend to require a formalized approach of some kind. The formalized approach that is most efficient is the one we have just used. The only difference between the structured design we used in preparing the quiche and the structured design programmers use to write programs is that programmers aim for a set of statements written in a programming language. The term used to describe any collection of programming language statements is *code*. The descriptions of the structured design steps we used in the quiche-baking problem—such as Prepare Dough and Prepare Quiche—are known as *pseudocode*. These brief, informal statements take the place of statements written in a computer language.

A completed computer program consists of two parts: the syntax (or structure) and the semantics (or meaning). Pseudocode is concerned only with semantics—the approach taken and how and why it should work. Once the pseudocode is written, it is a relatively simple matter to transform it into the syntax of whatever computer language you happen to be using (BASIC, Pascal, FORTRAN, C, or any other). Syntax errors are relatively easy to locate and remove; semantic errors are often hidden deep within the design of a program and are very hard to isolate and correct. That is why time spent on carefully constructed pseudocode saves time in the long run.

Our discussion of structured design touched on many important and powerful ideas. Among the ideas that are most useful in computer programming (as well as in quiche-baking) are the division of a problem into subproblems, the use of looping and conditional branching, and strict attention to detail. We will explicitly discuss code and programming in later chapters that contain no recipes for edible foods at all.

The reason this chapter has had so little to do with computers is that it deals primarily with a method of thinking. The approach to solving a problem should, at the first level, be independent of the machinery or tools used in the solution. At subsequent levels, solving the problem requires knowledge of the syntax of the computer language used—that is, the acceptable form for statements in the language. It may also require some knowledge of the type of computer that is being used. When a problem is first specified, however, all that exists is that problem.

In setting out to solve a problem, it is important to remember that computers will do only what they are told; they can't figure out what you want them to do and then find a way to do it. Thus, it is essential to write code that tells the computer exactly what to do. Almost no one can sit down and immediately write a complex computer program; a certain amount of thought and preliminary sketching is required. The more complex the program, the more important are such intermediate steps as the writing of pseudocode. Pseudocode also has the advantage that it requires planning and thus makes better and more efficient designs that are easier to encode in computer language. Spending time on the design of a solution saves time that otherwise would be spent debugging and correcting the program.

One study cited by Larry Constantine and Edward Yourdon singled out a military software system that uncovered as many as 900 bugs per month, each of which required an average of 17 modifications to rectify. Although it is unlikely that any large system could be rendered completely bugless, many fewer bugs occur when proper structured design features are used. Later we discuss a major success story in which Bell Laboratories used structured design in its ABM project.

The Air Travel Problem

Now let's work through another problem: traveling abroad. Suppose you have friends in Paris whom you decide to visit. Your problem is getting from where you are to where you wish to be. You brainstorm and come up with a partial list of necessary activities: finding a flight on a given day, packing, getting to the airport, and going through customs.

If this list were a computer program, you would be left on the ground—you forgot to put yourself on the plane, which will now take off without you. You also forgot to obtain a passport, without which you won't be allowed to enter France. Taking a more structured approach to your trip, you may decide on the following subgoals, depicted in Fig. 6.6: Find a Flight, Get a Passport, Pack, Go to the Plane, and Fly to Paris. Notice that one of the subgoals (Fly to Paris) need be subdivided no further. Assuming that you are not a pilot yourself, the actual flying of the plane can be left to those trained for the task.

Finding a flight divides easily into subproblems. You must first determine which airlines fly to Paris; you can do so by looking through the travel section of a newspaper and writing down the names of airlines that advertise such flights. The goal of your search is a list of air-

Figure 6.6
The Traveling Abroad problem divided into subproblems.

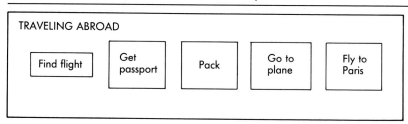

lines. Then you contact each of the airlines to find the lowest available fare. The goal of calling the airlines is a list of prices, one for each airline. You decide to select the airline that offers the lowest fare. Once you have found the least expensive flight, you call back the airline of your choice and make a reservation. The goal of calling back is the same as the end goal of the Find Flight procedure: to obtain a reservation on a flight to Paris. These steps are illustrated in Fig. 6.7.

Obtaining a passport is somewhat more complicated since you can apply in person for passports only in certain cities. (Passports can also be obtained by mail, but if you are in a hurry, you would have to visit a passport office; we'll assume you're in a hurry.) First, you find the nearest city where you can apply and then obtain an application and have passport photos taken. The application must be filled out and returned to the passport office along with the photos. The passport will

Figure 6.7
(a) The Find Flight procedure and (b) its complete pseudocode.

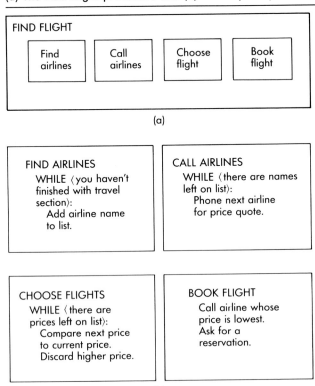

be sent to you in about a month. We leave you the job of drawing a diagram of this procedure.

You now have a flight and a passport; your day of departure is drawing nearer. Having decided to pack in a structured manner, you make a list of the clothing and other items you'll need. Because your Parisian friends are partial to California wines, you thoughtfully tuck a few bottles into your bulging suitcase. We leave you to pack as you wish; suffice it to say that you will discover, shortly after arriving in Paris, that you forgot something important you'd meant to bring with you—a bug in your packing algorithm. We leave you to your own devices for getting to the airport. Have a good time, and don't forget to write!

■ Problem-Solving Methods in Practice

Now that you have been introduced to structured problem-solving techniques, we can consider their direct application in a real-world example. One of the best examples of a large project that needed structured design was the antiballistic missile (ABM) research and development project carried out in the 1960s at Bell Laboratories. This project used the energy and time of several thousand people over a period of four years. The problem the ABM project team had to solve was to build a defense system that could detect incoming intercontinental ballistic missiles (ICBMs) and then launch missiles to destroy the ICBMs before they reached their targets. When the project was undertaken, it was not clear that a solution was possible.

Following the principles of structured design, the ABM project team broke down the problem into subproblems. These subproblems included early detection of incoming ICBMs, communications between detection equipment and ABM launching equipment, and in-flight tracking of the ICBM from the ABM. Because only a short amount of time would elapse between the first appearance of an ICBM on radar and the time when it could no longer be safely destroyed, it was critical that the system be extremely fast (processing perhaps 30 million instructions per second). Because of the tremendous threat of destruction from ICBMs, it was imperative that the ABM system be extremely reliable. It would hardly pay to have the computer "go down" at a critical time.

Another important feature of the ABM project was that the design was allowed to evolve so that methods of approaching the problem could be tested and the best one selected. The project proceeded from planning to simulation to testing, with each aspect carefully evaluated at many points. The project history prepared by Bell Laboratories concluded that "development of a large weapons system can be completed on schedule to prescribed performance specifications with effectively controlled costs."

Problem-Solving Teams

In the design process for computer software systems, the goal or the problem that must be solved is typically identified by users of the computers or people who speak for the users. The first step in building a working system to solve the problem involves a *systems analyst,* who strictly defines the problem and tentatively decides which types of hardware and software configurations are needed. A *systems designer* then breaks the problem down into subproblems and specifies the subproblems in detail, using the types of hardware and software tentatively chosen by the systems analyst. Programmers write the actual code that will ultimately make the system run. Other programmers test and debug the code, while still others are responsible for its maintenance.

The systems analyst generally deals with structured analysis of a problem, the systems designer with structured design, and the programmer with structured programming. (Structured programming is described in later chapters.) In many instances the jobs of systems designer and programmer overlap.

Frequently, large computer programs are written by many people under the supervision of one person. One structured organization of this type is called the chief programmer team, a team led by a *chief programmer,* who is responsible for the conceptual integrity of the system. The task is broken down into subtasks and sub-subtasks until it has been divided far enough so that one person can work on each subtask. At this level, it is vitally important that the supervisor know precisely what each person is working on and how the pieces are going to fit together.

SUMMARY

Structured design has a large variety of applications, from following recipes to designing and overseeing large projects to programming computers. In each case, the same basic techniques are used to evaluate a problem so that it can be solved in a logical fashion. The divide and conquer approach is used to break the big problem down into two or more basic pieces. Then stepwise refinement is used to further divide the problem into subproblems. The resulting subproblems can then be thoroughly described in pseudocode before they are translated into final form (a programming language or final outline of necessary steps). This method is crucial to the successful solution of complicated tasks.

FURTHER READING

ABM Research and Development at Bell Laboratories Project History (Whippany, N.J.: Bell Laboratories, Oct. 1975).

Larry Constantine and Edward Yourdon, *Structured Design* (Englewood Cliffs, N.J.: Prentice-Hall, 1979).

Edsger W. Dijkstra, *A Discipline of Programming* (Englewood Cliffs, N.J.: Prentice-Hall, 1976).

Edsger W. Dijkstra, *A Short Introduction to the Art of Programming*, folio EWD 316, August, 1971.

Tracy Kidder, *The Soul of a New Machine* (Boston: Little, Brown/ Atlantic Monthly Press, 1981).

ISSUES AND IDEAS

1. Select one of the following tasks and write pseudocode to tell another person how to carry it out. Your instructions should be specific enough that a person who has never performed the task can carry it out successfully, yet they should include no unnecessary detail.
   a) The steps required to locate and check out a particular book at your local library. You may assume the person knows how to get to the library.
   b) The steps required to select and purchase a meal at a local fast-food restaurant.

2. Devise a procedure to teach a 12-year-old child to operate an automatic teller machine.

3. Write a set of instructions to teach an adult how to operate a hi-fi or video cassette recording system. The adult is intelligent but has never seen this equipment before. Your instructions must be complete as well as concise.

4. Use structured design techniques to break the Prepare Dough procedure into manageable pieces. Then write pseudocode for each of the pieces. Finally, identify the algorithmic procedures (types of loops, conditional statements, and so on) used in your pseudocode.

5. Use a structured design approach to plan the preparation, serving, and cleanup of a four-course meal for a group of 30 people. The plan includes sending invitations, finding a place to hold the dinner, and so on, as well as preparing the food.

Programming Concepts in BASIC

Programming is one of the most fascinating games ever devised. Easier than
chess and more varied than bridge,
programming is both an intellectual
challenge and an act of personal domi-
nation over the machine.

DAVID CORTESI, *Inside CP/M: A Guide
for Users and Programmers*

■ Introduction

A computer may have great potential, but that potential can be realized
only with the proper software. *Software*, as mentioned earlier, is a collection of computer programs. Many people believe that writing such
programs requires knowledge and skills beyond the grasp of the average
person. It is our purpose to dispel this notion. We do that by introducing
some important programming concepts and illustrating them with examples. This introduction should demonstrate the enormous power that
can result from the use of simple programming concepts.

Of course, it is not necessary to become an expert programmer to
make good use of computers today. An understanding of programming,
however, can help provide an awareness of what computers can and
cannot do.

This chapter presents programming concepts in the BASIC language. BASIC, an acronym for Beginner's All-purpose Symbolic Instruction Code, was originally developed and implemented at Dartmouth
College in 1965 to teach programming to undergraduates. A widely used

language available on most low-cost microcomputers, BASIC is popular with people who have no programming experience.

Because BASIC was developed early, it does not include many of the constructs that help programmers write in a structured way—that is, it is not a structured programming language. Structured languages make it simple to write computer programs that are easy to read, understand, and modify. Although BASIC is not a structured programming language, it is possible to write BASIC programs in a structured way. We take a structured approach to BASIC in this chapter. Once a person learns to program in a structured way with BASIC, applying this knowledge to a more sophisticated language such as Pascal is a relatively simple task.

There are many different versions of BASIC, and they vary slightly in syntax. We examine the major concepts in the language and gloss over syntactic differences among versions. You may employ these major concepts when you use any of the slightly different versions of BASIC. We recommend that you buy a reference manual that gives specific syntactic rules for the particular version you will be using. Our programs are written in Microsoft BASIC, one of the most popular versions of BASIC for microcomputers.

■ What Is a Program?

A *program* is a series of instructions that tells the computer what to do. When a program is run, the instructions are executed one at a time. Since BASIC is an *interactive language,* the program is executed while you, the user, sit at a computer terminal and watch. If the program needs specific data to operate on, it will ask for the data when it is needed. The program may print out information on the CRT or the printer at any time. In contrast, some programming languages are *batch processing languages.* As you may recall, in batch processing, the program and its data are submitted to the computer together. Such programs cannot request input from a user sitting at a keyboard. Information is not printed out until the computer has finished running the entire program. With BASIC and other interactive languages, you can "watch" the program run; with batch processing languages, you cannot. Interactive languages are much more user-friendly because they permit users to observe the progress of programs and detect problems as they occur.

The following is an example of a simple BASIC program:*

```
LIST
  5 REM THIS PROGRAM PRINTS A SIMPLE MESSAGE
  8 REM
 10 PRINT "THIS IS A SIMPLE PROGRAM"
 20 PRINT "THE LINES ARE EXECUTED IN ORDER, ONE AT A TIME"
 25 REM
 40 END
```

The word *LIST* above the program is a command telling the computer to display a listing, an enumeration of the statements in the program. We have italicized words that the user types in, such as *LIST*, to distinguish them from the computer's response. The program itself contains a *comment* on the first line (line 5) for the benefit of anyone who reads or modifies it. The word REM (for remark) at the beginning of the line indicates that the line contains a comment intended only for human use; the computer skips over the remainder of that line and proceeds to the next. An exclamation mark (!) or an apostrophe ('), depending on the version of BASIC, is often used to indicate a comment as well; later in the chapter, we will use an apostrophe instead of REM. Comments make programs easier to read and modify; they serve as a road map to help people understand the logic behind computer programs. Comment statements are also used to produce blank lines to separate major sections of the program, as shown in lines 8 and 25. The program shown here closes with an END statement to denote the end of the body of the program. END statements are required in some versions of BASIC but not in others; to avoid confusion, we will use them throughout this chapter.

Each line of the preceding program contains one instruction for the computer. The numbers at the far left of each line are called *line numbers*. Line numbers specify the order in which the lines will be executed. Lines may be numbered with any positive integer, but it is convenient to order line numbers by fives or tens to provide space to insert new lines. For example, we could insert another comment at line 22 since 22 does not currently correspond to any BASIC instruction. The lines may be typed in any order; the computer will automatically place them in numerical order before listing or running the program. Lines 8 and 25 are blank lines, inserted solely to improve readability. They

---

* We use only uppercase letters in the BASIC programs we give here because many versions of BASIC permit only uppercase letters. Some versions, however, do permit lowercase as well.

are ignored by the computer. It is a good idea to separate major sections of code with blank lines.

Lines 10 and 20 are the only lines in this program in which an action is performed. They contain PRINT statements, which print messages on the screen as the program runs. Notice that quotation marks surround the phrases "THIS IS A SIMPLE PROGRAM" and "THE LINES ARE EXECUTED IN ORDER, ONE AT A TIME". The quotation marks cause the two sentences to be printed exactly as they appear in the program, but the quotation marks are not printed. Such phrases are known as *literals* because they are printed literally as they appear in the program.

After each PRINT statement, BASIC skips to the next line on the CRT screen or paper printout. We call such an action a carriage return, as we do when we use a typewriter. Of course, there are no carriages on many modern printers or on CRTs, but it is convenient to think of a carriage moving across the screen as the computer prints out information. Because the PRINT statement advances the carriage to the next line, our two literals will appear on separate lines. A sample *run* of the program would look like this:

```
RUN
THIS IS A SIMPLE PROGRAM
THE LINES ARE EXECUTED IN ORDER, ONE AT A TIME
```

The RUN command, typed by the user, tells BASIC to execute the program.

■ Variables

While the preceding statements constitute a legitimate computer program, they are not very useful because they do the same thing every time the program runs. To introduce some variety, programmers use variables. We can think of a *variable* as a storage place for a piece of information. A *variable name* is the name used to refer to the variable. In BASIC there are two types of variables: numeric and string. *Numeric variables* refer to numbers, and *string variables* refer to sequences of characters. A string variable may contain a letter, a word, a short sentence, or a number not intended for calculation.

Each variable has a unique name. In BASIC, variable names are used to differentiate between numeric variables and string variables. Variables that hold numbers for arithmetic purposes are given names beginning with a letter and consisting of letters, numbers, and periods. Examples of numeric variable names are SUM, PRICE1, INIT.TEMP, and

FINAL.TEMP. The names of string variables are formed in the same way except that they must end with a $. Examples of string variable names are OPTION$, NICKNAME$, FIRST.NAME$, and WORD1$. It is helpful to use *mnemonic* variable names—names that clearly indicate what kind of information is stored in the variable. For example, a variable that holds a person's name could be called NICKNAME$, one that holds the Fahrenheit temperature could be called TEMPF, and one that holds the Celsius temperature could be called TEMPC.

Assignment Statements

Information can be stored in variables in two ways: by use of an assignment statement or by use of an input statement. *Assignment statements* are used in a program to assign an initial value to a variable or to alter its present value. These statements look something like equations because they use equal signs, but their function is quite different. An assignment statement stores the value of the expression at the right of the equal sign in the variable named at the left of the equal sign.

The simplest form of assignment statement is used to assign an initial value to a variable—to *initialize* the variable. For example, the statement

TEMP = 25

would store the value 25 in the variable TEMP. Think of a variable as a labeled box in which a value can be stored; this statement tells the computer to take the value 25 and put it into the box labeled TEMP, as illustrated in Fig. 7.1.

Figure 7.1
The variable TEMP.

A second type of assignment statement performs a computation and assigns the result to the designated variable. For example, the statement

```
TEMP = TEMP + 20
```

would perform the calculation requested on the right-hand side of the equation and place the result into the variable specified on the left. BASIC performs addition and subtraction by using the familiar plus (+) and minus (−) operators. Multiplication is represented by an asterisk (∗), and division is denoted by a slash (/). Therefore, if TEMP equaled 25, TEMP + 20 would equal 25 + 20, or 45. The value of the right-hand side of the equation (45) would then be stored in the variable TEMP. (Remember, this is an assignment statement, not an equation.)

In computer programming, as in mathematics, numerical operations are performed in a certain order—multiplications and divisions first, then additions and subtractions. For example, if given the expression 2 + 3 ∗ 4 + 5 /6, the computer would first compute the multiplication (3 ∗ 4) and the division (5/6) and then the two additions. The value of the expression is 89/6. As is mathematics, parentheses can be used to change the order of operations. Our sample problem would have been computed quite differently if it had been written this way: (2 + 3) ∗ (4 + 5) / 6. The calculations within the parentheses would have been completed first, and then the remaining operations performed in the usual order of operations, for an answer of 15/2. If parentheses are used within parentheses, as in ((2 + 3) ∗ 4 + 5) /6, inside parentheses are calculated first. Thus, the value of this expression is 25/6.

▊ Input Statements

Another way to put information into a variable is with an input statement. Although the input statement is a type of assignment statement, it deserves separate mention since the value stored in the variable comes from the user and is not written as part of the program listing. An *input statement* tells the computer to temporarily stop running the program so that a user can enter information. In response, the computer types a question mark and waits for the user to type something in. Usually an input statement is preceded by a print statement. The computer executes this statement by telling the user what kind of information to type in. For example, the following program fragment will cause the computer to ask for a Fahrenheit temperature and then pause for input.

When the user types in a response, the program stores the response in the variable FAHR.TEMP.

```
10 PRINT "TYPE IN THE FAHRENHEIT TEMPERATURE"
20 INPUT FAHR.TEMP
```

The user must respond with a number because the variable specified is a numeric variable; if the user entered a character string, BASIC would print out an error message and refuse to store the character string in a numeric variable. With that one restriction, then, whatever is typed in will be stored in the variable specified by the input statement. For example, if the user typed in 68 when prompted by the program, the number 68 would be assigned to FAHR.TEMP. However, if the user typed YES, the computer would print out an error message and stop executing the program.

The next line of the preceding program might read:

```
30 CEL.TEMP = ((FAHR.TEMP − 32) * 5)/9
```

This statement performs a simple arithmetic calculation using FAHR.TEMP and assigns the result (20 when FAHR.TEMP is 68) to CEL.TEMP. Since statement 30 does not do anything to alter FAHR.TEMP, the value of FAHR.TEMP does not change. Again we see that in BASIC, multiplication is indicated by an asterisk (*) and division by a slash (/). Parentheses specify the order in which the operations are to be performed; the innermost set is executed first. Thus 32 is subtracted from FAHR.TEMP and the result is multiplied by 5 and then divided by 9.

If we add the following line:

```
40 PRINT CEL.TEMP
```

the computer would print the contents, or *value*, of CEL.TEMP—in other words, the Celsius equivalent of the number typed in by the user. When a variable name is specified without quotation marks in a PRINT statement, the contents of the variable are printed out. To print out a more informative message, literals and variable names can be combined as follows:

```
40 PRINT "THE CELSIUS EQUIVALENT IS", CEL.TEMP
```

The comma causes the "carriage" to move over one tab stop before printing the value of CEL.TEMP. This statement would produce the following output:

```
THE CELSIUS EQUIVALENT IS        20
```

To prevent the carriage from moving between the printing of the literal and the printing of the value of the variable, we use a semicolon in place of the comma:

```
40 PRINT "THE CELSIUS EQUIVALENT IS ";CEL.TEMP
```

This statement produces the following result:

```
THE CELSIUS EQUIVALENT IS 20
```

Notice that a blank space separates the closing quotation marks from the literal in line 40. This blank space simply ensures that the S and the value of CEL.TEMP will not run together. (Since BASIC uses the space preceding the number to specify whether the number is positive or negative, a space will be left before a positive number, such as 56, but not before a negative number, such as -56.) BASIC will print a blank space after the number.

Combining all of the preceding statements produces a complete program to convert a Fahrenheit temperature to its Celsius equivalent.

```
 1 REM THIS PROGRAM ASKS FOR THE FAHRENHEIT TEMPERATURE,
 2 REM AND PRINTS THE CELSIUS EQUIVALENT
 3 REM
10 PRINT "TYPE IN THE FAHRENHEIT TEMPERATURE"
20 INPUT FAHR.TEMP
30 CEL.TEMP = ((FAHR.TEMP - 32) * 5)/9
40 PRINT "THE CELSIUS EQUIVALENT IS ";CEL.TEMP
50 REM
60 END
```

This program can be run over and over, computing the Celsius equivalent of any Fahrenheit temperature typed in by the user. A run of the program might look like this:

```
RUN
TYPE IN THE FAHRENHEIT TEMPERATURE
?212
THE CELSIUS EQUIVALENT IS 100
```

Conditional Statements

To make this program even more useful, we could allow the user to request either a Fahrenheit-to-Celsius conversion or a Celsius-to-Fahrenheit conversion. We can allow for such variation by using a conditional statement—namely, the IF statement. The IF statement evaluates information and bases a decision on it. The statement takes this form:*

---

* Angle brackets are used to specify where (syntactically) a piece of a programming construct should appear. In this case, the angle brackets show where the condition and the statement should appear.

IF <condition> THEN <statement>

If the <condition> is true, the computer will execute the <statement>. If the <condition> is not true, the computer will not execute the <statement>. For example, the following piece of code asks the user whether it is his birthday and prints a birthday message if it is.

```
100 PRINT "IS TODAY YOUR BIRTHDAY?"
110 INPUT ANSW$
120 IF ANSW$="YES" THEN PRINT "HAPPY BIRTHDAY!"*
```

The condition, in this case, is ANSW$="YES". If the condition is true (if ANSW$="YES"), the statement (PRINT "HAPPY BIRTHDAY!") is executed. Note that the equal sign in the condition tests for equality between the value of ANSW$ and the literal YES; it does not constitute an assignment statement. (Performing such a test does not affect the value of the variable being tested. Thus, ANSW$ will have the same value before and after the test.)

What if we want the program to execute more than one statement if the condition is true? Microsoft BASIC allows us to specify more than one statement to be executed by stringing the statements together with colons (:) all on one line. The colon tells BASIC that these are separate statements to be executed together only if the condition is true. For example, if we want to ask the user his age only if it is his birthday, we can do the following:

```
100 PRINT "IS TODAY YOUR BIRTHDAY?"
110 INPUT ANSW$
120 IF ANSW$="YES" THEN PRINT "HAPPY BIRTHDAY!":PRINT "HOW
    OLD ARE YOU NOW?":INPUT AGE:PRINT "WOW!"
```

Let's modify this program so that it will print a consolation message if it is not the user's birthday. We can do this with two IF statements, one executed when ANSW$="YES" and the other when ANSW$="NO":

```
100 PRINT "IS TODAY YOUR BIRTHDAY?"
110 INPUT ANSW$
120 IF ANSW$="YES" THEN PRINT "HAPPY BIRTHDAY!":PRINT "HOW
    OLD ARE YOU NOW?":INPUT AGE:PRINT "WOW!"
130 IF ANSW$="NO" THEN PRINT "HAPPY UNBIRTHDAY!"
```

Another way to solve this problem is to use the ELSE construct:

```
100 PRINT "IS TODAY YOUR BIRTHDAY?"
110 INPUT ANSW$
```

(continued)

---

*When a new BASIC concept is introduced, it is highlighted in boldface within a program listing.

```
120 IF ANSW$ = "YES" THEN PRINT "HAPPY BIRTHDAY!":PRINT "HOW
    OLD ARE YOU NOW?":INPUT AGE:PRINT "WOW!"
    ELSE PRINT "HAPPY UNBIRTHDAY!"
```

The ELSE construct signifies a course of action to be taken when the condition is false. The difference between these last two program fragments is that the first will wish the user a happy unbirthday only if the user answers "NO", but the second will wish the user a happy unbirthday if the user answers anything but "YES". Thus if the user typed in "MAYBE" or "Y" or "I DON'T KNOW" or anything except "YES", the second program fragment will print "HAPPY UNBIRTHDAY"; the first program fragment will not print anything.

The only restriction on the Microsoft BASIC IF statement is that an entire statement cannot be more than 255 characters long. Sometimes 255 characters is sufficient; other times it is not. For example, think back to our temperature conversion program. We decided to use an IF-THEN statement to direct the computer to convert a Celsius temperature to Fahrenheit as well as a Fahrenheit temperature to Celsius. Unfortunately, the code required to do this takes far more than 255 characters. However, we can simulate a lengthy IF-THEN statement by using GOTO statements. The GOTO instruction directs the computer to move to a specific line and to start executing statements there. Used with the IF-THEN statement, the GOTO statement directs the program to one place if the condition is true and another if the condition is false. The following is a complete version of the temperature program incorporating the IF-THEN construct and GOTO statements. Notice that here we use the apostrophe (') to stand for REM.

```
10 'THIS PROGRAM ALLOWS THE USER TO REQUEST EITHER A
20 'FAHRENHEIT-TO-CELSIUS CONVERSION OR A CELSIUS-
30 'TO-FAHRENHEIT CONVERSION
40 '
50 PRINT "WOULD YOU LIKE A FAHRENHEIT-TO-CELSIUS"
60 PRINT "CONVERSION OR A CELSIUS-TO-FAHRENHEIT"
70 PRINT "CONVERSION?"
80 PRINT "TYPE 'FC' FOR F-TO-C OR 'CF' FOR C-TO-F"
90 INPUT CHOICE$
95 '
100 IF CHOICE$ = "FC" THEN GOTO 200          'F-TO-C
110 '
120 'OTHERWISE WE ASSUME CELSIUS TO FAHRENHEIT
125 '
130 PRINT "ENTER THE CELSIUS TEMPERATURE"
140 INPUT CEL.TEMP
150 FAHR.TEMP = (CEL.TEMP * 9)/5 + 32
```

(continued)

```
160 PRINT "THE FAHRENHEIT EQUIVALENT OF ";CEL.TEMP;
170 PRINT "IS ";FAHR.TEMP
180 GOTO 290 'END OF PROGRAM
190 '
200 'FAHRENHEIT TO CELSIUS
210 '
220 PRINT "ENTER THE FAHRENHEIT TEMPERATURE"
230 INPUT FAHR.TEMP
240 CEL.TEMP = ((FAHR.TEMP — 32) * 5)/9
250 PRINT "THE CELSIUS EQUIVALENT OF ";FAHR.TEMP;
260 PRINT "IS ";CEL.TEMP
280 '
290 END
```

This program executes statements in order until it encounters line 100. At line 100, it tests to see if CHOICE$ is equal to FC. If it is, the program jumps to line 200 and then executes lines 200–290 in order. These lines contain instructions to convert a Fahrenheit temperature to Celsius. If the condition is false (if CHOICE$ does not equal FC), the program assumes that a Celsius-to-Fahrenheit conversion is required and continues to execute instructions in numerical order until it reaches line 180. Line 180 contains a GOTO instruction that causes the computer to jump to line 290, the end of the program.

GOTO statements break up the sequential execution of program statements by redirecting the *flow of control*—the order in which the program statements are executed. In our earlier programs, statements were executed strictly in numeric order. Here they are executed in numeric order unless otherwise specified. Thus, after the command to GOTO line 200, line 220 is executed, then line 230, and so on until another GOTO is encountered or the program is ended. Liberal use of GOTO statements may cause confusion, since they tend to disrupt an otherwise orderly flow.

When BASIC was first implemented, most programming languages used GOTO statements; and it was not uncommon to find programs that were incomprehensible because they used so many such statements. We call programs of this sort examples of "spaghetti programming" because it is difficult to trace any one strand of the program from beginning to end. Computer scientists recognized this problem and created modern computer languages that reduce or eliminate the need for large numbers of GOTO statements. This helps people to program in a structured way. Many new languages, such as Pascal, make structured programming easy.

In many versions of BASIC, IF statements can also be *nested*; that is, one IF statement can be located within another. In the following program, note that one IF-ELSE construct is located totally within the body of another.* This is perfectly legitimate. The computer will match each ELSE statement with the most recent IF statement that does not already have an ELSE associated with it.

```
10 'THIS PROGRAM BLINDLY DECIDES WHETHER IT CAN SNOW
20 'BASED ON THE CURRENT TEMPERATURE AND HUMIDITY
30 '
40 PRINT "WHAT IS THE CURRENT TEMPERATURE IN FAHRENHEIT?"
50 INPUT TEMP
60 IF TEMP<32 THEN
      PRINT "WHAT IS THE PERCENTAGE OF HUMIDITY IN THE AIR?":
      INPUT HUMID:
      IF HUMID>90 THEN
       PRINT "IT WILL PROBABLY SNOW"
      ELSE PRINT "IT IS NOT HUMID ENOUGH FOR SNOW"
     ELSE PRINT "IT IS TOO WARM TO SNOW"
80 END
```

This program assumes that it will snow if the temperature is below freezing and the humidity above 90 percent. The program first asks for the temperature; if the temperature is below freezing, it asks for the humidity. Based on the humidity, the program decides whether it will snow. If the temperature is above freezing, the program informs the user that it is too warm to snow. Then the program ends. Here are a few sample runs:

```
RUN
WHAT IS THE CURRENT TEMPERATURE IN FAHRENHEIT?
?45
IT IS TOO WARM TO SNOW

RUN
WHAT IS THE CURRENT TEMPERATURE IN FAHRENHEIT?
?22
WHAT IS THE PERCENTAGE OF HUMIDITY IN THE AIR?
?95
IT WILL PROBABLY SNOW
```

(continued)

---

* For the nested IF statement to work in Microsoft BASIC, it must be typed in as one long line with one line number (in this case, 60). We have printed it on several lines with indentation to make it easier to read and have highlighted the IFs and ELSEs to make the nesting clear. However, the statement would be typed into the computer as follows:

60 IF TEMP <32 THEN PRINT "WHAT IS THE PERCENTAGE OF HUMIDITY IN THE AIR?":INPUT HUMID:IF HUMID>90 THEN PRINT "IT WILL PROBABLY SNOW" ELSE PRINT "IT IS NOT HUMID ENOUGH FOR SNOW" ELSE PRINT "IT IS TOO WARM TO SNOW"

```
RUN
WHAT IS THE CURRENT TEMPERATURE IN FAHRENHEIT?
?22
WHAT IS THE PERCENTAGE OF HUMIDITY IN THE AIR?
?55
IT IS NOT HUMID ENOUGH FOR SNOW
```

Loops

All of the programs in previous examples have one thing in common: they execute *once,* from top to bottom. Occasionally, this is acceptable—for example, if you wanted to convert only one temperature from Fahrenheit to Celsius or if you wanted to check only one combination of temperature and humidity to determine whether it will snow. However, if you want to convert 20 temperatures, you would have to run the program 20 times. Often, it is helpful for a program to perform the same action more than once automatically. This is accomplished by use of a *loop,* a programming construct that specifies that a block of statements is to be executed repeatedly.

Recall from Chapter 6 that there are two types of loops: definite loops and indefinite loops. A *definite loop* is executed a stated number of times, and an *indefinite loop* is executed until a certain condition is true.

WHILE Loops

In Microsoft BASIC, an indefinite loop is specified with the WHILE construct. A statement of the form WHILE <condition> indicates the beginning of the series of statements to be repeated, and a WEND (for WHILE-END) indicates the end. The following program uses the WHILE construct to allow the temperature conversion program to be repeated as many times as the user wants.

```
10 'THIS PROGRAM ALLOWS THE USER TO REQUEST ANY NUMBER OF
20 'FAHRENHEIT-TO-CELSIUS CONVERSIONS OR CELSIUS-
30 'TO-FAHRENHEIT CONVERSIONS
40 '
50 PRINT "WOULD YOU LIKE A FAHRENHEIT-TO-CELSIUS"
60 PRINT "CONVERSION OR A CELSIUS-TO-FAHRENHEIT"
70 PRINT "CONVERSION?"
80 PRINT "TYPE 'FC' FOR F-TO-C OR 'CF' for C-TO-F"
85 PRINT "OR 'Q' TO QUIT"
90 INPUT CHOICE$
```

(continued)

```
100 '
110 WHILE CHOICE$ < > "Q"
120   IF CHOICE$ ="FC" THEN GOTO 210
125 '
130                    'C to F
140   PRINT "ENTER THE CELSIUS TEMPERATURE"
150   INPUT CEL.TEMP
160   FAHR.TEMP = (CEL.TEMP * 9)/5 + 32
170   PRINT "THE FAHRENHEIT EQUIVALENT OF ";CEL.TEMP;
180   PRINT "IS ";FAHR.TEMP
190   GOTO 280    'ASK FOR ANOTHER TEMPERATURE
200 '
210                    'F TO C
220   PRINT "ENTER THE FAHRENHEIT TEMPERATURE"
230   INPUT FAHR.TEMP
240   CEL.TEMP = ((FAHR.TEMP - 32) * 5)/9
250   PRINT "THE CELSIUS EQUIVALENT OF ";FAHR.TEMP;
260   PRINT "IS ";CEL.TEMP
270   GOTO 280    'ASK FOR ANOTHER TEMP
280   PRINT "WHAT WOULD YOU LIKE TO DO NOW?"
290   INPUT CHOICE$
300 WEND
310 '
320 PRINT "GOODBYE. HOPE THE TEMPERATURE CONVERSION"
330 PRINT "WAS HELPFUL"
340 '
350 END
```

This program executes the body of statements between WHILE and WEND as long as the user continues to enter anything other than Q— until the condition CHOICE$ < > "Q" is false. Here the symbol < > means "not equal to." Consequently this condition means "while CHOICE$ is not equal to the string Q." The loop is executed until this condition is false, that is, until CHOICE$ *is* equal to Q.

Some versions of BASIC do not have explicit WHILE loops. In this case, the programmer simulates a WHILE loop by using GOTO and IF statements. This can be done in the following way.

```
10 'THIS PROGRAM ALLOWS THE USER TO REQUEST ANY NUMBER OF
20 'FAHRENHEIT-TO-CELSIUS CONVERSIONS OR CELSIUS-
30 'TO-FAHRENHEIT CONVERSIONS. IT USES GOTO STATEMENTS TO
35 'SIMULATE A WHILE LOOP
40 '
50 PRINT "WOULD YOU LIKE A FAHRENHEIT-TO-CELSIUS"
60 PRINT "CONVERSION OR A CELSIUS-TO-FAHRENHEIT"
```

(continued)

```
 70 PRINT "CONVERSION?"
 80 PRINT "TYPE 'FC' FOR F-TO-C, 'CF' FOR C-TO-F,"
 90 PRINT "OR 'Q' TO QUIT"
100 INPUT CHOICE$
110 '
120 IF CHOICE$ = "Q" THEN GOTO 350
    ELSE IF CHOICE$ ="CF" THEN GOTO 230
130 '
140                     'F TO C
150 '
160 PRINT "ENTER THE FAHRENHEIT TEMPERATURE"
170 INPUT FAHR.TEMP
180 CEL.TEMP = ((FAHR.TEMP — 32) * 5)/9
190 PRINT "THE CELSIUS EQUIVALENT OF ";FAHR.TEMP;
200 PRINT "IS ";CEL.TEMP
210 GOTO 310     'ASK FOR ANOTHER TEMPERATURE
220 '
230                     'C-TO-F
240 '
250 PRINT "ENTER THE CELSIUS TEMPERATURE"
260 INPUT CEL.TEMP
270 FAHR.TEMP = (CEL.TEMP * 9)/5 + 32
280 PRINT "THE FAHRENHEIT EQUIVALENT OF ";CEL.TEMP;
290 PRINT "IS ";FAHR.TEMP
300 GOTO 310     'ASK FOR ANOTHER TEMPERATURE
310 PRINT "WHAT WOULD YOU LIKE TO DO NOW?"
315 PRINT "ENTER 'FC' FOR F-TO-C, 'CF' FOR C-TO-F,"
316 PRINT "OR 'Q' TO QUIT"
320 INPUT CHOICE$
330 GOTO 120     'DO IT AGAIN
340 '
350 PRINT "GOODBYE. HOPE THE TEMPERATURE CONVERSION"
360 PRINT "WAS HELPFUL"
370 '
380 END
```

FOR Loops

Definite loops, unlike indefinite loops, are executed a predetermined number of times. For example, to print out a table of Celsius/ Fahrenheit equivalents for ten Celsius temperatures, we could use a loop made to execute ten times. A definite loop in BASIC is implemented with a FOR-NEXT construct. The following is a simple FOR-NEXT loop.

```
10 CEL.TEMP = 5
20 FOR COUNTER = 1 TO 10
30   FAHR.TEMP = (CEL.TEMP * 9)/5 + 32      'CONVERT TEMP
40   PRINT CEL.TEMP, FAHR.TEMP      'PRINT OUT INFORMATION
50   CEL.TEMP = CEL.TEMP + 5           'MAKE NEW CEL.TEMP
60 NEXT COUNTER
```

A FOR statement is used to initiate the loop and to specify the number of times the loop should cycle. It takes the form

```
FOR <variable> = <initial value> TO <final value>
```

The <variable> is a numeric variable that keeps track of how many times the loop is executed; such a variable is called a *loop counter*. Both <initial value> and <final value> are integers or variables that have integer values. The loop will be executed <final value> − <initial value> + 1 times. A statement of the form NEXT <variable> stops execution of the loop.

Our example uses a loop counter called COUNTER. The first time the loop is executed, COUNTER equals 1. Each subsequent time the loop is executed, the COUNTER is automatically increased by 1, until it has counted ten loops. Then execution of the loop is stopped.

Here is another example of a definite loop that is executed ten times. This loop uses the value of the loop counter for a calculation as well as for keeping track of the loop execution.

```
10 'THIS PROGRAM CONVERTS TEN CELSIUS TEMPERATURES
20 '(FROM 0 TO 9) TO THEIR
30 'FAHRENHEIT EQUIVALENTS AND PRINTS OUT BOTH THE
40 'FAHRENHEIT AND CELSIUS TEMPERATURES
50 '
60 PRINT "HERE IS A TABLE OF CELSIUS/FAHRENHEIT CONVERSIONS"
70 PRINT
80 'THE FOLLOWING STATEMENT PRINTS HEADERS FOR THE TABLE
90 PRINT "CELSIUS","FAHRENHEIT"
100 PRINT
110 '
120 FOR CEL.TEMP = 0 TO 9
130   FAHR.TEMP = (CEL.TEMP * 9)/5 + 32   'CONVERT TEMP
140   PRINT CEL.TEMP, FAHR.TEMP            'PRINT OUT TEMPS
150 NEXT CEL.TEMP
160 '
170 END
```

Lines 70 and 100 contain PRINT statements that specify nothing to print. They produce carriage returns, which print blank lines and make the program's output easier to read. The program produces the following output:

RUN

HERE IS A TABLE OF CELSIUS/FAHRENHEIT CONVERSIONS

CELSIUS	FAHRENHEIT
0	32.
1	33.8
2	35.6
3	37.4
4	39.2
5	41.
6	42.8
7	34.6
8	46.4
9	48.2

■ Arrays

When we know exactly how many values must be stored and when the number of values is small, variables are useful. For example, if you only have one name to store, you can keep track of it easily by using the variable NICKNAME$. Similarly, if you need to remember only two numbers, the variables NUMBER1 and NUMBER2 suffice. However, if we had to record a hundred names, we would not want to keep track of a hundred different variables. Similarly, writing a hundred different INPUT or PRINT statements to take in or print out the information in these variables would be tremendously time-consuming.

BASIC and many other computer languages provide a time-saving shortcut. They allow us to use *arrays*—sequences of variables accessed under a common name, with a specific number or *subscript* to refer to each individual element. If a variable can be thought of as a box in which the computer stores a value, then an array can be thought of as a row or column of boxes, each storing a value. Each box contains one array element (see Fig. 7.2).

Arrays, then, are used to store related information under a single name. To access the information stored in an array, we use the name of the array and the subscript that indicates which element of the array we want. For example, NUMBER$(2) is the second element of the array of strings called NUMBER$; 2 is the element's subscript. A feature that

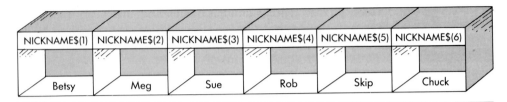

Figure 7.2
An array.

distinguishes array names with subscripts, such as NICKNAME$(1), from explicit variable names, such as NICKAME1$, is that array subscripts can be specified by variables as well as by specific numbers. For example, we could use NICKNAME$(COUNT) to access different array elements without specifying each by number.

Array names have the same format as variable names: they must start with a letter and may contain any number of numbers, letters, and underscores. All elements of an array must be of the same type (string or numeric), and arrays meant to store strings must have $ as the last character before the subscript. NICKNAME$(2), for example, is an element in the array NICKNAME$, an array of strings. NUMBER(2) is an element in the array NUMBER and is a number. If we tried to put nonnumeric characters into NUMBER(2), BASIC would print an error message and stop executing our program.

Creating an Array

In most versions of BASIC, we must explicitly tell the computer in advance what arrays, if any, will be used in a program. We do this with a DIMENSION statement placed near the beginning of the program. The DIMENSION statement (abbreviated DIM) is followed by the name of an array and, in parentheses, the largest subscript that will be used. The following example uses a small array.

```
10 'A SIMPLE ARRAY PROGRAM
20 '
30 'THE ARRAY IS DECLARED WITH A DIMENSION STATEMENT
40 '
50 DIM NICKNAME$(3)
60 NICKNAME$(1) = "JOHN"
70 NICKNAME$(2) = "FRED"
80 NICKNAME$(3) = "MARY"
90 '
100 'THE ARRAY IS PRINTED OUT WITH A LOOP
```

(continued)

```
110 '
120 FOR LOOP.COUNT = 1 TO 3
130   PRINT NICKNAME$(LOOP.COUNT)
140 NEXT LOOP.COUNT
150 '
160 END
```

Statement 50 defines the array and specifies that the largest subscript called for will be 3. Lines 60–80 assign values to the elements in the array. The values for NICKNAME$(1), NICKNAME$(2), and NICKNAME$(3) are printed with a FOR-NEXT loop (statements 120–140). If this program had tried to print out the element NICKNAME$(4), BASIC would have printed an error message and stopped the program because NICK-NAME$(4) was not created by the DIM statement and thus does not exist. (Some versions of BASIC allow us to use arrays of ten or fewer elements without first using the DIM statement.)

Common Uses of Arrays

Computer programmers often loop through arrays to find elements with certain values. This practice, called "searching an array," consists of comparing some specified value with the actual values of array elements. For example, if an array called STUDENT$ contains the names of a hundred students, the following program fragment can be used to find all students named John. Each time an element of the array STUDENT$ that is equal to JOHN is found, a message is printed.

```
90 'THIS IS A FRAGMENT OF CODE
95
110 FOR COUNT = 1 TO 100
120   IF STUDENT$(COUNT) = "JOHN" THEN
        PRINT "STUDENT NUMBER ";COUNT;"IS NAMED JOHN"
170 NEXT COUNT
```

Searching arrays becomes more useful when coupled with the concept of parallel arrays. *Parallel arrays* are two or more arrays set up so that elements with the same subscripts are related in some way. For example, you might have an array called FRIEND$ that contained the names of all your friends. An array called TELEPHONE$ could be set up to hold their telephone numbers. You would make the arrays parallel by ensuring that the telephone number in TELEPHONE$(1) belonged to the friend in FRIEND$(1). In other words, the telephone number of the person named in TELEPHONE$(COUNTER) must be the telephone number of the person named in FRIEND$(COUNTER) for each value of COUNTER, as shown in Fig. 7.3. To find the telephone number of a given friend (say Mark), you would simply search the array until you found

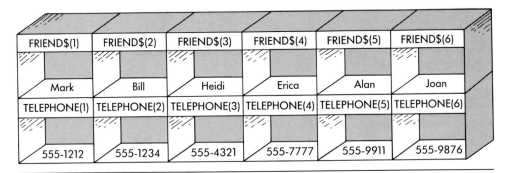

Figure 7.3
Parallel arrays.

the element that equaled MARK. When you knew the position of MARK in your FRIEND$ array, you would automatically know the position of his telephone number in the TELEPHONE$ array. The following segment of BASIC code would find Mark's telephone number by using two parallel arrays.

```
100 COUNTER = 1
105
110 WHILE FRIEND$(COUNTER) < > "MARK"
130   COUNTER = COUNTER + 1
140 WEND
145
150 PRINT "MARK'S TELEPHONE NUMBER IS ";
        TELEPHONE$(COUNTER)
```

Think about what this segment would do if MARK were not in the FRIEND$ array. What modifications would you propose to handle this situation?

Subroutines

A *subroutine* consists of a block of program statements that is logically distinct from the rest of the program. Subroutines save space and effort since they can be called on several times in a program; it takes only one line to call a subroutine, while it might take 20 lines to type it over. Using subroutines also helps make programs more comprehensible because it allows the programmer to outline the major actions of a program at the start and then specify them in detail in the subroutines.

Each time a subroutine is needed, the programmer places a GOSUB statement in the program. The GOSUB—for GOTO subroutine—statement takes the form GOSUB <line number>. The <line number> refers to the first line of the subroutine; it tells the computer where the subroutine is located. The computer jumps to the line number given in <line number> and executes the statements that follow. When it reaches a RETURN statement, it returns to the line after the GOSUB statement.

A GOSUB statement differs from a GOTO statement in that it is less disruptive to the flow of control. A GOSUB statement temporarily leaves the main program to execute the subroutine and then returns to the next line of the program. A GOTO statement, on the other hand, directs the computer elsewhere but does not restore an orderly flow of control.

The following program uses a subroutine to compute the user's age.

```
10 'THIS PROGRAM CALCULATES A PERSON'S AGE
20 'BASED ON YEAR OF BIRTH
30 '
40 PRINT "ENTER THE YEAR YOU WERE BORN"
50 INPUT YEAR.BORN
60 PRINT "ENTER THE CURRENT YEAR"
70 INPUT YEAR.CUR
80 GOSUB 130              'CALL SUBROUTINE TO COMPUTE AGE
90 PRINT "YOU ARE ";AGE;" YEARS OLD"
100 '
110 END
120 '
130 'AGE COMPUTATION SUBROUTINE
140   AGE = YEAR.CUR − YEAR.BORN
150 RETURN
```

The subroutine itself is located after the main body of the program. The END statement separates the two and prevents the computer from executing the subroutine except when it is called on. The subroutine is called in line 80 with the GOSUB statement, which specifies the line number with which the subroutine begins. The subroutine itself occupies lines 130–150. It ends with the RETURN statement, which signifies a return to the main program. Note that in this example the value of the variable AGE is only an approximation of the user's true age since the program fails to take into account whether or not the person's annual birthday has yet taken place.

When the program is executed, the computer follows the instructions line by line until it reaches line 80. The GOSUB statement there causes the program to jump to line 130. The computer then executes line 130 and all subsequent lines until it comes to the RETURN statement. It then jumps back to the line immediately following the GOSUB statement (line 90).

In this example, the use of the subroutine may not seem to be worth the trouble since the code contained in the subroutine is only one line long. However, when subroutines are several lines long, when programs consist of more than a page, or when the same block of code is used repeatedly, subroutines can be very useful. The following example uses a subroutine to save typing.

```
10 'THIS PROGRAM ASKS THE USER FOR THE HIGHEST
20 'AND LOWEST FAHRENHEIT TEMPERATURES OF THE DAY
30 'AND CONVERTS THEM TO CELSIUS. IT USES A
40 'SUBROUTINE TO CONVERT THE TEMPERATURE.
50 '
60 PRINT "HIGHEST TEMPERATURE OF THE DAY IN FAHRENHEIT?"
70 INPUT TEMPF
75 '
80 GOSUB 220                    'CONVERT FAHRENHEIT TO CELSIUS
90 HIGH.TEMPC = TEMPC
95 '
100 PRINT "LOWEST TEMPERATURE OF THE DAY IN FAHRENHEIT?"
110 INPUT TEMPF
115 '
120 GOSUB 220                   'CONVERT FAHRENHEIT TO CELSIUS
130 LOW.TEMPC = TEMPC
140 '
150 PRINT "THE HIGHEST TEMPERATURE OF THE DAY IN CELSIUS IS ";
160 PRINT HIGH.TEMPC
170 PRINT "THE LOWEST TEMPERATURE OF THE DAY IN CELSIUS IS ";
180 PRINT LOW.TEMPC
190
200 END
210
220 'SUBROUTINE TO CONVERT FAHRENHEIT TO CELSIUS
230   TEMPC = ((TEMPF − 32) * 5)/9
240 RETURN
```

Debugging

Often a program will not do what the programmer intended; such a program is said to contain bugs. *Bugs* are minor errors, and *debugging* is finding and correcting those errors. Few programs work perfectly at first, and as programs get larger they are increasingly likely to contain bugs.

Debugging, then, is as much a part of programming as problem analysis, program design, and code writing. Fortunately, debugging is a skill that is improved through practice; the more you do, the better you get. To help you practice, we have outlined some typical problems and solutions as well as common problem-locating techniques.

Typographical Errors and Similar Mistakes

Even if you are an excellent typist, check the typed-in version of your program against the handwritten version. (A word-for-word, line-for-line comparison carried out before you run the program is recommended.) In particular, check for skipped lines, improper syntax, and inconsistent variable names (WORD does not mean the same as WORD$; RESPONSE$ is not the same as REPONSE$). Make sure that all your FORs have NEXTs and all your WHILEs have WENDs. Make sure, too, that the programming constructs you use are syntactically correct (ELSE IF, for example, does not equal ELSEIF).

Keywords sometimes cause problems. A *keyword* is any word with a specific meaning in the programming language you are using (such as PRINT, END, IF, FOR, NEXT, WHILE, WEND in BASIC). Make sure not to use keywords as names for any of your variables. If you do find yourself with an unidentifiable bug or an error message you do not understand, scan a list of keywords to make sure that you have not accidentally used a keyword as a variable name. Some versions of BASIC do not allow the use of keywords even as prefixes for variables; in such versions, you should avoid variables with names like WHILECOUNT or FORCOUNTER.

Mistakes Related to Data Types

As you know, there are two kinds of data in BASIC: numbers and character strings. Numeric variables must be given names starting with a letter and consisting of alphabetic characters, numbers, and/or periods (examples include COUNTER, COUNTER1, COUNT.IT, LOOP.COUNT, and VALUE). Character string variable names follow the same conventions except that the last character in the name must be $ (examples are WORD$, SENTENCE$, REPLY$, FIRST.NAME$). Once you have named a variable, you can use it to manipulate only one kind of data. Watch for mistakes related to this rule.

Infinite Loops

Every loop must have an explicit exit condition or it will be executed indefinitely. WHILE loops in particular are subject to this problem; if the condition specified in the WHILE clause is never false, the loop will never stop cycling. Infinite loops are easy to recognize. If there is a PRINT statement within the loop, it will be executed over and over again; if there are no PRINT statements in the loop, the program will run silently until you step in.

Off-by-One Errors

Often loops contain loop counters to help determine how many times the instructions within the loop should be executed. Such counters are usually increased or decreased within the body of the loop. The initial value of the loop counter, the place where it is changed within the loop, and the placement of the exit condition all affect how often the statements within the loop will be executed. It is easy for the programmer to make a mistake in the placement of these statements. A mistake may cause the counter to be off by one on each execution of the loop; this, in turn, causes the loop to be executed one too few or one too many times.

Hand Simulation

Although the term sounds odd when you first hear it, *hand simulation* is a valuable technique for debugging. To hand-simulate your program, you work through it pretending to be the computer; to do that, you must act unintelligently. The computer knows only what you have told it. Since you have written the program, you are handicapped by the knowledge of what you intended to do. To simulate the actions of the computer by hand, you must try to forget your intentions and concentrate on what you have actually written in your program. Like the computer, you will need to know the values of variables and to change those values as your program would change them.

When an error cannot be found by other means, we recommend that you use the following hand-simulation technique. On a piece of paper, write down the names of all the variables used in your program. Now, start at the top of the program and execute each of the instructions in turn. When you come to an instruction that changes the value of a variable, write the new value under the variable's name on the paper; if the variable had an old value, cross it out. When you come to a statement that causes something to be printed out, write the result on a separate section of your paper. Although this is not an exciting process, you must proceed line by line and not jump ahead because you think you know what is going to happen next. The computer doesn't know what is going to happen next and you'll have to pretend to be as uninformed as it is. For hand-simulating loops and other such functions, follow the flow-of-control descriptions outlined in previous sections.

■ An Extended Example of Programming

Thus far, we've used simple programs to illustrate the concepts we've introduced. Now we'd like to show how a program can be written to solve a specific problem. Our approach combines the structured problem-solving techniques introduced in Chapter 6 with the programming concepts introduced in this chapter. The problem is as follows.

Imagine that you are the owner of a small variety store. For years, you've kept track of the current stock on the shelves by hiring a neighborhood girl to come in and replenish the items on the shelves twice a week. She would tell you when supplies got low, and you would order more. But the neighborhood has changed, and there are no longer teenagers available to hire. You've seen how large stores keep their shelves stocked by installing fancy computer systems that monitor inventory and speed up checkouts. Unfortunately, you cannot afford such a system for your small variety store. You do own a home computer, though, and think it might be possible to use it to deal with your problem. Armed with knowledge gained by reading Chapters 6 and 7, you decide to try writing a program.

The first step, of course, is to clarify what you want the program to do. After thinking about it, you decide that what you need is a way to keep track of the quantity of each item currently on the shelf. You would also like the computer to help you with checkout by subtracting the total from the customer's payment to help you make change and by printing a receipt. The best way to do this, you believe, is to store the current quantity of each item in the computer and then subtract items as they are bought, just as the supermarkets do when their laser scanners read the UPC (universal product code) number beneath the zebra stripe on prepackaged items. You realize that you can use the UPC numbers even without a scanner. Because each product has a unique code number, you can identify each item in the computer simply by typing in the UPC. The computer can then be used both to total bills and to keep track of your inventory.

You know that you need some way to keep track of all this information. Separate variables are not practical for such a task, but parallel arrays would be perfect. You need five arrays, and you name them as follows: the UPC array, which contains the UPC of each item; the ITEM.DESCR$ array, which contains a brief description of each item; the PRICE array, which contains the price of each item; the ON.SHELF array, which lists the number of each item currently on the shelves; and the STORAGE array, which lists the number of each item in storage. Since the contents of each array will have to be stored somewhere when the program isn't being used, you set up a separate computer file that, in part, looks like this:

	UPC	DESCR$	PRICE	ON.SHELF	STORAGE
1	10048	SNICKERS	.35	10	100
2	10001	TISSUES	.79	7	23

Now that you have a way to store the information, you return to the problem. You decide to break it down into three subproblems: updating the number of items on the shelves and/or in storage, updating prices, and checking out a customer's purchases. Your pseudocode looks like this:

```
Ask for choice of procedure
Execute desired procedure
```

You make another pass and subdivide the problem as follows:

```
Ask for choice of procedure
If choice = "inventory update" then
    Execute inventory update
Else if choice = "price change" then
    Execute price change procedure
Else
    Execute checkout procedure
```

Your problem has been divided into subproblems, each corresponding to a subroutine. Now all you have to do is write the three subroutines. First, however, you write pseudocode for each of them, as follows.

INVENTORY

```
Ask for UPC
Find UPC in array
Ask if user wants to record new shipment or restock shelves
If new shipment
    Update items in storage
Else if restock shelves
    Update items in storage
    Update items on shelf
```

(continued)

PRICE CHANGE

Ask for UPC
Find UPC
Ask for new price
Change price in array

CHECKOUT

While there are items to be checked out
   Ask for UPC
   Find UPC in array
   Add price to total
   Update number of items on shelf
Total bill
Make change

You may notice that each of these subroutines requires that you locate the subscript of the particular UPC you need in the UPC array so that you can access information pertaining to it. Since this operation requires several steps, it would make sense to write another subroutine to carry it out. You realize that each UPC will occur once and only once in the array. Your pseudocode might look like this:

FIND UPC

For each element in the array
   If the array element = desired UPC
      Store location of the array element

Since the problem has now been broken down into manageable pieces, writing the actual code should not be a problem. Remember that the arrays are stored in another file. One version of the variety store program might look like this:

```
10 'THIS PROGRAM KEEPS TRACK OF INVENTORY OF A SMALL
20 'VARIETY STORE AND HELPS WITH THE CHECKOUT PROCESS.
30 'IT HAS THREE MAIN SUBROUTINES—ONE TO UPDATE INVENTORY,
40 'ONE TO UPDATE PRICES, AND ONE TO CHECK OUT A CUSTOMER.
50 'THE PROGRAM ASKS WHICH PROCESS THE STOREKEEPER WOULD
60 'LIKE TO USE AND EXECUTES THE CORRESPONDING SUBROUTINE.
70 'A SURROUNDING LOOP ALLOWS THE STOREKEEPER TO USE MORE
80 'THAN ONE SUBROUTINE AT A TIME. THE LETTER 'Q' IS USED
90 'TO EXIT THE PROGRAM
95 '
100 PRINT "TYPE 'I' TO UPDATE INVENTORY, 'P' TO UPDATE A PRICE,"
```

(continued)

```
110 PRINT "'C' TO CHECK OUT A CUSTOMER, AND 'Q' TO QUIT."
120 INPUT CHOICE$
125 '
130 WHILE CHOICE$ < > "Q"
140   IF CHOICE$ = "I" THEN GOSUB 230   'INVENTORY SUBROUTINE
150   IF CHOICE$ = "P" THEN GOSUB 530        'PRICE PROCEDURE
160   IF CHOICE$ = "C" THEN GOSUB 660   'CHECKOUT PROCEDURE
170   PRINT "TYPE 'I' TO UPDATE INVENTORY, 'P' TO UPDATE A"
180   PRINT "PRICE, 'C' TO CHECKOUT A CUSTOMER, AND 'Q'"
190   PRINT "TO QUIT THE PROGRAM"
200   INPUT CHOICE$
210 WEND
215 '
220 END   'END OF MAIN PROGRAM
225 '
230 'INVENTORY SUBROUTINE
235 '
240 'THIS SUBROUTINE ALLOWS THE STOREKEEPER TO UPDATE STORE
250 'INVENTORY. EITHER A NEW SHIPMENT MAY ARRIVE
260 'OR THE SHELVES MAY BE RESTOCKED. IN EITHER CASE, THE UPC
270 'NUMBER IS REQUESTED, ITS LOCATION IN THE ARRAY IS FOUND
280 'AND THE APPROPRIATE NUMBERS ARE UPDATED
285 '
290 PRINT "ENTER THE UPC OF YOUR PRODUCT"
300 INPUT CUR.UPC
305 '
310 GOSUB 920   'FIND UPC IN ARRAY
315 '
320 PRINT "THERE ARE ";ON.SHELF(ELEMENT);"ON THE SHELF AND "
330 PRINT STORAGE(ELEMENT);" IN STORAGE."
340 PRINT "DO YOU WANT TO RECORD A NEW SHIPMENT ('N') OR"
350 PRINT "RESTOCK THE SHELVES ('R')?"
360 INPUT INV.CHOICE$
365 '
370 IF INV.CHOICE$ = "R" THEN GOTO 450
375 '
380 'CHOICE ASSUMED TO BE N
390 PRINT "HOW MANY NEW ITEMS HAVE ARRIVED?"
400 INPUT NEW.NUM
410 STORAGE(ELEMENT) = STORAGE(ELEMENT) + NEW.NUM
420 PRINT "THERE ARE ";ON.SHELF(ELEMENT);"ON THE SHELF AND "
430 PRINT STORAGE(ELEMENT);" IN STORAGE."
440 GOTO 520
```

(continued)

```
445 '
450 'CHOICE = R
460 PRINT "HOW MANY ITEMS SHALL WE ADD TO THE SHELF?"
470 INPUT TRANSFER
480 ON.SHELF(ELEMENT) = ON.SHELF(ELEMENT) + TRANSFER
490 STORAGE(ELEMENT) = STORAGE(ELEMENT) − TRANSFER
500 PRINT "THERE ARE ";ON.SHELF(ELEMENT);"ON THE SHELF AND "
510 PRINT STORAGE(ELEMENT);" IN STORAGE."
515 '
520 RETURN 'END OF SUBROUTINE
525 '
530 'PRICE SUBROUTINE
535 '
540 'THIS SUBROUTINE IS USED TO UPDATE THE PRICE OF ANY
550 'ITEM. IT ASKS FOR THE UPC, FINDS ITS LOCATION,
560 'ASKS FOR THE NEW PRICE, AND REPLACES THE OLD
570 'PRICE WITH THE NEW PRICE
575 '
580 PRINT "TYPE THE UPC OF YOUR PRODUCT"
590 INPUT CUR.UPC
595 '
600 GOSUB 920      'FIND UPC IN ARRAY
615 '
610 PRINT "THE OLD PRICE IS ";PRICE(ELEMENT)
620 PRINT "WHAT IS THE NEW PRICE?"
630 INPUT NEW.PRICE
635 '
640 PRICE(ELEMENT) = NEW.PRICE
645 '
650 RETURN   'END OF SUBROUTINE
655 '
660 'CHECKOUT SUBROUTINE
665 '
670 'THIS SUBROUTINE IS USED TO CHECK OUT A CUSTOMER. FOR
680 'EACH ITEM TO BE CHECKED OUT, THE SUBROUTINE ASKS FOR
690 'THE UPC OF THE ITEM, LOCATES THE ITEM, SUBTRACTS 1
700 'FROM THE NUMBER ON THE SHELF, ADDS THE PRICE TO
710 'THE RUNNING TOTAL, AND PRINTS THE INFORMATION ON A
720 'SALES RECEIPT. AFTER THE ITEMS HAVE BEEN TOTALED, IT ASKS
730 'FOR MONEY AND TELLS THE CASHIER HOW MUCH
740 'CHANGE IS NEEDED
745 '
750 TOTAL = 0     'SET TOTAL TO 0
```

(continued)

```
760 PRINT "TYPE UPC OF ITEM. TYPE 0 TO EXIT."
770 INPUT CUR.UPC
775 '
780 WHILE CUR.UPC < > 0
790    GOSUB 920                          'FIND UPC IN ARRAY
800    TOTAL = TOTAL + PRICE(ELEMENT)
810    ON.SHELF(ELEMENT) = ON.SHELF(ELEMENT) − 1
820    PRINT DESCR$(ELEMENT),PRICE(ELEMENT)
830    PRINT "NEXT UPC?"
840    INPUT CUR.UPC
850 WEND
855 '
860 PRINT "THE TOTAL IS ",TOTAL
870 PRINT "HOW MUCH MONEY DOES THE CUSTOMER HAVE?"
880 INPUT MONEY
885 '
890 CHANGE = MONEY − TOTAL
900 PRINT "THE CHANGE IS ",CHANGE
905 '
910 RETURN                               'END OF SUBROUTINE
915 '
920 'FIND LOCATION OF UPC SUBROUTINE
925 '
930 'THIS SUBROUTINE FINDS THE LOCATION OF THE UPC
940 'IN THE ARRAY. IT ASSUMES THAT EACH UPC CODE
950 'APPEARS ONCE AND ONLY ONCE IN THE ARRAY
955 '
960 FOR COUNTER = 1 TO 400
970    IF UPC(COUNTER) = CUR.UPC THEN
           ELEMENT = COUNTER            'MATCHING UPC FOUND
980 NEXT COUNTER
985 '
990 RETURN                               'END OF SUBROUTINE
```

A run of the program might look as follows, assuming that the arrays in the program have been given values. For example, the product SNICKERS might have been associated with the following values: UPC, 10048; items on shelf, 10; items in storage, 100; and price, $0.29 per unit.

```
RUN
TYPE 'I' TO UPDATE INVENTORY, 'P' TO UPDATE A PRICE,
'C' TO CHECK OUT A CUSTOMER, AND 'Q' TO QUIT.
?I
```

(continued)

```
ENTER THE UPC OF YOUR PRODUCT
?10048
THERE ARE 10 ON THE SHELF AND
100 IN STORAGE.
DO YOU WANT TO RECORD A NEW SHIPMENT ('N') OR
RESTOCK THE SHELVES ('R')?
?R
HOW MANY ITEMS SHALL WE ADD TO THE SHELF?
?90
THERE ARE 100 ON THE SHELF AND
10 IN STORAGE
TYPE 'I' TO UPDATE INVENTORY, 'P' TO UPDATE A
PRICE, 'C' TO CHECK OUT A CUSTOMER, 'Q' TO QUIT.
?P
TYPE THE UPC OF YOUR PRODUCT.
?10048
THE OLD PRICE IS 0.29
WHAT IS THE NEW PRICE?
?0.31
TYPE 'I' TO UPDATE INVENTORY, 'P' TO UPDATE A
PRICE, 'C' TO CHECK OUT A CUSTOMER, 'Q' TO QUIT.
?C
TYPE UPC OF ITEM. TYPE 0 TO EXIT.
?10048
SNICKERS   .31
NEXT UPC?
?10001
TISSUES    .79
NEXT UPC?
?0
THE TOTAL IS 1.10
HOW MUCH MONEY DOES THE CUSTOMER HAVE?
?3.00
THE CHANGE IS 1.90
TYPE 'I' TO UPDATE INVENTORY, 'P' TO UPDATE A
PRICE, 'C' TO CHECK OUT A CUSTOMER, 'Q' TO QUIT.
?Q
```

This program carries out the fundamental operations required but contains few error-checking devices: it assumes that the human users will always type in the correct UPC or price change or number of items. But what if the UPC typed in is not in the array? What if you want to look at the contents of one entry in the array? To make the program more user-friendly, you might want to write code to handle some of these special cases.

SUMMARY

BASIC is a programming language designed for use by beginning programmers. Since BASIC provides a limited number of commands, it is a language that is easily learned.

Simple BASIC programs can be built with nothing more than a few PRINT statements. Variables are used in more sophisticated programs as places to store values. BASIC recognizes two types of variables: those to store numbers and those to store strings. Variables receive values either from assignment statements or from input statements.

Programmers can write fairly sophisticated BASIC programs using conditional statements, loops, subroutines, and arrays. The conditional IF statement evaluates a condition to determine whether to execute a following statement or not. Some versions of BASIC allow an extension of IF, the IF-ELSE statement, that allows the program to select between one of two statements to execute. All versions of BASIC provide definite loops (FOR loops) and some also provide indefinite loops (WHILE loops). The first executes for a definite number of times, and the second executes until some condition is satisfied.

Subroutines are blocks of statements to which a program can branch and then return. Subroutines allow programmers to outline programs. They can simplify design and save time in typing since blocks of code used in more than one place in a program can be put in a subroutine and do not have to be retyped each time they are used.

Arrays permit programmers to store related information together under a common name. Individual elements in arrays are accessed with the array name and a subscript. Related elements can be kept in corresponding or parallel arrays under the same subscript. This facilitates retrieval of related information.

FURTHER READING

Margot Critchfield and Thomas A. Dwyer, *Microsoft BASIC: Programming Pocket Guide* (Reading, Mass.: Addison-Wesley, 1983).

Neil Graham, *Programming the IBM Personal Computer: BASIC* (New York: Holt, Rinehart and Winston, 1982).

ISSUES AND IDEAS

1. For each of the following pieces of data, tell what type of variable could contain it.

   Babbage   98765   9.8765   antidisestablishmentarianism   −98765

2. Carry out the following operations in the proper order.
   a) $6 + 5 \times 4 \times 3 - 2 \times 1$
   b) $(6 + 5) \times 4 \times (3 - 2) \times 1$
   c) $(6 + (5 \times 4)) \times (3 - 2) \times 1$
   d) $(6 + 5) \times (4 \times 3) - (2 \times 1)$

3. Write a simple program that carries on a conversation with the user by asking questions and then commenting on the user's responses. For example, the program might ask for the user's favorite food. If the user replied "strawberries," the program might respond, "I don't like strawberries. My favorite food is jello."

4. Write a program that takes in any number of numeric grades and prints out their average.

5. Write a program to balance a checkbook. The program should ask for the user's initial balance and should update the balance as transactions are made. It should be able to handle any number of deposits and checks. It should update the balance after each transaction and should charge $0.25 for each check processed. When the user is finished, the program should print out the final balance and the number of checks written.

6. Hand-simulate the BASIC code on page 164 using the following arrays. Execute the program statements one at a time, keeping track of the current value of each of the variables. If there is any output, print it out.

	FRIEND$	TELEPHONE$
1	STEVE	321–5432
2	HEIDI	987–6543
3	CAROL	789–1234
4	MARK	321–9876
5	CONNIE	543–9876

7. Modify the inventory program in the last section in this chapter so that it can deal with the following special cases.
   a) What if the UPC requested is not in the array? Modify the program to print out an error message and ask for another UPC.
   b) What if the user wants to view the contents of a single array entry? Write a subroutine to print out the entire contents of one entry in the array, including the UPC number, the product description, the price, the number of items on the shelf, and the number of items in storage.
   c) What if the user wants a listing of all the information about all the UPC codes? Write a subroutine to print out the entire array.
   d) What if the user tries to move more items from storage than are

actually there? The current program will allow the user to do this and will register a negative number of items in storage. Modify the program to prevent this situation from occurring.

e) What if the customer doesn't give the cashier enough money? Modify the checkout subroutine to print a warning message if the customer gives the cashier less money than necessary.

8. Write a program to act as an on-line thesaurus. The program should use two parallel arrays, one containing a set of words and a second containing their synonyms. The program should look up any number of words for the user by asking for a word and then printing out all synonyms of that word that appear in the array. If that word is not in the array, a message should be printed to inform the user. Any word may be in both arrays.

Programming Concepts in Pascal

Today, we're beginning to realize that the new media aren't just mechanical gimmicks for creating worlds of illusion, but new languages with new and unique powers of expression.

MARSHALL MCLUHAN, *McLuhan: Hot and Cool*

Introduction

Since a large amount of software is available for most computers, people can make good use of computers without acquiring expertise in programming. However, understanding the process involved in programming helps to demystify computers and also helps to provide an awareness of what computers can and cannot do.

In this chapter we introduce many important programming concepts using the programming language Pascal. Pascal is a procedure-oriented language, which means that it encourages the programmer to break programs into subprograms using the structured design methods discussed in Chapter 6.

Pascal was developed in Switzerland in the late 1960s by Niklaus Wirth. Wirth's goal was to develop a language that could be used to teach programming in a disciplined way. He wanted to produce a language that reflected the rules and methods of good structured design.

Although Pascal takes slightly longer to learn than BASIC, it is a much more powerful language. Furthermore, people who have learned to program in Pascal seldom have trouble learning other procedure-oriented programming languages. Pascal is also available on many personal computers. For these reasons, Pascal is taught in many introductory programming courses.

Pascal can operate as either an interactive or a batch processing language. Batch processing, you recall, requires that the program and all the data needed to run it be submitted to the computer before the program is executed. When the program is run, the computer generates a listing of the program and its output for the user to examine later. An interactive language, on the other hand, allows the user to interact with the program while it is being run—to submit data when required and to view the output as it is printed out. For our purposes, it doesn't matter whether Pascal is used interactively or as a batch processing language. To simplify the presentation, however, we explain all our examples assuming an interactive environment. Keep in mind that using Pascal as a batch processing language does not alter the concepts we present in this chapter, just the way in which they are used.

Because there are many versions of Pascal that differ slightly in syntax, we will concentrate on the major concepts in the language and ignore minor syntactic differences. However, the programs in this chapter have all been verified to run with versions of Pascal that are available on many personal computers. The interested reader may employ these concepts with any of the slightly different versions of Pascal. We provide the name of a reference book at the end of the chapter for readers who wish to study Pascal in more depth.

■ What Is a Program?

A *program* is a series of instructions that tells a computer what to do. When a program is *run*, these instructions are carried out by the computer, one at a time. Here is an example of a simple Pascal program:†

```
(*    --------------------------------------------------------------------    *)
(*                                                                             *)
(*    This program prints out two sentences.                                  *)
(*                                                                             *)
(*    --------------------------------------------------------------------    *)

program Simple(input, output);
```

(continued)

---

† The uses of capitalization and boldface type in the programming examples are our conventions and are not required by Pascal. We find that they make the programs easier to read.

```
begin
     writeln('This is a very simple program');
     writeln('All it does is print out two sentences')
end.    (* Simple program *)
```

At the beginning of this example is a brief description of the program, enclosed in a box consisting of parentheses and asterisks. This description is a *comment,* intended for human eyes only. Well-written comments make a program much easier to understand. The parentheses and asterisks at the beginning and end of each line indicate to the computer that these lines are not for its use, so it skips over them. This particular comment is called a *block comment* because it is essentially a block of several lines of comment statements (in this case, five comment statements); it is a *header comment* as well because it heads the program. Block comments may also appear within the body of the program. Each line of comment must begin with the symbols (* and end with the symbols *).

The program itself begins with the program statement, which names the program and specifies whether it will take input and whether it will produce output. This program is called Simple, and it takes input and output. The next line, the begin statement, marks the beginning of the executable section of the program—that is, the instructions that cause the computer to execute commands. The writeln instruction is used to print out information. The two writeln statements shown here print out two sentences, the strings of characters enclosed by apostrophes and parentheses. Finally the end statement terminates the program. Note the period immediately following the word end. It must be used to end the program.

A short comment appears on the last line of the program following the end statement. It is called an *in-line comment* because it appears in the same line as a Pascal command. Notice that it is enclosed by parentheses and asterisks, Pascal's punctuation for a comment. This comment tells us that the end statement on that line refers to the end of the program Simple. End statements are also used to end sections of programs; this one refers to the end of the entire program. You may have observed that some of the statements in this program are indented and that a blank line is left before the beginning of the executable section of the program. Indentation and spacing are conventions that make programs easier to read and understand.

You may also have noticed that some of the lines of the program end with semicolons. This is a Pascal convention: each instruction to be executed by Pascal must be separated from other statements with a semicolon (;). This punctuation tells the *compiler* (the program that translates Pascal to machine language) where one instruction ends and another begins. Semicolons do not follow begin statements and do not follow statements that precede end statements. In this program, for example, the last writeln does not end with a semicolon because it is followed by an end statement. No semicolon is necessary here because the end statement also marks the end of an instruction.† As noted above, the last statement in a Pascal program, the end statement, must end with a period. Thus, a Pascal program is punctuated like a sentence, with semicolons separating distinct phrases and a period at the end.

A run of the program would look like this:

```
This is a very simple program
All it does is print out two sentences
```

■ Variables

Our simple computer program is not terribly useful because it prints out the same two sentences every time it is run. It does not operate on information, but simply prints a message. Before we can write a program to operate on information, however, we must have some place to put the information and some means to identify it. In computer programming, variables serve these purposes.

A *variable* is a storage place for information. Unique *variable names* are used to distinguish one variable from another. We can picture a variable as a post office box. Each variable (like each post office box) has its own unique address to tell the computer where it is located. Electronic addresses can be difficult for us to remember (since the computer represents them as strings of 1s and 0s), so high-level languages such as Pascal allow us to refer to variables by name rather than address. The computer keeps track of where each variable is stored.

Variable names in Pascal may contain any combination of letters, numbers, and underscores‡ but must begin with a letter. (For example, name, name3, and name_of_person are all valid variable names.) Although it is possible to give variables one-letter names (such as x, y, or z), it is more helpful to use *mnemonic* names—names that correspond to the purpose or function of the variable. Without mnemonic names, it is often difficult for people to understand what a program is supposed to do. This chapter uses only mnemonic variable names.

Pascal identifies three basic types of variables, which correspond to three major data types: strings, integers, and real numbers. A *string* is

---

† Pascal will accept a semicolon preceding an end statement without printing an error message. Using semicolons before end statements, however, is not considered good programming style.

‡ Not all versions of Pascal permit underscores to be used in variable names.

a sequence of letters, numbers, blank spaces, punctuation marks, and/or special symbols. In Pascal a string is enclosed in single quotation marks (these marks are not part of the string). Examples of strings are 'string', 'this is a string', 'so is this!!', and '!@$%( )*&!!'. A string's length is equal to the number of characters it contains. The lengths of the strings above are, respectively, 6, 16, 12, and 10.

In many versions of Pascal, the maximum length of a string variable must be specified before the variable is used so that the computer will know how much space is needed to store the contents of the variable. Thus, a string variable that will begin by holding one character, expand to five, and then contract to three typically must be declared as a string with a maximum length of five. If a string variable is made to hold more characters than its maximum length, Pascal will issue error messages. Some versions of Pascal do not explicitly allow string variables but instead use separate characters joined together in what is known as a packed array. (We will consider examples of arrays later.) Other versions permit users to specify a string without stating its length.

Integer variables hold integers—positive and negative whole numbers such as 1, −3, 545, −2001, 0, and 11. *Real-number variables,* unlike integers, may contain decimal points and decimal fractions; 2.6, −1.3, 0.998, 4.000001, and −0.5 are all examples of real numbers. When programming in Pascal, it is important to distinguish between real numbers and integers. Although the contents of a variable may change, the type of information it stores (string, real, or integer) may not. Pascal will allow users to store integer values in real variables (for example, it would store the integer 3 as 3 in an integer variable but as 3.0 in a real variable) but will not allow users to store real values in integer variables. When an integer and a real number (say 3 and 1.4) are added, the result (4.4) will be a real number; attempting to assign such a result to an integer variable will result in an error message.

Before variables may be used, they must be *declared,* or defined, in a var statement. The var statement specifies the data type of each variable (integer, real, or string) and allots a storage space to the variable. It is located at the beginning of a Pascal program, underneath the program statement. Below the var statement should appear a list of variables. Each variable is placed on a separate line and is followed by a colon, the type of the variable, and a semicolon. Here is an example of the declaration of several variables:

```
var
    number:          real;
    name:            string[5];
    counter:         integer;
    num_of_students: integer;
```

In this example, number is a real number, name is a string with a maximum length of five characters, and counter and num_of_students are integers.

■ Reading and Writing

One way the computer gets the information to store in variables is by asking the user to supply it. Pascal uses the readln statement for this purpose. The readln statement tells Pascal to request information from the person using the program, to read that information from the keyboard, and to store that information in the memory space allocated to a specified variable. For example, the statement readln(price) would obtain a value from the user and store it in the variable price.

A programming language should be able not only to read data from the user but to send data from the program back to the user. For this purpose, Pascal has a method analogous to the readln command known as the writeln command. The writeln statement, as we saw earlier, can be used to print out predetermined messages specified by the programmer. It can also be used to print out the contents of a variable. For these contents to be printed, the variable name must be enclosed in parentheses following the writeln command. For example, the statement writeln(price) will print out the value of the variable price on the user's screen. To print out a predetermined string (referred to as a *literal* because its literal value is printed out), we surround the literal with single quotation marks and enclose it within parentheses following the writeln statement. For example, the Pascal statement

writeln('Remember Blaise Pascal from Chapter 2?');

produces this message on the user's screen:

Remember Blaise Pascal from Chapter 2?

The difference between a literal and a variable is that the contents of the literal will be the same every time the program is run, whereas the contents of the variable may be requested from the user and may therefore vary from run to run. The programmer can combine literals and variables in a writeln statement by enclosing both within the parentheses and separating them with a comma, as follows:

writeln('The loop counter equals', loop_count);

If loop_count had the value 4, the preceding statement would print on the user's screen the following message:

The loop counter equals4

The comma that separates the two different elements in our writeln statement holds the printer "carriage" in place between items so that the second item is printed directly next to the first. To prevent the literal and the variable from running together as they do in our example, we add a blank space to the end of the literal as follows:

```
writeln('The loop counter equals ',loop_count);
```

As a result, the computer will print a blank before printing the contents of loop_count, producing the following output:

```
The loop counter equals 4
```

Here is a statement that prints out two variables and two literals.

```
writeln('loop counter = ',count,' area = ',space);
```

If the variable count had the value 6 and the variable space had the value 4.9, the following message would be printed:

```
loop counter = 6 area = 4.9
```

■ Two Simple Programs

Let's combine the concepts of reading, writing, and variables in a short program:

```
(*   ----------------------------------------------------------------   *)
(*                                                                       *)
(*   This program reads in a number and prints it out with a            *)
(*   message. It illustrates the basic structure of a Pascal program.   *)
(*                                                                       *)
(*   ----------------------------------------------------------------   *)
program Number(input, output);
var
   num:real;

begin
   writeln('Please type in a number');
   readln(num);
   writeln('The number is ',num)
end. (* Number program *)
```

The first line of the program specifies that the program is called Number and that it takes input and produces output. This program uses one variable, a real-number variable named num. There are three executable statements in the program, the readln statement and the two writeln statements.

This program, of course, is not especially useful; all it does is read in a number and print it out again. A sample run might look like this (italics identify the user's response):

```
Please type in a number
11
The number is 11
```

Here is an example of a program that composes a sentence. Note that the program is named Sentence and that it uses two variables, a string variable named noun that can be up to ten letters long and a string variable named verb that can be up to eight letters long.

```
(*  ------------------------------------------------------------------  *)
(*                                                                       *)
(*   This program asks the user for a noun and a verb, forms a           *)
(*   sentence from the two words, and prints it out.                     *)
(*                                                                       *)
(*  ------------------------------------------------------------------  *)
program Sentence(input, output);
var
   noun: string[10];
   verb:  string[8];
begin
   writeln('Please enter a noun, ten letters or less');
   readln(noun);
   writeln('Please enter a verb, eight letters or less');
   readln(verb);
   writeln('The ',noun,' ',verb,'s.')
end. (* Sentence program *)
```

This program composes a simple sentence based on words given to it by the user. It asks the user for a noun and stores the response in the variable noun. It then asks the user for a verb and places that response in the variable verb. Finally it forms a sentence by printing the word *The*, the desired noun, the desired verb, and an *s* and a period to complete the sentence. The first two writeln statements are known as *prompts* because they prompt the user to supply the program with a particular type of information. A sample run might look like this:

```
Please enter a noun, ten letters or less
elephant
```

(continued)

Please enter a verb, eight letters or less
trumpet
The elephant trumpets.

Of course, the completed sentence will not always be a grammatical one. That depends on the particular noun and verb supplied by the user.

Assignment Statements

We have seen that one way the computer stores information in a variable is by requesting it from the user and reading it in by means of a readln statement. Another way to store information in a variable is to assign it to the variable in an assignment statement. An *assignment statement* consists of a variable name followed by the assignment operator : =, followed in turn by some value or the result of a computation. For example, the following assignment statements assign values to the variables total and name.

    total : = 8;

    name : = 'John';

The variable total is assigned the value 8, and the variable name is assigned the string John.

Numerical Operations

To create more useful programs, we can use numerical operations to manipulate numeric data. We will limit this discussion to the more well known and useful among these operations. Pascal performs addition and subtraction with the familiar plus (+) and minus (−) operators. Multiplication is represented by an asterisk (*), and division is denoted by a slash (/). These arithmetic operations are illustrated in the following discussion.

Consider first the following assignment statement:

    total : = 3 + 5;

The computer executes this statement by taking the result of the numerical operation 3 + 5 (namely, 8) and storing it in the variable total. Similarly, the assignment

    total : = total + 1;

means that the current value of total should be increased by 1 and the sum stored under the name total. Thus, if total's value had been 8, it would have become 9 after this statement was executed. Here is another example of a typical assignment statement in Pascal:

total := **price** * **quantity**;

The value of the variable price is multiplied by the value of the variable quantity, and the result is stored in the variable total. Thus, if price contained the value 0.39 and quantity contained the value 4, total would be given the value .39 * 4, or 1.56.

We should note that in Pascal, as in mathematics, operations are performed in a certain order—multiplications and divisions first, then additions and subtractions. For example, if given the problem 2 + 3 * 4 + 5 / 6, the computer would first compute the multiplication (3 * 4) and the division (5/6) and then the two additions (2 + 12 + 5/6), for an answer of 89/6. Parentheses can be used to change the order of these operations. Our sample problem would have been computed quite differently if it had been written this way: (2 + 3) * (4 + 5) / 6. The calculations within the parentheses would have been completed first and then the remaining operations performed in the order described above, for an answer of 15/2. If sets of parentheses, such as ((2 + 3) * 4 + 5) / 6, had been used, the calculation within the innermost set of parentheses would have been performed first, then the operations within the next set of parentheses, and so on, for an answer of 25/6.

Here is an example of a statement designed to compute the average of three test scores:

avg := (**score1** + **score2** + **score3**) / 3;

To execute this statement, the computer adds together the values of score1, score2, and score3 and divides the result by 3. The answer is stored in the variable avg. This statement appears in the following simple program, called Average:

```
(*  ----------------------------------------------------------------  *)
(*                                                                     *)
(*    This program takes three test scores and computes their          *)
(*    average.                                                          *)
(*                                                                     *)
(*  ----------------------------------------------------------------  *)
program Average(input, output);
var
    score1: real;    (*score of first student*)
```

(continued)

```
        score2: real;    (*score of second student*)
        score3: real;    (*score of third student*)
        avg:    real;    (*average student score*)

    begin
        writeln ('First score?');
        readln(score1);
        writeln('Second score?');
        readln(score2);
        writeln('Third score?');
        readln(score3);
        avg := (score1 + score2 + score3)/3;
        writeln('The Average score was ',avg);
    end.    (* Average program *)
```

This program asks the user for three test scores, averages the test scores, and prints out the average. Note that a comment follows each variable declaration. These comments form a *glossary* that tells anyone reading the program what function each variable serves. A glossary helps to make a program easier to read.

■ Conditional Branching

We can now write programs that request information from the user, operate on that information, and send information back to the user. One limitation, however, is that our programs will always operate on the data we give them in the same way. The Sentence program will always make a simple sentence out of the noun and the verb. The Average program will always average the three numbers typed in. But what if we want the program to follow different courses of action in different situations? What if, for example, we want the grade averaging program to check for a failing grade or to average two grades if the third grade is missing?

One of the concepts introduced in Chapter 6 was *conditional branching*, which allowed us to indicate what the computer should do next based on the existing conditions. Pascal provides a very easy way to perform such branching—the if...then statement. The if...then statement takes the form

    if <condition> then
        <statement>

Angle brackets indicate the type of information that should appear in their place. In this case, a condition should take the place of <condi-

tion> and a statement should take the place of <statement>. Here is an example of a simple program that uses the if...then construct.†

```
(*   --------------------------------------------------------------   *)
(*                                                                    *)
(*   This program asks the user what day of the week it is and        *)
(*   makes a comment if the day is Friday.                            *)
(*                                                                    *)
(*   --------------------------------------------------------------   *)
program Day(input, output);
var
   wkday: string[10];      (* the day of the week *)

begin
   writeln('What day of the week is it today?');
   readln(wkday);
   if wkday = 'Friday' then
      writeln('Thank Goodness it''s Friday!!!');
   writeln
end.   (* Day program *)
```

This program will print out the message Thank Goodness it's Friday!!! only if the day entered by the user is Friday. Otherwise, the program will end. This means that if the user enters a day other than Friday, such as Tuesday, the program will simply stop running without telling the user why. To allow the programmer to prevent such dead ends, Pascal provides a second part to the if...then statement—an else statement, which indicates the action to be performed if the condition is not true.

The if...then...else statement takes the form

```
if <condition> then
   <statement>
else
   <statement>
```

What happens when Pascal encounters an if...then...else statement? If the condition is true, the statement following then is executed. If the condition is false, the statement after else is executed. One of the two statements is executed each time the program is run.

Here is a modified version of the Day program that uses an if...then...else statement:

---

† In this program we use a double apostrophe within a literal expression to cause the literal to have a single apostrophe when printed.

```
(*   --------------------------------------------------------------   *)
(*                                                                    *)
(*   This program asks the user what day of the week it is and        *)
(*   prints a message.                                                *)
(*                                                                    *)
(*   --------------------------------------------------------------   *)
program Day2(input, output);
var
    wkday: string[10];                  (* the day of the week *)

begin
    writeln('What day of the week is it today?');
    readln(wkday);
    if wkday = 'Friday' then
        writeln('Thank Goodness it''s Friday!!!')
    else                                (* not Friday *)
        writeln('Have a good day!!')
end.    (* Day2 program *)
```

This program asks the user for the day of the week and stores this information in the variable wkday. It then evaluates the day typed in. If the condition wkday = 'Friday' is true, the program will print the message

Thank Goodness it's Friday!!!

If the condition is not true, the program will print out

Have a good day!!

With the Day2 program, we see the importance of the *flow of control*—the order in which the instructions are executed. In Day2, the first statement after begin is executed first. The third statement is an if statement. At this point, the condition following if is evaluated. If that condition is true, then the statement following then is executed, and the statement following else is ignored. If the condition is false, the statement under then is ignored and the statement under else is executed. It is very important for a programmer to have a clear and precise understanding of how a program functions and in what order its statements are executed.

Notice that there are no semicolons after the lines in the if...then...else construction; rather there is an end statement after the final clause. This is because Pascal treats the statement's four lines (from if to the end of the writeln under the else) as one statement.

A problem would develop, however, if you wanted to use more than one statement following the then clause (or the else clause) because Pascal expects a single statement. For example, suppose you wanted to print an additional message if wkday equaled Friday. Simply inserting another line before the else statement would make the program syntactically incorrect. However, Pascal will treat a block of statements as one line provided the statements are marked with a begin and an end. (The begin and end here act like parentheses, telling the computer that the lines they contain should be treated as if they were one statement.) Thus, we could modify Day2 as follows:

```
(*    -------------------------------------------------------------------    *)
(*                                                                           *)
(*    This is a modified version of the Day2 program that illustrates        *)
(*    that several instructions in an if...then...else construct can         *)
(*    be grouped together and treated as one statement.                      *)
(*                                                                           *)
(*    -------------------------------------------------------------------    *)
program Day3(input, output);
var
    wkday: string[10];                (* the day of the week *)

begin
    writeln('What day of the week is it today?');
    readln(wkday);
    if wkday = 'Friday' then

        begin
            writeln('Thank Goodness it''s Friday!!!');
            writeln('Have a good weekend.')
        end

    else                              (* not Friday *)
        writeln('Have a good day!!')
end.    (* Day3 program *)
```

In this case, if wkday = 'Friday' is true, the program will print out

```
Thank Goodness it's Friday!!!
Have a good weekend.
```

Notice that there is no semicolon after the begin...end block under the then clause, just as there was no semicolon in Day2 after the writeln statement under the if clause. Note too that statements in the begin...end block must obey ordinary Pascal syntax, ending with a semicolon if they are not part of a special construction such as if...then...else.

Pascal allows use of still another clause in conditional branching—

the else if clause. Let's modify Day3 further to illustrate this new construct.

```
(*   -------------------------------------------------------------------   *)
(*                                                                         *)
(*   Yet another version of Day, this program illustrates the             *)
(*   flexibility of conditional branching.                                *)
(*                                                                         *)
(*   -------------------------------------------------------------------   *)
program Day4(input, output);
var
    wkday: string[10];                    (* the day of the week *)

begin
    writeln('What day of the week is it today?');
    readln(wkday);
    if wkday = 'Friday' then

        begin
            writeln('Thank Goodness it''s Friday!!!');
            writeln('Have a good weekend.')
        end

    else if wkday = 'Monday' then

        begin
            writeln('Hope you had a good weekend.');
            writeln('Time to start another week.')
        end

    else                            (* not Friday or Monday *)
        writeln('Have a good day!!')
end.    (* Day4 program *)
```

Here are three separate runs of the Day4 program:

```
What day of the week is it today?
Friday
Thank Goodness it's Friday!!!
Have a good weekend.

What day of the week is it today?
Wednesday
Have a good day!!
```

(continued)

What day of the week is it today?
Monday
Hope you had a good weekend.
Time to start another week.

Notice that, under the else if clause, there is a begin...end block that serves the same purpose as the begin...end block under the if clause. Both enclose blocks of instructions that are to be executed if the particular clause is selected. Notice also that we have inserted some blank lines into the code. The blank lines, like the comments and the indentations, are ignored by the computer. We use them to divide the program visually into smaller pieces to help people understand what the program is doing. It is a good idea to use comments, indentation, and blank lines liberally if you wish other people to be able to understand your programs.

Although these examples of conditional branching may seem a bit silly, they illustrate the importance of the concept. Conditional branching is one of the crucial concepts of computer programming—it enables the computer to vary its actions based on the user's responses.

■ Looping

Another powerful concept introduced in Chapter 6 is looping. A *loop* allows a programmer to repeat an instruction or series of instructions several times without having to write out the instruction each time. If we wanted to use the Day4 program to check out all seven days of the week, we would be forced either to write out the main body of the program seven times (from the first writeln to the last writeln) or to run the program seven times. A loop simplifies this process immensely.

As we observed in Chapter 6, there are two types of loops—definite and indefinite. *Definite loops* are executed a specified number of times, while *indefinite loops* are executed until a given condition has been fulfilled. Pascal uses a different construction for each type of loop. The for statement is used for definite loops, the while statement for indefinite loops.

For Loops

The for statement is used to repeat a statement a specified number of times. It takes the form

```
for <variable1> := <number1> to <number2> do
    <statement>
```

Here variable1 is any integer variable (preferably not one that has been previously used, since its previous value will be lost), and number1 and number2 are any two integers or integer variables with number1 not greater than number2. This first line determines the number of times the statement under it will be executed. For example, consider the lines

```
for counter := 1 to 10 do
    writeln('I want candy!');
```

Here, the writeln statement would be executed ten times. The first time through the loop, counter would be set equal to 1 and then it would be set to 2, then 3, and so on until counter had exceeded 10, at which point Pascal would stop executing the loop. Here is a short program that uses a for loop to print a message.

```
(*  ------------------------------------------------------------------  *)
(*                                                                       *)
(*  This program asks the user for a number and prints out a            *)
(*  message the specified number of times.                              *)
(*                                                                       *)
(*  ------------------------------------------------------------------  *)
program Hunger(input, output);
var
    maximum: integer;      (* number of times loop will execute *)
    counter:   integer;    (* loop counter *)

begin
    writeln('Enter an integer, please.');
    readln(maximum);
    for counter := 1 to maximum do
        writeln('I am getting hungry')
end. (* Hunger program *)
```

This program asks for a number and prints out the message I am getting hungry the specified number of times.

The for loop is a special construction consisting of the for statement and the statement to be executed. Just as with conditional branching, if there is a block of more than one line to be executed by the for loop, begin and end must enclose the block. Thus, we could easily modify the Hunger program, as follows.

```
(*   ------------------------------------------------------------   *)
(*                                                                  *)
(*   This is a modified version of the Hunger program. It illustrates  *)
(*   how to use multiple statements within a for loop.              *)
(*                                                                  *)
(*   ------------------------------------------------------------   *)
program Hunger2(input, output);
var
    maximum: integer;         (* number of times loop is repeated *)
    counter:   integer;       (* for loop counter *)

begin
    writeln('Enter an integer, please.');
    readln(maximum);
    for counter := 1 to maximum do
      begin
        writeln('It is getting late');
        writeln ('I am getting hungry')
      end                       (* for Loop *)
end.    (* Hunger2 program *)
```

Here is a run of the program:

```
Enter an integer, please.
7
It is getting late
I am getting hungry
It is getting late
I am getting hungry
It is getting late
I am getting hungry
It is getting late
I am getting hungry
It is getting late
I am getting hungry
It is getting late
I am getting hungry
It is getting late
I am getting hungry
```

While Loops

For loops are great for repeating an action a given number of times. But what if you don't know in advance how many times the loop should be executed? Suppose, for example, that you wanted to write a program that would take any number of grades and compute their average. Since you will be doing something (reading in grades) over and over again, a loop will be needed. You don't know, however, how many times the loop will be used. That depends on how many grades you want to average. In this case we use an indefinite loop, which will loop as long as a certain condition is true. We use the while construction for indefinite loops. Its syntax is

```
while <condition> do
    <statement>
```

The statement will be executed as long as the condition is true. When the condition is false, the statement will not be executed, and Pascal will skip to the next statement not in the loop. As usual, the body of the loop may contain only one line, unless begin and end statements are used to designate a sequence of lines.

Here is a program to compute the average of a series of grades:

```
(*  --------------------------------------------------------------  *)
(*                                                                   *)
(*    This program reads in a series of grades and computes their    *)
(*    average.                                                        *)
(*                                                                   *)
(*  --------------------------------------------------------------  *)
program GradeAverage(input, output);
var
    grade:      real;      (* grade to be averaged *)
    sum:        real;      (* sum of the grades typed in *)
    count:      real;      (* number of grades entered *)
    average:    real;      (* average of the grades typed in *)

begin
    writeln('This program averages a list of numeric grades.');
    writeln('Type in the grades one at a time.');
    writeln('Type in a negative number when all of the grades');
    writeln('have been entered.');
    sum := 0;           (* sum is initially set to zero *)
    count := 0;         (* number of grades is 0 *)
    writeln('Grade:');
    readln(grade);

    while grade >= 0 do
```

(continued)

```
begin
  sum := sum + grade;
  count := count + 1;
  writeln('Grade:');
  readln(grade)
end; (* while loop *)

average := sum/count;
writeln('The average of the grades is ', average)
end.    (* GradeAverage program *)
```

This program starts by telling the user to type in grades one at a time and to type in a negative number when all the grades have been entered. Then it sets the values of the variables sum and counter to zero. Next it asks for the first grade and reads it into a variable called grade. Then it begins the loop. Each time the computer comes to the while statement, it pauses to evaluate the condition. In this case, the condition is grade $>= 0$, so the computer checks to see if the present value of grade is greater than or equal to zero. If it is, the computer executes the statements in the loop one at a time, adding the new grade to the cumulative sum of grades, increasing the counter by one, and reading in the next grade. When the computer reaches the end of the loop, it jumps to the top of the loop and evaluates the condition again. When the condition is no longer true (when grade < 0), the computer skips to the next statement not in the loop (the statement to compute the average of the grades typed in). The average is then printed out, and the program ends. Here is a sample run of the program:

```
This program averages a list of numeric grades.
Type in the grades one at a time.
Type in a negative number when all of the grades
have been entered.
Grade:
99
Grade:
76
Grade:
86
Grade:
77
Grade:
-1
The average of the grades is 84.5
```

In Pascal, there is another kind of indefinite loop construct called the until loop. It is similar to the while loop, except that the condition is evaluated at the bottom of the loop rather than at the top. The loop is executed until a condition is true. We won't elaborate on the until loop but will leave it to the interested reader to investigate.

Nested Loops

An important extension of looping is nested looping. A *nested loop* is a loop within a loop. Why would we want to use one loop within another? For one example, look back to our pseudocode for baking a quiche in Chapter 6. That pseudocode contained a loop to cut the strips of bacon. Now let's say we want to bake five quiches, one right after another. We want to repeat the entire quiche-baking process five times. So we put another loop around our quiche-baking pseudocode to loop five times, once for each quiche. The bacon-cutting loop now becomes a nested loop, since it falls within the larger loop to bake five quiches.

For another example, look back to our grade averaging program. It contains a loop to average a series of grades. But let's say we want to average several series of grades—say, one for each student. We put another loop around the first, a loop to be repeated for each student:

```
(*  ----------------------------------------------------------------  *)
(*                                                                    *)
(*   This program computes GPAs (grade point averages) for any        *)
(*   number of students. It asks for each student's name and          *)
(*   grades and prints out the average.                               *)
(*                                                                    *)
(*  ----------------------------------------------------------------  *)

program GradeAverage2(input, output);
var
    studname: string[25];    (* name of student *)
    grade:    real;          (* grade to be averaged *)
    sum:      real;          (* sum of the grades typed in *)
    count:    integer;       (* number of grades entered *)
    average:  real;          (* average of the grades typed in *)

begin
    writeln('This program averages each student''s grades to');
    writeln('compute individual grade point averages. It will');
    writeln('request a student''s name and grades.');
    writeln('When you are done using the program, type');
    writeln('Q when asked for a student''s name.');
    writeln('Student''s name:');
    readln(studname);
```

(continued)

```
while studname < > 'Q' do

    begin
        writeln('Type in the grades one at a time.');
        writeln('Type in a negative number when all the grades');
        writeln('have been entered.');

        sum := 0;          (* sum is initially set to zero *);
        count := 0;        (* number of grades = 0 *);
        writeln('Grade:');
        readln(grade);

        while grade > = 0 do
            begin
                sum := sum + grade;
                count := count + 1;
                writeln('Grade:');
                readln(grade)
            end; (* while loop *)

        average := sum/count;
        writeln(studname,' has a GPA of ', average);
        writeln('Student''s name:');
        readln(studname)
    end;
end.    (*GradeAverage2 program *)
```

This program contains two loops, one to loop once for each student and another to loop once for each grade. For each student, the computer executes the GradeAverage2 program until the user types Q to quit. A run of the program might look like this:

```
This program averages each student's grades to
compute individual grade point averages. It will
request a student's name and grades.
When you are done using the program, type
Q when asked for a student's name.
Student's name:
Donald Duck
Type in the grades one at a time.
Type in a negative number when all the grades
have been entered.
Grade:
76
```

(continued)

```
Grade:
92
Grade:
55
Grade:
– 3
Donald Duck has a GPA of 74.3333
Student's name:
Mickey Mouse
Type in the grades one at a time.
Type in a negative number when all the grades
have been entered.
Grade:
66
Grade:
77
Grade:
88
Grade:
99
Grade:
– 1
Mickey Mouse has a GPA of 82.5
Student's name:
Q
```

■ Procedures

The programs we've presented thus far have been fairly short and easy to read and understand, but not especially useful. Longer programs tend to be more useful but are also more complicated and therefore potentially more difficult to understand. Long programs tend to perform the same series of instructions in several places. To make these programs easier to write and to read, we use a programming construct called a procedure.

A *procedure* is a block of instructions designed to perform some task. For example, a program to draw geometric figures might have one procedure to draw circles, another to draw squares, a third to draw rectangles, and a fourth to draw triangles. Likewise, a word processing program might contain a procedure to print text in boldface, a procedure to print text in italics, a procedure to control the margins, a procedure for indentation, and so forth.

Procedures are placed in a program after the variable declarations and before the main body of the program. They are called upon when required. Procedures make programs easier to follow since in the body of the program procedure names can be used in place of the many program statements the procedures contain. Procedures can also save typing time when the same series of instructions is needed at several different points within one program. In addition, procedures make long programs easier to write and correct; a programmer can test each procedure separately to make sure it works properly before it is incorporated into the larger program. It is much easier to isolate an error in a 10- to 20-line program than to find it in a 1,000-line program. Finally, procedures encourage programmers to break problems into subproblems, since subproblems to solve problems may be incorporated into a procedure.

The following is an example of a procedure.

```
(*    ----------------------------------------------------------------   *)
(*                                                                        *)
(*    This procedure draws a 10 x 10 square of asterisks.                 *)
(*                                                                        *)
(*    ----------------------------------------------------------------   *)

procedure Square;
   var
      counter: integer;      (* loop counter *)

   begin
      for counter: = 1 to 10 do
         writeln ('*   *   *   *   *   *   *   *   *   *')
      end;   (* Square procedure *)
```

This procedure draws a 10-by-10 square of asterisks, as stated in the header comment, by printing out a string of ten asterisks ten times.

The syntax of procedures is similar to that of programs. Differences are that the word procedure replaces the word program and that the end statement is followed by a semicolon instead of a period (end;). Both procedures and programs may include a set of variable declarations followed by a begin...end block of instructions. Variables declared within a procedure are used only in that procedure. They are distinct from variables with the same names outside the procedure.

As suggested, procedures are called upon, or *invoked,* in the body of a program. This section, called the *mainline,* appears after all procedures have been set out. Here is an example of a program that uses the Square procedure:

```
(*   ----------------------------------------------------------------   *)
(*                                                                      *)
(*   This program draws a specified number of 10 x 10 squares of        *)
(*   asterisks. It illustrates how a procedure is defined and used      *)
(*   within a program.                                                  *)
(*                                                                      *)
(*   ----------------------------------------------------------------   *)

program Draw(input, output);

var
    count:      integer;    (* loop counter *)
    maxsquares: integer;    (* number of squares to draw *)


(*   ----------------------------------------------------------------   *)
(*                                                                      *)
(*   This procedure draws one square.                                   *)
(*                                                                      *)
(*   ----------------------------------------------------------------   *)

procedure Square;
  var
      counter:   integer;    (* loop counter *)

    begin
      for counter: = 1 to 10 do
        writeln ('*   *   *   *   *   *   *   *   *   *')
  end;   (* Square procedure *)


(*   ----------------------------------------------------------------   *)
(*                                                                      *)
(*   Mainline                                                           *)
(*                                                                      *)
(*   ----------------------------------------------------------------   *)

begin
    writeln('How many squares shall I draw for you?');
    readln(maxsquares);    (* find out how many squares to draw *)
    for count: = 1 to maxsquares do
    begin
        Square;
        writeln              (* prints a blank line to separate squares *)
    end   (* for loop *)
end.   (* Draw program *)
```

This program asks the user how many squares to draw and then prints that number of squares by executing the Square procedure the specified number of times. A run of the program might look like this:

```
How many squares shall I draw for you?
3
*   *   *   *   *   *   *   *   *   *
*   *   *   *   *   *   *   *   *   *
*   *   *   *   *   *   *   *   *   *
*   *   *   *   *   *   *   *   *   *
*   *   *   *   *   *   *   *   *   *
*   *   *   *   *   *   *   *   *   *
*   *   *   *   *   *   *   *   *   *
*   *   *   *   *   *   *   *   *   *
*   *   *   *   *   *   *   *   *   *
*   *   *   *   *   *   *   *   *   *

*   *   *   *   *   *   *   *   *   *
*   *   *   *   *   *   *   *   *   *
*   *   *   *   *   *   *   *   *   *
*   *   *   *   *   *   *   *   *   *
*   *   *   *   *   *   *   *   *   *
*   *   *   *   *   *   *   *   *   *
*   *   *   *   *   *   *   *   *   *
*   *   *   *   *   *   *   *   *   *
*   *   *   *   *   *   *   *   *   *
*   *   *   *   *   *   *   *   *   *

*   *   *   *   *   *   *   *   *   *
*   *   *   *   *   *   *   *   *   *
*   *   *   *   *   *   *   *   *   *
*   *   *   *   *   *   *   *   *   *
*   *   *   *   *   *   *   *   *   *
*   *   *   *   *   *   *   *   *   *
*   *   *   *   *   *   *   *   *   *
*   *   *   *   *   *   *   *   *   *
*   *   *   *   *   *   *   *   *   *
*   *   *   *   *   *   *   *   *   *
```

Note that the main program calls the procedure simply by naming it. The statement Square; is interpreted as meaning that the procedure called Square should be executed. Procedures may be called from other procedures as well as from the main program.

Arrays

Variables are very useful when we know exactly how many values need to be stored and when the number needed is small. For example, if we need to store one name, we can easily do so by using the variable name. Similarly, if we have only two numbers to store, we can use the variables number1 and number2. But what if we have a hundred names or two hundred numbers to store? We could use separate variable names (ranging from name1 to name100 or from number1 to number200), but that would be cumbersome, to say the least. Writing out two hundred different writeln statements just to print out all the numbers would be tremendously time-consuming. Fortunately, there is an easier way to solve this problem.

Pascal, like many other programming languages, provides special structures to organize data. An array is a simple example of such a structure. An *array* is a succession of variables accessed under a common name by a subscript. If a variable can be thought of as a box in which the computer stores a value, then an array can be thought of as a row or column of boxes, each containing one value identified by a subscript (see Fig. 8.1). Arrays are used when the programmer wishes to store related information under a single name. To retrieve the information stored in an array, we use the name of the array and the subscript that indicates which item of the array we want.

In Pascal, the array name is always followed by the subscript enclosed in square brackets, as in name[2]. The subscript can be either an integer or an integer variable. For example, name[counter] is the element of the array name whose subscript is equal to the contents of the vari-

Figure 8.1
An array.

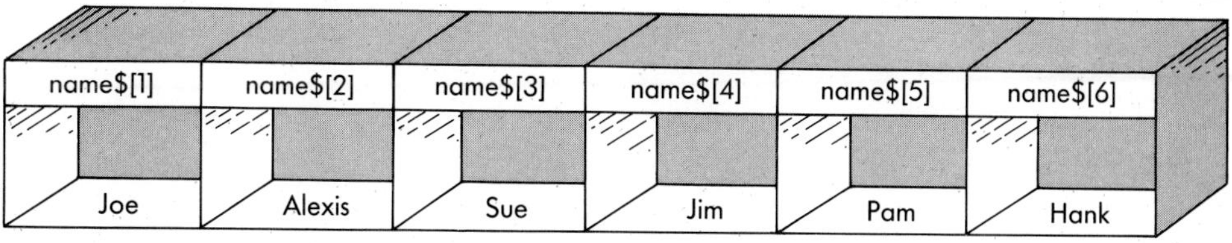

able counter. In particular, the second element in the array name is called name[2], where 2 is the value of its subscript. Array names use the same format as variable names (they must start with a letter and may contain any number of numbers, letters, and underscores). All elements of an array must be of the same type—string, integer, or real.

Arrays are declared under the var statement using the following format:

```
var
    name:       array[1..200] of string[5];
    id_number: array[1..30] of integer;
```

Here name is a 200-element array with subscripts ranging from 1 to 200 and strings containing five characters. The array of integers called id_number contains 30 elements and subscripts ranging from 1 to 30. These two arrays are depicted in Fig. 8.2. The first number in the square brackets is the lowest-numbered element of the array (usually this is 1, but it can be any number). The second number is the highest-numbered element. Following the word of is the data type for all of the array elements (integers for id_number, strings of length 5 for name). The word array, the two dots between the highest and lowest element numbers, and the word of must appear as shown; they ensure that storage space is reserved for each array element.

Arrays can be useful in programming. Suppose, for example, that we wish to sort alphabetically and print out a file containing 200 names. We might write a program in which the mainline reads the names into an array called name, a procedure sorts the array, and the following simple procedure prints out the names.

Figure 8.2
A parallel array.

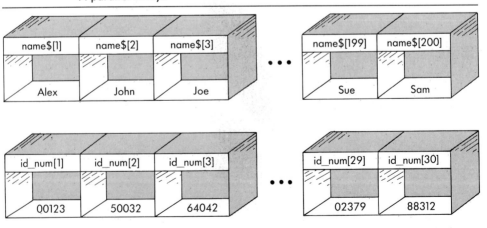

```
(*   --------------------------------------------------------------------   *)
(*                                                                          *)
(*   This procedure prints out the contents of an array of names.           *)
(*   The array contains 200 elements.                                       *)
(*                                                                          *)
(*   --------------------------------------------------------------------   *)

procedure Print;
var
    count: integer;              (* loop counter *)

begin
    for count := 1 to 200 do
        writeln(name[count])     (* print out array element *)
    end;   (* Print procedure *)
```

As you can see, a for loop is used to print out the array elements. The
loop is executed 200 times, once for each element in the array. Each
time the loop is executed, the counter is increased by 1 and the next
array element (the element with the subscript corresponding to the
counter) is printed out. Thus, the first time the loop is executed, the
contents of name[1] are printed out, the second time the loop is executed name[2] is printed out, and so forth until name[200] is printed out.
Programmers often use arrays in this way.

Another common use of arrays is for searching. Simple searching
involves moving through an array and comparing each of its elements
with a particular value until the value is located or until the entire array
has been searched. For example, the following procedure searches an
array called callee, which contains the names of 200 students, to find
persons named John.

```
(*   --------------------------------------------------------------------   *)
(*                                                                          *)
(*   This procedure searches an array of names and prints out the           *)
(*   subscript of any person named John.                                    *)
(*                                                                          *)
(*   --------------------------------------------------------------------   *)

procedure Findjohn;
var
    counter: integer;                          (* for loop counter *)

begin
    for counter := 1 to 200 do
```

(continued)

```
        if callee[counter] = 'JOHN' then
            writeln('callee numbered ', counter, ' is named JOHN')
   end;   (* Findjohn procedure *)
```

Parallel Arrays

Why, you may ask, would anyone want to search through an array for a particular name (such as John)? Why would we care where John's name was located in the array? Well, suppose we had another 200-element array that contained phone numbers, and suppose each phone number corresponded to the name in the callee array with the same subscript. (Suppose, for example, that Margaret was callee[7] and that her phone number was telno[7].) Then, if we knew where in the callee array a particular name was located, we could easily find that person's phone number.

When two or more arrays of the same size are set up so that elements with the same subscript are related to each other, we call them *parallel arrays*. For example, an electronic thesaurus might include one array that contained a list of words and another that contained their synonyms. Or one array might contain names; another, post office box numbers; another, telephone numbers; and a fourth, street addresses, so that a person's name, post office box, phone number, and street address would all have the same subscript. Or an airline reservation system might include one array for place of origin, another for place of destination, a third for departure times, and a fourth for arrival times. Each subscript would correspond to a specific flight so that for each flight a travel agent could determine origin, destination, arrival time, and departure time.

For a simpler example, let us return to our on-line telephone book. We'll assume that we have two arrays of 200 elements each—one array,

Figure 8.3
The callee and telno arrays.

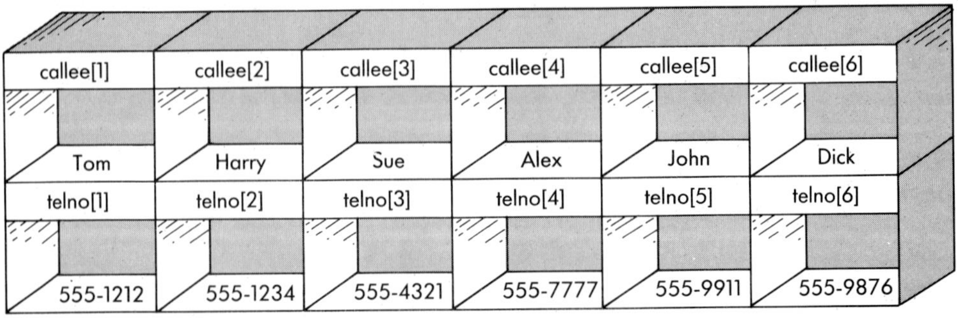

callee[1]	callee[2]	callee[3]	callee[4]	callee[5]	callee[6]
Tom	Harry	Sue	Alex	John	Dick
telno[1]	telno[2]	telno[3]	telno[4]	telno[5]	telno[6]
555-1212	555-1234	555-4321	555-7777	555-9911	555-9876

called callee, that contains names of people we may wish to call, and another, called telno, that contains their telephone numbers. The arrays are set up as shown in Fig. 8.3, with each telephone number corresponding to the name with the same subscript in the callee array. Here is a procedure that asks the user for a name, searches for the name in the callee array, and, if it finds the name, prints the corresponding telephone number.

```
(*   ------------------------------------------------------------------  *)
(*                                                                        *)
(*    This procedure attempts to find a person's telephone number,        *)
(*    given the person's name. It asks the user for a name and            *)
(*    searches for the name in the callee array. If it finds the name,    *)
(*    it prints the corresponding telephone number from the telno         *)
(*    array.                                                              *)
(*                                                                        *)
(*   ------------------------------------------------------------------  *)
procedure Telephone;
var
    counter: integer;        (* for loop counter *)
    name:    string[25];     (* name of person whose *)
                             (* phone number is sought *)

begin
    writeln('Enter name');
    readln(name);
    for counter := 1 to 20 do
        if callee[counter] = name then
            writeln('the phone number for ',name,' is ',telno[counter])
    end;    (* Telephone procedure *)
```

An Example of Structured Programming

Let's combine the structured problem-solving principles described in Chapter 5 with Pascal programming methods to write a program that solves a practical problem.

Suppose that you run a business that employs 50 people, all paid by the hour. In the past, your bookkeeping was done by a kindly old bookkeeper who has recently retired. You have decided this is the time to computerize. You are not pleased with the idea of spending several hundred dollars for payroll software, so you decide to write your own program in Pascal. First, in accordance with the structured problem-solving methods, you determine what you want the program to produce—a list of names and the amounts of paychecks due. You will need to know the names of the employees, the number of hours they worked per pay period, and their hourly wage rates.

Your problem breaks down into three subproblems: reading in the information, computing the pay due to each worker, and printing out the name and pay for each worker. Your initial pseudocode looks like this:

Read data
Compute pay
Print info

Before going any further, you need to know how to compute each worker's pay. Ordinarily, the pay would simply be the hourly wage multiplied by the number of hours worked. However, some employees work overtime (more than 40 hours per week), and their contract calls for them to receive time and a half for the extra hours.

Your pseudocode for computing pay might look like this:

COMPUTE PAY

IF hours > 40 THEN
   pay = wage × 40 + (hours − 40) × wage × 1.5
ELSE
   pay = wage × hours

Your pseudocode for reading in the value and printing out the final information might look like this:

READ DATA

Read name
Read wage
Read hours

PRINT INFO

Print name
Print pay due

Now you need only convert this pseudocode outline into syntactically correct Pascal. One version of such a program might look like the following one. Notice how closely the actual Pascal code corresponds to the initial pseudocode. Notice also that the procedure Computepay is called from the mainline and that Computepay in turn calls the proce-

dure Print. For this reason, Print must appear before Computepay in the
program.

```
(*  -------------------------------------------------------------  *)
(*                                                                  *)
(*  This program computes a payroll for a small business. It reads  *)
(*  in the information, calculates each employee's weekly pay,      *)
(*  and prints out the information.                                 *)
(*                                                                  *)
(*  -------------------------------------------------------------  *)

program Payroll(input, output);

var
    name:    string[15];      (* name of worker *)
    wage:    real;            (* hourly wage *)
    hours:   real;            (* hours worked *)
    pay:     real;            (* pay earned *)
    counter: integer;         (* for loop counter *)


(*  -------------------------------------------------------------  *)
(*                                                                  *)
(*  This procedure prints out the employee's name and the          *)
(*  corresponding amount of money.                                 *)
(*                                                                  *)
(*  -------------------------------------------------------------  *)

procedure Print;

begin
    writeln(name,' gets paid $',pay);
    writeln
end;   (* Print procedure *)


(*  -------------------------------------------------------------  *)
(*                                                                  *)
(*  This procedure computes an employee's weekly pay based on      *)
(*  number of hours worked and hourly wage.                        *)
(*                                                                  *)
(*  -------------------------------------------------------------  *)

procedure Computepay;
```

(continued)

```
begin
   if hours > 40 then
      pay: = (40 * wage) + (1.5 * wage * (hours − 40))
   else
      pay: =wage * hours;
   Print                          (* call Print procedure *)
end;   (* Computepay procedure *)


(*   ------------------------------------------------------------------   *)
(*                                                                        *)
(*    Mainline                                                            *)
(*                                                                        *)
(*   ------------------------------------------------------------------   *)
begin
   for counter: = 1 to 50 do          (* for each worker *)
      begin
         writeln('Enter employee''s name, wage, and hours worked.');
         readln(name, wage, hours);
         Computepay                 (* invoke Computepay procedure )
      end    (* for loop *)
end.   (* Payroll program *)
```

Here is an abbreviated sample run for the program. Rather than running the program for 50 employees as indicated in the mainline, we have run the program for five employees.

```
Enter employee's name, wage, and hours worked.
Jeff Franklin
6.50
45
Jeff Franklin gets paid $308.75

Enter employee's name, wage, and hours worked.
Deborah Chen
7.25
40
Deborah Chen gets paid $290.00

Enter employee's name, wage, and hours worked.
Elizabeth Giles
6.25
41
Elizabeth Giles gets paid $259.38
```

(continued)

Enter employee's name, wage, and hours worked.
Michael Goodman
7.50
42
Michael Goodman gets paid $322.50

Enter employee's name, wage, and hours worked.
Nancy Madison
6.25
50
Nancy Madison gets paid $343.75

▌Debugging

Often a program, although it runs, does not do what the programmer intended; such a program is said to contain bugs. *Bugs* are minor errors in a program, and *debugging* is discovering and correcting such errors. Debugging is as much a part of programming as problem analysis, program design, or code writing.

Debugging is a skill that is improved through practice; the more you do, the better you get. To help you gain some practice, we have outlined some typical problems and solutions as well as some common problem-locating techniques.

Typographical Errors

Even excellent typists sometimes make errors. To avoid having typographical errors ruin a program, carefully check the typed program against the handwritten version, word for word and line for line, before you try to run the program. In particular, check for missing lines, inconsistent variable names (such as respone instead of response), and improper syntax. Also make sure that the programming constructs you use are syntactically correct for Pascal (for example, else if is not the same as elseif).

Mistakes in Data Types

As mentioned earlier, there are three basic kinds of variables in Pascal—integers, real numbers, and character strings (letters, words, sentences, and numbers that are not meant to be used in calculations). Once you have declared a variable to be of a certain data type, you can use the variable only to manipulate that kind of data. For example, a string variable called num1 with the value "14" and another string variable called num2 with the value "12" cannot be added together to total 26. The computer will recognize them only as character strings, not as numbers for calculation.

Infinite Loops

An infinite loop is one that never stops looping either because no exit condition was specified or because the exit condition was never met. If there is a print statement within such a loop, it will be executed over and over again; if there are no print statements, the program will run silently until stopped. Here is an example of an infinite loop:

```
counter: = 1;
while counter < 10 do
   writeln('I am thirsty');
counter: = counter + 1;
```

Notice that the variable counter is increased outside the loop, not within it. The first time through the loop, counter has a value of 1. Nothing in the loop changes the value of counter, so it will be equal to 1 the second time through the loop as well. Since the value of counter is never changed by the loop, this fragment of code will continue to print "I am thirsty" until it uses up too much computer time and is stopped.

Off-by-One Errors

Often, loops use loop counters to determine how many times their instructions should be executed. Such counters are usually increased or decreased within the body of the loop. The initial value of the loop counter, the place where it is changed within the loop, and the placement of the exit condition all affect how often the statements within the loop will be executed. Try hand-simulating these two pieces of code, keeping in mind that hi is an array of strings with elements numbered from 1 to 3:

```
counter: = 1;
while counter < 3 do
   begin
      hi[counter]: = 'Hello';
      counter: = counter + 1
   end;

counter: = 1;
while counter < 3 do
```

(continued)

```
begin
    counter: = counter + 1;
    hi[counter]: = 'Hello'
end;
```

Note that different results are produced by these two very similar programs.

Errors in Initializing Counters

As just mentioned, many loops use counters to keep track of the number of times the loop has been executed. These counters must be initialized (assigned an initial value) *before* the program enters the loop. If they are initialized within the loop, they will be reinitialized every time the loop is run, and the loop will never stop.

Hand Simulation

You can find some errors in your program by working through the program just as the computer would. This process is called *hand simulation*. To hand-simulate a program, you must pretend to be the computer; in other words, you must act unintelligently.

Since you have written the program, you are handicapped by the knowledge of what you were trying to do. The computer will know only what you have told it. To simulate the actions of the computer by hand, then, you must try to forget your intentions and concentrate solely on what you have written in the program. Like the computer, you will need to know the values of variables and change these values as your program changes them.

A bug that proves particularly difficult to locate may be found with the following procedure. On a piece of paper, write down the names of all the variables you use in your program. Now start at the top of your program and "execute" each of the instructions in turn. When you come to an instruction that changes the value of a variable, write the new value under the variable's name on the paper; if the variable had an old value, cross it out. When you come to a statement that causes something to be printed out, write the result on a separate section of your paper. Although this is not exciting work, you must proceed line by line and not jump ahead because you think you know what is going to happen next. The computer does not know what will happen next, and you must pretend to be as uninformed as it is. Be sure to follow the outline for flow of control given in this chapter.

SUMMARY

Pascal is a structured programming language used in a great variety of applications. Although it is more difficult to learn than BASIC, Pascal provides much more power and versatility.

Very simple Pascal programs can be built with a program statement and writeln statements enclosed in a begin...end block. Variables are needed in most programs, however, as places to store values. Pascal recognizes several types of variables, including strings, integers, and real numbers. Each variable must be declared using the var statement. Variables receive values from either assignment statements or readln statements.

Programmers can use conditional statements, loops, procedures, and arrays to create more sophisticated Pascal programs. The conditional if...then statement evaluates a condition to determine whether to execute a following statement. The if...then...else statement allows the programmer to select one statement to execute if a condition is true and another if it is false. Pascal provides both definite loops (for loops) and indefinite loops (while loops). The first executes for a definite number of times while the second executes until some condition is satisfied.

Procedures in Pascal are blocks of programming statements designed to perform some specific task. They can simplify design and save typing time. Procedures also encourage programmers to write code that reflects the problem-solving methods outlined in Chapter 6.

Arrays are used extensively in Pascal. They allow programmers to store related information under a common name. Individual elements in arrays are accessed with the array name and a subscript enclosed in brackets. Related elements can be kept in corresponding or parallel arrays under the same subscript to facilitate retrieval of related information.

FURTHER READING

Arthur M. Keller, *A First Course in Computer Programming Using Pascal* (New York: McGraw-Hill, 1982).

Robert Sedgewick, *Algorithms* (Reading, Mass.: Addison-Wesley, 1983).

ISSUES AND IDEAS

1. Explain what variable type would be used for each of the following pieces of data.

   digit   12345   123.45   supercalifragilisticexpialidocious   −11

2. Carry out the following operations in the proper order:

$$1 + 2 \times 3 + 4 + 5 \times 6$$
$$(1 + 2) \times 3 + (4 + 5) \times 6$$
$$1 + 2 \times (3 + (4 + 5)) \times 6$$
$$(1 + 2) \times (3 + 4) + 5 \times 6$$

3. Write a simple program that asks the user for his name and prints out a greeting that incorporates the user's name. For example, if the user's name is Dave, the program might print out the message, "Hi Dave! Today may be your lucky day!"

4. Write a program that asks for three numbers and then prints out the largest and smallest of the numbers along with identifying messages.

5. Write a program that prints out the squares of the integers from 3 to 99.

6. Write a procedure to draw a right triangle of asterisks with a base and height of ten asterisks. Your program should contain nested loops, one instance of the writeln command, and one instance of the write command. [*Note:* The write command, which is not explained in the chapter, is identical to writeln except that it keeps the cursor on the current line while writeln causes the cursor to jump to the beginning of the next line.]

7. To answer the following questions, refer to the chapter's explanation of parallel arrays.
   a) How could you modify the telephone number procedure so that it could find phone numbers for any number of people?
   b) How could you modify the procedure so that it would tell the user if it failed to find the desired name in the array?
   c) How could you modify the procedure so that it would stop searching for a name once the name had been found?

8. Hand-simulate the following piece of code using the nums array shown below. In this instance, N will be 4 since there are four elements in the array.

```
procedure insertion
var
    element: integer;
begin
    for count1: = 2 to N do
        begin
            element: = nums[count1];
            count2: = count1;
```

(continued)

```
            while nums[count2 - 1] > element do
               begin
                  nums[count2]: = nums[count2 - 1];
                  count2: = count2 - 1
               end;
            nums[count2]: = element
         end
   end.
```

	nums
1	2
2	10
3	8
4	6

9. Write a program to help a library user locate a particular subject. Your program will use two arrays, one containing the first letter of the Library of Congress headings and the other containing subject headings. Since some letters represent more than one subject area, these letters may appear more than once in the first array. However, each subject area appears only once in the subject array. Your program should perform two functions. First, when given a letter, it should print out all of the subjects pertaining to that letter. Second, when given a subject, it should print the letter under which the subject can be found.

Programming Languages

In the past fifteen years, there have emerged from within the world of automation several hundred different entities characterizable as high-level programming languages. Such christening of a language implies that its expressive powers make it either a valuable communication vehicle, from the standpoint of a computer user, or an unrecognizable collection of nonsense, from the point of view of a computing machine.

MARK ELSON, *Concepts of Programming Languages* (1973)

■ Introduction

Computer programs, as we have seen, are written in computer languages. In this chapter we explore computer languages from several angles, examining what their purpose is, how the various levels of programming languages differ, why it is necessary to have more than one programming language, which language is most appropriate for different types of problems, and what the languages have in common. We also provide brief sketches of five popular languages—FORTRAN, COBOL, LISP, Smalltalk-80, and PROLOG.

You may recall that the only type of language computers understand consists of strings of binary digits (ones and zeros). This is called *machine language*. Since few people want to write programs in machine languages, other computer languages have been developed that allow the same concepts to be expressed in a form that is closer to the *natural language* that people use to communicate.

The progression from machine language to near-natural languages encompasses several language levels. Machine language is referred to as a *low-level language*. As languages get closer to natural language and further from machine language, they become *high-level* or *very-high-level languages.*

From Machine Language to a High-Level Language

The first programmers programmed in machine languages, a tedious and error-prone process. Imagine the possibilities for error when changing a single digit could alter the meaning of an instruction and cause the failure of an entire program or of the computer itself. Clearly, steps to simplify programming had to be taken. The first such step involved finding an alternative to the notation of 1s and 0s. Symbolic *assembly languages* provided this alternative. These languages are similar to machine languages and are not considered high-level languages. However, they do allow the use of *mnemonic codes,* names that help programmers remember what each instruction does. With assembly language, programmers no longer had to remember that 0101 signaled that two numbers should be added; instead, it was only necessary to remember the word ADD.

Further efforts to reduce the difficulty of programming led to the development of high-level languages. Indeed, computer scientists have designed hundreds of these languages. Different languages were developed to suit different tasks—for example, FORTRAN for scientific problem solving and COBOL for business applications. In each case, specific features of the language were designed to enable complicated operations to be performed with a minimal number of steps. Before we discuss high-level languages further, let us take a closer look at machine and assembly languages.

Machine Languages

When hardware engineers design a computer, they also design the machine language the computer will use. As explained in Chapter 3, a computer that stores programs in its memory fetches instructions from the program one at a time; each instruction describes a specific action for the computer to perform. In a simple computer, single binary words of a common length represent machine language instructions. Each word might contain two fields, one for the operation code and one for an address. The operation code specifies the operation to be performed. The address refers to a memory location that the computer will use in performing the operation; data may be stored in the memory location or retrieved from it. The binary word with its two fields can be represented this way:

| OP_CODE | ADDRESS |

(More sophisticated machines use more than one word per instruction and often rely on different formats for different instructions.)

Suppose our simple computer requires a word length of 16 bits. An engineer designing the machine language might reserve 4 bits for the OP_CODE and 12 bits for the ADDRESS. To specify an addition a programmer using this machine language might give an OP_CODE of 0101 (meaning ADD) and an ADDRESS of 001011010011. This would cause the number at this address to be added to a number in the accumulator. (The *accumulator*, you will recall, is a special register or storage place that can hold the results of a logic or numeric operation.) A 4-bit operation code allows 16 different patterns of 4 bits; so this machine could have at most 16 different instructions. Similarly, with a 12-bit address field, it could refer to at most 4,096 memory locations.

Machine language statements found in small computers include instructions to clear the accumulator before a new addition is begun (known by the mnemonic CLEAR); to load a word from memory into the accumulator (LOAD); to store the contents of the accumulator in a memory location (STORE); to perform arithmetic operations (ADD, SUB, MULT, DIV) on the contents of the accumulator and the contents of a memory location; to jump to a new memory location to locate the next instruction (JUMP); or to jump only when the number in the accumulator is positive (JPOS), negative (JNEG), or zero (JZERO). Assembly languages also have commands to permit a jump to a subroutine (JSUB), causing the machine to jump to a new address while saving the address of the next instruction. Another instruction (RETURN) at the end of the subroutine will return to the stored address and continue executing there. In machine language programming, of course, all of these commands are represented not by their mnemonic names but by strings of bits.

Assembly Language

Assembly languages allow programmers to write instructions with mnemonic names (such as those mentioned above) rather than binary strings. Assembly languages also make it possible to refer to addresses with decimal rather than binary numbers or to label addresses and then refer to them by their labels. Programmers can even attach labels to assembly language statements, such as the following:

TEST ADD 127

Here, TEST is a label that rerers to the address of the ADD statement in memory. Rather than remembering the address, the programmer can simply say

```
JUMP TEST
```

and the computer will find the address of the statement with label TEST and jump to it. Here is a simple program that uses TEST:

```
        CLEAR
        LOAD    342
TEST    ADD     127
        JNEG    TEST
        STOP
```

This program clears the accumulator, puts a number from memory location 342 into it, and then adds to that number the contents of a second memory location (127). The instruction ADD 127 is given the label TEST. Thus, JNEG TEST causes the program to jump back to the addition instruction until the addition results in a nonnegative number. When the result in the accumulator is not negative, the program stops.

Assembly language programs may be easier for a person to write, but a computer cannot act on them; it can act only on strings of binary digits. In order for an assembly language program to work, another program, called an *assembler,* must first translate the assembly language program into machine language. Such a program is called an assembler because it assembles, or combines, previously written sections of code. We now outline how an assembler works.

To simplify our outline of the operation of an assembler, we assume that each line of an assembly language program fits into one word of memory and that the first line is placed in the first location in memory. Each line in a program then has a memory address—1, 2, 3, and so on. The first phase of the assembly process is to replace all occurrences of each label with the actual address it represents. In our sample program above, the label TEST would be given the value 3 since it is associated with the third statement in the program. Next the assembler finds each *keyword,* such as LOAD, STORE, ADD, and JUMP, and replaces it with the appropriate sequence of bits. This completes the translation process. Because the labels and mnemonics for instructions translate fairly directly into machine language, assemblers need to be only moderately complex.

Translation of High-Level Languages

Like assembly language programs, programs written in high-level languages must be translated into machine language before the computer can run them. There are three major types of translation. Assembly, for assembly language programs, has already been described. The other two types, compilation and interpretation, are used with high-level language programs. Because compilation and interpretation are similar and because both are very complicated, we will focus on compilation but mention some differences between the two processes.

The compilation process consists of four phases—lexical analysis, syntactic analysis, optimization, and code generation—and is performed by a program called a *compiler*. This process is depicted as follows:

| LEXICAL | → | SYNTACTIC | → | OPTIMIZATION | → | CODE GENERATION |

In *lexical analysis*, the text of a program is scanned and its components are identified by type. In Pascal, for example, *reserved words* (if, else, while, end, and so forth) are identified, as are variables or constants that store data for use by the program. Compilers associate with each word a *token* to describe the category to which the word belongs (much as English grammar categorizes words as nouns, verbs, adjectives, and so on).

Once tokens have been assigned, syntactic analysis can begin. In *syntactic analysis*, streams of tokens are evaluated for the purpose of parsing the program. *Parsing* involves analyzing each statement according to specific rules about the "grammar" of the language. This process helps identify statements that violate these rules.

After it has completed syntactic analysis, the compiler "knows" the meaning of the program and can translate each statement into a machine language statement that the computer can understand. This step, called *code generation*, is the computer equivalent of the translation of an English sentence into a foreign language. Since computer languages, unlike human languages, are designed to be unambiguous and to follow rules without exception, code generation is a much simpler task than translation between two human languages.

Between the syntactic analysis and code generation phases is the optimization phase. *Optimization* is a process by which the compiler modifies a program slightly to improve its efficiency without changing its meaning.

Let us look at some of the steps involved in translating a for loop in Pascal.

```
for counter : = 1 to maximum do
    sum : = sum + counter;
```

The code requires that the CPU execute the body of the loop (one statement) for each value of the integer variable counter from 1 to maximum. The compiler must provide machine language statements to store the value of both counter and maximum in memory, to add 1 to the value of counter after each execution of the loop, to compare the new value of counter to the value of maximum, to loop back if counter does not exceed maximum, and to stop otherwise. Figure 9.1 illustrates the assembly language equivalent for this simple Pascal statement. (We use assembly language statements here instead of the machine language produced by a compiler because it is very similar to machine language but much easier to read.) Note that the compiler tests the condition counter ≤ maximum by subtracting maximum from counter. If the result is negative, the loop executes again, jumping to the symbolic address LOOP. When it converts the assembly language into machine code, the assembler assigns the address LOOP to the instruction that starts the loop.

This example illustrates the conversion of a simple Pascal for loop into a set of assembly language statements. From this point, it can easily be assembled into machine language. In higher-level languages it is not always possible to translate directly from token streams into assembly language, and considerable syntactic analysis may be necessary.

As we have seen, compilation is done all at once. The user may then run the resulting machine language program without seeing or modifying it. When the user modifies the high-level program, the translation process must be repeated and the entire program *recompiled.*

An interpreted language, on the other hand, has an associated translator, called an *interpreter,* that translates each statement individually. It keeps track of all of the information available to the program and translates a command only when the command must be executed. Thus, the user can change a command and immediately execute the

Figure 9.1
A simple loop program in assembly language.

LABELS	OP_CODES	ADDRESSES	COMMENTS
			Beginning of loop body
LOOP	CLEAR		Clear the accumulator
	LOAD	M10	Move SUM from M10 into accumulator
	ADD	M8	Add counter from M8 to accumulator
	STORE	M10	Move SUM plus counter back to M8
	CLEAR		Clear the accumulator
	LOAD	M8	Bring counter into accumulator
	INCR		Increment the value of counter
	STORE	M8	Store the incremented value of counter
	SUB	M9	Subtract maximum at M9 from accumulator
	JNEG	LOOP	If accumulator contents (counter − maximum) are negative, jump to LOOP
			Otherwise, continue to next instruction.

program without having to recompile it entirely, as is required for a compiled language. Interpretation permits programmers to construct and debug programs rapidly, but compilers produce machine language programs that generally run much more quickly. This is because an interpreted program is translated as it is executed.

Although many languages may be both compiled and interpreted, some traditionally use one method or the other. BASIC, LISP, Smalltalk, and PROLOG are typically interpreted languages, while FORTRAN, Pascal, and COBOL are compiled. Today LISPs (there are many dialects) generally have both interpreters and compilers, so programmers may write programs in the interpreted mode and perform final runs in the compiled mode.

Families of Languages

Before discussing individual languages in detail, let us briefly consider how types of languages differ. As mentioned earlier, computer scientists classify programming languages by level, speaking of low-level, high-level, and very-high-level languages. The level of a language reflects how far removed its instructions are from the machine language understood by the computer. Thus, we consider assembly languages low-level, and FORTRAN, Smalltalk, COBOL, Pascal, BASIC, LISP, and Ada high-level. The high-level languages received that label when computer scientists first began to assign levels to languages; people classifying these languages today might call them intermediate-level languages. The label *high-level* stuck, however; so another term was needed to indicate higher-level languages. Therefore, PROLOG belongs to the class known as very-high-level languages.

We can also describe languages by the *conceptual model* reflected in their construction. Figure 9.2 classifies a number of languages ac-

Figure 9.2
Language levels and conceptual models.

LEVEL	PROCEDURES	SYMBOLS	OBJECTS	RULES
Low	Assembly			
High	FORTRAN, COBOL ALGOL, BASIC, Pascal ADA, Modula-2	LISP	Smalltalk	
Very high				PROLOG

cording to conceptual models as well as levels. Assembly language, FORTRAN, COBOL, Pascal, BASIC, and Ada are largely *procedure-oriented* languages; they focus on the process required to solve the problem. Programmers using these languages are encouraged to view programs as extended CPUs that take data from memory, operate on the data, and return the results to memory.

LISP, by contrast, supports the conceptual model of *symbol manipulation*. LISP cannot distinguish between data and program instructions, just as computers at the lowest level cannot tell whether strings of bits represent data or an instruction. In LISP every object, be it program, data, or a mixture of the two, is a *symbolic expression*, that is, a list of symbols. LISP is a language designed expressly to solve problems in artificial intelligence, which involves activities that simulate intelligent behavior, such as using logic, reasoning, and responding to questions based on previously recorded factual information.

The language Smalltalk is *object-oriented*. It views the world as a set of communicating objects each with its own internal methods of operating on data. Users request action via messages to objects; the objects then return messages containing the results of the action. This model of computation encourages a structured and organized style of programming.

The conceptual model reflected in the very-high-level language PROLOG is *rule-based*. The programmer states deductive rules, gives some specific data on which the rules operate, and then makes an inference. The system examines various ways of applying the rules to see if it can confirm or reject the inference. The programmer tells the program what to do, not how to do it. This is an example of a *nonprocedural language*. Other examples are given in Chapter 10.

■ Important Programming Languages

The conceptual models just described suggest the purposes for which languages were invented. FORTRAN was designed for scientific calculation and COBOL for business purposes such as file handling. Procedure-oriented languages are well suited to performing such straightforward tasks. LISP was introduced to solve problems in the field that is now known as artificial intelligence. Problems in this area deal with symbolic information as opposed to the numerical information used in scientific computation. Thus, LISP uses symbolic expressions. All three of these languages are described in more detail later in the chapter.

FORTRAN, COBOL, and LISP were among the first high-level languages developed. Other languages that are important historically include ALGOL-60 and PL/I. The design of ALGOL (for *algo*rithmic language), a language for scientific computation, was completed by a small international team of computer scientists in 1960. Their objective was to produce a standard scientific programming language that would meet three conditions: it would be largely machine-independent, that is, capable of being run on a great variety of computers; it would be understandable by anyone familiar with mathematical notation; and it would be readily translated by a machine. If the language could meet these conditions, it could be used by scientists all over the world on many different computers. ALGOL was a great scientific success; it introduced many new concepts to programming language and set a standard for language design that is still used today. ALGOL failed commercially, however, in part because it did not provide commands for input and output (these were left to programmers of individual machines) and in part because IBM chose to support its competing scientific programming language, FORTRAN, rather than to adopt ALGOL.

PL/I (an acronym for Programming Language/One), developed in the early 1960s, combines features of FORTRAN, COBOL, and ALGOL-60. It is a very large language—some say too large—that has been widely used for a great variety of scientific and business applications. Not only is the language large, but it must be learned in its entirety to be used confidently. It is possible to learn and use small portions of it, but there are often subtle and unpredictable interactions between instructions, and such side effects occasionally produce unexpected results. For these reasons it has been unpopular with many influential computer scientists.

About the time PL/I was being developed, a team at Dartmouth University was developing BASIC as a teaching language. BASIC, described in Chapter 7, is widely used today on microcomputers. Although the original version, a highly simplified version of FORTRAN, was limited in its usefulness, later versions included many features that make it more useful for serious programming. The language does not lend itself well to the use of structured programming techniques, however.

Pascal, described in Chapter 8, was developed in the late 1960s. Its developer sought to keep the better features of ALGOL, discard the others, and incorporate new methods of describing data to make the language suitable for handling nonnumeric data. Thus, it would be useful for both business and scientific applications. The developer also hoped to create a language that could be translated efficiently into machine language and that would be a good vehicle for teaching programming languages. Pascal's success is demonstrated by its growing popularity.

Smalltalk, described later in this chapter, was designed to make the computer accessible to the nonspecialist. Alan Kay developed the first version of Smalltalk, called Smalltalk-72, in the early 1970s. Kay sought to emulate the success of LOGO, a language used by small children for simple tasks (described in Chapter 11). Smalltalk is object-oriented; objects communicate with one another through messages that send and request information. As a result, the language is more conversational, unlike procedural languages, in which the programmer must command the machine. At this time, Smalltalk is a scientific but not a commercial success. It continues to influence language development but is used only experimentally.

Ada, named in honor of Ada Augusta, Countess of Lovelace, is a very recently developed language commissioned by the U.S. Department of Defense to cope with a "software crisis" that emerged in the 1970s. Programs were growing rapidly in size and complexity, yet the number of computer scientists trained to write them was inadequate. Ada, completed in 1980, is distinctive because it was the first prominent procedural language to provide a facility for abstract data types. *Abstract data types* consist of variables for storing data and methods for accessing the data. The only way for an external procedure to access the variables in an abstract data type is to use one of the methods provided by the abstract data type. The actual implementation of the method is unknown outside the abstract data type, although the effect of using it is known.

It is not clear what the future holds for Ada. It is a large and rich language with many features that have not been fully tested in smaller languages. In the short run, the support of the U.S. Department of Defense will undoubtedly ensure that Ada is widely used.

Modula-2 is another language that supports data abstraction through the use of the module concept. It was developed by Pascal's creator around the same time the definition of Ada was completed. Modula-2 shares many features with Pascal; however, it also provides modules with separate definition and implementation parts so that the details of implementation need not be specified by the user. Modula-2 is a considerably smaller language than Ada. As a result compilers for Modula-2 exist today on many different machines, whereas compilers for Ada have been slow to appear and then have generally been slow to compile. Modula-2 is becoming a popular language for instruction.

A language designed to simplify programming in mathematical logic, PROLOG, is also receiving considerable attention. The Japanese may make it the programming language for their fifth-generation computer project, discussed in Chapter 12. Using PROLOG, a programmer can state problems without having to describe how the problems should be solved. This is an attractive feature for those who would like to write programs very quickly. However, the style of programming required in PROLOG is quite different from that used with conventional programming languages. As yet the language has not been widely used, so it is not clear whether it will gain widespread acceptance. PROLOG is discussed in more detail in the last section of this chapter.

■ The FORTRAN Language

In the 1950s, a number of programming languages were developed for scientific and business applications. Through trial and error, languages of lasting importance, such as FORTRAN and COBOL, emerged.

FORTRAN (for *formula translating* system) was developed under the leadership of John Backus of IBM and released in 1957. With only a few minor modifications, the programming community enthusiastically accepted FORTRAN by 1958, and FORTRAN IV, a dialect completed in 1966, is still the most widely used language for scientific computation. Its success can be attributed to three factors: excellent documentation provided with the first release of FORTRAN, a compiler that produced very efficient machine language, and the adoption of FORTRAN as a standard IBM language. Another factor in FORTRAN's continued popularity is that a large number of programs have already been written in it.

FORTRAN has much in common with Pascal, although a few sophisticated features of Pascal are absent from FORTRAN. A simple FORTRAN program, given in Fig. 9.3, should allow you to compare some features of FORTRAN, Pascal, and BASIC. Comment statements are set off by the character C in the first column. This program prints a triangle of characters (the exact character determined by the value of the variable ANYCHAR) in a two-dimensional four-by-seven array. All elements of the array that are not part of the triangle contain the value of the variable BLANK, the second variable read in from the keyboard. The first row of the triangle consists of a single centered instance of ANYCHAR, and the second, third, and fourth rows contain, respectively, three, five, and seven centered ANYCHARs. The remaining characters in the four-by-seven array are the value of BLANK. This is illustrated in Fig. 9.4, which shows three executions of the compiled program. In the first, ANYCHAR is & and BLANK is #; in the second they are (blank space) and *; and in the third they are * and (blank space). Here % is the prompt and a.out is the name of the compiled program.

```
C    ------------------------------------------------------------------------------  C
C                                                                                    C
C    THIS PROGRAM READS TWO CHARACTERS. IT PRINTS                                    C
C    A 4×7 TRIANGLE OF THE FIRST CHARACTER                                           C
C    USING CHARACTERS OF THE SECOND TYPE AS SPACERS                                  C
C                                                                                    C
C    ------------------------------------------------------------------------------  C

             DIMENSION TRIANGLE(7)
             LENGTH=7
             MID=(LENGTH + 1)/2
             WRITE(6,5)
5            FORMAT('TYPE ANY TWO CHARACTERS ON THE SAME LINE')
             READ(5,10),ANYCHAR,BLANK
10           FORMAT(2A1)
C
C    SET ALL ENTRIES IN THE ARRAY TRIANGLE TO 'BLANK'
C
             DO 40 J = 1, LENGTH
40           TRIANGLE(J) = BLANK
C
C    SET THE MIDDLE ENTRY TO 'ANYCHAR' AND PRINT THE ARRAY
C    THEN SET THOSE ON EITHER SIDE TO 'ANYCHAR' AND PRINT
C    THE ARRAY. REPEAT THE ABOVE STEP UNTIL ALL ENTRIES
C    IN THE ARRAY ARE 'ANYCHAR'
C
             DO 50 I = 1,MID
             LLOWER = MID - (I-1)
             LUPPER = MID + (I-1)
             TRIANGLE(LLOWER) = ANYCHAR
             TRIANGLE(LUPPER) = ANYCHAR
C            NOW WRITE OUT THE ARRAY TRIANGLE
50           WRITE(6,60) (TRIANGLE(K), K = 1, LENGTH)
60           FORMAT(7A1)
             STOP
             END
```

Figure 9.3
A FORTRAN program to print a triangle.

```
TYPE ANY TWO CHARACTERS ON THE SAME LINE
& #
# # # & # # #
# # & & & # #
# & & & & & #
& & & & & & &
```

```
TYPE ANY TWO CHARACTERS ON THE SAME LINE
  *

*** ***
**   **
*     *
```

```
TYPE ANY TWO CHARACTERS ON THE SAME LINE
*
    *
  ***
 *****
******
```

Figure 9.4
Sample executions of the FORTRAN program in Fig. 9.3.

The program of Fig. 9.3 uses a DIMENSION statement to specify the length of an array, just as BASIC does. Input to the program comes from a READ statement, and output occurs with a WRITE statement. The lines labeled 10 and 60 contain format statements that help determine the nature of the output. This program also demonstrates the use of a DO loop, the FORTRAN equivalent of Pascal's for loop and BASIC's FOR-NEXT loop.

The FORTRAN statement

    DO 40 J = 1, LENGTH

will cause all statements following DO up to and including the statement on line 40 to be executed in a loop. J is a loop counter whose value starts at 1 and increases by 1 each time the loop is executed. When J exceeds the value of LENGTH, the execution of the loop ends. FORTRAN also allows the use of subroutines, functions, and conditional branching.

Figure 9.5 shows another FORTRAN program. This one performs

```
C    --------------------------------------------------------------------------  C
C                                                                               C
C    THIS PROGRAM READS IN A SERIES OF                                          C
C    GRADES AND COMPUTES THEIR AVERAGE                                          C
C                                                                               C
C    --------------------------------------------------------------------------  C


         SUM = 0
         COUNT = 0
C
         WRITE(6,1)
1        FORMAT('THIS PROGRAM AVERAGES A LIST OF NUMERIC GRADES')
         WRITE(6,2)
2        FORMAT('TYPE IN THE GRADES ONE AT A TIME')
         WRITE(6,3)
3        FORMAT('TYPE IN A NEGATIVE NUMBER WHEN ALL OF THE GRADES')
         WRITE(6,4)
4        FORMAT('HAVE BEEN ENTERED')
C
10       WRITE(6,20)
20       FORMAT('GRADE: ')
         READ(5,30) GRADE
30       FORMAT(F5.2)
C        GO TO 50 IF NEGATIVE GRADE ENTERED. OTHERWISE CONTINUE
         IF (GRADE) 50, 40, 40
40       SUM = SUM + GRADE
         COUNT = COUNT + 1
         GOTO 10
50       AVERAGE = SUM/COUNT
         WRITE(6,60) AVERAGE
60       FORMAT('THE AVERAGE IS ',F5.2)
         STOP
         END
```

Figure 9.5
A grade-averaging program.

the same task as the Pascal GradeAverage program in Chapter 8. The COBOL program given in Fig. 9.6 closely resembles this FORTRAN program.

Although more recent languages are easier to learn, FORTRAN remains a popular language for scientific purposes, perhaps because of the large number of programs already written in it.

```
IDENTIFICATION DIVISION.
PROGRAM-ID.                                  GRADE-AVERAGE.
ENVIRONMENT DIVISION.
CONFIGURATION SECTION.
SOURCE-COMPUTER.                             IBM-370.
OBJECT-COMPUTER.                             IBM-370.
INPUT-OUTPUT SECTION.
FILE-CONTROL.
      SELECT CARD-FILE ASSIGN TO UT-S-CRDFL.
      SELECT PRINT-FILE ASSIGN TO UT-S-PRTFL.
DATA DIVISION.
FILE SECTION.
FD CARD-FILE
    LABEL RECORDS ARE OMITTED
      DATA RECORD IS GRADE-CARD.
*
01   GRADE-CARD.
     02 NUMBR                                PIC 999V99.
     02 FILLER                               PIC X(75).

FD PRINT-FILE
     LABEL RECORDS ARE OMITTED
     DATA RECORD IS OUTPUT-LINE.
*
01   OUTPUT-LINE.
     02 FILLER                               PIC X(20).
     02 AVERAGE                              PIC 99999.99.
     02 FILLER                               PIC X(106).

WORKING-STORAGE SECTION.
77   TOT                                     PIC 99999V99.
77   CNTR                                    PIC 999.
*
PROCEDURE DIVISION.
      OPEN INPUT CARD-FILE,
      OUTPUT PRINT-FILE.
      MOVE ZEROS TO TOT, CNTR.
*
010-START-OF-LOOP.
      READ CARD-FILE
      AT END GO TO 020-FINISH.
      ADD NUMBR TO TOT.
      ADD 1 TO CNTR.
      GO TO 010-START-OF-LOOP.
020-FINISH.
      MOVE SPACES TO OUTPUT-LINE.
      DIVIDE TOT BY CNTR GIVING AVERAGE.
      WRITE OUTPUT-LINE AFTER ADVANCING 2 LINES.
      CLOSE CARD-FILE,
            PRINT-FILE.
      STOP RUN.
```

Figure 9.6
A sample COBOL program.

■ The COBOL Language

COBOL (for common business-oriented language) was developed in a six-month period, between June and December 1959, by a team of representatives from business, academia, and the U.S. Department of Defense. The team came together to design an English-like business-oriented language that they hoped would become a standard for business computation. This goal has been met many times over. Not only has the Department of Defense adopted COBOL as a standard, but programmers now have written more lines of code in COBOL than in any other language. It is still very widely used today.

In an early demonstration of COBOL, several companies in 1960 produced translators for COBOL and then ran the same program, only slightly modified to reflect local conditions, on different computers and got the same results. At that time this was a considerable achievement. The involvement of the Department of Defense and its insistence on compatible translators ensured COBOL's success as a standard language. Except for a few modifications, the version of COBOL used today is the same as the original version, providing English-like phrases in a procedure-oriented environment.

The designers of COBOL set as their goal the development of a language that was as much like English as possible so that novices could learn it quickly. The result is a verbose language that results in a "self-documenting" code. Figure 9.6 illustrates this feature as well as the four main components of COBOL programs—the identification division, the environment division, the data division, and the procedure division. The identification division provides the name of the program. The environment division describes the type of computer on which the program will be translated (SOURCE-COMPUTER) and the type on which it will be run (OBJECT-COMPUTER). It also describes the devices on which input will be found and on which output will be placed, as well as the input/output techniques that will be used. The data division describes the data the program will use while running and allocates a fixed space for each piece of data. In the example, two file descriptors (FD) are used to describe the input and output files. Both files are said to be unlabeled. The data records are given names (GRADE-CARD and OUTPUT-LINE) and the format of the records defined. For example, the entry NUMBR is shown (by PIC, or picture) to be a decimal number with three digits before the decimal point (indicated by V) and two after it. The procedure division contains the executable statements.

This program averages a list of grades by adding them together and dividing the sum by the number of grades. Within the procedure division the program opens input and output files. This means that it tells the operating system that it wants data from the file CARD-FILE and that it will send data to the file PRINT-FILE. It then sets the two variables TOT and CNTR to zero and begins a loop. TOT will be used to hold the cumulative sum of the grades, and CNTR will contain the number of grades read in. The loop reads one line from the CARD-FILE, checks to see if this is the last line of the CARD-FILE, and goes to the line labeled FINISH if it is. If it isn't, the first entry on the current line of the CARD-FILE, NUMBR, is added to the variable TOT. CNTR is then incremented by 1, and the loop is repeated. When the loop has been completed, spaces are put in the output file and the value of TOT is divided by the value of CNTR, giving the result AVERAGE, which is printed after two lines have been skipped. Finally, the two files that were open are closed, and the program is stopped.

Because everything in a COBOL program must be described before the program statements can be written, writing programs in COBOL can take longer than writing programs in other procedure-oriented languages. (Compare, for example, the length of this COBOL program with the length of the Pascal grade-averaging program in Chapter 8, which performs almost the same function.) To write different programs for the same machine in COBOL, much information must be repeated from program to program. A more modern approach allows compilers to provide this sort of information for the machine, freeing the programmer to concentrate on programming the computer.

■ The LISP Language

LISP (for *list p*rocessing language) is a language for symbol manipulation. It was developed in the late 1950s by John McCarthy to support research in artificial intelligence. The language, distinctive for its elegance, simplicity, and coherence, models programs and data as lists. LISP can build complex commands by applying the results of one command to another. Because it is an interpreted language, commands are translated into machine language as they are executed, greatly simplifying the process of modification and debugging. LISP programs can also be compiled for efficiency.

LISP represents both data and programs as lists called *S-expressions* (for symbolic expressions), which can contain subexpressions or lists. The lowest-level unit in the language is the atom, which can be an integer (such as 5), a function (such as PLUS), or a string of one or more letters and digits. An example of LISP data is '(A B C D), in which A, B, C, and D are atoms. An example of a LISP function is (PLUS 2 3). If a user types this expression while using LISP's interpreter, LISP will print out the sum of 2 and 3, as follows:

```
% (PLUS 2 3)
5
%
```

The percent sign (%) is LISP's *prompt,* indicating that the program is waiting for the user to type something in. Notice that the function name, PLUS, appears first in the S-expression, followed by the relevant values. This is an example of *prefix notation,* in which the operator precedes the values to be operated on.

LISP has a number of arithmetic functions, such as TIMES and QUOTIENT, which are used exactly as PLUS is. Programmers can *nest* S-expressions, using the result of one S-expression in the body of another:

```
(QUOTIENT (TIMES 2 3) (PLUS 1 2))
```

LISP interprets this expression as $(2 \times 3) / (1 + 2)$. Note that LISP evaluates a function by evaluating each of its parts and then applying the function to them, repeating the procedure as often as necessary, depending on the degree of nesting. An expression that is not meant to be evaluated in this way must be *quoted,* or preceded by an apostrophe, as in '(A B C D).

CAR and CDR are two list operators that play very important roles in LISP. CAR prints out, or returns as a result, the first element in a list, and CDR returns the list of remaining elements. Thus, CAR returns an element of a list (which might also be a list) and CDR always returns a list. The empty list, known as the atom NIL or (), is another important feature. NIL appears at the end of a list when the list is exhausted. For example, when evaluating (CDR '(A)), LISP returns the value NIL because the list is exhausted after the first element has been deleted.

To construct lists, LISP provides a small set of list constructors. One of these, CONS, combines two items, attaching the second item to the first and returning the new list:

```
% (CONS '(A (B C)) '(E F (G (H I))))
((A (B C)) E F (G (H I)))
%
```

LISP includes several predicate functions that return T for true and NIL for false. (Note that () or NIL does double duty, serving as both the end-of-list symbol and the Boolean value false.) These predicate functions can decide whether given S-expressions are atoms or can test if one number is greater than another.

LISP assigns values to atoms as a side effect of the function SET.

The statement (SET 'A '(B (C D))) returns the value (B, (C D)), assigning this value to the atom A. When a user subsequently types in A, LISP evaluates it and returns the response (B, (C D)).

You may have noticed that LISP uses many functions. A *function* is a name for a series of steps. The use of a function's name causes the steps in the function to be executed. In the following illustration, DEFUN (*def*ine *fun*ction) indicates that a function is being defined:

```
(DEFUN F-TO-C (TEMP)
   (QUOTIENT (- TEMP 32) 1.8))
```

This function is called F-TO-C because it converts a temperature from Fahrenheit to Celsius. The name of the function appears just after DEFUN. The expression (TEMP) indicates that TEMP is a *parameter* of this function, that is, data used by the function for computation. Next comes the definition of the function, in which 32 is subtracted from TEMP and the result is divided by 1.8. Once the function F-TO-C has been defined, it can be used in programming. The command (F-TO-C 68), for example, will convert 68 degrees Fahrenheit to its Celsius equivalent, 20 degrees.

It is common in LISP to use functions to operate on lists. The function SENTENCE-MOD, which modifies a sentence by replacing a noun with a noun phrase, illustrates this procedure. SENTENCE-MOD takes two parameters, NOUN-PHRASE and SENTENCE, both of which are lists, and replaces the second element in SENTENCE with the elements in the list NOUN-PHRASE. For example, if NOUN-PHRASE is (LITTLE GIRL) and SENTENCE is (THE BOY JUMPED UP), the result is (THE LITTLE GIRL JUMPED UP).

The function SENTENCE-MOD is defined as follows:

```
(DEFUN SENTENCE-MOD (NOUN-PHRASE SENTENCE)
(APPEND (CONS (CAR SENTENCE) NOUN-PHRASE) (CDR (CDR SEN-
TENCE))))
```

The command APPEND joins the elements of separate lists into a single list. It operates on the results of the two commands that follow it. The first of these commands, (CONS (CAR SENTENCE) NOUN-PHRASE), builds a new list consisting of the first element of the list SENTENCE and the elements of the list NOUN-PHRASE. The next command, (CDR (CDR SENTENCE)), returns a list that is the list SENTENCE with the first two elements removed. The action of this function on a string is illustrated by the following example:

```
% (SET 'NEWSENTENCE '(THE BOY JUMPED UP))
(THE BOY JUMPED UP)
% (SENTENCE-MOD '(LITTLE GIRL) NEWSENTENCE)
(THE LITTLE GIRL JUMPED UP)
```

The first line sets the atom NEWSENTENCE to the string (THE BOY JUMPED UP). LISP responds with the value of the resulting expression. Then we apply the function SENTENCE-MOD to the string NEWSENTENCE with the parameter (LITTLE GIRL). The value returned is shown on the last line.

LISP includes many other language constructs, but space does not permit us to present them here.

The Smalltalk-80 Language

Smalltalk-80 is the product of about a decade of research and development by the Software Concepts Group at the Xerox Palo Alto Research Center. It owes its existence to the vision of Alan Kay, who formulated the first version of the system, Smalltalk-72, in the early 1970s. Smalltalk-80 provides an interactive programming environment that depends heavily on the use of computer graphics and personal workstations. It is most interesting as an attempt to create not just a new language but a new programming environment. The Smalltalk environment was the first to extensively use the concept of windows. *Windows* are portions of the computer screen in which different activities can be performed; with several windows "opened," a user can read electronic mail in one, write a program in another, and perform other operations in others. Smalltalk also encourages a modular approach to programming, which generally leads to well-designed programs.

Smalltalk-80 embodies an idea introduced in an earlier language called SIMULA. This idea is the concept of an object, an entity that consists of some memory and a set of operations. The memory, called *private memory*, is used only by that object; it cannot be used by other objects. Objects send messages to one another and receive messages in return. Objects can represent numbers, dictionaries, programs, text editors, or anything else one cares to define. Through messages, objects request services from other objects. These services typically require access to and modification of the private memories of objects. However, a requesting object cannot itself access or modify that memory. Instead the owning object does this using its local procedures. The effect is to hide the exact representation of data within objects and the methods objects use to access it. Thus, a request can be provided in one of many ways. A text editor object may request a list of words with the prefix *histo* from the dictionary object; however, it need not know how this list is obtained by the dictionary object. A consequence of the fact that objects have no direct access to the private memory of other objects is that no sharing of data between objects is possible.

Objects in Smalltalk-80 have names. The object named *frame* might contain information about the frame around the active window (the window containing the cursor) on a personal workstation. This frame has position and size. Messages also have names. The message named center might refer to a message that could be sent to the object frame by some other object. It would return the coordinates of the center of frame. Smalltalk-80 provides a set of rules for creating messages. These rules result in expressions. For example, the two-word expression frame center means send to the object frame the message center. The result will be a return message to the sender containing the coordinates of the center of the frame.

Consider another example. In Smalltalk-80 there are no variables outside of objects. If one object needs a value that is held by another object, it must send a message to that object to retrieve it. Suppose an object called index is an integer, and another object would like to increase it by some value, say the value held by the integer offset. The expression index + offset will produce the desired effect. The message that is returned to the sender is the sum of the integers associated with these objects. The sum then must be sent to index to replace the old value.

Smalltalk-80 also includes *assignment statements* for assigning values to variables inside objects. The statement newcenter ← frame center, for example, assigns to the variable newcenter the result of the message center applied to the object frame.

In addition to objects and messages, Smalltalk-80 employs a concept known as class. An object within a class is called an *instance* of that class. Classes are useful in much the same way as arrays. If a programmer plans to use many instances of an object that are identical except for names and private memories, then it makes sense to define a class to include these instances. That way, the programmer will not need to retype the entire definition of the object for each instance. For example, if the two objects index and counter are both examples of integers, both definitions will have to include methods to increase and decrease them and report values. The programmer can create a class called Integer and make index and counter instances of that class. Then they can share definitions.

Again, since objects in Smalltalk-80 cannot share variables, values that are going to be shared must be located inside objects, and methods must be available to access and modify them. As suggested, each instance of a class has a private memory recorded in its instance variables. When a message is sent to an object, a method is invoked. A *method* is a procedure used inside an object to operate on its instance variables and to return results.

Figure 9.7 shows an example of a class called Point. Instances of this class record internally the coordinates of a point in two dimensions.

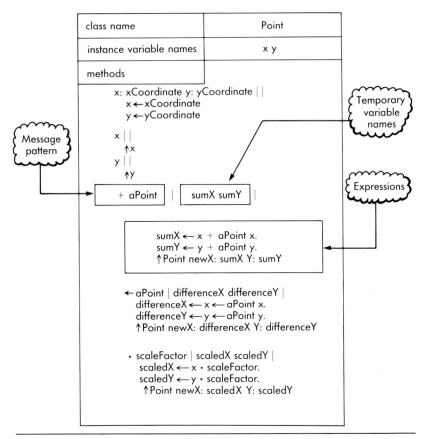

Figure 9.7
A simple Smalltalk class template. (Printed with permission of the Xerox Corporation)

Each instance has a unique name and unique values for instance variables. The instance variables for this class, x and y, record the point's two components. Six methods are associated with the class, and every instance of the class includes each method. The first method is x:_ y:_, which consists of the keywords x: and y:, each followed by an integer. When a message that takes the form x:_ y:_ is sent to an object of the class Point, the object resets its x and y coordinates, as indicated by the notation x ←xCoordinate, y ←yCoordinate at the top of Fig. 9.7. The second and third messages in the figure are simply x and y and return the values of these two components. (Vertical bars in the figure separate various sections.)

The last three methods are similar to one another, so we describe only one of them: + aPoint. Here + denotes a message and aPoint is an instance of the class Point. It has two coordinates, aPoint x and aPoint y. The method associated with this message updates the x and y coordinates of the instance in question. To do so, it must use instance variables, called sumX and sumY. The method updates the instance variables and then with the expression ↑Point new X: sumX Y: sumY replaces the old values of the coordinates with the new values.

As indicated earlier, Smalltalk-80 provides an environment as well as a programming language. The environment runs on personal workstations equipped with high-resolution displays, a keyboard, and a mouse. It is very user-friendly, employing overlapping windows, pop-up menus, and many advanced graphical interaction techniques.

■ The PROLOG Language

Philippe Roussel developed PROLOG in 1972 to support programming in mathematical logic, usually called *logic programming.* In the parlance of artificial intelligence research, PROLOG leads to *rule-based programming.* Both terms imply that the programmer supplies rules of inference for the program to use, initial data or hypotheses, and goals whose truth the program will test. The programmer does not specify how the truth of the goals will be tested because PROLOG contains built-in truth-testing methods.

Pure PROLOG, unmodified to account for the efficiency of execution, is a truly *nonprocedural language.* As mentioned, the programmer has no way to state the procedures for testing a goal; PROLOG may follow the rules given in any order. For those seeking truly high-level languages that nonprogrammers can use, PROLOG is very attractive. Researchers in the Japanese fifth-generation computer project (discussed in Chapter 12) have decided to use a language that allows logic programming and are considering some form of PROLOG for this purpose.

The language is best understood from an example, which we give in Fig. 9.8. The figure shows a PROLOG program with three sections separated by blank lines. The first section contains rules of inference, the second contains the initial hypotheses, and the third contains the goal. Rules of inference specify the rules for deducing relationships. Hypotheses provide particular information or data. Goals are conditions we hope can be met.

The purpose of this program, as stated by the goal, is to determine whether john is the parent of a child with a sibling named virginia. Another way to put the question is this: Does john have a child virginia and, if so, what are the names of her siblings? The rules of inference state

```
parent(Name, Childname) :- father(Name, Childname).
parent(Name, Childname) :- mother(Name, Childname).
sibling(Childname1, Childname2) :- mother(Mothername, Childname1),
                                    mother(Mothername, Childname2),
                                    father(Fathername, Childname1),
                                    father(Fathername, Childname2).


father(john, edmund).
father(john, kevin).
father(edmund, paul).
father(edmund, virginia).
father(edmund, richard).
mother(ann, virginia).
mother(ann, paul).


?- parent(john, UnknownName), sibling(UnknownName, virginia).
```

Figure 9.8
A sample PROLOG program.

conditions that determine whether a person is the parent of a child. To be a parent, a person must be either the father or the mother of a child. Since either condition establishes parentage, the conditions are stated on separate lines that end with periods. The rules of inference also state that for two persons to be siblings, they must have common parents.

Let's now examine each of the rules of inference. The first rule states that the person with name Name is the parent of the person with name Childname if Name is the father of Childname. (The pattern :- between the two parts of this line is called an arrow. A statement to the left of an arrow is true if all the statements to the right are true.) The second rule states the same condition for mothers. Since the two conditions appear separated by periods, Name is the parent of Childname if either rule applies. The third rule defines the sibling relationship by stating that two siblings must have the same father and mother. Because the conditions that specify the sibling relationship are preceded by only one arrow and are separated by commas, all these conditions must apply if the statement to the left of the arrow is to be judged true.

The data on which the rules can operate follow in the hypothesis section, which provides the particular information to be used by the rules of inference to determine whether the goals can be satisfied. (For example, john is said to be the father of edmund.) The third category of information in this example is a single goal. This goal is to determine the name of the person or persons, if any, who have john as parent and who are siblings of virginia.

The PROLOG system is free to pursue any of the rules and hypotheses in any order as it tries to match them against the conditions stated in the goal. Basic types of matching include *bottom-up* and *top-down*. The top-down approach starts with the goals; the bottom-up approach, with the hypotheses.

The top-down approach compares the left-hand side of the rules with the goals and selects preconditions that must be true. For example, a comparison of the goal conditions parent(john, UnknownName) with the first and second rules suggests that either father(john, UnknownName) or mother(john, UnknownName) must hold. Since neither of these subgoals matches the left-hand side of a rule, however, PROLOG must try matching against the hypotheses. Clearly, the second subgoal, mother(john, UnknownName), is not consistent with the hypotheses; but the first produces father(john, edmund) and father(john, kevin), either of which may be true, since both are consistent with parent(john, UnknownName). Thus, this subgoal produces two potential values for UnknownName, namely edmund and kevin.

Comparing the second half of the goal, sibling(UnknownName, virginia), with the right-hand side of the third rule produces the subgoals mother(Mothername, UnknownName), mother(Mothername, virginia), father(Fathername, UnknownName), and father(Fathername, virginia). All these subgoals must be met, as explained earlier. None of the subgoals can be matched against the left-hand side of the rules, so the program again attempts to match against the hypotheses, producing mother(ann, UnknownName), mother(ann, virginia), father(edmund, UnknownName), and father(edmund, virginia). There is only one solution for UnknownName other than virginia, namely paul. However, this value for UnknownName does not correspond with the two values provided by the first subgoal. Therefore the goal itself is not obtainable.

Like the top-down approach, the bottom-up approach generates many subgoals. These arise when the hypotheses are substituted into the left-hand sides of the rules—just the reverse of the top-down procedure. We will not present all of the steps in the bottom-up approach here.

The top-down and bottom-up approaches can differ greatly in the time they take. It is known that for fairly simple problems one method can take much more time than the other. Thus, even though PROLOG is said to be nonprocedural, most practical versions of PROLOG provide the programmer with methods to control the type of searching that will be used. Thus, a purely nonprocedural language is not a practical possibility.

Although PROLOG may seem to be a fairly simple language, it is in fact very powerful, encompassing everything that can be done in LISP. In fact, every procedural language can be encoded within

PROLOG. However, PROLOG does have limitations on execution speed. The possibility that the Japanese fifth-generation computer project may use PROLOG means that the language will probably receive a great deal of attention in the near future.

SUMMARY

Programming languages are sets of instructions to direct the activity of computers. They range in complexity from machine language, the lowest-level language understood by a computer, to very-high-level languages in which a problem is stated without providing a procedure for solving it. A great variety of programming languages has been developed to serve a great variety of needs.

Machine language instructions are strings of ones and zeros understood by the computer. Each instruction contains an operation code; most instructions also contain an address. An operation code tells the computer which of its instructions is to be executed, and an address specifies the location in which to find a value on which to operate. Since machine languages are very difficult to use, assembly languages were developed. They permit programmers to use mnemonic names for binary operation codes and to refer to program statements with labels rather than by the addresses of the statements in memory. These two features greatly reduce the chance of errors in programming. Assembly languages have the structure of machine languages and so are easy to translate into machine languages.

High-level language programs must also be translated into machine language before they can be executed. There are two types of translators for high-level languages: compilers and interpreters. A compiler produces a machine language program from a high-level program by translating all of the statements in the program in one step. This has the disadvantage that a change in a high-level program requires that the program be recompiled. It has the advantage that a compiled program will run fast once it has been translated. An interpreter produces a machine language program by translating each statement individually into machine language. This has the advantage that a change in a high-level program is incorporated immediately, but it has the disadvantage that the program is translated as it is executed, making execution much slower than for a compiled language.

Programming languages can be classified into different families based on the conceptual model that they embody. These families include procedure-oriented languages, symbolic-expression languages, object-oriented languages, and rule-based or nonprocedural languages.

Within each family, languages are distinguished by several factors, including their level.

This chapter has examined five languages in some detail: FORTRAN, COBOL, LISP, Smalltalk-80, and PROLOG. FORTRAN and COBOL are both high-level procedure-oriented languages developed in the 1950s and widely used today. FORTRAN is used primarily for scientific computations; COBOL is used in business. LISP, a high-level symbolic-expression language, was developed in the late 1950s to support research in artificial intelligence, and it continues to be the primary vehicle for developing software in this field.

Smalltalk-80 is a high-level object-oriented programming environment that relies on graphics and the personal workstation. It was developed with the specific goal of making computers accessible to nonspecialists. PROLOG is a very-high-level nonprocedural language and will be instrumental in the next generation of computers. Programs in PROLOG are stated in the form of rules. A built-in search procedure is used to determine whether a given hypothesis is consistent with the rules.

FURTHER READING

Adele Goldberg and David Robson, *Smalltalk-80: The Language and Its Implementation* (Reading, Mass.: Addison-Wesley, 1983).

Bruce J. MacLennan, *Principles of Programming Languages: Design, Evaluation, and Implementation* (New York: Holt, Rinehart and Winston, 1983).

Richard L. Wexelblat, ed., *History of Programming Languages* (New York: Academic Press, 1981).

Patrick H. Winston and Berthold K. Horn, *LISP* (Reading, Mass.: Addison-Wesley, 1984).

Niklaus Wirth, *Programming in Modula-2* (New York: Springer-Verlag, 1983).

ISSUES AND IDEAS

1. In Chapter 3 we described the pocket calculator computer (PCC). Invent mnemonic names for commands used by the PCC.

2. Explain why a programmer would prefer to write a program in assembly language rather than in a high-level language such as Pascal.

3. Compilation and interpretation are two ways to translate programs in high-level languages to machine language. Explain the advantages of each method.

4. Programming languages are classified by conceptual models in Fig. 9.2. Describe a problem that is particularly well suited to each model. Justify your answers.

5. Modify the FORTRAN program in Fig. 9.3 to print an inverted triangle.

6. Define a LISP function to modify a sentence containing a noun and a verb by replacing the verb with a verb phrase. Such a function would be similar to the one in the text that replaces a noun with a noun phrase.

7. Write a simple PROLOG program to determine whether the grandfather relationship holds between individuals. Pattern your solution on the example in Fig. 9.8.

Software Systems

Knowledge is power, and the computer
is an amplifier of that power.

EDWARD FEIGENBAUM and PAMELA
McCORDUCK, *The Fifth Generation*

■ Introduction

Most computer users do not write their own programs. Instead, they
rely on special-purpose programs written by others. Through a process
akin to natural selection, the better-prepared or better-advertised software has succeeded in the marketplace. The result is readily available
software that in most cases is vastly superior to that which individuals
could produce themselves.

In Chapter 4, we discussed one of the most popular areas of commercial software, word processing. In this chapter, we describe four
other popular types of applications software: graphical editors for producing and manipulating pictures and drawings; electronic spreadsheets for making business calculations and forecasts; charting programs
for producing charts and graphs; and database management systems for
storing, organizing, and retrieving data. Good commercial software allows people to expand their personal resources, increase their level of
knowledge, and channel their creativity while saving time and effort.

■ Computer Graphics

The field of *computer graphics* is concerned with the generation by computer of graphs and pictures. Graphics make computers easier to use
because they allow the user to display information pictorially. Animation of routine computer tasks makes computer use more interesting.
In addition, graphical representations help humans digest large quantities of information; without graphs and charts, we have a hard time
making sense out of avalanches of numbers.

Graphics have proved to be an effective communication medium
in many areas, such as office automation, publishing, commercial art,
simulation and animation, computer-aided design, and video games. The
medium has many applications in commercial art—such as generation
of logos—and its popularity in the movie industry is illustrated by the
large number of films that rely on sophisticated computerized special
effects. Computer graphics are also important in computer-aided design, the field in which engineers design products interactively with
sophisticated graphical software systems that use animation and color.
(Computer-aided design is discussed in Chapter 13.) Computer graphics
are finding their way into many everyday applications as well.

In this section we provide a short description of the way pictures
are created through computer graphics. We then introduce graphical
editors and paint systems, illustrating them with MacPaint, a paint system developed for Apple's Macintosh computer.

Graphics Hardware

The hardware of computer graphics consists of video displays and computers for the generation and storage of pictures. A video display uses
a *cathode ray tube* (CRT). Inside the CRT is an electron beam that
sweeps out rows, or *raster lines*, on the screen, as shown in Fig. 10.1.
As the electron beam sweeps the screen, it can light up some picture
elements, or *pixels*, and leave others dark. The *resolution* of a video
display is measured by the number of such pixels per square inch. The
higher the resolution, the more detailed and accurate the displayed pictures.

Early video displays did not use the raster scan technology; instead,
they were *vector graphics* displays that drew points and sets of lines.
When a line was to be drawn, the electron beam was turned on and
moved from one point on the screen to another. The beam filled in
every point it passed. Thus, vector graphics displays always produced
drawings that looked like stick drawings because each consisted of a
collection of lines (see Fig. 10.2). Raster graphics allow production of

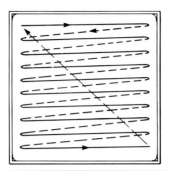

Figure 10.1
The raster display scan pattern.

more realistic drawings (depending, as noted, on the resolution of the display screen). This is because the electron beam sweeps every pixel and can illuminate pixels in any pattern. Drawing a picture on a raster graphics display amounts to a type of *pointillism*, the technique used by the Impressionist painter Seurat at the turn of the century to construct drawings from many small dots. Figure 10.3 shows a drawing made on a raster graphics display. In spite of their shortcomings, vector graphics were used in the early days because they generally needed less storage to remember a picture. Only the lines drawn had to be remembered, whereas in raster graphics displays each pixel has to be remembered.

There are two types of video displays, those with full color and those without. Those without are usually black-and-white displays, al-

Figure 10.2
A vector graphics line drawing. (Courtesy of Calcomp Corporation)

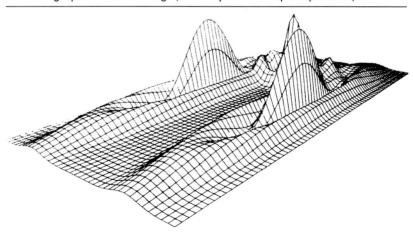

Figure 10.3
A drawing made on a raster graphics display. (Courtesy of Janet Watt)

though they may be black and green. The color of the screen is determined by the phosphor that lines the inside of the display. In color displays each pixel is really a set of three dots, one red (R), one green (G), and one blue (B). A set of three electron guns directed at the RGB dots can generate a great variety of colors.

Graphical Editors

A *graphical editor* is a program to create and modify a picture on a computer screen. The editors discussed here are assumed to use raster displays. Thus, each editing operation ultimately affects the color or intensity of one or more pixels on the screen. Such editors require a keyboard and a pointing device, usually a mouse or a stylus, with which to draw.

There are two principal types of graphical editor programs—paint systems and layout editors. A *paint system* provides direct control over pixels. It views an image as a set of pixels, each with a specific color or intensity. In its memory, the paint system stores a *bitmap*, a two-dimensional representation of the picture in which pixels, represented as bits, are on or off. A *layout editor*, in contrast, understands the concept of *object*—a specific portion of a picture, such as a tree, a flower, or a kite. Layout editors display an object by setting the pixel values that correspond to it. If the object is moved to another part of the screen, the layout editor can reconstruct previously obscured portions of the picture, as shown in Fig. 10.4. By contrast, paint systems do not store

Figure 10.4
When an object is moved with a layout system, the program reconstructs
previously obscured portions of the background. In this example, the robot
was at the right-hand side of the screen and was moved to the left.

objects as separate entities and cannot restore anything previously covered by an object, as shown in Fig. 10.5. Layout editors are considerably
more complex than paint systems because of these differences in capability.

All graphical editors provide the user with the ability to move
around in a document and to cut, paste, and copy from within it.
Graphical editors also provide users with a palette of colors (or patterns,
if the display is black and white). Brush sizes and shapes allow users to
simulate the physical process of painting. Users may draw freehand with
brushes or fill the screen with generic geometric figures, usually including straight lines, rectangles, circles, and ellipses. In addition, it is
common to have a *fill command* to fill up an entire region with a given
color or pattern. Fill commands eliminate the tedious job of filling in
a region by hand. Both paint systems and graphical editors may provide
grids to aid in the placement of drawings. Within the grid, *grid gravity*
pulls the cursor to grid points, eliminating small alignment errors found
in hand drawings. This speeds up the drawing of figures that contain
many straight-line segments. Text, in a variety of fonts and sizes, can
often be inserted into a drawing. Finally, users can store drawings or
objects in electronic libraries for easy retrieval and reuse.

Paint systems are designed primarily for artistic work. Advertising
agencies use them to touch up photographs for commercials or printed

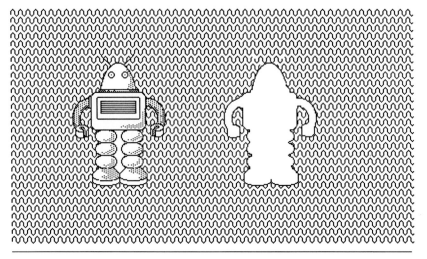

Figure 10.5
When an object is moved with a paint system, the program does not
restore the background previously covered by the object.

advertisements. Some computers can read a photograph into memory
and digitize it, reducing the original picture to a set of pixel values.
Artists can then change the colors of objects in the picture, blend together rough edges, or alter backgrounds. Using a paint system, an artist
might remove an unwanted street sign, for example, or change the color
of a carpet. Special effects could be added, such as twinkles or sparkles,
to make a product more appealing. Paint systems are also used to design
cartoon backgrounds against which characters are moved.

Layout editors, on the other hand, are used by graphic designers;
they contain many tools to help produce professional graphics quickly.
A layout system gives the designer much more freedom and control
over the layout of the final picture than does a paint system. A designer
using a layout system can move objects around or copy objects in different sizes or colors. Layout editors are used widely in television for
headings and titles, station logos, weather reports, and news backdrops.
Since the news changes constantly, layout systems are of crucial importance to the designers of news program graphics, who must be able
to produce high-quality, effective graphics quickly. Layout editors are
also used for circuit and architectural drawings and for charts and slides
in business and education.

The MacPaint Paint System

Figure 10.6 shows a computer screen displaying the Edit menu of
MacPaint, a paint system developed for the Macintosh computer by Bill
Atkinson of Apple Computer, Inc. Along the top of the MacPaint dis-

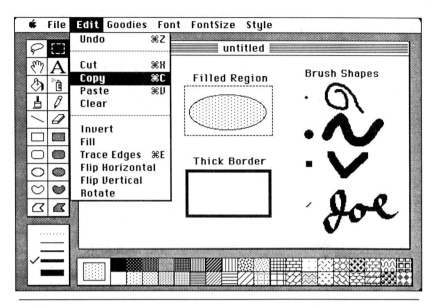

Figure 10.6
The Edit menu of a MacPaint display.

play is a menu bar similar to that used in MacWrite, the word processing program we discussed in Chapter 4. Menus in MacPaint pull down
in the same fashion as MacWrite menus. The left-hand side of the
MacPaint screen contains 20 icons that represent actions available to
users. The bottom of the screen contains a choice of patterns with which
to draw or fill areas. The center of the screen shows a portion of the
painting "canvas."

Among the icons that represent actions is a group associated with
various painting techniques. To use them, we position the cursor over
the appropriate icon and click the mouse button. To paint with a brush,
for example, we click on the paint brush icon, then move the cursor
onto the canvas and move the mouse while holding down the mouse
button. The movement of the mouse is reproduced on the canvas as a
stream of paint. Figure 10.6 shows four brush patterns as well as a sample shape drawn with each.

Another group of icons on the left represents geometric figures such
as lines, rectangles, and ellipses. We select one of these icons just as we
select a painting technique. To select the open rectangle, for example,
we move the cursor to the open rectangle box and click the mouse
button. Then we move anywhere on the canvas and press the mouse
button to mark one corner of the rectangle. An open rectangle appears
on the screen starting at the point where the button was pressed. Moving the mouse "stretches" the rectangle. Releasing the button determines the far corner of the box, which remains stationary on the canvas.

Figure 10.6 shows an open rectangle drawn with this method. We selected its thick border by clicking on one of the boxes containing lines in the lower left-hand corner of the display.

Users can draw ellipses, circles, and polygons in a similar fashion. Figure 10.6 shows a filled ellipse drawn with this technique. To fill a figure, we select one of the patterns shown in the large square at the bottom of the screen. We can select another pattern by clicking the mouse button over one of the smaller squares. Ambitious users can even design their own patterns.

The Edit menu in Fig. 10.6 highlights the option of copying a figure. To indicate which object to copy, the user must enclose the object in a flashing outline, with either a lasso icon or a dashed-box icon. The lasso differs from the dashed box in that it "tightens" over whatever it surrounds until it just covers the outline of the enclosed object. After enclosing the object, the user can cut, copy, or move it.

Figure 10.7 shows the word CUBES outlined in boldface. Users insert text such as this by selecting the icon with the letter A, moving the cursor to any point on the canvas, and clicking to indicate the starting point of the text. Text can then be typed in from the keyboard in any number of font styles and sizes, just as it can with the MacWrite word processor.

As mentioned above, graphical editors usually provide grids to help

Figure 10.7
A MacPaint display with grid.

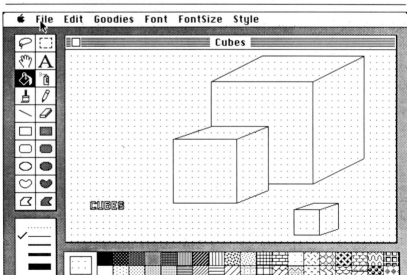

align objects within drawings. Figure 10.7 shows a MacPaint display with a dot placed at each grid point. The figure also shows three cubes drawn by connecting dots. Users draw straight lines by selecting the line icon on the left and then moving the cursor to an endpoint of the line and holding down the mouse button. The point where the button is released marks the other endpoint of the line. Grid gravity has forced the endpoints of all the lines in Fig. 10.7 to fall on grid points.

MacPaint provides a magnification facility to enlarge a picture and modify it at a high level of detail. The FatBits entry on the Goodies menu allows a user to enlarge a portion of the canvas so that its pixels appear as small squares, as illustrated in Fig. 10.8. In the upper left-hand corner of the screen is the portion of the canvas chosen for magnification. Using the pencil and clicking over a square will turn the pixels represented by the square on or off.

The last feature of MacPaint illustrated here is the Show Page feature, also selected from the Goodies menu. The canvas shown on the MacPaint screen is actually smaller than the paper on which the drawing will be printed. What appears on the screen, then, is a viewing window containing only about a third of the complete canvas. See Fig. 10.9. The Show Page shows the viewing window's relation to the entire page. Users can move the viewing window by dragging it up or down while holding down the mouse button.

Figure 10.8
The use of FatBits in MacPaint to magnify a portion of a picture.

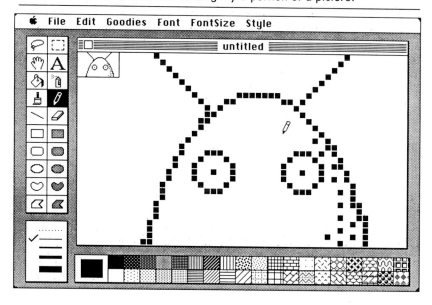

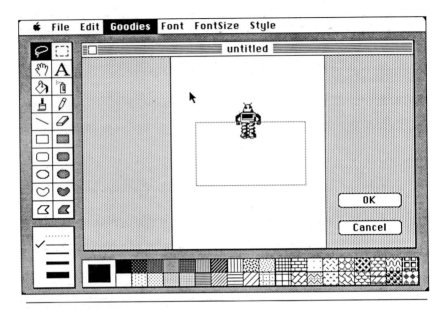

Figure 10.9
The Show Page feature of MacPaint. The rectangle identifies the portion of
the full page that appears on the canvas in the viewing window.

MacPaint has many other features not described here, including
methods to move figures, to save them for later use, and to reflect and
rotate them.

■ Electronic Spreadsheet Programs

A *spreadsheet* is a type of table used in business for a variety of purposes,
including sales forecasts, cash flow projections, calculations of all kinds,
and estimates of production and inventory growth. Conventional
spreadsheets use paper ruled into columns and rows to display data for
analysis. Columns of a table might correspond to quarters in a business
year and rows to the sources of income and expenditures. Data displayed in such a table might show the financial health of a company.
The spreadsheet allows individuals to evaluate "what-if" questions as
a basis for business decisions. A business analyst could, for example,
determine the effect of a change in a product's price on units produced,
consumer demand, and a company's profitability.

An *electronic spreadsheet* is a computer program that displays on a
terminal screen an electronic table that looks much like a conventional
spreadsheet. The first electronic spreadsheet, VisiCalc, was developed

by Dan Bricklin of Harvard and Bob Frankston of MIT. Many other electronic spreadsheet programs now exist. The electronic spreadsheet is an important innovation that simplifies the entry and analysis of data and makes evaluation of "what-if" questions much easier.

Electronic spreadsheets offer many advantages. For one thing, paper spreadsheets can be tedious to use because a change in one entry often causes several other entries to change. Avoiding errors when changing all these entries requires considerable care. With electronic spreadsheets, relationships between items can be built into the program. Users can specify such relationships by formulas whose results the computer will calculate, display, and update. Consequently, when an entry changes, all calculations dependent on that entry change automatically. A total, for example, might be the sum of all the preceding entries in a column; when any one entry changes, the total will change accordingly. Similarly, if interest payments are the product of an interest rate and a principal, a change in either interest rate or principal will immediately be reflected in an altered interest payment.

The electronic spreadsheet's program screen acts as a viewing window through which a portion of the spreadsheet is visible at one time. (Such viewing windows are similar to the windows used with the editors discussed in Chapter 4.) The program uses a table to receive input and produce output. The table is divided into indexed rows and columns. The intersection of a row and a column is called a *cell*, and each cell can contain a label, a constant, or the result of a formula. Using row and column indices, the users may refer to any entry and specify its use in a computation. We describe the features of spreadsheet systems in general, using VisiCalc as our example.

VisiCalc

VisiCalc tables have 254 rows and 63 columns. The rows are indexed from 1 to 254, and the columns from A to Z, AA to ZZ, and BA to BK, in that order. To refer to a cell, we specify a letter for the column and a number for the row; H121, for example, denotes the cell in the 8th column and the 121st row. We can move from cell to cell by using cursor movement keys or by typing in a cell number and jumping to it with a special command. Since the table is larger than the displays on most terminals, the screen provides a viewport through which part of the table is visible. Users may move the viewport to provide access to any section of the table.

Figure 10.10 shows a VisiCalc display that contains a portion of the table as well as useful information on table entries. The display contains edit, prompt, and entry contents lines. The edit line displays information typed in by the user. This information moves to the entry contents

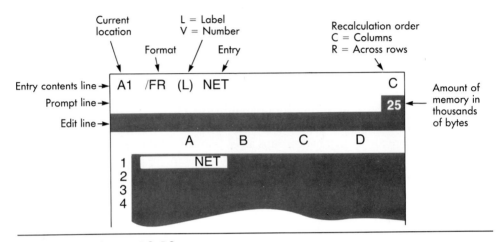

Figure 10.10
The VisiCalc display, with the cursor in cell A1. (From Carol Klitxner and Mathew J. Plociak, Jr., *Using VisiCalc: Getting Down to Business*, p. 61; copyright 1983 John Wiley & Sons, Inc.)

line after the user strikes the RETURN key. The entry contents line also displays any information already contained in the cell over which the cursor currently lies. In Fig. 10.10, the spreadsheet highlights the cell containing the cursor, cell A1. The cell contains the label NET. The entry contents line contains, along with other information, the symbols /FR, indicating that the cell's format is "right justify," a formatting choice that aligns the cell's contents with the right margin.

To enter information in VisiCalc, we first move the cursor to a cell, where we can enter a number, a label, or a formula. To enter a label, we type its name on the edit line, as suggested in Fig. 10.11, and hit

Figure 10.11
Entering a label in the edit line of a VisiCalc display. (From Carol Klitxner and Mathew J. Plociak, Jr., *Using VisiCalc: Getting Down to Business*, p. 35; copyright 1983 John Wiley & Sons, Inc.)

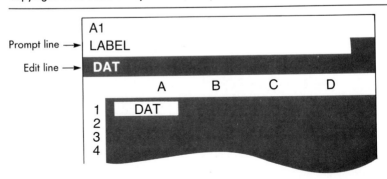

RETURN. If we type in DAT with the cursor in cell A1, for example, that label will appear in the cell A1, and the entry contents line will change to read A1 (L) DAT. VisiCalc knows that DAT is a label (denoted by L) because it begins with a letter. VisiCalc also clears the prompt and edit lines when we hit RETURN. If we wish to enter a number, we simply type it and hit RETURN. To enter a formula, we type + followed by the desired equation. Here, since the system finds values based on the formula, VisiCalc displays the letter V (for value) instead of L (for label) on the entry contents line. Figure 10.12 shows that the value of cell A6 is the result of a formula summing the contents of cells A1 through A5. We can assemble fairly complicated formulas with Visi-Calc, using addition, subtraction, multiplication, and division. VisiCalc evaluates all expressions from left to right unless they contain parentheses; this is different from the order of operations used in traditional mathematics. For example, VisiCalc calculates 6 + 4 / 2 by summing 6 and 4 and then dividing the result by 2; traditional practice would compute the division before the addition, yielding a result of 8 rather than 5. The order of evaluation by VisiCalc can be altered through the use of parentheses.

VisiCalc provides a set of built-in functions for common tasks such as summing elements in a row or column, averaging such quantities, and finding the minimum or maximum element in such a set. Other features include copying and deleting cells; inserting, deleting, and moving rows and columns; clearing the table; saving, deleting, and restoring files from disk; printing a rectangular portion of the table on a

Figure 10.12
The cell entry is a formula, the result of which is entered in the cell, A6. (From Carol Klitxner and Mathew J. Plociak, Jr., *Using VisiCalc: Getting Down to Business*, p. 32; copyright 1983 John Wiley & Sons, Inc.)

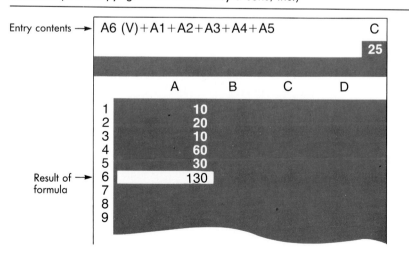

printer; fixing titles either vertically or horizontally; and splitting the screen to show two portions of the table at one time. Users may also specify the formatting of individual cells or of the entire table, indicating whether dollar signs should appear, whether particular entries should be integers, and whether labels should be left- or right-adjusted in their cells. Typing the symbol / calls up a menu, which displays the abbreviations for the commands available.

Although VisiCalc is the best known and most popular spreadsheet system, others do exist, varying widely in features and cost. Some, such as 1-2-3, a product of Lotus Development Corporation, incorporate a simple database management system, a spreadsheet program, and a charting program. Data entered into the database can be accessed by the spreadsheet, and the results of computations can be shown graphically as line charts, pie charts, or bar charts. A limited amount of text formatting is also possible. Undoubtedly more and richer integrated systems will appear in the future.

■ Charting Programs

It is often difficult to interpret large tables of numbers. They make much more sense when displayed pictorially in graphs or charts. Graphs and charts are widely used in business, politics, news reporting, education, and many other fields. Creating charts and graphs, however, can be a costly and time-consuming process. Charting requires a good eye, a steady hand, a ruler, a compass, a T-square, and careful calculations. Often several attempts are necessary to produce a good-looking chart. Further, changes in data usually necessitate redrawing entire charts.

Computerized charting programs simplify this task immensely. Given a set of data and a format, such programs can produce a finished chart in a matter of seconds. When data are updated, charting programs can redraw the chart instantly. They provide many formatting options with different backgrounds, shadings, and layouts. Some programs even provide a wide range of colors.

There are six basic types of charts—line graphs, area charts, pie charts, bar charts, column charts, and scatter charts—which are illustrated in Fig. 10.13. Line charts consist of points plotted on x-y axes and connected by one or more lines. Area charts add emphasis to line charts by shading various regions. Pie charts represent the pieces of a whole as segments of a circle. Bar charts represent numbers with horizontal bars, while column charts use vertical bars. Scatter charts, like line and area charts, plot points on x-y axes, but they do not connect the points with lines.

Although creating a chart with the help of a computer program is far easier than drawing one by hand, it is still a multistep process. First

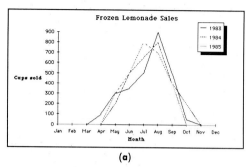

(a)

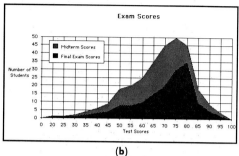

(b)

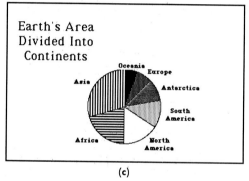

(c)

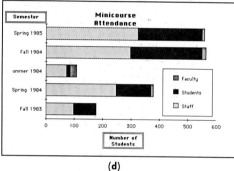

(d)

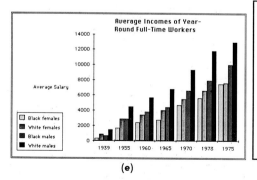

(e)

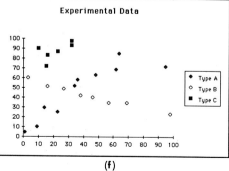

(f)

Figure 10.13

Computer-generated charts: (a) a line chart; (b) an area chart; (c) a pie chart; (d) a bar chart; (e) a column chart; (f) a scatter chart.

the user must enter the data, either by typing it in by hand or calling it up from the results of a compatible spreadsheet or database program. Then the user must decide on the type of chart and the specific format (including shading, background color, connecting lines, and placement of headings). The user must label the axes with descriptive headings and subheadings or number increments. Sometimes a legend is needed to explain the significance of the shading of the graph. Finally, the user must give the chart a title.

■ Database Management Systems

Before computers were introduced, enormous quantities of records were stored in file cabinets. People who wished to use the information contained in these records had to physically inspect the file cabinets or maintain their own files. This required much duplication of effort, a great deal of storage, and large expenditures of time and effort to locate and update files. Today, the centralized computer database offers a convenient alternative.

A *database* is a collection of information organized in a way that makes it highly accessible. The contents of databases can vary greatly. Private databases owned by individuals or organizations may maintain up-to-date mailing lists, inventories of stocks and supplies, or catalogs of books, periodicals, phonograph records, or cassette tapes. Today, there are also hundreds of commercial databases that contain information about such diverse topics as colleges, stock market prices, mail order catalogs, books in print, and computer software. This information may consist of articles, news stories, book reviews, entire newspapers and magazines, a complete encyclopedia, business reports, bibliographies on various subjects, and biographies of millions of individuals. Specialized commercial databases cover law, medicine, engineering, the physical sciences, art, biology, and many other fields. Microcomputer users with telephone lines and modems can generally gain access to commercial databases from their homes and offices.

A *database management system* (*DBMS*) consists of a database and software to operate it. A *query language* for use in retrieving or changing items stored in the database must also be included. Suppose, for example, that a database contains information on flights scheduled by airlines servicing North America. A database management system might permit travel agents to find information concerning schedules, seating, and tariffs; to make reservations; and to submit special customer requests, such as meatless meals or portable baby cribs. Transactions by these travel agents would involve queries, insertion of new information, and, in some cases, updating of previous entries. These are the principal actions taken by users of any database.

A computerized database can be quite complex because it generally stores and cross-indexes many different items. Keeping track of who may see the information stored in the database and who may change items in it requires organization, clarity, and creativity. Simple databases may be maintained by a single person. More complex databases require supervision by computer programs as well as individuals.

Of these individuals, one person, the *database administrator*, usually has overall responsibility for the database system. The administrator determines the format used to present and access data and specifies which items are available to which groups of users. An employer, for example, may have access to every employee's personnel information (such as salary history) while each employee may have access only to her own information.

One important responsibility of the database administrator is en-suring that no unauthorized viewing or modification of the database occurs. To make sure that no unauthorized persons access the database, the administrator can issue each authorized user a password. *Audit trails*—continuously generated histories of all changes made to the data-base—can be set and monitored so that all actions can be traced to specific users. In addition, information stored in the database can be periodically copied to other storage media to minimize data loss due to sabotage or equipment failure. In case of damage or loss, restoring the database would require reentering only the changes made since the last copy (or backup) was made. Depending on the importance of the in-formation in the database and the frequency with which the informa-tion is changed, a backup might be made every week, every day, or even every hour.

In addition to data, databases also record relationships between data, a very important function. People use relationships to organize infor-mation into manageable blocks, and a good DBMS is similarly orga-nized. Grouping data in ways that reflect typical requests will likely result in more efficient retrieval from physical storage. For example, if queries about employees almost always involve requests for the em-ployee's name, number, and department, then it is unwise to treat these three as unrelated data items, since unrelated items may be placed at different locations on a disk, requiring time-consuming searches for each query.

The relationships between data items are often more difficult to record than the data itself. Capturing such relationships in a way that users find helpful is an art. *Conceptual models* for the database are used to record relationships. Models need not show how data are physically organized in memory; instead they provide an abstract representation of all of the information in the database and the relationships between pieces of information. Such a model is a great aid to users working with the database.

Examining conceptual models helps provide an understanding of the differences between various database management systems. The *hierarchical model* organizes the data into one or more treelike structures, resembling family trees, that store information on each branch. To use a hierarchical database, a user must be familiar with its structure to know which branches lead to which information. Another model, the *network model*, organizes the data in groups with links connecting one group to another. Again, the user must know where each link leads in order to use the system. Both of these models can be difficult to use. In contrast, the *relational model* is based on the familiar concept of tables. Their ease of use has made relational databases very popular.

The Relational Database Model

The relational model of a database treats information as if it were contained in tables. Figure 10.14 shows a representative table containing several entries from an airline database. These tables are easily displayed on a computer terminal, unlike the trees and networks in other models. Since information is often more easily understood when contained in a table, relational databases are very attractive. Remember, though, that the tables represent the user's perspective; the computer may actually store the data in some other form.

The relational database Query-by-Example, or QBE, utilizes tables exclusively. Users request information with tables and QBE provides the results in tables. Other relational databases, although they use tables as the basis of their conceptual models, may not accept queries or display results with tables. Because it directly reflects its conceptual model, QBE is much simpler to understand than many relational database systems. We use QBE as our primary model for describing relational databases, although we also present two other popular relational databases, SQL and dBASE II.

Figure 10.14
A typical table in a relational database.

FLIGHTS				
AIRLINE	**FLGHT_NO**	**DEPT_TM**	**ARRVL_TM**	**DATE**
UNITED	14	1300	1515	186
AMERICAN	72	0815	1437	350
EASTERN	04	2003	2210	015

Each table in a relational database has several columns, known as *fields*. These columns have headings called *attributes*. For example, the attributes for the FLIGHTS table in Fig. 10.14 are AIRLINE, FLGHT_NO, DEPT_TM, ARRVL_TM, and DATE. (The times use the 24-hour clock, and the date is the number of the day, counting from the first day of the year.) Each row in a table has a single value for each attribute. The FLIGHTS table, for example, has three rows. It is necessary that each table have a *primary field*, one column in which no entry is repeated. For example, in Fig. 10.15, the FLGHT_NO field is a primary field because no flight number appears more than once; the PILOT_ID field, in contrast, is not a primary field because one PILOT_ID (3216) appears twice. Each field in the FLIGHTS table is a primary field. The use of primary fields ensures that each row in a table can be identified by a unique value for at least one attribute.

Three basic operations are used to retrieve information from the tables in a relational database: selection, projection, and join. *Selection* is the process of choosing rows from a table. Selection, applied to a table, generates a new table containing the same fields and attributes as the old table, but only for the selected rows. We could, for example, create a new table containing information about the pilots Smith and Green by selecting rows from the PILOT_DATA table in Fig. 10.16.

Projection is the process of selecting columns from a table. Projection generates a new table containing only specified fields and attributes. A table containing names and years of birth of pilots, for example, could be formed by projecting the NAME and YOB attributes from the PILOT_DATA table in Fig. 10.16.

Join is the act of combining two tables. Tables can be joined only if they share one field with the same name or attribute. New rows are formed by joining rows with a common entry in the shared field. For example, if the tables in Figs. 10.15 and 10.16 were joined on the PILOT_ID field, the resulting table would contain seven fields and three rows: the first row of Fig. 10.15 joined with the first row of Fig. 10.16; the second row of Fig. 10.15 joined with the first row of Fig. 10.16; and the third row of Fig. 10.15 joined with the second row of Fig. 10.16.

Figure 10.15
PILOT_ASSIGNMENT table.

PILOT_ASSIGNMENT		
PILOT_ID	**FLGHT_NO**	**DATE**
3216	72	350
3216	04	015
0126	14	186

PILOT_DATA

PILOT_ID	NAME	YOB	FLY_TM	AIRCRAFT
3216	T. SMITH	1933	22,000	747
0126	N. JONES	1933	36,450	DC3
0451	R. GREEN	1925	45,100	CONCORDE

Figure 10.16
PILOT_DATA table.

The third row of Fig. 10.16 would be dropped because its PILOT_ID is not repeated in Fig. 10.15. Figure 10.17 shows the table created by such a join.

The following sections give examples of fairly complex queries on relational databases. Each query can be expressed as a combination of selection, projection, and join.

The Query-By-Example System

Query-by-Example (QBE) is one of the most attractive relational database management systems available. It was developed by M. Zloof of IBM and is now an IBM product. QBE allows users to update or query the database simply by filling out sample tables. This is illustrated in Fig. 10.18.

To pose a query, a user begins with an empty table whose name is that of a table in the database; by convention, the first column of a table contains its name. Then the user makes sample entries in rows and columns to indicate the information he requests. These entries can be particular or example values of attributes, conditions, or commands to print and update entries.

A particular value is a value that can be taken by an attribute. When a particular value is placed in a column of a table, the rows of the table retrieved must have that value in the selected column. Figure 10.18 shows the skeletons of three tables of the database with sample entries. The user has specified that all rows that are retrieved from the table

Figure 10.17
New table resulting from a join between the PILOT_ASSIGNMENT table and the PILOT_DATA table.

PILOT_ASSIGNMENT_DATA

PILOT_ID	NAME	YOB	FLY_TM	AIRCRAFT	FLGHT_NO	DATE
3216	T. SMITH	1933	22,000	747	72	350
3216	T. SMITH	1933	22,000	747	04	015
0126	N. JONES	1933	36,450	DC3	14	186

FLIGHTS	AIRLINE	FLGHT_NO	DEPT_TM	ARRVL_TM	DATE
	P._PSA	_FLGHT_NUMBER	>1130	P._TIME	
	P._PSA	_FLGHT_NUMBER		P._TIME	<200

PILOT_ASSIGNMENT	PILOT_ID	FLGHT_NO	DATE
	_ID	_FLGHT_NUMBER	

PILOT_DATA	PILOT_ID	NAME	YOB	FLY_TM	QUAL_LVL
	_ID		1933	<40,000	

Figure 10.18
Sample compound query in Query-by-Example (QBE).

PILOT_DATA must have for the YOB (year of birth) entry the particular value 1933. Conditions are also used here. In the sample table FLIGHTS the condition >1130 is used to select rows that have a value for DEPT_TM that is larger than 11:30, an hour of the day. Also, the condition <200 selects rows that have DATE less than 200, the 200th day of the year.

If more than one row is given in a sample table, then all rows in the table that meet the conditions stated in any of the sample rows will be retrieved unless the rows are linked by example values. An *example value* is similar to a variable in that it holds no particular value, but it is used to represent a particular type of value. The names of example values must begin with an underscore (_) but otherwise need not bear any relation to the names of the fields in which they are used. In Fig. 10.18 the example values _PSA, _FLGHT_NUMBER, and _TIME in the FLIGHTS table do link sample rows. They require that all rows retrieved from FLIGHTS have the same value for AIRLINE, FLGHT_NO, and ARRVL_TM.

Example values may also be used to join tables. They link rows selected from one table to rows in another table that have the same attribute value. In the tables FLIGHTS and PILOT_ASSIGNMENT, the example value _FLGHT_NUMBER joins rows retrieved from the two tables that have the same value for FLGHT_NO. Similarly, the use of the example value _ID in the tables PILOT_ASSIGNMENT and PILOT_DATA joins rows that have the same value for the attribute PILOT_ID.

It is now possible to state in words the query represented by the tables in Fig. 10.18. We seek the rows of the table FLIGHTS that have a departure time later than 11:30 on a day preceding the 200th day where the flight number is that of a flight for which the pilot is born in 1933 and has no more than 40,000 hours of flying time. Since not all of the fields in the table FLIGHTS are needed, the FLIGHTS table contains print or project statements (P.) to print or project out only some of the fields of the table. Thus, this query will produce the table of Fig. 10.19, which

AIRLINE	ARRVL_TM
UNITED	1515
EASTERN	2210

Figure 10.19
Response to the query in Fig. 10.18.

has columns with attribute names AIRLINE and ARRVL_TM. These are the columns of the table FLIGHTS that are projected out by the instances of the print command.

In addition to providing answers to queries, QBE allows updating of entries in the database. The command U., for update, will update the database when placed in the field to be changed along with the updated value. Figure 10.20 shows a query to update the departure time of flight 72 to 930. In addition to changing information in existing rows in tables, QBE allows creation of new tables, deletion of old tables, and creation and deletion of rows within existing tables.

Other Relational Database Management Systems

Although QBE is one of the easiest relational database systems to use, several other relational database systems are also popular. These other systems provide similar features but communicate with users through a textual rather than a table-based method. We provide examples of queries in two of these systems, SQL and dBASE II. SQL (for Structured Query Language; pronounced "sequel") is a system developed at IBM for medium to large machines; it is currently marketed by several companies. dBASE II is a product of the Ashton-Tate Corporation and was developed for use on small personal computers.

SQL and dBASE II, like QBE, permit users to create, retrieve, and modify tables. While QBE is nonprocedural (that is, it allows users to tell the system what to do but not how to do it), both SQL and dBASE II allow the use of some constructs of programming languages. In this way, SQL and dBASE II offer more flexibility and allow users to exercise greater control over the way in which the DBMS operates. We will fo-

Figure 10.20
Updating entries in QBE.

FLIGHTS	AIRLINE	FLGHT_NO	DEPT_TM	ARRVL_TM	DATE
		72	U.930		

cus here on operations similar to those illustrated for QBE, providing
a sample of the syntax of each system.

In SQL, the SELECT command displays specified rows and columns
of a table. An asterisk following SELECT causes all rows and columns to
be printed. Thus, the following command prints an entire table:

```
SELECT*
FROM FLIGHTS
. . .
```

If the names of specific attributes such as AIRLINE and ARRVL_TM replace the asterisk, then the query produces only those columns of the
specified table. For example, to produce a table similar to Fig. 10.17,
SQL requires the following commands:

```
SELECT AIRLINE, ARRVL_TM
FROM FLIGHTS
WHERE FLGHT_NO =
      (SELECT FLGHT_NO
      FROM PILOT_ASSIGNMENT
      WHERE PILOT_ID =
           (SELECT ID
           FROM PILOT_DATA
           WHERE    YOB = 1933
                    AND FLY_TM <40,000
      )
      )
AND (DEPT_TM > 1130
     AND
     DATE <200)
```

Like programming languages, SQL executes the operations within the
innermost set of parentheses first. Thus, the query first finds the flight
number for pilots who were born in 1933 and have less than 40,000
hours of flying time. SQL executes the innermost SELECT command,
using the attribute PILOT_ID to find values from the PILOT_DATA table.
These values then help the database system select values for the attribute FLGHT_NO from the PILOT_ASSIGNMENT table. From this table
of flight numbers, SQL finally identifies the airlines and flight numbers
for all flights whose departure time is later than 11:30 and whose departure date falls before the 200th day of the year.

The syntax in dBASE II is more complex. It recognizes that two
tables, called PRIMARY and SECONDARY, can be active at one time. Any
table in the database can be made the primary or secondary table with
the USE command. For example, to make the secondary table a copy of
PILOT_ASSIGNMENT, we first use the command

.SELECT SECONDARY

and then issue the command

.USE PILOT_ASSIGNMENT

Here the period (.) is the dBASE II prompt. The command

.SELECT PRIMARY

followed by

.USE FLIGHTS

will make the primary table a copy of FLIGHTS.

Once the primary and secondary tables in dBASE II have been assigned values it is possible to perform joins on them. The following fragment of code in dBASE II joins the two tables PILOT_ASSIGNMENT and FLIGHTS together to form a new table called TEMPTABLE, which has fields called AIRLINE, ARRVL_TM, and PILOT_ID. It joins the two tables under the following conditions: the values of attribute FLGHT_NO in the primary table and attribute FLGHT_NO in the secondary table (denoted S.FLGHT_NO) must be equal; DEPT.TM in the primary table must be greater than 1130; and DATE in the primary table must be less than 200.

```
.SELECT SECONDARY
.USE PILOT_ASSIGNMENT
.SELECT PRIMARY
.USE FLIGHTS
.JOIN TO TEMPTABLE FIELDS AIRLINE, ARRVL_TM, PILOT_ID
 FOR FLGHT_NO = S.FLGHT_NO
.AND.DEPT.TM > 1130
.AND.DATE < 200
```

The table TEMPTABLE that is created by this fragment of dBASE II code from the data in Figs. 10.14, 10.15, and 10.16 is shown in Fig. 10.21.

We can now use TEMPTABLE to complete the query that is stated above for QBE and SQL. We set the secondary table to PILOT_DATA and the primary table to TEMPTABLE. We then join the two to form the table FINALTABLE with fields AIRLINE and ARRVL_TM by joining rows with identical values for PILOT_ID such that YOB in the secondary table is 1933

Figure 10.21
The table TEMPTABLE.

TEMPTABLE	AIRLINE	ARRVL_TM	PILOT_ID
	UNITED	1515	0126
	EASTERN	2210	3216

and the number of hours of flying time in the secondary table is less than 40,000. The following fragment of code carries out these operations.

```
.SELECT SECONDARY
.USE PILOT_DATA
.SELECT PRIMARY
.USE TEMPTABLE
.JOIN TO FINALTABLE FIELDS AIRLINE, ARRVL_TM
FOR PILOT_ID = S.PILOT_ID
   .AND.S.YOB = 1933
   .AND S.FLY_TM < 40000
```

Finally, to print out the result we use the following two commands:

```
.USE FINALTABLE
.DISPLAY ALL
```

This example shows why QBE is so much easier to use than other relational database systems.

SUMMARY

For computer users who lack the time or experience to write their own software, a variety of commercial programs are available. This chapter describes four popular types of applications software: graphical editors, electronic spreadsheets, charting programs and database management systems.

A graphical editor is a program to create and modify pictures on a computer. Graphical editors can be either paint systems or layout editors. Paint systems permit the user to modify the color or intensity of pixels. MacPaint is an example of a paint system described here. Layout editors deal with objects, which can be moved and partially obscured without losing information about them.

An electronic spreadsheet is a computer program that displays a table on which values, categories, or relationships between items can be stored. VisiCalc, the first spreadsheet program, has been one of the most popular programs available for personal computers. Spreadsheets allow easy manipulation of numbers. However, since people often have difficulty understanding large quantities of numbers, charting programs have become popular. Charting programs convert numerical information into pictures, which often can be more easily understood than numbers.

Database management systems consist of databases to hold information, software to process the information, and a query language to retrieve or change the information. In addition to storing data, databases can record relationships between data, making the information easier to understand. Relational databases treat all data as if they were stored in tables. The Query-by-Example (QBE) system is one relational database management system. Other types of relational database systems, such as SQL and dBASE II, communicate in a textual rather than a table-based manner.

FURTHER READING

J. E. Bingham, *1-2-3 Go!* (Reading, Mass.: Addison-Wesley, 1984).

C. J. Date, *Database: A Primer* (Reading, Mass.: Addison-Wesley, 1983).

C. Klitzner and M. J. Plociak, Jr., *Using VisiCalc* (New York: John Wiley & Sons, 1983).

ISSUES AND IDEAS

1. What are the advantages of color graphics displays over black-and-white displays? What are the disadvantages?

2. List three examples of computer graphics that you have encountered in the past week. Discuss the characteristics of each example and describe methods that might have been used to design them.

3. Differentiate between layout editors and paint systems. For what uses would layout editors be more appropriate? For what uses would paint systems be more appropriate?

4. Describe three tasks other than those mentioned in the chapter in which an electronic spreadsheet could be used. For each task, describe the advantages and disadvantages of using an electronic spreadsheet rather than a conventional one.

5. Represent the following data with a line graph, an area chart, a bar chart, a column chart, and a pie chart:

October sales:

Rakes	$43
Sunglasses	$23
Popcorn	$88
Books	$45
Mustard	$5
Cookies	$158

6. List two advantages to using tables as opposed to text to access information stored in a database.

7. Discuss the difference between selections, projections, and joins.

8. List two tasks that entail working with large quantities of information. Discuss how an electronic database would change the work involved. How would it make each task easier? How would it complicate the work required?

Education

The computer is the Proteus of machines. Its essence is its universality, its power to simulate. Because it can take on a thousand forms and can serve a thousand functions, it can appeal to a thousand tastes.

SEYMOUR PAPERT, *Mindstorms*

■ Introduction

The U.S. educational system is currently undergoing major reevaluation. Several detailed studies have been conducted, addressing such issues as the current state of education, its problems, and suggestions for improvement. These studies have uncovered disturbing facts. In 1983, the National Commission on Excellence in Education (NCEE) found that 13 percent of all 17-year-olds are functionally illiterate. The general level of literacy in the United States is so low that business and military leaders complain that they must spend millions of dollars for remedial education and training in basic skills such as reading, writing, spelling, and computation. The NCEE study concluded that "if an unfriendly foreign power had attempted to impose on America the mediocre educational performance that exists today, we might well have viewed it as an act of war. As it stands, we have allowed this to happen to ourselves."

These are complicated problems requiring a major reevaluation of the goals and methods of the U.S. educational system. This reevaluation should include examination of the potential role of the computer in schools. The computer is not a panacea; it cannot replace good schools and teachers. It can, however, help ease teachers' loads and provide new environments and new tools for learning. Although computers can by no means solve all the problems of education, they can provide alternatives and opportunities unavailable until now.

To illustrate the possibilities and limitations of computer use in the schools, we present in this chapter an overview of present and future uses of computers in education. Our purpose is not to provide a comprehensive discussion of the vast array of available software or approaches but rather to construct a framework, illustrated with specific examples, in which to evaluate the computer's potential educational value. Our framework identifies two major approaches to education: structured learning and experiential learning.

Structured learning, organized for the student by the teacher or textbook writer, consists of specific tasks or exercises that address a concrete goal. Traditional tools of structured learning include flash cards, workbooks, drill exercises, and multiple-choice tests. Computer-based structured learning consists not only of the automation of these pedagogical aids but of sophisticated tutorial programs that present and test ideas in a structured way.

Experiential learning, in contrast, allows the student to learn through experimentation and discovery. Goals of experiential learning are much broader than those of structured learning; the process of discovery is more important than a measurable result. Experiential learning is typically more prevalent in the education of younger children, who are encouraged to learn through play, than in the education of older students, who are expected to absorb information at a rapid rate. Often older students' experiential learning may be limited to writing and research projects where they discover information for themselves, though still in a prescribed fashion. The computer can make experiential learning more feasible for older students by providing new resources and learning environments.

After illustrating this framework as it applies to computer-based education, we conclude with a discussion of the computer's potential to aid students whose special needs may not be met by a conventional classroom—the physically handicapped, the cognitively handicapped, and the gifted.

Historical Perspective

Formal education is a relatively modern invention. Prehistoric people probably acquired basic skills of survival through experience and under the tutelage of parents and elders of a community. Such learning was an active process; one learned by doing or by imitating someone else, much as a preschool child does today. With the increased complexity of society and the gradual accumulation of knowledge, other forms of learning developed. Memorization became an important skill through which accumulated wisdom and history could be passed on to succeeding generations; there was no other way to preserve information.

The introduction of writing materials gradually produced important changes in the way knowledge was acquired and transmitted. Memorization and learning through experience declined in importance. Around 1440, the invention of the printing press made mass education possible; with this new technology large quantities of information could be recorded and distributed at a reasonable cost. Two hundred years after the invention of the printing press, the textbook came into existence, and with it the role of the teacher changed. The teacher as tutor was replaced to a large extent by the teacher as interpreter of written documents. Within another two hundred years, roughly by the end of the eighteenth century, the public school became a reality in many countries.

In most public schools today, computers play an insignificant role in the educational process. This is primarily because there are not enough computers to have a major impact. With one or two personal computers serving a school of hundreds of students, the computer must remain a novelty, a toy that may add some variety to the day but that cannot change the way classwork is done because the amount of time any one student can spend using the computer is minimal. As schools acquire more computers, because of decreasing costs, gifts, and discounts from computer manufacturers and the fund-raising efforts of parents and students, students will be able to spend more time using computers. The problem, then, will be the availability of innovative, educationally sound, affordable software.

The creation of innovative educational software requires the talents of people well versed in both software development and educational theory. It also requires development of new teaching methods. Much of the educational software available today merely translates established methods to the computer; for example, a program may enable students to use a keyboard and CRT screen instead of pencil and paper to drill multiplication tables. Obviously, such software does not take advantage of many of the computer's unique capabilities. Developing new computer-based methods, however, is complicated by the fact that computers provide a new graphical and dynamic medium that we are just beginning to understand. Much experimentation and hard work will be required before computers find their place in the classroom.

■ Structured Learning

There are many aspects to computerized structured learning. In this section we examine testing by computer, computer-aided instruction, and specialized tools for learning that can be used in the classroom, such as programs to plot curves, compose music, and provide an on-line dictionary. We also examine structured educational games that provide motivation to acquire basic mathematical and word skills and programs that teach by simulating science experiments and simple business situations.

Computer-Managed Instruction

When computers were first introduced in education, they were primarily used for testing. Centralized databases of tests were created along with plans of study for individual students based on their performance on the tests. Teachers accessed the databases via terminals. A student's responses to questions were entered, and immediately a plan of study was generated to guide the student and the teacher. This was called *computer-managed instruction* (CMI). Today the term has come to include on-line testing, that is, testing in which a student answers questions directly through a terminal or personal computer, perhaps testing in some areas more than others depending on the student's responses. Such testing is done on a large scale with the PLATO system.

On-line testing can help both teacher and student identify areas that need attention and then can prompt the student to spend more time developing those areas, perhaps through on-line instruction. Computerized testing does have its problems, however. It takes a large amount of data to determine the level of difficulty of a particular question and much experience to decide which question should logically follow another.

Computer-Aided Instruction

Computer-aided instruction (CAI) is the most widespread and well known use of computers in education. Here, as the name suggests, the computer is used as an aid or replacement for traditional instruction. Simple CAI programs automate the process of drill and practice; more sophisticated programs serve as private tutors. They often include a tutorial with computer simulations, language or music tapes, synthesized music, slides, or video films. A great variety of CAI courses have been developed since the field blossomed in the 1960s. They range from accounting to zoology and serve preschoolers as well as adults. CAI courses are offered at some universities in topics as diverse as mathematical logic and Old Church Slavonic.

Sophisticated CAI programs tailor their presentation and test material according to the responses given by the student. Such tutorial programs are called *dialogs* because they mimic the teaching method used by Socrates, in which he led a dialog with his students. Figure 11.1 shows a sample dialog designed to teach students about chemistry.

Dialogs can be particularly valuable in mathematics and science, where the goal is to convey a method of thinking as well as a body of information. A program can lead the student through the problem-solving process, prompting for the appropriate information. For example, if the student is learning to solve algebra word problems, the program can help him to determine what information is required, what information is available, and what procedures are necessary to solve the problem. In subjects such as physics and chemistry, where the solution to a hypothetical problem can be obtained through experimentation, the computer can provide simulations to illustrate results graphically. For example, if the student's task is to determine the angle and speed at which an arrow must be shot to hit a given target, the computer can simulate the arrow's path according to the student's specifications and illustrate the results.

The largest, most well developed, and oldest of the CAI systems is PLATO, developed at the University of Illinois and now commercially available through the Control Data Corporation. PLATO programs are usually run on large mainframe computers and thus have the advantage of large storage capacities not available with microcomputers. For this reason, PLATO programs tend to be more sophisticated than most other CAI programs. PLATO programs are run on special terminals that can display pictures as well as text. The terminals are also equipped with touch-sensitive screens, making the system easier to use for people without computer experience because users can indicate a choice simply by touching the appropriate place on the screen.

Currently more than 8,000 hours of instructional material exists for this system in about 150 different subject areas, including tutorial programs, simulation systems, and educational games. PLATO courses range from a basic skills course designed to provide functional literacy (eighth-grade reading, language, and math skills) to high school–level and college-level courses in agriculture, botany, biology, engineering, medicine, music, physics, and many other subjects. An example of a PLATO screen is shown in Fig. 11.2. The developers of PLATO created what they consider a complete learning environment, where on-line lessons are often supplemented by workbooks, texts, or videotapes. PLATO

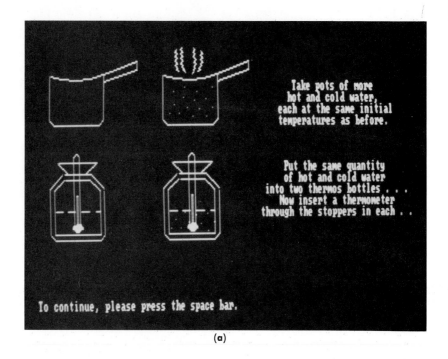

(a)

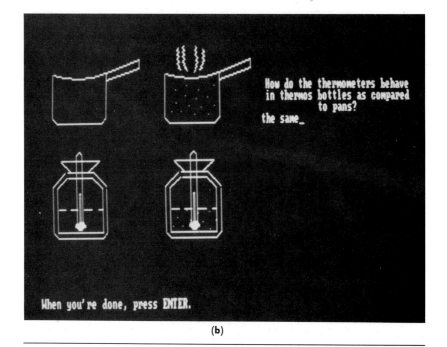

(b)

Figure 11.1
Example of a chemistry dialog. (Courtesy of University of California Regents)

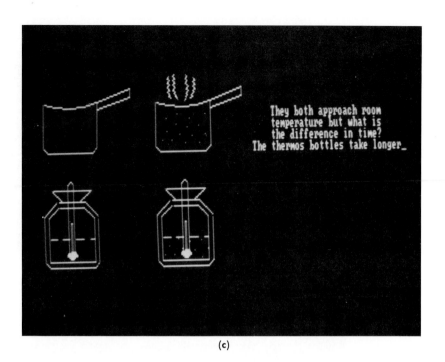

(c)

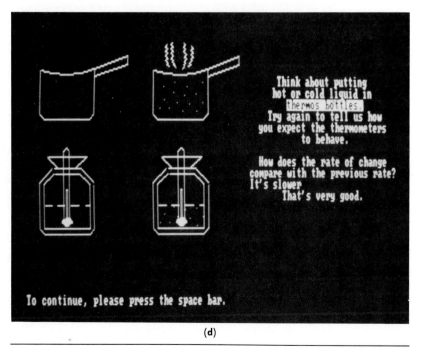

(d)

Figure 11.1 (*Cont.*)

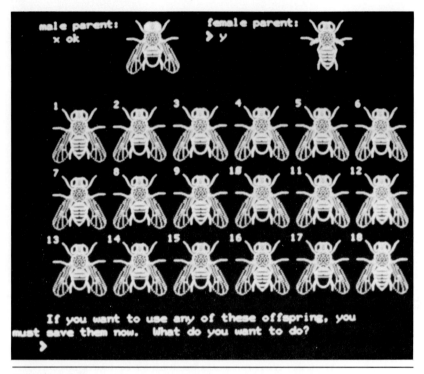

Figure 11.2
A PLATO screen showing a simulation of a fruit fly experiment. (Courtesy
of Control Data Corporation)

can provide hints to problem solutions before displaying the answer and
can explain why answers are incorrect. In addition, special electronic
aids are available to users; a computer literacy program, for example,
offers an on-line glossary that can be accessed at any time during the
course. Recently, some PLATO software has been rewritten for personal computers. Because of the limited memory capacity of microcomputers, this software is necessarily inferior to the mainframe versions;
the teaching strategies are simpler and more limited.

CAI has met with diverse reactions from educators and students.
Proponents feel that sophisticated uses of CAI help restore learning to
a more active process. Since the material is presented in small pieces
and since the student is constantly asked to respond to material as it is
presented, more information is assimilated with CAI than through reading a textbook or listening to a lecture. Each student has the constant
and undivided attention of the computer program and so can progress
at her own pace, receiving individualized and immediate feedback for
each response given. Although the process is structured, it requires

much more involvement of the student than lectures or textbooks. Also, the very fact that lessons are presented on a computer, especially if the lessons are accompanied by interesting graphics, can provide extra motivation for some students. Finally, CAI offers courses in some areas, such as highly specialized languages, for which it is uneconomical to offer lecture-based courses.

Opponents argue that many CAI programs lack flexibility. Although they respond to each student individually, their structure may be too rigid for creative learning. CAI is not especially user-friendly; the only responses many CAI programs allow are answers to multiple-choice questions. Also, the programs seldom recognize misspellings or answers that do not follow the required format (for example, the answer "of course" instead of "yes"). Because only answers in the expected format solicit positive feedback from the computer, such programs discourage creativity. Instead, they require compartmentalization of knowledge into small bits of information that can be easily tested. This is a limiting process: not all knowledge can be compartmentalized into multiple-choice or true-false questions.

Since there will always be a need for drill and practice, CAI has at least a limited function to serve in those areas. It also has a place in tutoring individuals in specialized areas (such as Old Church Slavonic) in which other courses of instruction may not be readily available. How big a role CAI will play in schools and universities depends in part on future developments in CAI systems.

Some researchers hope that through the use of artificial intelligence techniques (discussed in Chapter 12), CAI systems of the future will provide much more effective and attractive learning environments. Currently students have little or no ability to question a CAI program or request more information from it. More conversation between computer and student may eventually be possible when artificial intelligence methods are applied to CAI programs. Whether this hope will be realized remains to be seen. Researchers in artificial intelligence have often underestimated the difficulty of replicating intelligent behavior.

Some progress has been made in the development of intelligent CAI (ICAI) systems. Some systems, for example, can list new skills for the student to acquire, ranking them according to the student's level of knowledge. A beginning student will first receive help in using the system itself. Once he has acquired more experience, he will be coached in various strategies and approaches to problems. This shifts the program's emphasis from tutoring and drilling to coaching and guiding.

Such programs may someday be able to advise students on problem solving and to identify the types of errors students make in solving problems. The designer of this type of intelligent system will need considerable knowledge of the way people learn and solve problems. Much effort will also be needed to encode this knowledge into a computer system. It will be some time before it becomes apparent whether such systems can be created.

A technological development that may add power to CAI programs is the videodisk. Like videotapes, videodisks store images. Unlike videotapes, they allow the user to gain access instantly to any frame of stored information simply by specifying its location. A videodisk is to a videotape what a phonograph record is to a cassette tape: songs on the record and frames on the videodisk can be accessed instantly, while the cassette or videotape must be advanced or rewound to the appropriate place. One disadvantage is that videodisks, like records, can be recorded only by professionals and cannot be rerecorded, while tapes can be altered by the user.

A videodisk can hold approximately 100,000 frames of pictures, which can add realism to a computer presentation. Videodisks store photographs as well as pictures previously created with computer graphics systems. Dynamic computer graphics in which images are created in real time may be satisfactory in many instructional situations, but only the most powerful and expensive graphics systems can provide the degree of realism possible with videodisks. Very large amounts of computation are needed to provide realistic pictures dynamically. For areas in which graphical detail is important, such as art history and science, videodisks can be used to control photograph-quality images, both still and moving pictures. Videodisk technology has already been incorporated into CAI programs used by medical schools.

Creating CAI Courses

The range of systems available for creating CAI course materials is large. At one end of the spectrum are *template-based systems*, in which the designer fills in a series of templates to construct a lesson. Each template typically lists the question to be asked, the response required, and, based on the response, which template the program should advance to. Such systems provide little flexibility to a course designer, but are relatively easy to use. At the other end of the spectrum are *authoring systems*, which provide a great deal of control over the design of the lesson but which are far more difficult and time-consuming to use. Authoring systems are essentially specialized programming languages, providing facilities geared toward the creation of CAI tutorials. They typically include six principal components: calculational capabilities to support calculations of all sorts; sequencing routines to control the flow of a lesson; answer-judging capabilities to permit the author to specify acceptable answers, including those with spelling errors; graphics capabilities to support the creation and display of illustrations; data manipulation facilities to record student responses, grades, and other pertinent data; and external device control commands to provide control over such equipment as audio and video cassettes, speech synthesizers, lightpens, mice, and switches. Several good authoring systems are available for microprocessors and mainframes.

Even with the best tools, writing CAI programs is difficult and time-consuming. It is estimated that a person experienced in use of an authoring system and in a subject must spend about 40 hours to develop a script for a single 45-minute lesson. About 100 hours more are needed to turn that script into a program, and an additional 20 hours are needed to test the program and fix errors. The program is then typically tested on a small group of students for several weeks. Any errors uncovered by students must be fixed before the program can be published. Developing a simple 45-minute lesson can thus take 13 to 15 weeks. The time and difficulty involved make CAI program development a job primarily for professionals. Experts in this field hope to spend the next decade developing many complete CAI courses.

Computer Learning Tools

The computer learning aids described above—CMI and CAI—provide a structured learning environment. These programs attempt to assume some of the more mundane duties of a classroom teacher, such as testing and drilling, allowing the teacher the time for more uniquely human contributions. A second category of structured learning can be addressed under the heading "computer learning tools." A learning tool is any object or program that can extend a teacher's or student's learning capabilities. A chalkboard is a tool, as are a pencil, a ruler, and a paintbrush. Like these traditional tools, well-designed computer programs are neutral entities—their effectiveness depends on how well they are used. These computer tools can be used in either structured or experiential environments; we include them in this section because they can be used effectively without an experiential approach. Software packages in this category generally extend the boundaries of the classroom and thus the power of the individual student. They range from the almost trivial use of the computer as a pocket calculator to much more complicated uses, some of which are described in the following discussion.

Statistical analysis programs are widely used by decision makers in the business world. Similar programs can help children learn the significance of numbers and how to analyze them in a meaningful way. The Minnesota Educational Computing Consortium (MECC), one of the chief suppliers of educational software for personal computers, offers a series of mathematical programs that concentrate on concepts and minimize the "busy work." A graphing program, for example, draws a graph of a given equation; an integration program calculates definite integrals in calculus in three different ways and shows the results from each method. From these programs, students can make discoveries about the nature of the graphs or methods of integration. The computer also can automatically plot graphs of scientific experiments or draw bar graphs or histograms. This frees the student from the time-consuming task of plotting points by hand; the time saved can be used in studying what the numbers and graphs mean. With spreadsheet programs, such as those described in Chapter 10, several variables can be manipulated at once, and the result is instantly visible.

Another promising approach uses the computer as a book. An electronic book may not seem an improvement over the paper version, but when supplemented by an on-line dictionary it can help improve a reader's vocabulary. The reader can simply move a cursor to an unfamiliar word and push a button to request a definition. The definition appears on the screen while the text is still visible. This makes finding definitions easy, encouraging readers to use a dictionary. Systems of this sort are not in wide use at the moment because of the high cost of storing and retrieving an on-line book and an on-line dictionary, but decreasing costs and increasing capacities may make them more common in the future.

Computers can also be used as creative tools, especially in music and art. They give children the chance to explore these appealing media at an earlier age, before most have had time to learn to play a musical instrument or develop the motor control to handle a pen or paintbrush. They are, however, sophisticated enough for experienced artists as well. A *music compositional facility* usually consists of an input device (either a "piano" keyboard, a traditional typewriter keyboard, or a pointing device), a computer, a CRT to display musical notation, and an audio output device to play the music and produce the sound. Together these components can be used to compose music. A composer can view a composition graphically on a computer screen and hear it played electronically at the same time. This makes it possible to compose a melody, listen to it, and then try different harmonizations, tempi, dynamics, key signatures, instrumentations, and articulations. When a pleasing combination is found, it can easily be reproduced many times. With the aid of a printer, the composer can print out a finished piece in musical notation.

Similarly, artists can "paint" on a sophisticated system that provides a limitless range of colors, brush sizes, and strokes. Such a system typically allows freestyle drawing with a pointing device as well as the capacity to draw precise lines, angles, and curves. Most important, artists have the freedom to experiment and change their minds. Like the music composition program, the paint system allows users to experiment until they create something they like. Both music composition and paint systems are currently available for microcomputers.

Structured Educational Games

From spelling bees to essay contests to numbers games to hangman and Scrabble, teachers have often used educational games as rewards for achievement or as supplements to the basic curriculum to provoke interest and encourage competition. As the popularity of video arcades demonstrates, computers are particularly effective game players. Their graphics, animation, and sound capabilities make them exciting opponents, and their computational abilities can match the pace of any human player. Video games are popular, as are electronic versions of chess, checkers, backgammon, and other traditional games. As a result of this popularity, many educational computer games have appeared on the market. Not only do these games appeal to children; they also appeal to parents and educators who believe that their children and students should be using computers, but are uncertain how.

A wide variety of games is available, with many different educational objectives. Some games are geared primarily toward educational goals, others primarily toward fun. Some concentrate on adding novelty to rote memorization and drill exercises; others have more sophisticated aims. While we cannot describe all the games on the market, we can classify them in a few broad categories. One of the categories is described here; the rest are less structured and are described in the section on experiential learning. All the games described in this chapter are available for personal computers.

One category of educational games is modeled after arcade games, combining teaching with colorful graphics, amusing sound effects, and a variable pace. Spelling games challenge children to spell correctly the name of a pictured object before it explodes or is eaten by some animated creature. Arithmetic games present a problem and a choice of answers. When the right answer is selected, a graphical reward such as a balloon appears; when the wrong answer is selected, a graphical punishment such as a dragon shooting fire at buildings appears. Typing programs teach touch typing by displaying animated letters on the screen, perhaps floating on a cloud from one side of the screen to the other. To score, the user must type the letters before the cloud disappears. Most of these games include various speeds and levels so that players of different skill levels can use them. They make previously boring tasks challenging and fun, and their sounds and pictures hold players' attention. Because they are computer games, they also move quickly and provide constant stimulation.

Models and Simulations

A *model* is a simplified representation of reality designed by a human.
A *simulation* is the use of a model to imitate or predict reality. Since
computers are such powerful tools and since computer calculation time
is less expensive than human calculation time, computer simulations
have widespread use, particularly in weather forecasting, economics,
social sciences, and physical sciences. They also have great potential in
education.

Educational models and simulations can be purchased ready-made
or can be designed by a teacher and class for a particular purpose using
a specially designed language such as MicroDYNAMO. Suppose, for
example, a teacher wants to teach a class about pond life. The class
could visit a pond to observe the various types of wildlife there, the
depth and circumference of the pond, and the condition of the water.
Using data from past years and some knowledge of pond life, the class
could then build a model with which to predict the condition of the
pond in a given number of years.

Prepackaged educational simulations come in a variety of forms for
a variety of purposes. Simulations of science experiments, particularly
in chemistry and physics, can take the place of actual experiments or
can serve as a preparation for lab experiments, giving students a chance
to observe the expected results before trying experiments themselves.
For example, a chemistry experiment in which students heat various
gases to see how quickly they expand can be animated and displayed
graphically on a personal computer screen (see Fig. 11.3). Similarly, a
physics experiment in which a projectile is launched at a specific angle
and velocity can be animated to show the projectile's path.

The computer can also be used to simulate scientific phenomena
otherwise invisible to the human eye. With sophisticated computer
graphics, for example, the structure of atoms and molecules can be
viewed in three dimensions and their movement animated. Similarly,
in biology, animated computer models of functioning organs can be
viewed and rotated. With a high-resolution graphics system, these
models can be far more convincing than textbook photos. Although
high-quality graphics systems of this kind are still too expensive for the
average chemistry or biology classroom, films of such simulations are
readily affordable and can be distributed for classroom use until high-
quality graphics systems become affordable.

Simulations are also used in areas of social study. In economics, for
example, computer programs allow children to pretend to own small
businesses and test their business sense. One classic and simple example of this is a lemonade stand simulation program designed for el-

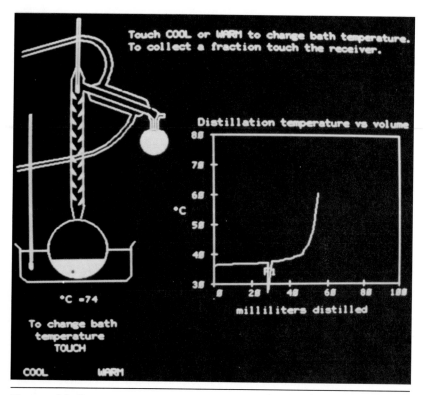

Touch COOL or WARM to change bath temperature.
To collect a fraction touch the receiver.

Distillation temperature vs volume

°C

°C =74

To change bath
temperature
TOUCH

COOL   WARM

milliliters distilled

Figure 11.3
A snapshot from a chemistry CAI course. (Courtesy of Control Data
Corporation)

ementary school children. The children oversee several lemonade stands
over a series of days. Each child starts with a certain amount of money
and a lemonade stand and must decide how much money to allot for
advertising, how much to charge per glass of lemonade, and how many
glasses of lemonade to prepare. The children are told how well each
stand fared after a day of operation and are allowed to change advertising budgets, lemonade prices, or quantities prepared. If they do well,
they earn money to use for the next round; if not, they lose money and
will probably change their business strategy. The computer alters the
scenarios slightly from one round to the next, sometimes warning that
the weather is unusually hot or cold. The cost of lemonade may also
change, depending on whether sugar is provided by the parents or purchased by the children. Although this program has only a few variables,
it provides an enjoyable introduction to the free enterprise system.

■ Experiential Learning

All the applications previously discussed serve as supplements to the materials usually found in a classroom. They provide additional teaching tools, perhaps taking some of the drudgery out of repetitive tasks such as memorization. However, they do not necessarily alter the established classroom structure, where the teacher is an authority figure supervising the students, who are expected to follow directions. While CAI ideally allows students to work at their own pace, it does not challenge the belief that there is an established body of knowledge that all students should learn before they advance. Some critics argue that CAI "programs" the child and that the reverse should be true—the child should program the computer. We now turn to several very different approaches to the use of the computer in education, approaches that reject the traditional methods and propose instead to change the role of teacher and classroom to help children learn actively and effectively by giving them the freedom to explore and to discover for themselves.

LOGO

One of the major proponents of experiential learning is Seymour Papert of MIT. Papert has been heavily influenced by the theories of the Swiss psychologist Jean Piaget, who believed that learning occurs largely through play and action. With colleagues at Bolt, Beranek and Newman, Inc. and at MIT, he developed the programming language LOGO to facilitate active learning through play and experimentation, with particular emphasis on mathematical concepts. Papert emphasized mathematics because, in his view, traditional methods of teaching present mathematics in such an abstract and meaningless way that few people can see past the drill to find the reason behind the process. In contrast, Papert has developed what he considers a more humanistic and concrete approach, which he hopes will put an end to what he calls "mathophobia," the fear of mathematics.

Papert and his colleagues set out to create a programming language that was syntactically simple, easy to learn, and powerful to use and that would help students think logically about mathematics. The result was LOGO, a language meant to make learning to communicate with the computer a natural process. With a few simple commands, the child using LOGO can control a drawing device called a *turtle*, which allows the child to draw an endless variety of pictures.

The turtle is intended to be an "object to think with." It comes in many forms, often either a mechanical computer-controlled device on wheels holding a pen or an arrow on a computer screen that draws lines at the user's request (see Fig. 11.4). With the basic commands FOR-WARD <a given number of spaces>, RIGHT <a certain number of de-grees>, PENUP (to lift the pen off the paper to move it without leaving a trace), and PENDOWN (to put the pen back down on the paper), the user can draw almost anything by "teaching" the computer a new word—that is, by writing a procedure to execute the desired instructions.

For example, a child can teach the turtle to draw a square by defining the word SQUARE with the actions shown below:

```
TO SQUARE
    FORWARD 100
    RIGHT 90
    FORWARD 100
    RIGHT 90
    FORWARD 100
    RIGHT 90
    FORWARD 100
    RIGHT 90
END
```

Once the word SQUARE has been defined, it can be used any time the child wishes to draw a square with 100 units to a side. To simplify the program, a repeat command similar to the BASIC or Pascal FOR loop can be used:

Figure 11.4
(a) Floor and (b) screen turtles used with LOGO. (Courtesy of Dr. Robert W. Lawler)

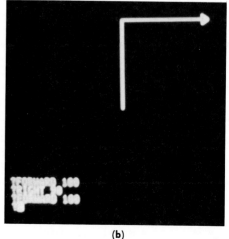

(a)   (b)

```
TO SQUARE
  REPEAT 4
    FORWARD 100
    RIGHT 90
  END
END
```

Finally, to write a more general procedure that can draw squares of varying sizes, the child can introduce a variable called :SIZE and define SQUARE as follows:

```
TO SQUARE :SIZE
  REPEAT 4
    FORWARD :SIZE
    RIGHT 90
  END
END
```

This procedure draws a square with sides of length :SIZE. Thus the request SQUARE 50 will draw a square with sides 50 units long.

Why is this simple idea so powerful? First, the child learns about numbers and basic geometry by using them to achieve a desired goal. A 90-degree angle *means* something to a child trying to draw a rectangle. Similarly, the child can *see* that a 20-unit line is twice as long as a 10-unit line. A child drawing a complex picture must be able to estimate lengths and angles—to predict how the computer will react to a command. And since the concepts are being used toward a desired end, mathematics becomes a useful tool rather than simply a set of repetitions. At the same time, LOGO encourages the logical process of breaking down a problem into manageable pieces, which is useful in many types of problem solving. A child who wants to draw a flower, for example, will have a much easier task if he figures out how to draw one petal and duplicates the operation for each petal.

Further, the LOGO turtle makes mathematics a more concrete subject because the child can think of the turtle's movement in terms of her own body's movements. To find the bug in a program, for example, the child can simply "play turtle" and walk through the instructions line by line. To figure out how to solve a new problem, such as drawing a circle, the child need only try to perform the operation herself by walking through it. To draw a circle, she would need to step forward a little and turn a little repeatedly until the circle was complete. Examples of pictures drawn with LOGO are given in Fig. 11.5.

The action of debugging offers another advantage. Debugging, a necessity in programming, encourages the child to evaluate rather than discard misjudgments. There are no mistakes in LOGO, just misjudgments and surprises. The child is not stifled by the usual right/wrong

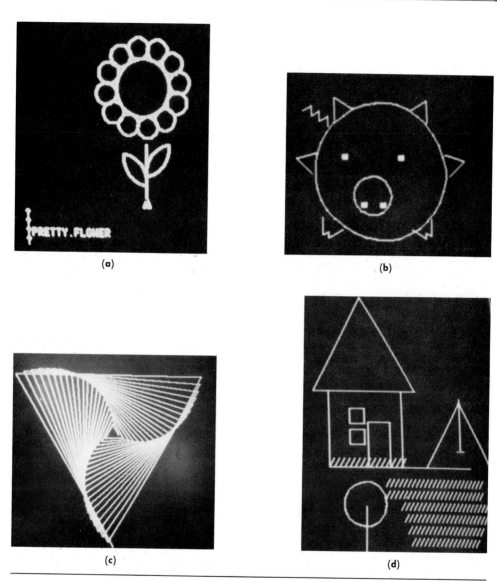

Figure 11.5
Pictures drawn by children with LOGO. (Courtesy of Dr. Robert W. Lawler)

distinction. Instead, the *process* becomes as important as the result, and the child becomes an epistemologist of sorts, thinking about thinking and learning about learning.

LOGO the programming language is much more extensive than these examples suggest. Besides turtle graphics, it also includes a full-list processing language that is almost identical with LISP (see Chapter

9) except that its command names more closely reflect the purpose they serve. For example, the name CAR (a LISP command) is replaced by FIRST because this command selects the first element on a list; and CDR (another LISP command) is replaced by BUTFIRST because this command gives all but the first element of a list.

Turtle graphics encourage children to experiment with LOGO, a process that may lead them to try to use the list-processing features of the language. Papert reports on one child, Jenny, who could not understand the importance of grammar until she used LOGO to construct "poems." To do this she formed lists of words—nouns, verbs, adjectives, and so on. She then formed sentences by randomly selecting words from the various lists. She could construct a simple sentence, for example, by selecting a word from the noun list and a word from the verb list. Since she had to make use of syntactic categories, such as noun and verb, she began to understand the role that grammar plays in our language. A sample of Jenny's poems is shown in Fig. 11.6.

When LOGO is used as intended, the role of the teacher changes from an authoritarian to a cooperative one. The child and the teacher are engaged in a partnership, and often the teacher knows no more than the child about how to solve a particular problem. Teachers are still essential to the learning process, but their importance is in the support and guidance they give as children build their own intellectual structures.

Word Processors and Other Writing Aids

Another experiential use of computers in the classroom is that of word processors to teach writing. Poor writing skills have been a recent cause for worry among educators and employers. Several reevaluations of current methods of writing instruction have concluded that they fail in part because they stress the end product. Critics point out that it is not enough to read the works of great writers and expect somehow to assimilate their skill; it is also necessary to examine the process and prac-

Figure 11.6
An example of Jenny's poetry, constructed with LOGO. (From *Mindstorms: Children, Computers, and Powerful Ideas* by Seymour Papert. © 1980 by Basic Books, Inc., Publishers. Reprinted by permission of the publisher.)

INSANE RETARD MAKES BECAUSE SWEET SNOOPY SCREAMS
SEXY WOLF LOVES THATS WHY THE SEXY LADY HATES
UGLY MAN LOVES BECAUSE UGLY DOG HATES
MAD WOLF HATES BECAUSE INSANE WOLF SKIPS
SEXY RETARD SCREAMS THATS WHY THE SEXY RETARD HATES
THIN SNOOPY RUNS BECAUSE FAT WOLF HOPS
SWEET FOGINY SKIPS A FAT LADY RUNS

tice the craft of writing. As part of this reevaluation, many educators have turned to the word processor and its potential as a writing tool.

As explained in Chapter 4, a word processor is either a computer program used on a general-purpose computer or a special-purpose computer used for word processing. In either case, it is designed to make typing, rewriting, and formatting text relatively painless. The first generation of word processors, though powerful tools, were difficult to master, often requiring special training or the patience to wade through nearly incomprehensible manuals. Now, however, software designers have become more concerned with user-friendliness, and new word processors are available that are easy to use and are designed to adapt to the user. Some are intended for specific audiences: the Bank Street Writer, discussed in Chapter 4, for example, was written especially for children. Using it requires very little guidance from an instructor since the menu of available choices can always be displayed on the screen. Once an option has been selected, easy-to-follow step-by-step instructions are provided to lead the user through the process; and, in general, the results of a command can be undone if necessary. In Bank Street Writer the act of word processing is divided into three distinct stages, or modes, that correspond to the three phases of writing—write mode, edit mode, and transfer mode (in which the text is stored, retrieved from storage, or printed). A typical Bank Street Writer screen is shown in Fig. 11.7.

Figure 11.7
A Bank Street Writer screen. (Courtesy of Broderbund and Bank Street College)

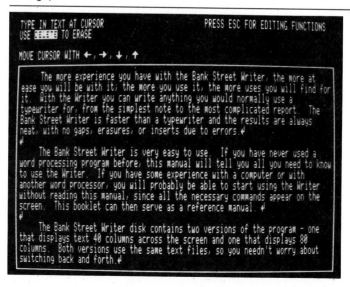

Proponents of the use of word processors in teaching believe that writing should be an experiential process, not just a means to produce finished products. One of the major causes of so-called writer's block is that people become so obsessed with the necessary perfection of the final product that they cannot bring themselves to commit a less-than-perfect first draft to paper. For children in particular, the physical act of writing and recopying is so laborious that drafting a piece is a painful process, and revision is even more tiresome. If a student has no easy way to revise, an important part of the writing process may be lost. Furthermore, if a writer does not have the security of easy rewriting, even the original drafting of the text can involve added pressure because the writer may be trying to edit in her head a text that has not yet been written.

Advocates believe that with a word processor, these frustrations are alleviated. Writers have the freedom to experiment, to concentrate on content and ideas rather than wording and grammar, and to revise and rework. The draft is always neat and pleasant to look at, no matter what the stage of drafting. Many professional writers find the word processor to be a freeing medium—they find that they write better and faster with it. Educators have found the same of their students; freed from the permanence of paper and pencil, students take risks, experimenting with both ideas and modes of presentation. By concentrating on the process, some students produce superior products.

Objections can be raised to this use of the word processor, however. Some objections are reactionary, asserting that our present methods of teaching writing are adequate or that a machine could not possibly help with a process meant to be done with pen and paper. Other objections are based on the present lack of available computers—a real but temporary problem. Still others are concerned with whether word processors will be used to their fullest potential, as more than electronic typewriters. After all, teachers with only a few computers may be able to let students type only final drafts on the word processor. This renders the rewriting process as laborious as ever; the final product may look nicer but is no less painful to draft. Also, teachers who have enough machines but who continue to view writing as an end product may not make full use of the word processor's unique capabilities. Other opponents worry about the time required to learn to type, the disintegration of handwriting skills, and the possible tendency to accept badly written papers because they look attractive. As always, the technology presents an opportunity that can be either used or abused; we must decide how to use it beneficially.

In addition to word processing programs, some teachers are using other writing aids to help students improve their writing. Increasingly common are spelling-check programs, which compare each word of the text with entries in an on-line dictionary of properly spelled words. Such programs typically highlight words that appear in the text but not in the dictionary and give the writer a chance to change them. The responsibility for correct spelling is still in the hands of the writer; such programs merely draw attention to unusual spellings. Some spelling-check programs allow the user to add commonly used words, names, and acronyms to the dictionary.

Other writing aids include programs that highlight uses of the passive voice, programs that draw attention to overused words and phrases, and programs that count the number of letters in words, words in sentences, and sentences in paragraphs. These devices make writers more aware of their writing style and hence help them to become more effective writers.

Another problem with current writing instruction is a general lack of motivation on the part of the students. Topics for writing exercises are assigned by the teacher, and the finished product is read only by the teacher or perhaps by family and friends. Such exercises offer students little to get excited about, even when a word processor is available. However, when the students are encouraged to write for a purpose—to communicate with their peers—they have motivation to write.

Encouraging students to write for a purpose is the aim of QUILL, a program developed by Bolt, Beranek and Newman, Inc. to provide a writing environment for third through sixth graders. QUILL offers not only a word processor but an integrated writing environment consisting of an electronic mail system, a planner that encourages brainstorming and prewriting, and a database that allows students to write articles on topics that interest them or their peers and to make these articles available to others. Articles can be retrieved by their name, subject, or author. The Electronic Mailbag, as it is called, allows students to send mail to any one person, to a predetermined group of people (say, to all the members of a softball team or reading group), or to everyone in the class. With the aid of a modem and telephone, students can communicate with students in other schools in different parts of the country as electronic pen pals. Finally, a Confidential Chat program allows a student to present a problem anonymously for others to discuss—a sort of Dear Abby in the classroom.

Preliminary field tests conducted in three different schools compared the writing improvement of children in a traditional classroom with the improvements of those in a QUILL classroom. Their results suggest the QUILL students not only improved their expository and persuasive writing skills more than their peers but also substantially changed their attitudes toward writing. Children who used QUILL got more excited about writing, did more writing and revising, and were more interested in learning how to improve their writing. Some students even asked to stay in at recess or come in before or after school to work on their writing. If computer environments can continue to succeed in making reading and writing more enjoyable, they may help reverse the trend toward increased illiteracy in the United States.

Experiential Educational Games

An earlier section described fast-paced, arcade-type games that make routine memorization less tedious. This section concentrates on games that require complex thought and experimentation.

Some educational games work to develop sophisticated skills, such as reasoning and logic. One example is a game series called Snooper Troops, in which players emulate detectives. The child, as a Snooper Trooper, rides around in a Snoopmobile, follows suspects, reports to Headquarters, and collects clues. In the process he must read maps, take notes, retrieve information from a simple database, and organize the information to solve the mystery. A time limit is imposed to encourage children to work together in small groups to solve the mystery since it is difficult for one child to solve it alone under the given time constraints.

Another category of educational games includes simulations that allow children to pretend to be somewhere or someone else. A geographically accurate flight simulator program, for example, allows children to pretend to fly a plane around the United States. Sophisticated computer graphics and sound effects create the illusion of flying as the program reacts to movements of the joystick or instructions to change the position of the plane's flaps.

Adventure games take children to another time or place. Fantasy games modeled after the popular Dungeons and Dragons game present a fantasy world to explore. The child directs the computer with simple natural language commands. If the program does not understand the child's command, it will ask for clarification. In addition to developing problem-solving skills, these games encourage verbal development by requiring reading and writing rather than illustrating the game with graphics. An example of an adventure game is given in Fig. 11.8. In contrast to games that create a world of pure fantasy, an Oregon Trail program, written from diaries of pioneers who traveled the Oregon Trail, takes a child across the wilderness in a covered wagon. The child must decide what to spend money on (ammunition, food, clothing) and when to spend it. In addition, the child chooses when to rest, eat, hunt, and so forth. The object of the game is to withstand the natural dangers of the country and arrive alive at the end of the trail. Although the program does reduce a life-threatening experience to a simple computer

You are in an open field west of a big white house with a boarded front door. There is a small mailbox here.

Look in the mailbox.

The mailbox is closed.

Open it, please.

Opening the mailbox reveals a leaflet.

Take the leaflet.

Taken.

Walk southwest.

You are in a dark forest with tall trees on all sides. Tied to a high branch on the nearest tree is a rope which dangles almost to your waist. On the ground there is a pot of gold.

Figure 11.8
The beginnings of a computer adventure game. The player's responses are in italics.

game, it may encourage children to do further research to gain a more accurate view of pioneer life.

Math games encourage children to experiment with numbers and mathematical concepts by providing motivation in the form of graphics and sound. The program Darts, for example, helps children to develop an intuitive sense of fractions. Balloons are situated between integers on a number line. To burst a balloon, a child estimates the fractional distance between the balloon and the integers surrounding it (see Fig. 11.9). In another math game, a number of "green globs" are positioned on coordinate axes. The object is to hit as many globs as possible by writing equations for the computer to graph. If the line that represents an equation runs through a glob, the glob is hit (see Fig. 11.10). The active use of these concepts promotes an understanding hard to duplicate with rote exercises.

Another family of games offers a brief tutorial in the use of animated tools and machines and challenges the player to use this equipment to complete some task. One game graphically illustrates the patterns of holes made by various stamping machines and then shows the player a strip of material stamped by a set of these machines. The player must discern which machines make up the set. Another chal-

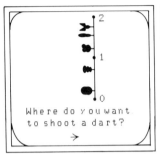  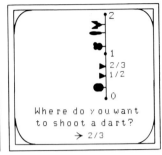

Figure 11.9
Darts: a math game that teaches fraction concepts. (From E. Paul Goldenberg et al., *Computers, Education, and Special Needs,* © 1984, Addison-Wesley, Reading, Massachusetts. Figs. 4.3, 4.4, 4.5.)

lenging game, Rocky's Boots, presents the player with a set of machines that recognize colors and shapes and a set of connectors for these machines that represent the operations of AND, OR, and NOT, described in Chapter 3. The object of the game is to assemble the set of recognizers and connectors so that when a series of objects such as triangles, squares, and circles of various colors pass by the connected compo-

Figure 11.10
Green Globs: a math game that teaches graphing concepts. (From E. Paul Goldenberg et al., Computers, Education, and Special Needs, © 1984, Addison-Wesley, Reading, Massachusetts. Figs. 4.12, 4.13.)

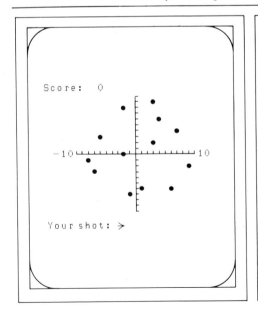 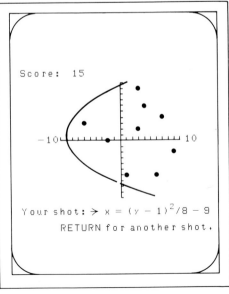

nents, Rocky's Boot will kick out of the series only those objects being sought, such as red squares or circles. These two games force the player to think logically to solve nonelementary logic problems.

Teaching Computer Programming

Computers are also being used in innovative ways to teach programming concepts. At Brown University, a special auditorium allows instructors to teach programming dynamically. The auditorium houses approximately 60 *personal workstations* (described in Chapter 3)—powerful personal computers connected by a cable network. Each student sits in front of a workstation, and the instructor has a workstation at the lecture podium. When discussing a new concept, the instructor can illustrate it by running a demonstration program on each student's screen. For example, to explain a program to alphabetize the elements in an array, the teacher can run a program that animates the array elements being sorted. The program is displayed in one window, with the current instruction highlighted; the changing values of variables are displayed in another window; and the actual output is shown in a third window. After the demonstration, the instructor can allow the students to modify the program, altering variables and constants and then running the revised program to note the effect of these changes. For complex algorithms, such as the sorting of numbers and words and the searching of the sorted lists, it is very helpful to be able to see the program run and very tedious to simulate a run by hand. A variety of software tools have been developed to facilitate instruction of this kind, including a package called BALSA, for Brown ALgorithm Simulation and Analysis. Figure 11.11 illustrates a BALSA demonstration.

■ Computers and Special Education

Special education is a broad term encompassing a variety of learning situations. It refers to the education of all students whose needs cannot be met in the traditional classroom. If such students' special needs can be satisfied, their "handicaps" disappear and they can be educated within a normal curriculum.

The computer can play an important role in special education. It can liberate the physically disabled, granting them a degree of independence and access to the world around them that otherwise would be difficult or impossible to obtain. The learning disabled child can find stimulation and motivation from computer programs that are engrossing and nonjudgmental, while the gifted child can be stimulated by advanced educational software.

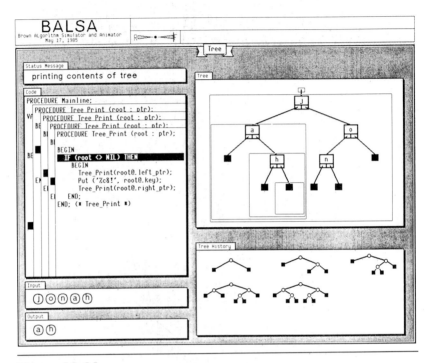

Figure 11.11
BALSA simulation of a Pascal program under execution. (Courtesy of Marc Brown and Robert Sedgewick)

Computers and the Physically Disabled

Computers can help the physically disabled in a number of ways. This discussion will focus on computer systems that help the handicapped to communicate and to process information since these abilities are vital to educational achievement.

Electronic devices can greatly enhance a handicapped person's self-sufficiency, making it possible for him to live alone or with minimal assistance. Robots can help him eat by himself, turn the pages as he reads a book, set up a typewriter and paper, and dial a phone number and hold the receiver. One example of a liberating device is an *ability phone* which allows some severely handicapped people to live outside the nursing homes and institutions to which they might otherwise be confined. The ability phone can dial up to six emergency numbers when the help key is pressed, playing an electronic message when the phone is answered and waiting for a response. It will dial until someone responds. It can monitor the state of the user by asking at predetermined times, "Are you okay?" and dialing emergency numbers if there is no response within five minutes. It can also answer the phone automatically. The ability phone, combined with an electric wheelchair, electric door opener, and a computerized voice synthesizer, made it possible for one young man, a quadriplegic who is unable to talk, to live in a college dormitory and earn a college degree.

Electronic devices can also help severely handicapped people to communicate with other people and with a computer. Pointing devices and touch-sensitive screens are useful to persons who have some motor control but not enough for typing. Special pointing devices are available for persons who have little motor control. A person can signal the computer by hitting the keyboard with any part of his body, by hitting particular keys with a headstick or mouthstick, or even by raising an eyebrow, blowing on a device, making a noise, or blinking an eye. These signaling devices are often used with *scanners* (see Fig. 11.12). A scanner presents the user with a menu of choices and automatically scans the choices by advancing the cursor from one to the next. The menu may consist of a set of simple requests, the letters of the alphabet, or a list of phonetic representations. The user's job is to signal the computer when the desired choice is highlighted. The speed of the scanner can

Figure 11.12
A rudimentary scanner to help a physically handicapped person communicate with a computer. (From *Technology for Special Children,* E. Paul Goldenberg, University Park Press, 1979, Fig. 2, p. 37)

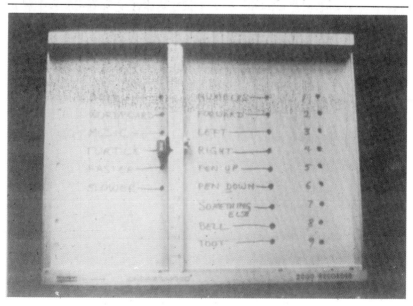

be adjusted to meet the person's pointing ability. A two-dimensional array of choices allows the user to select from a large number of possibilities more rapidly by selecting first a row and then the appropriate column within the row.

Scanning even a two-dimensional array can be a time-consuming and frustrating process, particularly if the goal is to spell out a sentence. One method that simplifies this task is anticipatory text selection. *Anticipatory text selection*, as the name implies, tries to anticipate the user's message, thus making it unnecessary for her to spell out the message letter by letter. An anticipatory letter selector anticipates the next letter in the word based on the previous letters and presents the most probable letter choices for the user's approval. The scanner then highlights the possibilities, one by one, so the user can indicate the desired letter. If the letter is not among those presented, another menu of letters is supplied. An example is shown in Fig. 11.13. A word anticipator helps the user complete the word once the first few letters have been chosen by providing a list of common words that begin with the chosen letters. An example of this is shown in Fig. 11.14. If the desired word is among them, the user can simply point to it; if not, she can continue to spell it out, letter by letter. The completed word will then be added to the database of choices in case it is used again later.

A number of systems have been developed to help people with more limited disabilities, such as the blind and the deaf. Blind people may be able to communicate orally but are restricted in their written communication; they cannot read printed text, and most seeing people cannot read Braille. Furthermore, blind people obviously cannot read a CRT screen. Several devices facilitate written communication between blind and blind, blind and seeing, and blind and computer. Braille keyboards are available for input, and Braille printers for paper output. A

Figure 11.13
Anticipatory letter selection helps handicapped people communicate by suggesting the letters of words they wish to write. (From Craig W. Hockathorne and Dudley S. Childress, "Anticipatory Text Selections in a Writing Aid for People with Severe Motor Impairment," *IEEE Micro*, June 1983, p. 20, Figure 3)

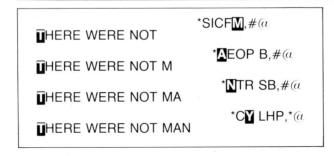

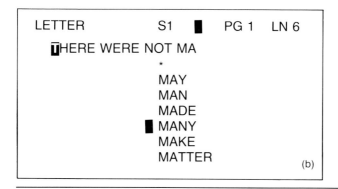

```
LETTER              S1   ■   PG 1   LN 6
   ▯HERE WERE NOT MA
             *
          MAY
          MAN
          MADE
        ■ MANY
          MAKE
          MATTER
                                        (b)
```

Figure 11.14
Anticipatory word selection helps handicapped people by providing choices of possible words to complete sentences they wish to write. (From Craig W. Hockathorne and Dudley S. Childress, "Anticipatory Text Selections in a Writing Aid for People with Severe Motor Impairment," *IEEE Micro*, June 1983, p. 21, Figure 4)

special device even produces "soft copy" by raising small pins to give an instant Braille representation of the computer screen. Since many blind people do not read Braille, however, this system is not always useful. Of use to all blind people are talking calculators and computers that can verify what has been typed in and communicate output. In addition, machines now exist that can read a printed text aloud.

Computers have an exciting role to play in teaching the deaf to read. Reading is taught to hearing children by building on their spoken language; but for deaf children, this is not a viable method. The program CARIS (Computer Animated Reading Instruction System) provides an interesting alternative. It typically gives the student a list of a dozen nouns and verbs from which to choose. The child selects a noun, perhaps with a lightpen or touch-sensitive screen, and a cartoon picture of the noun appears on the screen. The child chooses a verb, and the picture is animated according to the verb choice. For example, if the child selected the noun *dog* and the verb *runs*, the dog would run across the screen. Even implausible selections are illustrated; for example, if the noun *house* and the verb *runs* were selected, the house would run across the screen.

This system is useful because it encourages exploratory learning by creating a play environment. The child is free to make mistakes without either penalty or adult intervention. Limitations on the system are primarily hardware-based; storing the cartoons and their animations requires a great deal of electronic storage space. For this reason, the number of nouns and verbs available on current systems is limited. This problem should be alleviated in time, as further advances in hardware development make storage cheaper and more compact and retrieval faster.

The Computer and Cognitive Disabilities

Since education requires communication with the world around us, even slight impairments in the ability to communicate may have a great impact on success in learning. For example, children who are constantly distracted, even if they are very bright, have problems adjusting to traditional classroom environments. It has sometimes been assumed that children with short attention spans lack intelligence. Often this is not the case; they may suffer from an unusually strong need to be stimulated and so may constantly seek stimulation. Arcade-style computer games have a great deal of appeal for children, and they have been known to completely engage children with attention disabilities. As a result, the children have increased their attention spans so that they can engage in other forms of learning.

A more serious disability is autism. Autistic children have short attention spans and also are unresponsive to gestures, facial expressions, and sound. While it is difficult for autistic children to learn on their own, it is often more difficult for them to learn from others. For them exploratory learning is often more successful than imitative learning. The computer offers an attractive learning environment for such children because it requires their involvement. In addition, its use of color, sound, and animation can be captivating. With proper programming, an engaging educational environment can be created for the autistic child. LOGO, for example, has in some instances been effective in reaching such children.

Gifted Children

Gifted children may not always be treated with the same sympathy as handicapped children. However, a gifted child in a normal classroom is handicapped every bit as much as an average sixth grader placed in a second-grade classroom would be. When gifted children are not given special attention, they may become bored with learning and fail to make full use of their natural talents. Indeed, the National Commission on Excellence in Education found that over half the population of gifted students did not match their tested ability with comparable achievement in school. The computer does not provide an answer to the problem of education for the gifted, but it does offer some new possibilities.

Usually attempts to provide special opportunities for gifted students involve removing them from their classrooms, either to attend classes for gifted students, to attend classes with older students, or to study with private tutors or advisors. These opportunities may satisfy such children intellectually, but they involve the risk of making it more difficult for gifted children to associate with their peers. A computer can provide challenging opportunities and advanced courses without requiring children to leave the building. CAI courses, though limited in some respects, can act as stepping stones to further learning. For example, a child who is ready to study chemistry before the rest of her class can begin by using a good CAI program with graphic simulations of chemistry experiments. In contrast, a personal computer with a powerful programming language such as LOGO or Pascal can give the child a whole new world to explore, a world in which the only limitations are the memory size of the computer and the child's imagination. If the child is interested, he can write programs to help his peers with what they are learning in class, thus integrating his learning experiences with those in the classroom rather than isolating them. Finally, when computers become more widely used, electronic mail can facilitate question-and-answer exchanges between child and advisor, especially if the advisor is at another school.

SUMMARY

We have identified two types of learning, structured and experiential, to describe a variety of educational uses of computers. The principal form of computer use in structured learning is computer-aided instruction. PLATO is the largest and richest such system in existence; many hundreds of courses have been developed for it. The creation of CAI software, however, is very tedious and time-consuming and requires the efforts of many people. Computer-based tools to support structured learning include statistical software, electronic books, electronic games, and simulations.

LOGO is the prototypical environment for computer use in experiential learning. Children can use their understanding of body movement to compose instructions to direct the motion of a turtle. They can also use LOGO to compose sentences since it is a language that is well suited to dealing with symbols. Word processors, especially when combined with tools to encourage writing and communication, also provide experiential learning. Some educational games that require logical thinking and discovery serve the same purpose.

Finally, the computer can play an important role for the physically handicapped by increasing their mobility and communication skills. The computer also has an important role to play in the education of gifted students, providing them with opportunities not otherwise present in their classrooms.

FURTHER READING

Alfred Bork, *Learning with Computers* (Bedford, Mass.: Digital Press, 1981).

P. Coburn, P. Kelman, N. Roberts, T. F. R. Snyder, D. H. Wyatt, and C. Weiner, *Practical Guide to Computers in Education* (Reading, Mass.: Addison-Wesley, 1982).

L. D. Geoffrion and O. P. Geoffrion, *Computers and Reading Instruction* (Reading, Mass.: Addison-Wesley, 1983).

E. P. Goldernberg, *Special Technology for Special Children* (Cambridge, Mass.: University Park Press, Bolt Beranek and Newman, Inc., 1979).

E. P. Goldernberg, S. J. Russell, and C. J. Carter, *Computers, Education and Special Needs* (Reading, Mass.: Addison-Wesley, 1984).

P. Kelman, A. Bardige, J. Choate, G. Hanify, J. Richards, N. Roberts, J. Walters, and M. K. Tornrose, *Computers in Teaching Mathematics* (Reading, Mass.: Addison-Wesley, 1983).

S. Papert, *Mindstorms—Children, Computers, and Powerful Ideas* (New York: Basic Books, 1980).

P. Suppes, ed., *University-Level Computer-Assisted Instruction at Stanford: 1968–1980* (Stanford, Calif.: Institute for Mathematical Studies in the Social Sciences, Stanford University, 1981).

R. P. Taylor, ed., *The Computer in the School: Tutor, Tool, Tutee* (New York: Teachers College Press, Teachers College, Columbia University, 1980).

ISSUES AND IDEAS

1. Describe four different educational experiences that you have had, identify them as either experiential or structured, and describe their effectiveness or lack of effectiveness.

2. Sophisticated CAI tutorials use techniques that are akin to the Socratic method. State why such tutorials are likely to be either more or less effective than the Socratic method practiced by humans.

3. Is CAI an active or passive learning environment? Justify your answer.

4. Explain how LOGO may encourage experiential learning. Then describe how LOGO could be used in a structured fashion. State which of these two uses you think would be most effective and why.

5. Describe how word processors could be used innovatively in the teaching of poetry and biology.

6. Give several advantages and disadvantages to teaching computer programming using a network of workstations.

7. Propose two new educational games, one that supports structured learning and one that supports experiential learning. After describing them, justify their educational value.

Artificial Intelligence

The Analytical Engine has no pretensions of original thought. It can only do what we tell it to do.

ADA AUGUSTA, COUNTESS OF LOVELACE
(1842)

■ Introduction

The advent of electronic computers was a stimulating intellectual development. Many thoughtful and creative individuals sought to discover and exploit the potential offered by these extremely fast computational engines. In fact, some perceived correctly that these machines could deal not only with programs and text but also with logical concepts. Thus was born the field of artificial intelligence, commonly known as AI.

Information of any kind can be stored in a computer. We can store data, as well as rules for accessing and manipulating that data. If the data represent logical quantities, such as statements that are true or false, and if the programs represent rules for deducing new true statements, then a step in the direction of artificial intelligence has been taken.

In this chapter we bring together a number of different topics that are usually said to constitute the field of artificial intelligence. These include the nature of intelligence, problem solving, natural language understanding, representation of knowledge, vision, expert systems, game playing, and intelligent programs. We also discuss the Japanese fifth-generation computer project, an ambitious effort to simplify computer use through the application of artificial intelligence. Some of these topics lie squarely in the field of computer science, while others overlap with linguistics, cognitive psychology, and philosophy.

What Is Intelligence?

Woody Allen, the American writer, director, actor, and comedian, tells an apocryphal tale about his father's being laid off from a job in a factory. The company replaced the elder Allen with a small machine that could do anything he could do and do it better, faster, and cheaper; the next day, Allen's mother ran out and bought one for herself.

This story captures a basic fear that many people hold about computers: the fear that machines will one day become so efficient, inexpensive, and intelligent that they will take over, making human labor obsolete, creating widespread unemployment, destroying the means for self-fulfillment for many people, and enslaving us all to tireless and demanding machines. The reality, however, is that computers cannot take over because they are incapable of original thought—incapable, in fact, of any kind of thought at all. In spite of this, extensive research has been carried out in artificial intelligence, a field whose goals include the design of machines that can behave intelligently.

The very idea of intelligent machines offends many people who believe that humans are unique in the possession of intelligence. Central to any debate on this issue is a clear understanding of what is meant by intelligence. However, attempts to define intelligence have met with little success.

Perhaps the simplest test of intelligence is the ability to understand human language. This is an inadequate test, however, since dogs and other animals can be trained to respond to verbal commands. If a dog responds to a command to sit, few would be so foolhardy as to claim that the act of sitting is anything more than a conditioned response. Since we cannot know what goes on in the dog's head, it is impossible to determine whether the dog is behaving intelligently. Of course, tests can determine how well a dog can learn specified actions, but that is a far cry from deciding whether the dog is intelligent.

Intelligence is clearly more than the ability to understand and communicate with others. Perhaps, then, we can equate intelligence with the ability to understand and form abstract ideas. These are activities that humans perform, and we may be tempted to use them in a definition of intelligence. However, if we cannot communicate with animals or ask a machine what it is thinking, then the test is useless, since we do not know whether they have these abilities.

Arriving at a concrete definition of intelligence seems a difficult task. Perhaps it is also an unnecessary one. It may make more sense to focus on what appears to be *intelligent behavior* than to focus on intelligence itself. But what is intelligent behavior?

This question also presents problems. We do seem to know instinctively, however, what kind of behavior is not intelligent. A person who deliberately crosses a busy street with her eyes closed is not behaving intelligently. It may be fair to say, then, that intelligence is typified by behavior that mimics that of individuals whom we classify as intelligent. The circularity of this definition reflects our inability to give a precise definition of intelligence.

One of the more profound thinkers to study AI realized this point quickly. Alan Turing, whose fundamental contributions to computer science are discussed in Chapter 2, conducted inquiries into the nature of intelligence that classify him as one of the first AI researchers. In an influential article in the philosophical journal *Mind* in 1950, Turing suggested a practical application of the argument given above. To determine whether a machine was intelligent, he proposed a test, later called the *Turing test*. A machine or program would pass the test when a human being was incapable of differentiating between human (and therefore intrinsically intelligent) behavior and machine behavior.

The Turing test would place a person in a room with two teletype machines, one connected to a computer and the other connected to another person. The person in the room would be allowed to ask any sort of question or communicate in any way with either of the teletypes. To prevent questions such as "Are you the computer?" the computer could behave in a distinctly human manner—it could lie. There would be no time limit to the interrogations. When the person in the room could not determine from the responses which respondent was human and which was mechanical, the computer would have passed the Turing test and could be said to have behaved intelligently.

■ Building Electronic Brains

At the time Turing published his article, machines were far from passing his test. Most early AI research focused on attempts to build "giant brains." Many researchers believed that computer circuitry could work in the same way as the neurons that make up the brain—and thus that computers could be built that learned in the same way as the brain does. In 1943, Warren McCulloch and Walter Pitts proposed that the brain be emulated by a net of computer neurons, a giant mathematical model of the nerves of the brain.

One project launched in the 1960s to test the neural net approach was the perceptron project at Cornell, led by Frank Rosenblatt. An early version of the perceptron system was supposed to mimic the eye and its associated nerves in the brain; its task was to learn to recognize letters by sight. First, light struck a grid of photocells, the machine's "eye." Next, the photocells emitted impulses received by associator units, simulating the firing of neurons. Finally, the associator units signaled response units, where recognition of a letter occurred.

Although the perceptron project achieved some successes (a perceptron did, for example, learn to recognize letters), it also drew criticism. Marvin Minsky and Seymour Papert of MIT, in their book *Perceptrons*, refuted Rosenblatt's assertion that a general problem-solving perceptron could be built based on the limited perceptrons in existence. In other words, it was fine to build a program that could recognize the letters of the alphabet, but building an intelligent machine on the same principles was another matter. Minsky and Papert believed that more knowledge of how humans learn was needed before an intelligent machine could be built. Partly as a result of their book, the study of mechanical models of the brain quickly ground to a halt.

Problem Solving

Another important area of research in AI concerns general methods for solving problems. Allen Newell, Herbert Simon, and J. C. Shaw in 1957 developed a program they called the General Problem Solver (GPS). GPS was the first program whose problem-solving processes required no knowledge about the particular type of problem to be solved. The program would use the same general methods to solve a calculus problem as it would to predict the weather.

To solve a problem, GPS required three different types of information—the initial state, the goal state, and rules for the system to change its state. For example, to solve a bridge design problem, GPS would need to know the size the bridge would have to be, the materials available, the desired final result (including such factors as how much weight it would have to support), the rules of physics that described bridge building and supports, and so forth.

GPS utilizes a technique known as *means-ends analysis* in solving problems. The program operates in a current state (when the program starts, the current state is the initial state). It then generates potential successor states and evaluates them to see which is more likely to move

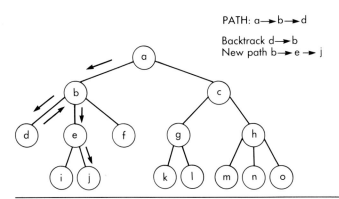

Figure 12.1
Backtracking to reach a desired goal in a tree diagram.

it toward its goal state. As it progresses, the program may discover that it is moving away rather than toward its goal state. In this case it backs up to a previous step and chooses a different successor state. This is called backtracking. The series of moves it takes can be visualized as moves on a tree of alternatives, generally moving forward but occasionally having to step back to find a path to the goal state. To enable the program to retrace its steps, a great deal of memory is required. Figure 12.1 illustrates the tree diagram of backtracking.

GPS succeeded in solving 11 different types of problems, including some problems in calculus and several different puzzles. The need for memory proved the program's downfall: GPS succeeded only in solving simple problems. On complex problems, it simply ran out of memory space and had to stop before it could solve the problem.

■ Language Translation

An early topic of research in artificial intelligence was the automatic translation of *natural language*, those languages used by human beings. English and French, for example, are natural languages, while Pascal and BASIC are computer languages. Although translators for computer languages were successfully constructed in the 1950s, natural languages presented important challenges that are still unmet. Many factors must be taken into consideration in language translation, such as differences in grammar, the importance of word order and case, and the precise relationships between words. Word-for-word translation has proved inadequate because it does not capture many fine points of language. Translation is also complicated by the fact that words generally have several meanings and by the use of idioms. (Consider, for example, the expression "He jumps to conclusions." A program must be able to differentiate between the physical act of jumping and the mental act of forming conclusions from incomplete information.) Thus, clarifying the meaning of ambiguous words requires some knowledge of context. Such knowledge is very difficult to impart to the translating program.

In 1949, Warren Weaver formulated a theory of language translation that borrowed from linguistics the concept of Interlingua, a hypothetical language that serves as the basis for all human languages. Weaver suggested that the way to translate from English to French, for example, was to translate first from English into Interlingua and then from Interlingua into French. Weaver proposed that research on computerized language translation concentrate on discovering this intermediate language for machine translation, a universal machine interlingua he called "machinese."

Several years later, A. G. Oettinger designed a program that would perform word-for-word translation by dictionary lookup, a more complex form of array searching. To translate Russian to English, the program used two parallel arrays, one containing Russian words and the other containing corresponding English words. The program searched through the Russian array until the proper word was found and then printed as a translation the corresponding word in the English array. When Oettinger's program translated Russian phrases into English, it listed all possible translations. For example, the following output typified the program's results:

> (In, At, Into, To, For, On) (last, latter, new, latest, lowest, worst) (time, tense) for analysis and synthesis, relay-contact, electrical (circuit, diagram, scheme) parallel-(series, successive, consecutive, consistent) (connection, junction, combination) (with, from) (success, luck) (to be utilized, to be taken advantage of) apparatus Boolean algebra.

A human translator would then sort through the output and clean it up so that it would appear in a readable and comprehensible form. The jumble above, correctly translated, would read:

> In recent times, Boolean algebra has been successfully employed in the analysis of relay networks of the series-parallel type.

Clearly, Oettinger's word-for-word approach is not what we desire from machine translation. By failing to take into account such factors as tense, context, and word order, it does a less than perfect job of language translation. Approaches that require human assistance based on machine-generated possibilities of translations have many advantages, however. A person can prevent the computer from straying too far from an accurate translation.

In 1973, Yorick Wilks developed a program that stressed the semantic links between words in a sentence rather than the syntactic relationships—that is, the words' meanings rather than their order. The program can translate short English phrases into relatively good French. The program works by converting the English phrase into an intermediate semantic representation (much like Weaver's machinese) and then into the final translated text.

Wilks' system first takes the English sentence as input, treating it as one long string. After breaking the string down into words, it replaces each word with an internal formula that represents the various possible meanings of the word. The formulas use elements to express these meanings. Elements are the most fundamental unit in Wilks' system, representing basic conditions, qualities, and actions that underlie much of human communication. There are 60 elements in all, in four classes: entities, states, qualities, and actions. Elements from Wilks' entities class include MAN and STUFF. The actions class includes the elements CAUSE and FLOW.

Elements, then, are a basis for determining what words mean. For example, the word *drink* is an action that CAUSES STUFF, namely liquid, to FLOW. When a word has more than one possible meaning, it is represented by more than one formula. The formulas are then compared against bare templates, sets of standard rules for word interaction. These templates represent typical ways in which words interrelate in a sentence. An example of a template is MAN-DO-THING. Where words are ambiguous, bare templates help decide which meaning is most correct. For example, the word *pitcher* used as an object with the word *drink* (as in "we drank a pitcher of lemonade") would have as one of its bare templates CONTAINER-OF-STUFF; if used as a subject in a sentence about baseball (as in "the pitcher struck out six batters"), the word would use the template MAN-DO-THING. By comparing the bare templates for the word *pitcher* with the bare templates of other words in these sentences, the program determines the appropriate meaning.

If after matching against the templates, more than one interpretation remains, the program calls on a more detailed evaluation procedure that takes into account probabilities about interrelationships between words. The system finally uses some knowledge of the world, programmed in previously, to determine whether the interpretations selected make sense. Finally, a text generator puts the sentence back together in reasonably good, grammatical French.

As this example indicates, natural language translation is a difficult subject. A great deal of information about usage and context must be made explicit if we are going to develop adequate methods of machine translation.

Game Playing

Some of the more fruitful research in AI has involved programs that play games in an intelligent, or apparently intelligent, way. It was long believed that if computers could be made to play games, they would have come a long way toward behaving intelligently. Charles Babbage once proposed building a special version of the analytical engine to play chess, thinking that such a machine would command enough attention to finance the construction of the engine. Similarly, Arthur Samuel set out in 1947 to design a checkers-playing machine as a way of earning enough money for the University of Illinois to build a big computer.

Samuel started his project with the belief that checkers was a simple game, but he soon found that the project presented frustrating complexities. After adding features that would enable his program to "learn" from its mistakes, he set about learning from experts in the game. Samuel solicited the assistance of several world-class checkers players who described their thought processes and methods to him. Unfortunately, such description is very difficult. Many of the experts, fearing that prolonged examination of methods would make them too self-conscious, eventually distanced themselves from the project. With the loss of his experts and with little knowledge of checkers (he didn't play very well), Samuel decided to take a different tack. Instead of asking himself how humans would solve the problem and then trying to duplicate the process in the "giant brain" of a computer, he looked at the technology and speeds available on computers and then tried to determine what the best method of solving the problem would be.

Samuel eventually was able to develop a successful program. Like most game-playing programs, it used the concept of "look-ahead"; that is, it evaluated the positions that would result from each move, the positions likely to result from the best response to each move, and so on. (This is not too difficult to do in checkers because not many moves are possible and all pieces, except kings, are treated the same.) The program's ability to learn from experience proved a valuable asset. When the program encountered a position it had previously faced, it would remember the outcome of the game in which the position had occurred and use that knowledge to evaluate the strengths and weaknesses of the position. This method of evaluation proved to be much more effective than merely evaluating each possible move based on positions two or three moves in the future. In fact, Samuel's program became so sophisticated that it eventually could beat world-class checkers players.

Samuel's success at checkers may be contrasted with the experience of Alex Bernstein, who worked at developing a chess-playing program starting in the late 1950s. Samuel was not a good checkers player; Bernstein, however, had been captain of his chess team at the Bronx High School of Science, and he intended to write a program that would use his knowledge of the game. Bernstein realized that the number of possible moves in chess was too great to evaluate in detail. For example, there are 18 possible opening moves and 18 possible responses—324 possible situations after only two moves. (To examine all the board positions possible in a complete game of chess would require more time than the estimated life of the universe.) Bernstein's program evaluated potential moves by looking ahead. General principles helped guide the program toward useful moves and away from obviously unfruitful ones. This procedure was thought to coincide with human methods of problem solving. If the program could eliminate a whole class of possible moves without examining each one individually, the number of potential moves to be evaluated would be greatly reduced. (This is nicely illustrated by the way we look for a telephone number in a telephone book. If the name of the person whose number we want is Jones, we ignore the early sections of the book, proceeding directly to the J's and thus considerably reducing the number of pages to be searched.)

By eliminating some of the moves to be examined, Bernstein was able to have his program examine the remaining moves in greater detail. Bernstein's program also took into account such factors as control of certain sections of the board, mobility of the remaining pieces, and control of the area around a king. The program also reflected some of the more important rules of chess. Despite the sophisticated nature of the parts of Bernstein's system, the program as a whole was not tested as thoroughly as he might have hoped. At the first public trial of the program, it resigned before making a single move, deeming the board position hopeless. After several additional years of work, Bernstein's program was able to play a respectable beginner's game. The program was a disappointment, however, because it was neither as fast nor as good as expected.

In 1976, David Slate and Larry Atkin of Northwestern University developed a program called Chess 4.5, the first program capable of beating class B players (class C players are superior to novices, but not very good; class B players are good; and class A players play at the championship level). The program did not incorporate any particularly new or revolutionary methods of problem solving; it simply took advantage of improvements in computer technology that had led to greater memories and faster speeds. Thus, the success of Chess 4.5 is not a victory for AI but rather a demonstration that technology coupled with fast search methods can be effective. Progress in the field has continued to the point where chess programs like Belle, created by AT&T's Bell Laboratories, have been classified as "master" chess players.

One objective of research on chess-playing programs is to discover the techniques that humans use so effectively to play chess. This is very difficult, however. Introspection is insufficient to determine what thought processes are actually involved in playing chess, and we know of no other means to get this information. Thus, there is reason to doubt that truly intelligent chess programs—programs that would play the way humans play—can be designed in the near future.

■ Programming Systems for Artificial Intelligence

Before the 1950s, all computation used batch processing. In this mode of operation, a program is prepared, submitted together with all necessary data to a computer, and then run to completion. Users do not interact with a program while it runs, and each program in turn can use all the resources of the machine for its run. John McCarthy, an important figure in artificial intelligence research, was an early advocate of another mode of operation, *time sharing*. When time sharing is used, several users or programs are active simultaneously, and each is allocated small *time slices* periodically. Each user's program behaves as if it had the entire machine at its disposal, except that the machine's speed has been reduced.

McCarthy's research in artificial intelligence also led him to the development of the programming language LISP. He had designed (but never completed) a program called the Advice Taker that would accept advice from a user and react accordingly. Of course, such a program could be used in a meaningful way only if a user could engage in an ongoing dialog with it. Also, the designer of a program could more easily improve it if he could modify it quickly. These needs called for *interactive computing*, that is, the ability to communicate with the program during its execution. In interactive computing, the programming language translator translates individual statements in a program into machine language just before they are executed. This makes it possible to modify the program and have the modification take effect immediately, not after the entire program has passed through the translator, as is true for compiled languages. (For more information on this subject, see Chapter 9.) LISP is the language that McCarthy designed for this purpose.

■ Conversation with ELIZA

One AI program that became widely known was DOCTOR, written in
LISP by Joseph Weizenbaum of MIT. The program conducts a conversation with the user, asking questions related to the user's previous
responses. The most famous version of DOCTOR is ELIZA, which emulates a Rogerian psychiatrist attempting to elicit further conversation
by repeating all or most of the "patient's" comments. Figure 12.2 illustrates a simple dialog with ELIZA.

Figure 12.2
A conversation with ELIZA, a computer program that simulates a Rogerian
psychiatrist's conversations with a patient.

```
*>   eliza
     WELCOME TO LISP/MTS
>    ELIZA
*>
>    TYPE: HALT TO LEAVE ELIZA!
>
>    WHAT CAN I DO FOR YOU TODAY?
*>   i feel sad
>    TELL ME MORE ABOUT SUCH FEELINGS
*>   i don't feel well
>    DON'T YOU REALLY FEEL WELL
*>   no
>    YOURE BEING SOMEWHAT SHORT WITH ME
*>   i feel sick to my stomach
>    YOUR STOMACH
*>   i don't want to get up in the morning
>    WHY DON'T YOU WANT TO GET UP IN THE MORNING
*>   i hate mornings
>    YOU SAY YOU HATE MORNINGS
*>   i just don't like them
>    CAN YOU ELABORATE ON THAT
*>   i don't like mornings
>    DO YOU WISH TO BE ABLE TO LIKE MORNINGS
*>   no
>    ARE YOU SAYING 'NO' JUST TO BE NEGATIVE
*>   no
>    YOU DON'T SEEM VERY TALKATIVE TODAY
*>   no
```

(continued)

```
>   YOU ARE BEING A BIT NEGATIVE
* >   no
>   I MUST INSIST THAT YOU STOP REPEATING YOURSELF!
* >   i hate you
>   PERHAPS IN YOUR FANTASY WE HATE EACH OTHER
* >   you are evil
>   NORMAN'S MOTHER IS EVIL
* >   who is norman's mother?
>   WHY? IS NORMAN'S MOTHER RESPONSIBLE FOR YOUR PROBLEM?
* >   I don't want to talk about mothers
>   HOW DO YOU FEEL ABOUT THE REST OF YOUR FAMILY?
* >   I don't understand you
>   DON'T YOU REALLY UNDERSTAND I
* >   halt
>
>
>
>           GOOD-BYE
>
```

Figure 12.2 (*Cont.*)

Notice that Eliza uses some very easy "tricks." The program focuses on several key words—*mother* and *evil*, for example. For responses without these words, ELIZA tries to echo the response back, changing first-person pronouns to second-person pronouns if necessary. There is a major problem with such methods, however. Since the second-person object pronoun is the same as the second-person subject pronoun (*you*), ELIZA cannot know which is which. It assumes that the *you* is always a subject; thus its mistake "Don't you really understand I?" rather than "Don't you really understand me?"

In spite of the technical problems with ELIZA, it seems to have generated favorable responses from the general public. Versions of ELIZA have been written in many different languages for many different computers; several versions are currently available for use with popular microcomputers. Individuals have been found to talk to ELIZA, confiding in it as if it were actually a human being and not a computer. This and the suggestion that computer programs be used instead of human psychiatrists were most disturbing to Joseph Weizenbaum, the author of ELIZA. He has unequivocally opposed this possibility and tends to be generally skeptical about the many promises made on behalf of AI by its adherents.

■ Current Research in Artificial Intelligence

Vision

One of the most important areas of current AI research involves vision. The task of making a computer "see" involves giving it the ability to identify objects within some scene, as observed by a television camera. It can then take action based on this information. An image from a television camera is converted into a series of picture elements (*pixels*), each of which has a value corresponding to its degree of brightness. Figure 12.3 shows a picture made up of pixels. The task of a computer program is to read the pixels and classify objects according to the information it has received. For example, if the objects within the range of the camera are blocks, then the scene recognition program will attempt to find corners and edges to determine the heights and positions of the blocks. Other important areas in vision research include developing programs to understand what is seen and draw inferences that aid in understanding.

While vision is an easy and natural process for human beings, getting a computer to see and understand a scene is very difficult. For

Figure 12.3
Example of "vision" with pixels. (From *Fundamentals of Interactive Computer Graphics*, J. D. Foley and A. VanDam, © 1982, Addison-Wesley, Reading, Massachusetts, p. 92, plate 26. Reprinted with permission.)

example, in a drawing of two blocks, one in front of the other, one block may have a face that appears to be a triangle because some of its lines are hidden. To understand such a scene, the computer would have to know not only what was there but also rules about how to interpret objects that were only partly visible. Light can also create many problems. The positioning of a light source, for example, can make similar objects appear different by hiding or making ambiguous various surface areas.

Another problem in making computers see is that tremendous quantities of memory are required to store simple pieces of visual information. A photo digitized into pixels measuring 3,000 by 3,000 would require 9 megabytes (9 million characters) of memory (assuming 8 bits per pixel). A procedure to find straight lines might require that 10 operations be performed on each pixel; such a procedure would involve performing 90 million operations to find all the straight lines in the photograph. Since understanding a scene requires many different operations, the amount of memory and processing required is obviously very large.

Analyzing pictures poses a difficult problem, but recognizing moving objects is even more difficult. If we think of a moving scene as a series of still photographs (just as movies are made up of many still pictures), then we can imagine the problems discussed above to be multiplied as we increase the number of pictures that must be processed.

Vision has great potential for use in the field of robotics. Robots in turn offer great potential for increases in industrial productivity. At the moment most robots used in industry have no capacity for vision; they must be programmed to perform repeatedly the actions that they carry out. Blind robots continually weld at a certain spot under the assumption that the part to be welded will appear at the right time and place; they are much less useful than robots that can sense something of their environment. Sensing robots can tolerate errors in placement of parts and can refuse to weld unless the needed part is present.

Natural Language Understanding

Another important area of AI is natural language understanding. If computers can be taught to understand human or natural language, it should not be necessary for humans to learn computer languages, such as Pascal or BASIC, to communicate with a machine. "Instead of programming computers, we will tell them what to do," says Edsger Dijkstra, one of the major proponents of structured programming. This remark is offered in jest, of course, since programming is no more than a way to tell computers what to do. Nevertheless, communicating with computers by using a natural language would be much easier for most people than programming. Natural language understanding deals with many of the same issues as language translation does. The desired result, however, is not to translate a statement from one human language into another but to translate the statement into a form that the computer will understand.

One of the most innovative natural language understanding systems was offered by T. Winograd in his 1971 Ph.D. thesis. Winograd's system understands statements in a very limited context, that of the "blocks world," a world in which blocks and pyramids are stacked on one another, as illustrated in Fig. 12.4. The person using the system may pose questions such as "What is the pyramid supported by?" and the system will either know how to respond or will query the user. It can also respond to commands such as "pick up a big red block." In this case, a robot "arm" (represented in the figure by the vertical line with horizontal member) will move down and pick up the big red block. To implement this system, Winograd dealt with objects, such as blocks and pyramids; relations between objects, such as being supported by or

Figure 12.4
Objects in a blocks world. (Adapted from Patrick Henry Winston, *Artificial Intelligence,* © 1977, Addison-Wesley, Reading, Massachusetts, p. 158. Reprinted with permission.)

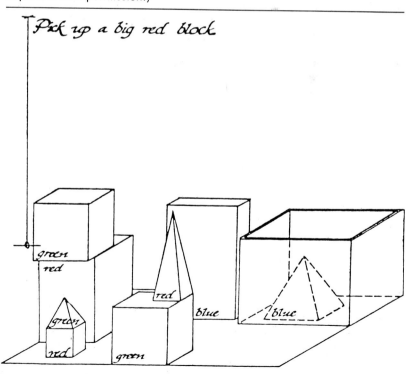

being behind a block; properties of objects, such as color and shape; and actions, such as picking up or putting down an object. This system demonstrates the power of natural language systems when restricted to a small domain.

Knowledge Representation

Related to the problem of natural language understanding is the problem of representing knowledge. Programs need large amounts of knowledge to understand discourse with humans. Many AI programs, especially programs that play games, concentrate on what is called state-space search to process large quantities of knowledge. Under the state-space search system, the program knows the original state and how to move from one state to another. The program also has a set of criteria by which to evaluate each possible new state. The one judged best is picked as the next state. Using state-changing rules, the program then picks the action that will produce the desired result. As we have seen, in certain cases the number of possible states to be examined grows extremely fast with the depth of the search. This is an example of *combinatorial explosion,* a situation that precludes the use of state-space search.

Another method of representing knowledge, one with many applications for expert systems (discussed in the next section), predicates the existence of semantic frames, illustrated in Fig. 12.5. A frame is a basic structure whose details can be filled in according to the particulars of any situation. For example, a frame for *dog* might have a space for general characteristics of dogs (four legs, tail, ears, and so on) as well as a space for specific characteristics to be filled in to fit any number of particular dogs (color, size, and the like). Frames are never completely empty; they contain certain default values filled by expectations. When you say *dog,* you conjure up an image of a dog that will have certain details filled in but others left unclear so as to give you something specific as well as a more general outlook on dogs as a class. The frame thus emerges as a very basic idea that corresponds to Wilks' concept of the bare template.

Still other methods of representing knowledge exist. A popular method utilizes logic and inference: All dogs have tails. Fred is a dog. Therefore Fred has a tail. Knowledge contained in small subroutines representing information such as this is known as a *procedural representation.* Another method of knowledge representation uses semantic nets. In a *semantic net,* pointers connect related objects; the set named *dogs* might point to a specific breed of dog, as suggested by dogs→cocker spaniel, or it might point to a property of dogs, as suggested by dogs→have tails. Still another method of knowledge, representation uses

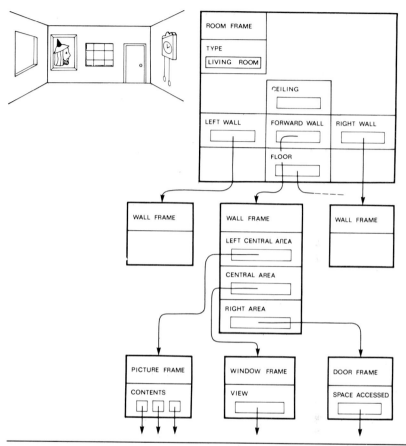

Figure 12.5
A collection of connected semantic frames each having slots filled with factual data or with a pointer to another frame. (Adapted from Patrick Henry Winston, *Artificial Intelligence*, © 1977, Addison-Wesley, Reading, Massachusetts, p. 186. Reprinted with permission.)

production systems, in which a condition triggers a response. For example, a typical statement in a production system is IF <condition> THEN <action>. Such a statement could be used to record the rule IF hungry THEN eat.

Expert Systems

One of the most promising areas of AI research for the near future involves expert systems. An *expert system* is a computer program or system that incorporates the knowledge of many experts in a given field, providing the nonexpert with the collected knowledge of experts. Such systems have been developed to do calculus, provide advice on problems in internal medicine, answer questions on bacterial infections, advise prospectors on mineral deposits, explore the molecular structure of atoms by analyzing spectral data, and help computer salespeople configure complicated computer systems before a sale.

The advantage of an expert system is that it incorporates the knowledge of many experts and greatly expands the number of people who will be able to gain access to this knowledge. Such systems are also useful because they never tire and will not make mistakes (except for those designed into them). A tired doctor or geologist may overlook certain data, but a program given the same information will not. An expert system in internal medicine that knows about rare tropical diseases will call them to the attention of a doctor living in a temperate zone, reminding the doctor of the possibility of some rare occurrence.

An expert system, of course, is not a substitute for knowledge and expertise in a field. There are many connections and deductions that are impossible for computers to make today. Computers are limited in their ability to analyze tasks requiring strategy and planning, as suggested in our earlier discussion of chess.

One of the earliest and best known expert systems is SAINT, developed by James Slagle at MIT to do calculus at the level of an average freshman calculus student. Newer systems, such as the MACSYMA system, also developed at MIT, can outperform any human at calculus problems because of the immense amount of information they contain and the speed at which they perform. MACSYMA is currently used by hundreds of researchers to solve complex mathematical problems.

Medicine seems particularly well fitted for expert systems, partly because so much information is needed to make decisions in medicine. INTERNIST, developed at the University of Pittsburgh by H. Pople, a computer scientist, and J. Myers, a specialist in internal medicine, accepts a list of symptoms and formulates hypotheses about their probable causes. INTERNIST knows when to expect certain symptoms and knows, too, that the absence as well as the presence of symptoms may be a key in discovering what ails the patient. The program's output is a list of probable diseases; it leaves the exact diagnosis to the human doctor. INTERNIST today contains information about 500 different diseases and 3,500 manifestations of diseases, covering 80 percent of internal medicine.

MYCIN is a medical expert system that conducts interviews with doctors to help diagnose infectious diseases. It asks the doctor general questions, such as the age and sex of the patient, and more specific questions about cultures taken and symptoms exhibited. Doctors must treat bacterial infections before all blood and urine tests have been completed, for if they wait until results of all tests are known, the patient may become much sicker. Like cultures and blood tests, MYCIN is a diagnostic tool, allowing doctors to make accurate diagnoses more quickly and thus to prescribe proper medication sooner. MYCIN offers conclusions about the cause of infection using a complex set of production system rules such as IF the infection is primary-bacteremia and the site of the culture is one of the sterile sites and the suspected portal of entry is the gastrointestinal tract, THEN there is suggestive evidence (the probability is greater than 70 percent) that the identity of the organism is bacteroides. By printing out probabilities as well as conclusions, MYCIN is more helpful than a program that merely lists conclusions.

An expert system that helps chemists is DENDRAL, developed in 1964 by Joshua Lederberg at Stanford. This system finds the set of molecular structures of known atoms that could account for a given spectrographic analysis of an unknown molecule. The system saves chemists from having to visualize and then recall complex molecular structures. Since the task of extracting exact molecular formulations from experts was thought to be a possible stumbling block, another program, called meta-DENDRAL, was developed that, given a set of rules for mass spectrometry, would generate rules that in turn would generate models of mass spectrometry of known elements. This is a step beyond traditional expert systems because it greatly reduces the need to supply large quantities of information to the system.

Another expert system of great practical value is PROSPECTOR, developed by Richard Duda and Peter Hart to help geologists explore problems in hard-rock mineral exploration. PROSPECTOR asks certain questions about a site and, based on the responses, matches the site against models of specific types of deposits. Since the data are not assumed to be complete or extensive, the conclusion is printed as a probability, as in MYCIN. In its first real test, in February 1980, PROSPECTOR predicted the presence of a molybdenum deposit on Washington's Mt. Tolman. The prediction was later confirmed by drilling.

Reactions to expert systems have been mixed. Some, recognizing their usefulness, welcome them with open arms. Others, afraid of trusting unknown and unseen experts and computer scientists, have avoided them. While the final verdict is not yet in, it does seem that expert systems have an important role to play in some areas. As long as they are constructed according to high professional standards and their weaknesses are clearly spelled out, they can serve as useful assistants. However, they must be used with care. If such a system has a programming error or if a newly discovered fact has not been incorporated into it, it can give misleading information or advice. Care must be taken when the system is used in life-or-death situations or where large financial investments are involved.

▪ Objections to AI

Expert systems are not the only facet of AI to come under criticism. Some people object in principle to the possibility that intelligence can be designed into machines, preferring to think of intelligence as a uniquely human property. More practical objections have also been voiced. In a famous report written in 1972, Sir James Lighthill of Cambridge University recommended to the Science Research Council in the United Kingdom that research in pure AI not be given further funding. Lighthill complained that there had been no remarkable successes in the field and that the partial successes that had occurred were not equal to the claims of potential impact made by AI researchers. Lighthill's objection is as true now as it was in 1972; no working models of truly intelligent machines exist. It should be noted, though, that the lack of economical alternatives to internal combustion engine automobiles does not stop people from looking for such alternatives.

It may have been true during Ada Lovelace's time that machines could do only what people programmed them to do; it is no longer strictly the case. For example, chess programs do not need to be told explicitly what to do in each case but are given rules for determining valid alternatives and methods for evaluating the relative worth of each alternative. If such programs could be taught to learn from their mistakes and modify their rules accordingly, could they still be said to do only what they were told to do?

▪ Fifth-Generation Computers

The modern computer age has thus far spanned four computer generations. The first was characterized by electronic vacuum tube computers. The invention and incorporation of the transistor into computers marked the second generation. The grouping of many transistors on silicon chips through large-scale integration (LSI) led to the third computer generation. Advances in integration techniques allowed hundreds of thousands of transistors to be placed on a single integrated circuit. This very-large-scale integration (VLSI) gave birth to the fourth computer generation. A current project in Japan seeks to usher in a fifth generation of computers.

The Japanese fifth-generation computer project seeks to create new computers that use new methods to produce dramatically improved results. In fact, the fifth-generation computers are often referred to as KIPS, or knowledge information processing systems. KIPS will ideally be able not only to gather, store, and link tremendous quantities of information but also to communicate in natural language, speak, and understand speech. Such goals call for different approaches to computing.

One difference between fifth-generation machines and conventional computers will be the method by which they operate. Conventional computers perform one action at a time, starting on a new subtask only after completing the previous one. KIPS will utilize parallel processing and will work on separate parts of a problem at the same time,

Figure 12.6
Diagram for a knowledge information processing system (KIPS). (Adapted from Edward A. Feigenbaum and Pamela McCorduck, *The Fifth Generation,* © 1983, Addison-Wesley, Reading, Massachusetts, p. 112. Reprinted with permission.)

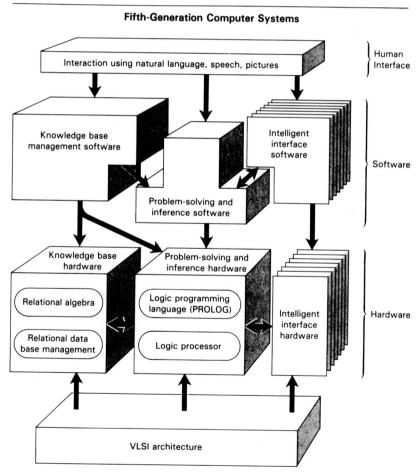

thus drastically reducing the total time required to solve a problem. While today's computers perform 10,000 to 100,000 logical inferences per second (LIPS), the Japanese expect to build machines that can perform 100 million to one billion LIPS. Such speed requires great advances in hardware. To meet the need for such advances, KIPS machines will use silicon chips that contain 10 million transistors; current chips contain several hundred thousand transistors.

Figure 12.6 illustrates the components of a KIPS machine. The KIPS user will see a machine that communicates easily in natural language using sophisticated graphics. A large database will hold all the auxiliary information the computer needs to interact with the user and solve problems. Large relational databases and a sophisticated rule-based programming language such as PROLOG will help the sophisticated hardware solve problems.

The Japanese seek nothing less than to revolutionize society by completely changing the computer and the role it plays. By introducing systems that are both powerful and easy to use, the Japanese hope to painlessly insert the computer into every aspect of society. Various experts have criticized the Japanese project as unrealistic. Others are cautiously optimistic, correctly pointing out that the computer field changes enormously from year to year. For this reason, it is virtually impossible to determine what might or might not be possible ten years from now. Clearly, by embarking on such a program, the Japanese have taken the first steps toward leadership in the computer field. Whether or not they can continue making progress remains to be seen.

SUMMARY

This chapter examines attempts to make computers behave intelligently. As many people have observed, defining intelligence is problematic. Although we generally know what we mean when we discuss intelligence, it is difficult to find a precise definition. Alan Turing, a seminal thinker in AI, devised a test for machine intelligence. The test stipulates that a machine or program is intelligent when people communicating with it cannot tell the difference between the computer and a person.

Research in AI has led in many different directions. Early in the computer age, researchers focused on attempts to create electronic brains. More recent research has dealt with problem solving, vision, knowledge representation, and language translation. A particularly interesting branch of AI, and one that illustrates many AI techniques, involves designing computer systems to play games.

A very popular AI program is ELIZA (also known as DOCTOR), which emulates a Rogerian psychiatrist. Although ELIZA is not very complex and can easily be fooled, a first encounter is often a fascinating experience.

Expert systems, computer systems containing much specialized information on particular topics, are becoming increasingly popular. Expert systems are used in a variety of fields, including medicine, geology, and chemistry.

The Japanese fifth-generation computer project represents one of the most ambitious industrial projects ever undertaken. Japanese researchers hope to develop knowledge information processing systems (KIPS) that will use multiprocessing and advanced AI techniques to solve difficult problems and communicate in natural language with their users.

FURTHER READING

Avron Barr and Edward Feigenbaum, eds., *The Handbook of Artificial Intelligence*, vols. 1 and 2 (Los Altos, Calif.: William Kaufman, Inc., 1981).

Eugene Charniak and Drew McDermott, *Introduction to Artificial Intelligence* (Reading, Mass.: Addison-Wesley, 1985).

Paul Cohen and Edward Feigenbaum, eds., *The Handbook of Artificial Intelligence*, vol. 3 (Los Altos, Calif.: William Kaufman, Inc., 1982).

Edward Feigenbaum and Pamela McCorduck, *The Fifth Generation* (Reading, Mass.: Addison-Wesley, 1983).

Andrew Hodges, *Alan Turing: The Enigma* (New York: Simon and Schuster, 1983).

Pamela McCorduck, *Machines Who Think* (San Francisco: W. H. Freeman, 1979).

David Marr, *Vision* (San Francisco: W. H. Freeman, 1982).

A. G. Oettinger, "The Design of an Automatic Russian-English Technical Dictionary," in W. Locke and A. Booth, eds., *Machine Translation of Languages* (New York: Technology Press of MIT and Wiley, 1955), pp. 47–65.

Allen Turing, "Computing Machinery and Intelligence," *Mind* (October 1950), pp. 433–460.

Joseph Weizenbaum, *Computer Power and Human Reason* (San Francisco: W. H. Freeman, 1976).

ISSUES AND IDEAS

1. Discuss the difficulties involved in determining whether computers can think. Propose new criteria for making such determinations.

2. Is the Turing test really a test of intelligent behavior? Justify your answer.

3. Describe the difficulties involved in translating one human language into another.

4. For some board games computers do not perform as well as humans. Explain why.

5. LISP is widely used by the artificial intelligence community. Using the material in Chapter 10 on LISP, explain this phenomenon.

6. How might a program such as ELIZA be useful to a psychiatrist? What might be appropriate uses of a program of this kind?

7. Should limits be put on the use of expert systems? Justify your answer.

8. In your view, is AI research desirable? Why or why not?

Automating the Factory and the Office

"Automation? Depends on how it's applied. It frightens me if it puts me out on the street. It doesn't frighten me if it shortens my work week. . . . Machines can either liberate man or enslave 'im, because they're pretty neutral. It's man who has the bias to put the thing one place or another."

MIKE LEFEVRE, steelworker, in Studs Terkel's *Working* (1972)

■ Introduction

Computers and automation are producing revolutionary changes in the workplace. Industry is restructuring and computerizing manufacturing. Robots are replacing human workers by performing repetitive and dangerous jobs in the factory. Designers, engineers, and salespeople are being linked electronically to activity on the factory floor. Computerization is similarly transforming the office. Electronic communication, computerized filing systems, word processing, and tools for calculation and charting are redefining the nature of office work.

In the next decade, technological change will have a substantial impact on the numbers and types of jobs available and on the nature of employment itself. To exercise some control over these developments, we must be knowledgeable about the nature and potential societal impact of coming technological developments. This chapter provides an introduction to these issues as they arise in industry and the office.

■ Computerization in Industry

Current trends indicate that by the year 2000, computerization will have produced dramatic changes in the manufacturing industries of technologically advanced nations. The availability of small, powerful, and inexpensive computers and sophisticated software assures the eventual computerization of most segments of business and industry. Computers will become essential tools for designers and for office and factory workers. Formerly distinct workplaces (such as those of the production worker, the manager, and the designer) will become tightly integrated, with data flowing easily from one area to another.

Computerization of industry is producing what is called *computer-integrated manufacturing* (CIM). CIM has three major components: *computer-aided design/computer-aided manufacturing* (CAD/CAM), factory automation, and administrative systems. CAD/CAM is the application of computers to all aspects of product design as well as to the implementation of design in the manufacturing process. *Factory automation* refers to the use of computers and robots in the actual process of manufacturing. *Administrative systems* record information about the manufacturing process and oversee production, inventory, and shipping.

CIM can substantially increase efficiency in manufacturing. Experts predict that savings will come from two factors. First, a general automation of the manufacturing process will reduce waste of facilities, raw materials, and labor. Second, a more efficient flow of parts and raw materials will reduce the time such materials spend sitting idle in storage. Through computerization, planning and manufacturing can be more tightly integrated, increasing the efficiency of production.

Computer-Aided Design and Manufacturing

Industries currently utilize CAD/CAM systems in such diverse fields as mechanical drawing, stress analysis of mechanical systems, electrical circuit design, programming of robots, optimization of the use of raw materials, and preparation of reports, charts, and computer-generated plots. In each of these applications, a computer workstation helps the human worker to solve complex problems. These workstations feature sophisticated computer graphics for display and electronic storage of documents. Designs, which are often displayed in color, can be retrieved at any time for immediate use or modification. Figure 13.1 shows a typical CAD/CAM workstation.

CAD/CAM workstations greatly extend the potential of human designers. Figure 13.2 shows a complicated three-dimensional mechanical

Figure 13.1
A CAD/CAM workstation. (Dick Luria, Science Source/Photo Researchers, Inc.)

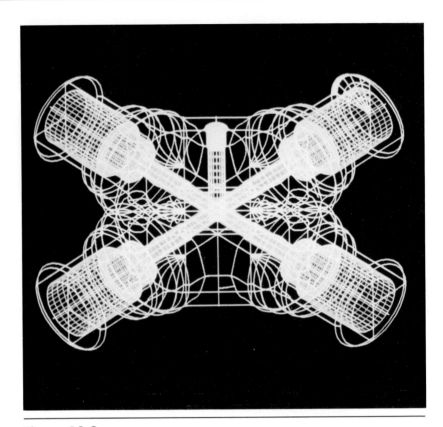

Figure 13.2
A mechanical drawing developed on a CAD/CAM system. (Courtesy of
Computervision Corporation)

drawing developed on a CAD/CAM system. Graphical editors (described in Chapter 10) greatly simplify the creation and manipulation
of such drawings. Previously, a draftsperson spent long hours in the
laborious creation of one set of drawings. When simple changes were
made, it was necessary to redraw the entire picture. Creating the original drawing with a graphical editor may require as much time as creating the same drawing on paper. However, once the initial design is
stored electronically, it is much easier to manipulate. The editor can be
used to rotate the design and show details of it from any perspective.
Just as word processors greatly reduce the time required to update textual documents, graphical editors greatly reduce the time required to
modify designs. This feature can in turn greatly increase the speed with
which a concept is transformed into a design, a production plan, and
finally a product that can be distributed and sold.

Computerization of the design process offers other practical advantages. Once a drawing of an object is stored electronically, useful data about that object can be extracted. Some CAD/CAM systems, for example, automatically generate a variety of calculations of physical properties, such as center of gravity. Finding an object's center of gravity without a computer can often be difficult and time-consuming.

Engineers use electronically stored designs in *process planning*, deciding exactly how a given design will be produced. For example, engineers might use their workstations to simulate the production of a part with different lathes and milling machines. Experimenting with different production methods in this way can help determine which is most cost-efficient without wasting time or raw materials on the building of physical models or prototypes. Once the method of production has been chosen, administrators can use design and process planning data to create lists of necessary materials. Supplies can be ordered from such lists, and shipments received can be checked against them. Thus, it becomes possible to obtain precise control of all materials on hand.

An interesting use of CAD/CAM is *solid modeling*, the drawing, coloring, shading, and lighting of three-dimensional objects. Solid modeling is used to provide realistic views of an object's design. Those models can then be rotated on a display screen so that they can be viewed from all angles. Solid models are often so realistic that they appear to be photographs of the manufactured object. Examples appear both in the color plate section of this book and in Fig. 13.3.

A very important application of CAD/CAM, one commonly called *computer-aided engineering* or (CAE), involves the use of computer-aided design in engineering analysis. CAE has been applied to many fields, including mechanical and electrical engineering. A typical application in mechanical engineering is analysis of the mechanical properties of an object. An artificial hip joint, for example, can be analyzed as shown in Fig. 13.4 to determine how much it will bend and what stress it will undergo when force is applied to it. Computer graphics help to animate the simulation, making it easier to interpret the results. As a consequence, many of the properties of the joint can be discovered before it is experimentally used in animals or humans. Since human beings have limited powers of visualization and find it difficult to interpret large quantities of numbers without pictures, the ability to graphically display the results of computer simulations is a great aid. Many important mechanical systems, including nuclear reactor containment vessels and the front ends of automobiles, have been studied with this method. Figure 13.5 shows the use of CAE to study stresses at various points in the ducts of an engine.

Any complex design and manufacturing activity can benefit from CAD/CAM. Figure 13.6 shows a CAE system used to analyze computer circuits so that time and money need not be spent in building proto-

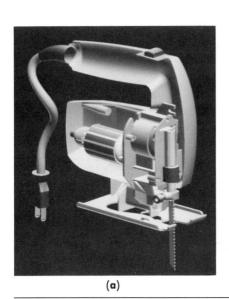
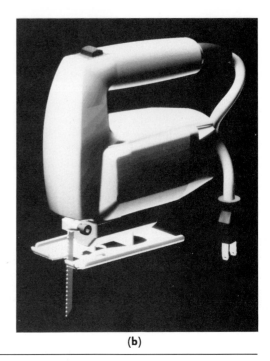

(a)   (b)

Figure 13.3
A figure created with a solid modeling program. (Courtesy of
Computervision Corporation)

types. The system can perform tests on logical and electrical circuits
and record the results. This ability can prove invaluable to an electrical
engineer since circuit design is a complex, error-prone task. Again,
graphical output is valuable because it helps the designer locate errors.
Current CAD/CAM systems can even produce all the information necessary to manufacture complex circuits directly from descriptions and
designs entered at a workstation. This direct link between production
and design eliminates many errors that occur in the transfer and implementation of designs.

CAD/CAM can also play an important role in increasing the efficiency of the use of materials. For example, when cutting sheet metal
for refrigerators, manufacturing engineers attempt to minimize the
amount of wasted material by cutting as many pieces as possible from
each sheet. This "cookie cutter" approach is another difficult task that
can be simplified with graphical editors. The designer can use an editor
to place items so as to minimize waste.

As is apparent, CAD/CAM systems generate large quantities of data
that can be used productively in many parts of the design, manufac-

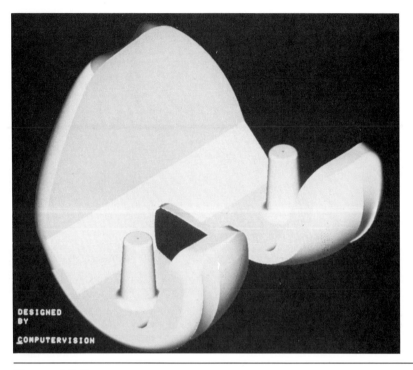

Figure 13.4
An artificial knee joint drawn with a CAD/CAM system. (Courtesy of
Computervision Corporation)

Figure 13.5
A model of an engine duct created on a computer-aided engineering
system. (Courtesy of Computervision Corporation)

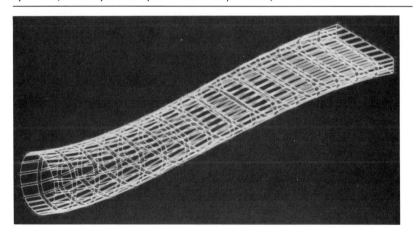

Figure 13.6
Circuit design with a CAE workstation. (Courtesy of Mentor Graphics)

turing, and maintenance aspects of production. Having recorded this data electronically, the systems transport it to each step in the production process. The data can also serve as a basis for future designs and plans.

Since CAD/CAM experts estimate that only 20 to 30 percent of all engineering designs are completely new, ready access to existing designs through centralized databases can greatly increase productivity. This has been shown in the few cases where such databases have been installed. These databases will be the warehouses of data and ideas within an industrial organization. Because of their importance, however, the contents must be carefully protected from loss, damage, and competitors.

In 1981 about 6,500 CAD/CAM systems were in use worldwide with approximately 22,000 attached workstations. They were used for the design and development of automobiles, aircraft, machinery, and computers; for oil exploration and mapmaking; and in many other fields. As shown in Table 13.1, some experts expect these numbers to grow eight times larger by 1990. Such systems and workstations may be essential to companies hoping to remain competitive.

Table 13.1 ☐ Installed CAD/CAM Systems and Workstations by Application, Estimated Year End Units

	1981		1985		1990	
	Systems	Workstations	Systems	Workstations	Systems	Workstations
Mechanical	2850	10400	13600	50000	25000	92000
Electronic	2400	7700	9300	25000	16000	42000
Architectural and engineering	750	3200	3200	12000	5500	20000
Other	500	1100	900	5000	1500	8000
Total	6500	22400	27000	92000	48000	162000

Source: International Technology Marketing

The Automated Factory

In the United States today, 75 percent of total industrial output is batch produced. In batch production, materials often lie idle on the shop floor or in storage between production steps. According to recent studies, the amount of time factories directly use any given part (or piece of raw material) is less than 5 percent of the total time the part spends in the factory. Since companies running factories own these parts, a substantial investment is sitting idle; if companies could reduce the time parts sit idle, it would mean a greater return on investment. Experts estimate that an integrated approach to manufacturing could reduce inventory costs by 50 to 75 percent as well as cut labor needs. Automated factories provide this integrated approach.

The automated factory combines the traditional machinery of production (such as welding equipment), new production technologies (such as robots), and systems that transport and store raw materials. The computer plays a central role in the automated factory, linking the diverse elements of production. It is a complex environment, containing facilities for the control and transportation of materials, quality control sensors, programmable robots, workstations, inventory control systems, facilities for communication with other factories, and a control center for plant supervisors.

A major reason for automating factories is to reduce the cost of production. For automation to be effective, raw materials must be delivered when needed and then transported directly to work areas so that costly inventory does not stand idle. Another major reason for automating factories is to increase the quality of products. If each step of the manufacturing process is done by a machine and all machines are running correctly, then the products produced will be of a uniform quality. If a plant is designed well, then the quality will be high. Both the delivery of parts and the control of the quality of the manufacturing process require sophisticated computer systems.

Robots in the Automated Factory

A key element in the automated factory is the robot (a word that comes from the Czech *robota*, meaning "forced labor"). Although many people equate robots with industrial automation, installation of robots alone does not make an automated factory. If robots do not receive materials on the production line, if materials lie idle on the plant floor, or if production quality is not controlled, robots will have little effect on productivity. Thus, designers of automated factories must pay attention to the entire environment of production. Also, managers and workers must be informed in advance about the nature of the automated factory and the changes it will create so that they can better adjust to these changes.

Most factories are divided into stations that perform specialized tasks. Each production station or *work cell* must itself be carefully designed to handle all of the tasks to be completed at that cell. This means that if a robot is to drill and mill material at a certain cell, the cell must contain the set of necessary metalworking tools for drilling and milling. If the robot is to manufacture more than one product, there must be some means to change the tasks the robot performs. In addition, since all manufacturing processes involve wear and tear on tools, the automated factory requires a system for monitoring wear and tear and for scheduling maintenance. Figure 13.7 shows the layout of a typical automated system for metalworking. It has many machining centers containing programmable machine tools and connected by an automatic delivery system.

Robots today are of limited use. Few have the ability to inspect a scene visually and react accordingly; instead, most perform the same actions again and again without checking the appropriateness of the actions. Thus, a welding robot welds in the same place repeatedly, whether or not a piece of metal is there. Furthermore, a robot must be programmed in a language specifically created for that robot; there is currently no standard language for robot programming. Simply telling the robot what to do, then, can be difficult and time-consuming.

Robots are further limited by their physical design. A typical robot has up to five or six degrees of freedom; in other words, it can move its components independently in up to five or six directions or angles. These components may be arms that move up and down or turn on an axis, or they may be grippers with jaws that turn or hold an object. The controlling computer program must specify how the robot is to move in each direction. Newer, more sophisticated robots are equipped with sensors that may make it easier to program them. These sensors can

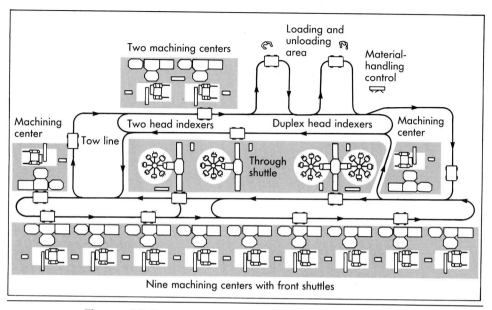

Figure 13.7
An automated system for metalworking. (Adapted from Eric J. Lerner, "Computer-Aided Manufacturing," *IEEE Spectrum*, Nov. 1981, pp. 36–37, Figure 2)

determine, for example, how much pressure to apply with grippers; they can also test for the presence of a piece of metal before welding. Thus, the robot can be told to move until a particular pattern is found by its camera, such as a pattern painted on a piece of metal, and to close its grippers until the pressure reaches a certain level. This is easier to specify than the exact position of the arm and the exact size of the gripper opening; in older robots, both have to be measured and inserted into the program as fixed parameters.

In many cases robots are programmed with handheld units called *teach boxes*; a human manually takes the robot through each required movement to ensure correct performance on the factory floor. The movements are then recorded and played back when there are no errors. This method of robot programming, called *on-line programming*, can be very time-consuming. Figure 13.8 shows on-line programming in process. Figure 13.9 illustrates the technique expected to be most widely used in the future for robot instruction, *off-line programming*. In off-line programming, a factory worker with a CAD/CAM workstation manipulates an electronic simulation of a robot and a work cell. The worker takes the model through a series of steps, which are interpreted by the CAD/CAM system. Once the program is complete, hu-

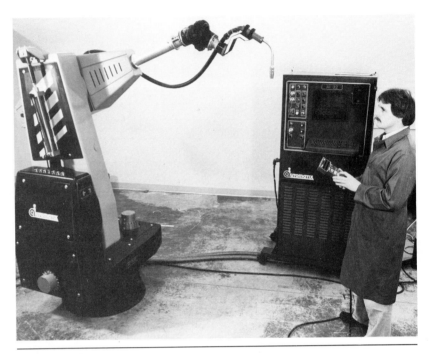

Figure 13.8
A robot and a handheld training unit. (Courtesy of Automatix Inc., the Adaptive Automation Company)

man inspectors can check its accuracy with the robot on the factory floor. Such systems also permit the designer to create a three-dimensional model of a work cell to ensure that robots within the cell do not collide with each other or with an immovable part of their work cell.

The Effects of Factory Automation on Employment

In 1983, there were only 6,500 robots in use in the United States, while the Japanese had installed more than 30,000. General Motors, the U.S. auto manufacturer, was the world's single largest user of robots, with 1,800 installed. GM expects to have 14,000 robots installed by 1990. By that time, as many as 100,000 robots could be in use in the United States. However, the increase in industrial robots does not necessarily spell doom for production workers.

The degree to which robots will replace human workers will depend on the economics of automation. A robot today can cost more than $40,000; when it is outfitted with equipment to hold, rotate, and load parts from an assembly line, the cost can triple. As more robots are produced, however, the costs should decline substantially.

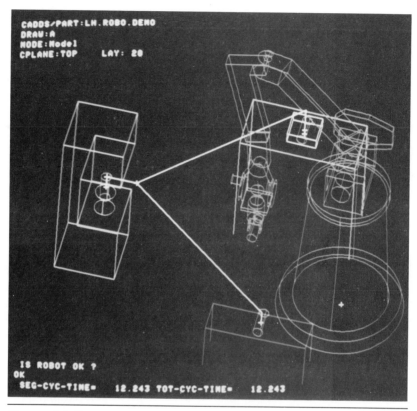

Figure 13.9
A CAD/CAM system for off-line robot programming. (Courtesy of
Computervision Corporation)

In some cases, workers have actually welcomed robot replacements
because robots are well suited to perform many dirty, dangerous, and
repetitive jobs. However, the possibility of large-scale unemployment
due to robots is frightening to many workers, union leaders, and others.
In fact, the International Association of Machinists and Aerospace
Workers union has proposed adoption of a Worker's Technology Bill of
Rights, calling for the imposition of a "tax on all machinery, equipment
and production systems that displace workers and cause unemployment." Given the permanent loss of jobs in many heavy industries, there
is much cause for concern.

However, it is not yet clear whether automation will cause permanent large-scale unemployment or will simply alter the type of work
humans perform. Supporters of industrial automation are quick to compare the robotics revolution they anticipate with the first industrial revolution. In the latter, the introduction of machines had some

unexpected consequences. The pin-making industry provides an example. Before machines were used, a pin maker working very efficiently could manufacture one or two pins per day. The introduction of machines that cheaply produced up to 5,000 pins per day should have driven many pin makers out of work, since one worker with a machine could outproduce thousands of manual pin makers. But as the cost of pin making fell, the price of pins was slashed, and it became economical to use pins in many new ways. The increased demand for pins helped save jobs in the pin-making industry. This story might be taken to heart by modern workers: automation does not automatically lead to unemployment. With increased automation will likely come new demands and new markets for products, creating more jobs in other areas and helping to offset the number of workers displaced by automation.

Office Automation

The automated office relies on the creative use of computers and electronic communications. The technologies behind office automation products are not new, but a rapid decline in the cost of electronics and computers has led to the introduction of many new products geared specifically toward office work. The result is a significantly different working environment.

The typical office worker performs many functions—communicating in various oral and written forms, filing and retrieving information, scheduling and planning, and preparing documents and graphs. New products transform each of these tasks and create new opportunities and problems. Included in these new opportunities are the possibility to work at home and the opportunity to conduct business meetings with people at many different sites through teleconferencing. Among the problems is the need to restructure lines of communication and division of work. The following scenario illustrates some of the problems found in the typical office of the present; later we illustrate how they are solved in the office of the future.

Life in the contemporary office is filled with interruptions. If you were a manager, a typical day might consist of the following events: A co-worker from a neighboring office stops by to see if you have a file she needs, but you have already passed it on to someone else. Five minutes later, your secretary knocks on your door; he is taking an inventory of office keys and needs to know what keys you have in your possession. You spend hours trying to reach a resource person to find information for a report you must prepare. First, he is on another line; then you step out of your office minutes before he calls you back. When you finally get through, you discover that his job has changed and he is no longer responsible for the information you need. He directs you to the appropriate person and you begin the communication runaround anew. Meanwhile you spend an hour painstakingly plotting a graph that you need for an afternoon meeting, only to discover that one of the numbers you have used is wrong and that the entire graph must be plotted again. An important memo that you have written must be completely retyped after each revision, a process that introduces new errors each time. Finally, a paper you must read before your meeting fails to arrive, even though it was mailed several days ago from a branch office in another city.

As this scenario illustrates, most businesspeople spend a substantial amount of time collecting, evaluating, preparing, and relaying information. Although hired for their thinking skills and managerial abilities, they spend a major portion of their time on busywork. The office is an area where computers and electronic communication can prove most helpful, since they provide information storage, retrieval, and evaluation as well as powerful communication, text-formatting, and data manipulation tools.

Let's look at the above scenario replayed in an office of the future. The co-worker who needs to look at your file can request that a copy of it be displayed on her terminal or workstation; she need not have physical possession of the file. The secretary who is taking inventory can send his inquiry through electronic mail, and you can respond at a convenient time. Better yet, the department conducting the inventory can automatically send mail to all key holders, thus eliminating the secretary's intermediary role. Meanwhile, electronic mail spares you the frustration of "telephone tag" since the resource person can respond to your questions while you are out of your office. Furthermore, he can automatically forward a copy of your note to the appropriate person so that your question can be answered as quickly as possible. A desk-top computer plots your graph effortlessly and revises it instantly when you enter the new, correct data. With a word processor, your secretary will have no trouble typing an error-free letter since he need only correct errors; the rest is not altered. The availability of a word processor may also encourage you to type letters yourself instead of dictating them to a secretary. Finally, the information you need for your afternoon meeting would have been available days ago if it had been sent electronically.

This scenario is an oversimplification, of course. Life in a conventional office is not always so harried, and life in an electronic office will not be so carefree. Solutions to old problems invariably lead to new and unexpected ones, and the new technologies are certain to offer surprises. For example, a person might unintentionally destroy files while learning how to use a word processor. As for electronic mail, its speed has sometimes encouraged office workers to send messages or respond to them too hastily. An ill-considered message or an angry response may cause problems within the office bureaucracy. Further, some workers may find themselves unable to perform their jobs when their desk-top computers malfunction. These are but a few examples of the consequences of office automation; there will be many others.

All of the above-mentioned technology is available and in use today, and most of it was described in technical detail in Chapters 4 and 5. However, let us again take a brief look at the type of computer facility required for the office of the future.

A *personal workstation*, as described in Chapter 3, is a powerful personal computer with several added features. It has a high-resolution screen, which means that it can display detailed graphical output as well as traditional text, and a pointing device used to move the cursor, facilitating use of a menu-driven editor of the kind described in Chapter 4. Menu-driven editors are easier to learn to use than editors based only on keystrokes since commands are selected from menus rather than memorized.

The workstation uses a *window manager* to provide the user with several different windows, each representing a different piece of work. Windows make it possible for a person to work on several tasks at once by keeping each one in a separate area of the display screen. The workstation is connected to other workstations and computer facilities through some type of electronic communications network. In an office situation several workstation users would probably share a printer, and all would have access to a central data storage facility where common files would be stored. Files would be protected from unauthorized users. Furthermore, there may be different degrees of protection—some people may be allowed both to read files and to update them (*read/write privileges*), while others may be permitted only to read files (*read-only privileges*).

Let us now take a closer look at the role of automation in the office. For the sake of convenience, we have divided office utilities into five areas: communication, text preparation, information retrieval, analytical tools, and personal support tools. In addition to these areas we will discuss telecommunications in the electronic office and describe possible effects of office automation on bureaucratic organizations and on workers' health.

Electronic Communication

There are two major kinds of electronic communication—simultaneous and nonsimultaneous. Simultaneous communication is commonly used for impromptu conversations or quick and urgent questions because the message is sent immediately and arrives on the recipient's screen a fraction of a second after the RETURN key has been pressed. A conversation of sorts is possible since both users can send messages in this way. Messages can be as distracting as knocks on the door, however, because they interrupt whatever the recipient happens to be doing. For this reason, some operating systems (see Chapter 5) provide a command allowing a user to refuse to accept incoming messages. In this case, the sender is informed that the intended recipient is not receiving messages. Figure 13.10 shows a message system in operation on the UNIX operating system, described in Chapter 5. One user's portion of the conversation is shown in regular type, the other's is in italics, and our comments are in square brackets. Sue types write as to open a conversation with Alex and then types the first line of conversation on the next line. A bell is sounded at Alex's terminal and he initiates a conversation with Sue in the same fashion. His messages appear on Sue's screen in italics.

Sending messages in this way works well for brief exchanges but has drawbacks for longer conversations. People often send and reply to electronic messages quickly without taking the time to think about what they are saying. Since voice inflection and body language cannot be used in this form of communication, misunderstandings are more frequent; it is often more difficult to determine whether a message is serious or sarcastic. Furthermore, the act of typing can detract from the conversation, particularly if one of the participants is a slow typist. Often, electronic conversations become so muddled that they can only be continued in person or over the telephone.

A more common form of electronic communication is nonsimul-

Figure 13.10
A simultaneous electronic communication.

%write as   [Sue initiates a conversation with Alex whose ID is as.]
Alex? This is Sue.   [This is the first line of Sue's message to Alex.]
Message from as on ttyn2 at 1350 . . .   [Alex responds.]
Hi. What's up?
Can we change our 2:30 meeting time
to 3:30? I want to run an errand at University
Hall before they close.
If you have to . . . I've got an appointment at
4:00, though.
So we'll talk fast. Thanks — I'll check with
John and get back to you.
Bye.
Bye.

taneous communication, commonly known as *electronic mail.* Electronic letters, as described in Chapter 5, do not instantly appear on the recipient's screen but collect in an electronic mailbox until the recipient wishes to read them. Mail can be sent through a small computer network (in an office or company, for example), through telephone lines, or through a larger computer network such as Telenet or Tymnet. Electronic mail saves paper and time and can eliminate distraction and "telephone tag." The sender knows that the message has been sent and will be read, and the receiver knows that he will not be interrupted every time someone wishes to ask a question.

Electronic mail also involves serious disadvantages. Since it can be sent cheaply and easily, the volume of mail people receive is likely to increase. (It is often as easy to send a hundred copies of an electronic letter as it is to send one.) This can either ensure that more people will be better informed or that they will be subject to a larger volume of junk mail. As a result, important mail may be unintentionally overlooked. Fortunately, priority systems may become part of future electronic mail systems. Such systems can sort mail messages either according to the priority of the sender (so that mail from your boss will be read before mail from your squash partner) or according to a priority imposed by the sender (so a message marked "to be read immediately" will be read before a message marked "to be read at your convenience").

If memos are easy to prepare, people are likely to write and send them in haste. Hastily written mail may be unintentionally ambiguous, causing more confusion than clarification, or may be insulting, causing unnecessary friction within an organization. People tend to react to electronic mail impulsively, drafting responses immediately without taking the time to think through a letter and a response; electronic arguments often result. The ability to communicate clearly through writing becomes more important as written communication replaces face-to-face or telephone conversations. Finally, it should be noted that electronic mail is less personal than many other forms of communication, a fact that often disturbs new users.

An extension of an electronic mail system is electronic news. Rather than posting notices of general interest on a bulletin board, computer users can send them to a general news facility accessible to other users. These facilities are often called electronic bulletin boards. Groups of people with common interests—movies, popular music, or sports events—can create special news groups or bulletin boards through which to discuss those interests. News groups can also help to display company news and promote community spirit within an organization. Electronic mail and message systems are discussed in more detail in Chapter 5.

Text Preparation

Word processing software has greatly reduced the time and effort required to revise paper and electronic documents, although the time to create an original document may not have changed much. In Chapter 4 we described in detail how word processors work. Here we concentrate on how they can be used.

As is probably obvious by this time, word processors are valuable tools because they allow people to create specially formatted professional-looking documents with a minimum of effort. Spelling programs can weed out many misspelled words (they cannot, of course, detect mistakes that occur when a word is properly spelled but improperly used—*there* used in place of *their,* for example). The user can revise quickly and easily by inserting, deleting, and rearranging as needed; it is not necessary to retype the entire text. Experimenting with output formats is as easy as altering a few key commands—type size and style can be changed, margin width altered, and spacing varied, all with a minimum of effort. Templates of standard memos or letterheads can be stored electronically, minimizing the amount of repetitive typing required (Fig. 13.11 illustrates a letter template). In general, less time and energy are necessary to produce a more attractive document.

Figure 13.11
A typical electronic letter template.

---

123 Main Street
Anywhere, USA 12345
INSERT CURRENT DATE

INSERT NAME
INSERT STREET ADDRESS
INSERT CITY, STATE ZIP

Dear *INSERT NAME*,

Thank you for your letter of *INSERT LETTER DATE*. As you know, I consider *INSERT SUBJECT* to be one of the fundamental issues affecting our society, and one that I expect to address as your representative. I hope that I can count on your continued interest in my campaign.

Sincerely,

John Q. Publicservant
Candidate

On the other hand, the ease of formatting often leads to hastily prepared documents whose neat appearance may camouflage the poor quality of the text itself. And often, word processors are not easy to use but require special training and practice. Older word processors use long lists of commands whose functions are not apparent from their names. This problem is being alleviated as second-generation user-friendly word processors appear. Some of these programs use more mnemonic command names, while others are menu-driven, displaying all choices on the screen.

Information Retrieval

Chapter 10 includes a technical description of databases; here we briefly discuss their place in an office. Offices, as mentioned earlier, are primarily concerned with organizing and managing information. Until recently, the best form of organization consisted of file folders and drawers. Filing systems were generally based on somewhat arbitrary classifications of information, since each folder could only have one place in a drawer. Even if a file pertained to three different subjects, it could be filed under only one, and the people who used it would have to remember where it was. Furthermore, with only one copy of a folder, only one person at a time could use the information it contained.

Electronic filing changes all this. Not only can the file cabinets be taken away; but the classification systems can be more logical and more varied, since each file can be marked by several key words. Several people can look at the file at once, and there is no need to worry about the files being lost or misplaced. Further, people may have different privileges in using any one file—some may only look at it, while others may also modify its contents.

As with all technological developments, we humans must learn to cope with databases, to readjust our working habits to meet the new possibilities and limitations. Databases make large quantities of information easily accessible, a situation that involves obvious advantages and less obvious disadvantages. Suddenly a plethora of information is available for the asking. This availability can cause information overload; the problem at hand may become obscured by the vast amount of related but irrelevant information retrieved from databases. The availability of information can also lead to abuses, which we discuss in Chapter 14.

Analytical Tools

Under the heading of analytical tools fall those applications programs specifically designed to aid in business decision making. Electronic spreadsheet programs such as VisiCalc, described in Chapter 10, and statistical analysis packages such as the Statistical Package for the Social Sciences (SPSS) help businesspeople perform numerous calculations. Because these systems can easily test the effects of small changes in the data, they are great aids in business forecasting.

Analytical tools, like other computer tools, can cause problems. As performing calculations becomes simpler, people may be tempted to give data more importance than it deserves or to produce unnecessary or misleading information. As always, computers and programs are merely tools. There is no substitute for asking the right questions and for interpreting data with common sense.

Personal Support Tools

Personal support tools range from the obviously useful to the apparently trivial. An alarm clock on a computer may seem frivolous, but to a person who does not have an alarm on his clock or wristwatch and who is in the habit of arriving late at meetings, such an electronic reminder can be a valuable aid. Similarly, an electronic diary might not seem to offer many advantages over a paper one, but for a person who writes better when she types, it may be suitable.

An especially useful device is a calendar system. People with busy schedules may find it much easier to keep their appointments in order with an electronic file. The computer can automatically print entries in users' calendars for the current day each time they log on. This is of great value to managers whose secretaries schedule many of their meetings; since both manager and secretary can have constant access to the most recent copy of the calendar, double scheduling can be avoided. Furthermore, if a central computer program has access to the calendars of people who often meet together, it can find a common meeting time, thus simplifying the job of scheduling. The only drawback to this system is that an electronic calendar is awkward to carry around (although small microcomputers may alleviate this problem). Also, if the computer stops working, people are left with no way to read their calendars.

Telecommunications and the Electronic Office

As you know, computers can be linked not only through internal networks but also through telephone lines with the aid of a modem. This technology makes possible a new type of office work—teleworking, in which people work at home on computers and use a modem to communicate with computers at the office. Physically handicapped persons, parents of young children, and people caring for home-bound relatives may not be able to travel to a distant office; teleworking provides one possible solution. Teleworking also saves commuting time and fuel and has been shown to increase productivity among certain types of clerical workers. It can save office space and can use computer time more efficiently since people can work when the computer might otherwise lie idle. Most important, it may give people more control over their lives because their working hours become more flexible.

On the other side of the coin, teleworking poses new problems. Workers may feel isolated from officemates; for those who rely on the comaraderie of others for energy and motivation, this system may not be appropriate. Some people, too, may feel the need to physically get away from home when they work; they may not feel a part of the business if they are not actually present at the office. In addition, there may be no one around to answer technical questions, as there would be in an office. Relationships with superiors are also affected. In-home workers may not get as much praise and recognition as their colleagues, and there is a loss of management supervision. This may have either positive or negative effects, depending on the work habits of the employee and the type of work required. Another disadvantage appears in companies that treat their teleworkers as part-time employees, denying them the fringe benefits given to full-time employees. Working at home may also encourage workaholism since workers may have more difficulty physically separating themselves from their work. Furthermore, teleworking may disrupt traditional family roles. If both parents are at home during the day or they work irregular hours, it may become more difficult to separate work from family life. Finally, sending important information through telephone lines leaves a company more vulnerable to security breaches. (See Chapter 14 for more on security problems.)

Teleworking is not for everyone, and special support systems will be necessary if it is to become a viable alternative to traditional office work. One method of teleworking that is gaining popularity divides an employee's time between home and office; the worker can travel to work two or three days per week and work at home during the remaining time. This arrangement can sometimes make it possible for two working parents to continue working and take care of their children at the same time.

Another alternative to traditional office practices made possible by modern technology is *teleconferencing*, the two-way transmission of audio and video signals, along with data, pictures, and computer graphics, over long distances. This technology makes it possible for a business to conduct meetings between groups of people at different places. Participants communicate from specially equipped conference rooms that typically contain audio and television transmitters and receivers, high-resolution color screens for display of graphics, high-definition copiers for hard copies, and other equipment, including computers (see Fig. 13.12).

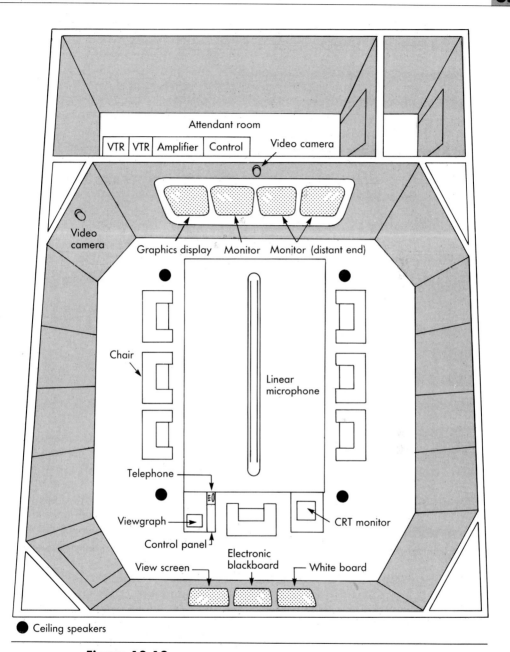

Figure 13.12
A typical teleconferencing facility. (Adapted from *Datamation*, Jan. 1983, p. 81)

Although teleconferencing has been technically feasible since the early 1970s, it has not been used widely until recently. One reason is its cost. A single teleconferencing system can cost more than one million dollars. Since large volumes of data must be transmitted to support teleconferencing, earth stations are often used to send and receive satellite transmissions. They add to the cost of teleconferencing. Even after the initial equipment has been paid for, the transmission costs themselves can be quite high.

Office Automation and Bureaucracy

In many organizations, bureaucracies are necessary. Since bureaucracies were introduced to manage large volumes of information and since the computer is a useful tool to manage and analyze information, it is appropriate to consider here the effect office automation can have on a bureaucracy.

Bureaucracies evolved as a communications device. When an organization becomes too large for everyone to communicate with everyone else and still have time to do work, a communications ladder is created to regularize the flow of information: supervisors request information from their subordinates, who break the request into manageable parts and request information from their subordinates, and so on. In organizations structured this way, the highly specialized information gatherers at the bottom have very limited knowledge of the original problem and are unable to provide more than partial answers. Information gathering and decision making take place on a sort of human assembly line, in which workers are often treated as automata rather than as people. What will happen if the computer is brought into this situation?

Paul A. Straussman, president of Xerox Information Products Group, was quoted in *Technology Review* (July 1983) as stating that the situation is likely to worsen if such hierarchies continue as they are: "If you take a traditional bureaucracy and give it computers, then instead of generating 30 useless pieces of paper, you generate 300. You may be worse off." Furthermore, if the work at the lower rungs becomes too specialized, as it is likely to do, mistakes proliferate, and time that could be spent in productive work must be spent correcting errors. Thankfully, this situation is not inevitable.

If a business takes the time to evaluate existing conditions and reorganize if necessary before introducing computers, office automation can have a positive effect. In several businesses, bureaucracies in which thousands of people performed single repetitive tasks were broken down into more autonomous units. Rather than having ten people performing small tasks, all of which contributed to a single operation, the new systems might have the ten people sharing responsibility for the entire operation, dividing the responsibility as they saw fit. This way, they could see how the operation functioned as a whole and could take more satisfaction in their work.

An example of this type of reorganization occurred in Citibank's letter-of-credit department. Citibank began to use computers in the 1960s. It was only after its efficiency decreased that the departments underwent the type of reorganization described above. In the letter-of-credit department a single letter verifying that a customer's credit with the bank was good was processed by some 50 clerks in six different areas, leaving great room for error. If an error did occur, the customer would have no idea where it had happened, and the problem would be sent to customer service. With the aid of a computer and a major reorganization, it became possible for one clerk to complete the entire process for a customer. The letter-of-credit clerks could take pride in seeing the job through from beginning to end. They were able to communicate directly with the customer, who knew where to turn if problems arose. The number of clerks necessary was reduced by almost two-thirds; the rest were transferred to other jobs within the company.

This example raises the question of job displacement, a very real concern. Karen Nussbaum, director of 9-to-5, a national association of working women, estimated in 1983 that automation would eventually jeopardize 20 million U.S. office jobs. With numbers such as these, retraining and reallocation will be crucial to the millions of employees adversely affected by automation as well as to the efficiency and productivity of automated businesses.

Computers and Health

Several major studies have concluded that working in front of computer terminals for prolonged periods of time can result in health problems. Perhaps the most common health problems associated with computer workers involve the eyes. Secretaries and others who must spend eight hours a day working at a computer or a computer terminal often report blurry vision, fatigue, nausea, or eye strain. In addition, people who stare at green letters on a CRT may see afterimages of the letters in pink when they look away. A 1981 study by the U.S. National Institute of Occupational Safety and Health (NIOSH) showed that clerical workers who used CRTs reported abnormally high levels of visual problems as well as musculoskeletal and emotional problems. Although NIOSH has concluded that sitting in front of a CRT involves no radiation hazard, many people continue to express concern that prolonged exposure to computers could cause cataracts or birth defects in fetuses whose mothers work regularly with CRTs.

Hearing problems frequently result from the high-pitched hums emanating from computers or from noisy air-conditioning units required to cool computer equipment. Many workers are not aware of such noises because of other background noise in the workplace—conversations, typing, traffic around the office, and mechanical noises in the building, for example. Whether or not they are apparent, however, these noises can cause hearing problems and can also contribute to stress, making workers less productive.

Stress is also increased when computers are used to monitor the amount of work being done by clerical workers. Computer systems can count how many times a telephone rings before an employee answers it, how many phone calls an employee handles per hour, and how many keystrokes a typist types per hour. If a worker is having an off day—after recovering from an illness, for example—the computer monitoring system will register only the decrease in productivity and not the circumstances that led to the decrease. Understandably, many workers resent this sort of evaluation.

Emphasis on using computers to increase the quantity of work may threaten the quality of work and of the workplace. While efficiency is a reasonable goal, the quest for efficiency can be pushed to unreasonable lengths. Many employees feel that their inability to reach management goals represents a personal failure; thus, they push themselves, increasing the amount of stress associated with their jobs.

Some situations may be avoided when employees are involved in decision making about the role of new technologies in the office. These employees feel less stress working in an automated office than do their counterparts who were not allowed to participate in planning and decision making. Frequent time away from the computer screen can further reduce stress as well as decreasing the health risks described above.

SUMMARY

Computers and automation are transforming the factory and the office. In the factory, computer-aided design permits engineers to specify designs with advanced graphical tools and in many cases to avoid redesign by using previous designs stored electronically. It also permits them to give a faithful graphical rendering of products without having to physically construct them. Computer-aided engineering permits designers to simulate the behavior of complex systems and avoid costly experiments. Computer-aided manufacturing simplifies the process of planning and coordinating the manufacturing process. These methodologies are being combined to produce highly computerized factories in which the results of design and simulation can be sent directly to the factory floor and used to direct the manufacturing process.

The robot is an important component in factory automation. It remains to be seen how much of an impact robots will have. They are expensive and must be programmed to carry out tasks. Programming of robots is itself labor-intensive. Robots may have a substantial negative impact on employment, although this is uncertain because as they become more widely used, the market for goods may change in ways that increase employment.

The computer is transforming the office in a similar manner. It is changing the way people communicate, prepare documents, update and retrieve information, analyze data, and generally manage their lives. Computers are making it possible to perform office work at home. They are also likely to have a noticeable impact on office bureaucracy as tasks and responsibility for information are reassigned. There is some concern that the technology of the office may have a negative effect on the health of office workers.

FURTHER READING

James S. Albus, "Robots in the Workplace," *The Futurist* (February 1983), pp. 22–27.

Craig Brod, *Technostress* (Reading, Mass.: Addison-Wesley, 1984).

John A. Byrne, "Whose Robots Are Winning?" *Forbes* (14 March 1983), pp. 154, 158.

Vary T. Coates, "The Potential Impacts of Robotics," *The Futurist* (February 1983), pp. 28–32.

Peter F. Eder, "Telecommuters: The Stay-at-Home Work Force of the Future," *The Futurist* (June 1983), pp. 30–35.

"How Computers Remake the Manager's Job," *Business Week* (25 April 1983), pp. 68–77.

Jan Johnson, "Pushing the State of the Art," *Datamation* (February 1982), pp. 112–114.

Laton McCartney, "Teleconferencing Comes Down to Earth," *Datamation* (January 1983), pp. 76–81.

Jonathan Schleffer, "The Automated Factory: More Than the Sum of the Parts," *MIT Technology Review* (February/March 1983), pp. 82–83.

Jonathan Schleffer, "Office Automation and Bureaucracy," *MIT Technology Review* (July 1983), pp. 32–40.

Special Issue on Robotics and Automation, *Computer* (December 1982).

Steve Turner, "When the Robots Punch In," *The Progressive* (August 1983), pp. 22–24.

ISSUES AND IDEAS

1. Describe how CAD/CAM may integrate design and manufacturing processes.
2. Find three companies that extensively use CAD/CAM. Compare and contrast their uses of CAD/CAM.
3. List three advantages and three disadvantages of using robots in the factory.
4. In your opinion, how will factory automation affect employment and the economy? Support your answer.
5. List five electronic tools you would expect to find in an automated office. Which would be used primarily by secretaries? By executives? Equally by both?
6. Describe the two basic types of electronic communication. List three advantages and three disadvantages for each. What steps could be taken to offset the disadvantages?
7. Discuss how technology could change the work environment in an office setting. How might people interact differently? How might their specific jobs change?

Protection and the Loss of Privacy

Where did that knowledge exist? . . .
If all records told the same tale, then
the lie passed into history and became
truth.

GEORGE ORWELL, *1984*

■ Introduction

As advances in technology solve old problems, they typically create new ones. For example, the city of New York, suffering from an excess of horse manure on its streets at the turn of the century, welcomed the automobile. New Yorkers could not have known that one day tens of thousands of people would die each year in automobile accidents or that the internal combustion engine would cause severe pollution. When Alexander Graham Bell developed the telephone, he expected it to be used to transmit important messages; he probably never suspected that his invention could be used to commit computer crimes or to harass people in the middle of the night. At the dawn of the atomic age, proponents of the peaceful use of nuclear power as an alternative energy source did not anticipate the problems of radioactive waste disposal, core meltdown, or the many problems of dismantling reactors that are no longer useful. Similarly, it is unlikely that some of the problems that the computer has introduced could have been anticipated by Charles Babbage in 1850.

One of the computer's greatest assets—speed—makes it dangerous as well as useful. Because a computer can perform millions of operations per second, it can be used to establish complex correlations that would previously have been difficult or impossible to find. For example, given separate lists of information about income levels, political contributions, automobile registrations, and magazine subscriptions, a computer can easily produce the names of all individuals who earn more than $50,000 a year and contribute to the Communist Party or the names of all the people from California who subscribe to *Newsweek* and own a Volkswagen. In the first instance, the information could be used to form a political profile; in the second, the information might help determine the effectiveness of an advertising campaign. One of the most difficult ethical issues raised by the computer revolution is deciding when it is proper to use such information. Consider the following examples.

■ *Item*: General Motors built 1981 Cadillacs with microprocessors to control the air-fuel ratio for maximum performance. If the microprocessor discovered a problem that required the attention of a trained mechanic, a CHECK ENGINE light on the instrument panel would light up. The microprocessor would then keep track of how many times the car was driven faster than 85 miles per hour and how many times the engine was started after the light went on. This information would be available to the mechanic examining the car. Was General Motors protecting itself from having to honor a warranty on a car that had been abused or was the company spying on the consumer? Would a police officer be justified in pulling a driver off the road, checking this device as a matter of course, and writing a ticket if she found the driver had been speeding at some earlier time even if he *wasn't* speeding when he was pulled over?

■ *Item*: Banks, landlords, and others who need to know about a person's credit history buy such histories from companies that specialize in credit reports and summaries. Such reports form the basis for many of the decisions banks make concerning creditworthiness and the granting of loans. Although the companies disseminate huge quantities of information, they usually do little or nothing to verify the accuracy of the information they receive. For example, TRW, a company that processes 35 million credit reports each year, has stated that it has no obligation to check the accuracy of the information it keeps on file.

■ *Item*: The most expensive part of many computer systems is the software. People who belong to computer clubs and other informal organizations often copy programs from one another instead of buying the programs themselves. This deprives software writers of the royalties they should receive from the use of their ideas. So-called software piracy is one of the fastest growing phenomena in the computer field.

■ *Item*: Many computer networks can be accessed by people anywhere in the country. They need only a telephone, a modem, and a terminal. Computer systems require methods of protecting information on the system from unauthorized users. For example, insurance companies need some way of safeguarding the policy and medical records of their customers from competitors or others who might use the information for personal gain.

This chapter deals with privacy and what can be done to preserve it in the computer age. We examine the need to protect information sent by electronic mail, stored in large databases, and transmitted from remote automatic teller machines (ATMs) to nearby banks. We look at efforts to protect sophisticated computer systems and valuable commercial software from intruders, thieves, or pranksters. Finally, we explore the attempts to deal legislatively with the effects of this new technology.

The Need for Privacy and Protection

In our modern society, sensitive audio equipment can pick up conversations in closed rooms tens of miles away. Monitoring equipment can record at great distances all telephone calls made from any given phone, noting the number called as well as the call's duration. Cable television systems can automatically keep track of how long each subscriber's TV set is on and what channels are tuned at what times. Information about credit card purchases and ATM transactions coupled with electronically stored bank records helps form financial profiles of almost all citizens. When all these items are put together, our society has the means to form an electronic profile of the movements, lifestyle, and habits of any individual. Paradoxically, coupled with all of these potential intrusions is the unprecedented amount of freedom of movement and speech that we now enjoy. But we should be aware that such a state could easily change.

In the past, when almost all records were kept on paper, the sheer size and bulk of records prevented them from being stored indefinitely. As more paper records were generated, old records were destroyed. With increased computerization, however, records occupy relatively little space and can conceivably be kept forever. From the moment of a person's birth, extensive medical, academic, marital, legal, and professional records may form a gigantic shadow of that person's existence.

Clearly, some of these records should remain confidential. For example, most of us would not want our bank to publish our financial records. Other examples of information that should be kept confidential include personal, medical, tax, and employment records. Since many of these records contain some of the same identifying information (such as names and social security numbers), it is important to set up a system by which people can gain access only to those pieces of information that are relevant to what they are doing. For example, it may be helpful for your new physician to have access to your medical records, but it would not be appropriate for a potential employer to have access to those same records.

Often, such information is stored in databases or in computer systems. There is a clear need for such data to be protected. Later we examine common protection methods; for now, we focus on two examples that illustrate the need to protect information to preserve individual privacy. Our first example is the automatic teller machine, introduced in Chapter 1; the second is electronic mail, introduced in Chapter 5.

Figure 14.1 shows a typical ATM. It consists of a slot into which the consumer inserts a special ATM card, a set of buttons to determine what type of transaction will take place, a set of numerical buttons to determine the value of deposits and withdrawals, a small CRT to display messages and commands, a withdrawal drawer, a deposit drawer, and a dispenser for receipts. The consumer inserts her ATM card in the slot. The card has a magnetic strip on the back to store information such as

Figure 14.1
A typical ATM. (Photo by Darlene Bordwell)

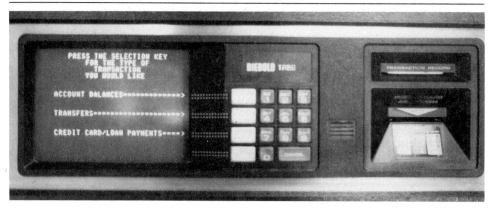

the name of the consumer and the type of account she has as well as the account number. The ATM prompts the customer for the necessary information, such as her personal code number. Once this information is correctly supplied, she is able to complete the transaction.

As you recall, ATMs offer many advantages to banks and their customers. Because ATMs are electronic devices and are directly connected to a bank computer, valuable employee time need not be spent entering data about deposits and withdrawals. The ATM itself generates this information and relays it to the bank's computer during each transaction. Since the ATM makes fewer demands than human tellers, banks consider ATMs a good investment. For the banking public, one of the greatest advantages of these machines is that they don't sleep. Consumers are no longer obligated to bank during "bankers' hours"—they can now bank whenever they wish.

ATMs are not, however, without problems. There must be some way for ATMs located a distance from the bank to communicate with the computers at the bank, notifying them how much to deduct from or deposit into which account. The medium most often used to transport such information is the telephone line. Thus, in theory, anyone who has tapped into a telephone cable can tap into the electronic messages being sent to and from automatic teller machines. This might not pose a problem if the messages were transmitted in code or otherwise disguised.

Unfortunately, most of the ATM data that speed through telephone cables are uncoded and could be tapped into by anyone with a few tools. The fact that most long-distance telephone communication occurs with microwave radio or satellite transmission makes this problem especially acute. Anyone with an antenna can receive such transmissions. Speech, as well as data, is vulnerable, given the reliance of telephone systems on satellites and microwave relays. Encoding data provides some protection. Telephone speech starts as nondigital information; to be securely transmitted, it must first be converted into digital form, then encoded, transmitted, received, decoded, and finally reconverted into its original nondigital form.

It is difficult to encode information so as to guarantee that it cannot be intercepted and decoded by unauthorized listeners. The U.S. Bureau of Standards introduced its data encryption standard (DES) several years ago as a means of ensuring uniformity in the encoding of digital data. Some observers have criticized the DES code as being too easily broken, although they estimate that months might be required to break an individual message.

Even safe transmission, however, does not guarantee the privacy of information. Protecting the privacy of electronic mail, for example, requires protecting the message after it has been sent as well as during the actual transmission. In one variant of electronic mail, the U.S. Postal Service sends electronic mail from one computer (or computer system) to a Postal Service computer near the message's destination. The message is then sent as a piece of paper mail. This service costs the Postal Service and the consumer less than an ordinary letter and usually arrives more quickly. One of the major disadvantages of the system, however, is that no laws restrict access to such messages. With regular letters and packages, rules and regulations specifically state who can open mail, what procedures must be followed, and how it must be reported. No such regulations exist for electronic mail.

Also, the Postal Service (as well as other commercial providers of electronic mail, such as GTE, Tymnet, Graphnet, and Western Union) generally keeps electronic files of all mail messages for at least six months. During that time, the message, complete with the names of the author and recipient, is available to anyone who has access to the computer system storing the files. Simple programs allow any user to receive information about how much mail a person has sent or to retrieve the text of any stored mail messages.

These two examples involve potential interception or alteration of confidential information. In each case, the information could be protected. With the ATM, encryption of the data before transmission would decrease the chances of information being intercepted or falsified. With electronic mail, messages could be stored in such a way that only authorized personnel may read them. We discuss this "shielding" of data in a later section.

■ Protection in Computer Systems

The popular press frequently carries stories about "hackers" who use home computers to violate the security of remote computers. Although these hackers are frequently bright youngsters who treat the violation of computer security as a game, they often damage systems by tampering with information. Unfortunately, any computer that can be accessed legitimately by telephone can be broken into by telephone. Many systems contain too little protection against this threat.

A typical large system requires anyone establishing contact with it to furnish some sort of login identification and a corresponding password. Sometimes users of such systems may mistype their passwords or login identifications, so most systems allow users to try again if they make a mistake the first time. Users occasionally make a mistake the second time they try to type in the information. Rarely does a legitimate user make three consecutive mistakes trying to log in to the system. One of the most sensible things to do to protect a system, then, is to break the telephone connection if three unsuccessful attempts are made to provide a valid login identification and corresponding password. Many computer systems, however, do not do even this. Some systems allow a user unlimited attempts to log in to the system. Hackers, then, can program microcomputers to try every possible password for a given login identification, making access to these systems easier.

Even with systems that provide protection against the average hacker, there are other security problems. Too often passwords are chosen carelessly and can be easily guessed. Some people reveal their passwords to others. Designers of operating systems frequently provide methods for responsible administrators of computer systems (called "superusers") to override certain system protections; such methods may be discovered by hackers. A very popular operating system for large computers was programmed so that knowledge of a single password would grant superuser privileges on any machine running that operating system.

Within many large computer systems, users are required to share the same storage space. Two examples of such systems are the time-sharing systems that characterized an earlier age of computing and the newer networks of workstations that characterize the current age of computing. Clearly, users need to protect their files from being read, modified, or destroyed by others.

The password system makes it possible for each person to have control over the files she creates. Many computer systems allow a user to specify who can have *read-only access* to a file (the ability to see the file), who can have *read/write access* to a file (the ability to see and to modify the file), and who can have no access at all. This method is very useful, for example, when several people are collaborating on a project. All the collaborators can have read/write access to files used in the project, while each collaborator's personal files can be kept private.

When the security of computers is evaluated, cost is an important consideration. The more secure the system, the higher the price. For some systems, such as those that control, monitor, and launch nuclear weapons, it is reasonable to spare no expense where security is concerned. For other systems, a lower level of security is adequate. In all cases, minimal security should be taken. To protect many large computer systems, it is necessary only to make breaking into them so complex, time-consuming, troublesome, or frustrating that hackers will leave them alone.

Large Databases and Privacy

Databases store much of the data kept in computers. Suppose we set up a fictional database with fields for name, sex, and age. Here is an example of a record from our imaginary database:

Name	Sex	Age
Jonathan Quagmire	Male	26

This record seems innocuous, and no great harm would result if the information contained within it were made public. Let's enlarge our database slightly, adding four new items as fields—employer, salary, phone number, and social security number.

Name	Sex	Age	Employer	Salary	Phone	Soc. Sec. No.
Jonathan Quagmire	Male	26	Consultants, Inc.	26,000	863-3300	123-45-6789

By now, the database contains information that should not be public knowledge. Without adequate protections on databases, any person who knows a key piece of information (such as a social security number) can gain access to any record that contained that piece of information. Someone might access our database to determine, say, the names, ages, and home phone numbers of people earning more than $75,000. This information could be useful for those hoping to collect charitable contributions as well as those interested in robbery. Since the information in the database could be used improperly, steps must be taken to prevent unauthorized access to it.

In addition to the general issues of privacy discussed above, there are more specific reasons why data should be protected. Often data from various sources are used to form an abstract picture or profile of a person. If data are not protected, inappropriate material may be included in such a profile. For example, information on political affiliation should not be used in making hiring decisions.

Let's look back to Jonathan Quagmire's record in our database. With *shielding*, all this information would be accessible to Quagmire; he would be able to examine it at will for inaccuracies. To local officials, the name, sex, age, and phone number fields would be available. However, the only information available to most users would be the name and sex fields. Under this system of masking certain fields from unauthorized persons, the privacy of the record is secured. Such a technique becomes much more useful as the number of fields in each record and the types of information represented in the fields increase. You may want to try thinking of twenty or thirty pieces of information that could be obtained about a person and then listing which of these items should be available to the person's family, to co-workers, to a reporter from a local newspaper, to owners of local stores, to the IRS, and so on.

Another problem associated with unprotected data is the possibility that intruders might tamper with the data. Alterations—for better or worse—could be made to bank balances or to academic or employment records. Further, there is the simple but serious problem of data entered incorrectly or entered correctly but not updated.

For example, a database might list Jonathan J. Quagmire guilty of a crime actually committed by Jonathan K. Quagmire; or the database might include the information that Jonathan J. Quagmire had been arrested and charged with robbery but might not include the fact that he had been tried and acquitted. Although Quagmire was found innocent, the database, because it contains only the information on his arrest, suggests he is guilty. There should be some way for people to examine their records and delete such incorrect or misleading information. Unfortunately, most databases do not allow this kind of checking.

The problem of inaccuracy is compounded by the tendency to share information between databases. Thus, a bank record may be shared with a database on renting, and the information will become part of a record in the renting database. The renting database may then be accessed by a credit-rating database; so the original information will become part of a third database. This process can conceivably continue indefinitely, with a record from a single database becoming part of many other databases and eventually part of the officially accepted truth. Clearly, this may cause problems if the information in the first database is incorrect.

Suppose, for example, that the bank database incorrectly lists Jonathan Quagmire as owing $75,000 in back payments of loans. This information is passed to a database on apartment rentals and then to a credit-rating database. When Quagmire decides to move into a larger apartment, his prospective landlord checks with the credit-rating service and decides that Quagmire, despite a record as a perfect tenant, would be a poor risk since he owes a bank $75,000.

Of course, Quagmire is bound to discover the bank's mistake when he reads his monthly statement. After a great deal of negotiating, he will probably get his record in the bank database corrected. But databases that share information with other databases are not required to share corrections of such information. Even after Quagmire has corrected the information about himself in the bank database, incorrect information will still exist in both the rental database and the credit-rating database. When Quagmire returns to the landlord of the new apartment, a second credit check will produce the same result as the first, based on the same incorrect information. This is a frustrating situation, but one that is unlikely to improve without specific legislative guidelines covering information stored in databases.

The above example illustrates the trust that many people place in information stored in a computer. People often believe that information stored in a computer is inherently more valuable than information found in other places. Of course, data do not suddenly gain legitimacy simply by being stored in a computer. All information, whether stored in computers or elsewhere, is only as good as its source; losing sight of this fact can have tragic results. In *The Rise of the Computer State*, David Burnham offers the following illustration: In the spring of 1969, U.S. Secretary of Defense Melvin Laird and the Chairman of the Joint Chiefs of Staff Earle Wheeler signed a top-secret memorandum directing the U.S. Air Force to falsify records about B-52 raids against Cambodia. The memorandum ordered that a computer program process bombing reports so that raids against Cambodian targets would appear to be raids against Vietnamese targets. Computer-generated bombing summaries were later submitted to the Senate Armed Services Committee as proof that the United States was not bombing Cambodia. Because the information came from a computer, many people assigned it more value than it deserved. Not until four years later did the U.S. Congress learn about this attempt to use computers to lie. If falsehoods—or even inaccuracies—are programmed into computers, the information the computers produce will also be false. This point, obvious as it may seem, is vital to any discussion of databases and privacy.

■ Databases and the Law

Fortunately, a few specific legislative guidelines covering databases do exist. In an amendment to the U.S. Crime Control Act of 1973, Congress ruled that (1) criminal history information disseminated with the use of federal funds should contain conviction as well as arrest information; (2) procedures should be changed to keep such information as current as possible; and (3) information should be used only for law enforcement, criminal justice, and "other lawful purposes." However, a questionnaire distributed by the U.S. Office of Technology Assessment in 1980 determined that 80 percent of the states had never audited their criminal history records to determine either how current or how accurate the records were.

Another attempt at the federal level to alleviate some of the problems caused by new technologies was the Privacy Act of 1974. In its original form, the act would have applied to all firms that use databases to keep records. However, the law eventually enacted applied only to federal agencies and private organizations that do business with federal agencies. Instead of creating a permanent independent commission to study new technology and issues of privacy, Congress created a temporary group to study information systems and to make recommendations for future legislation.

The Privacy Act does provide protections to individuals that represent some improvement over the unlegislated anarchy that previously reigned. Federal agencies, under the law, can collect only information that is directly relevant and necessary to ongoing investigations. To the greatest extent feasible, this information should be obtained directly from the individual about whom the information is sought. Federal agents are required to inform the individual (1) why the information is being sought, (2) how the information will be used and disseminated, (3) what penalties would be imposed if the individual refused to cooperate, and (4) under what authority the information is being sought.

Some countries have legislative guidelines far broader than those in the United States. One such country is Sweden. Under legislation dating back to 1973, Sweden has set up a central organization to deal with privacy issues related to computing. This organization, called the Data Inspection Board (DIB), is headed by a director general who is given a lifetime appointment as a way of protecting the board from political pressures.

The DIB oversees the gathering, correcting, and disseminating of information stored in computers. All citizens have the right to demand to see printout of any files kept on them in any databank and to correct any information that is in error. Furthermore, if an error is discovered, the correction must be sent to anyone who was sent the incorrect information. In addition, the DIB has the sole right to grant licenses to organizations wishing to start computerized databanks. (The law does not apply to databases that are not computerized.) Swedish law also grants the DIB the right to revoke licenses of record keepers who do not follow the guidelines. In addition, the DIB has the power to set up specific rules for each record keeper, including what types of records can be kept and what type of action must be taken to safeguard the personal rights of individuals to privacy. For more sensitive types of data, the DIB may require that the record keeper inform the individual each time a change is made in his records.

The United States might do well to follow the lead of Sweden and confront the problem of privacy directly. This area is so important that we cannot afford to ignore it in the hope that it will go away. It may not be enough to rely on the good intentions of people using and compiling databases; we may need definite legal standards for the protection of our privacy.

Software Piracy

At the moment, the most important part of a computer system is the software. In part because the price of the software is still relatively high, many computer hobbyists and users seem to believe that it is reasonable for them to copy the software they buy and share it with their friends. As mentioned earlier, there are some serious problems with such an attitude. The people who write programs devote enormous quantities of time and energy to the creation of new software (just as authors devote much time and energy to the creation of new books). Software authors, like book authors, rely on royalties from the sales of their products to compensate them for their work. To copy software that is copyrighted is to deprive software authors of their fair royalties.

People feel justified in copying software for a number of reasons. Because the field of home computing is relatively young, many computer users think of themselves as pioneers. Pioneers, because they march through uncharted territories, are not bound by the same rules that bind others. Further, in the early days of home computers, a small quantity of software was being manufactured, and the programs that existed often required extensive modification before they would work on particular machines. Early enthusiasts could not choose from a wide selection of software and frequently shared their software with other enthusiasts. Many computer hobbyists became accustomed to receiving software free; perhaps this feeling led many not to feel bound by copyright laws. Nevertheless, the unauthorized copying of copyrighted software is clearly a crime.

Too many discussions of software piracy leave out the ethical question involved, concentrating instead on how pirates operate or on what precautions are commonly taken to stop them. Although crimes involving computers may be different in some respects from other crimes, they still represent unethical behavior. The medium may be different, but the act, that of infringing on someone else's rights, is the same. It is important for us to realize this and to act accordingly.

A reason that many are tempted to copy copyrighted software is that it is often very expensive. Copying software is somewhat analogous to the problem of taping record albums rather than buying them. Buying new records costs about six times more than making high-quality cassette copies of the records. With software, the price differential is much greater. Buying spreadsheet and word processing programs, for example, costs a hundred times as much as copying them. Given such savings, consumers would probably never buy any software if copying it were simple. Fortunately for the manufacturers of software, there are ways of protecting programs. These protection methods, however, are far from perfect.

Protection of Data on Floppy Disks

At the heart of the piracy issue is the floppy disk and the disk drive, the machine that reads material from the disk into the computer or writes material from the computer onto the disk. As long as disks are unprotected, anyone with two disk drives can copy the material from one disk onto a second disk. To combat copying, manufacturers of software have worked diligently to invent new methods of protecting software.

One of the simplest methods is to rearrange the way the information is stored on the floppy disk. Rather than arranging the information sequentially so that all of it appears in order, the programmer can arrange the information nonsequentially. When the disk is read, part of the program instructs the drive head where to find the information needed to run the next part of the program. When the disk is copied, however, the instructions to the drive head would become camouflaged, leaving the copier with a jumbled, unusable program.

This type of protection has proved easy to discover and break, however, and has provided only a temporary delay for software pirates. Although more sophisticated protection systems have been developed, most have eventually fallen prey to those pirates. Indeed, many people who produce software believe it is impossible to design a foolproof protection scheme.

Of course, there are legitimate reasons to copy software. People usually wish to have backups—additional copies of programs they own— in case something should happen to the disk on which the purchased program is stored. Since most programs are protected against copying, it can be difficult for owners of software to make backups. To alleviate this problem, a new software item was introduced in 1980 to the horror of many software manufacturing companies and the delight of many owners of software. The program is called Locksmith, and its basic purpose is to make an exact duplicate of a program regardless of the precautions taken by the manufacturer. Software houses were outraged; no longer did a person need to spend a long time learning how to copy programs—now a computer program would do it for him!

There are two approaches to dealing with the problem of software piracy. The technological approach calls for a search for an unbreakable code, a foolproof method to stop people from copying software. The ethical approach emphasizes the development of a different way of looking at piracy. Instead of regarding it as harmless, we should work to develop the notion that software piracy is wrong; it is nothing but a high-tech method of theft. We should also urge software producers to discourage piracy by decreasing the cost of software.

SUMMARY

This chapter provides an overview of how computers affect privacy and the attempts made to protect this privacy. We illustrate the need for protection of confidential information with two specific examples—the ATM and electronic mail. Information generated by each of these systems can be intercepted or falsified unless it is protected in some manner, such as through encryption. Furthermore, once the information is received, some method, such as shielding, is needed to protect against unauthorized access.

Computer systems are vulnerable to the attacks of hackers and other unauthorized users. Although it is not possible for any system to be completely foolproof, some simple methods of security, such as password protection, can help safeguard the information stored in the system.

Computer databases store much information. When information shared between databases is incorrect, the information needs to be corrected in each database that has shared the information. Failure to do so can result in the dissemination of misinformation; since people tend to believe information more readily when it comes from a computer, this can have serious consequences.

Many computer users break the law by copying software. Because it is easy to copy software, many people ignore the fact that software piracy is stealing. In this case, the technological advances have exceeded the capacity of the law to deal with them. More legislative attempts are needed to clarify legal issues involving computerized information and privacy.

FURTHER READING

David Burnham, *The Rise of the Computer State* (New York: Random House, 1983).

"Electronic Mail," *The Progressive* (November 1982).

Lee Gomes, "Secrets of the Software Pirates," *Esquire* (January 1982), pp. 58–65.

John Wicklein, "How Sweden Keeps Its Computers Honest," *The Progressive* (November 1980), pp. 34–38.

ISSUES AND IDEAS

1. List three advantages and three disadvantages of ATMs. Suggest feasible methods of overcoming the disadvantages.

2. List each point at which electronic mail sent via the Postal Service could be read by unauthorized persons.

3. Discuss the need for protecting computer systems and list several methods that can provide protection. Are these methods foolproof?

4. List as many databases as you can think of that might contain information about you. How much of that information would you want to remain private? How much could be shared with others in business? How much would you not mind seeing on the front page of a newspaper?

5. What is shielding, and how can it be used?

6. In addition to the Privacy Act of 1974, many cities and states have passed laws concerning computerized storage and dissemination of information. What laws exist in your area? What modifications would you propose to those laws?

7. What factors contribute to the problem of software piracy? What measures can you think of that would ease the problem? Who currently "pays" for software piracy? Who should pay?

Afterword

Expectations is the place you must
always go to before you get to where
you're going. Of course, some people
never go beyond Expectations.

NORTON JUSTER, *The Phantom Tollbooth*

The first computers were the province of a small elite of computer specialists. These giant machines required constant care and attention from a new priesthood whose members spoke to their charges in incomprehensible computer languages. All that has changed. Today computers are available to everyone, novices and experts alike. They no longer need constant attention from specialists, and a person does not have to be a computer scientist to make good use of them. Nonetheless, the computer still holds many mysteries. Our purpose in writing this book has been to dispel these mysteries by providing a conceptual understanding of computers, their applications, and their implications.

Using the solid base of knowledge developed in this book, you can now question the various uses of computers and anticipate some of their consequences. To prepare you for this task, we present some important issues that have not yet been raised in this book. They involve our growing dependence on computers and its widespread results. We present these topics to provoke thought and discussion rather than to provide detailed information. The topics represent important issues that each of us should examine as we enter the computer age.

■ The Ubiquitous Computer

Computer technology has certainly affected many more aspects of modern life than Charles Babbage could have dreamed. From his idea for a general-purpose calculating device have sprung machines for writing, drawing, composing, and communicating—activities that at first glance have little to do with calculation.

- *The computer is ubiquitous.*

Computers are everywhere—in our homes, businesses, stores, theaters, and concert halls, in our wristwatches, cars, and telephones. It has become difficult to spend an entire day without some contact, direct or indirect, with a computer. We use computers for functions both mundane and revolutionary; their speed and storage capacity take some of the drudgery out of routine tasks while making possible some activities that could never have been done without them.

- *The computer has become virtually irreplaceable.*

If we were to suddenly remove computers from the planet, our society would suffer a serious setback. Most organizations could not function today without computers. Neither could many individuals whose jobs are linked to computers.

Our dependence on computers is at once fascinating and frightening. It is fascinating to see the evolution of the myriad applications found for computers. It is frightening to observe how thoroughly dependent on them we have become. Unfortunately, most of us are only dimly aware of this historic development, and few of us have the time or energy to pause and reflect on its meaning.

- *Computerization has had many unintended consequences.*

All new technologies have some unintended consequences. These are due largely to the difficulty of predicting the future; they also result from an unwillingness to make projections from the information available. The consequences of widespread computerization deserve, at least, thoughtful attention. In many cases these consequences require action to protect against unwanted side effects.

■ The On-line Computer

An on-line computer is designed to run almost continuously. It has many applications in business, industry, government, medicine, and academia. On-line computers make possible airline reservation systems, automatic teller machines, electronic security systems, and major databases. They must be continuously available if we are to depend on them.

■ *On-line systems have become essential in industry and commerce.*

Many organizations are completely computerized. All information on which they operate is entered and accessed through computers. If the computer is out of order, work comes to a standstill. In an automated office, for example, workers cannot get information, prepare documents, or send or receive electronic mail without a computer; if they keep their calendars on the computer, they will not even be able to schedule appointments. The automated factory falls prey to similar problems when computers control the manufacturing process, schedule production based on sales, order parts, and ship new designs to the factory floor. When the computer stops working, the cost to an automated factory can be staggering, as much as thousands of dollars per minute.

If computers fail often, or if they are sabotaged, a computerized organization may suffer substantial economic losses. In some cases, such as in the telephone business, only the most infrequent failures, measured in mere minutes per year, can be tolerated. Telephone customers are not accustomed to finding the telephone out of order when they wish to place a call. Again, if we are to depend on such services, they must be consistently available.

■ *Malfunction of computers used as controllers may have serious consequences.*

An important type of on-line computer is the controller. Controllers are specifically responsible for overseeing a particular operation. Such computers run petrochemical plants and serve as automatic pilots and cardiac monitors. A petrochemical plant, such as an oil refinery, contains hundreds of active components that must be controlled. If one temperature is allowed to become too high, an explosion may result. Similarly, if a cardiac monitor fails to detect a loss of heartbeat, the person being monitored may die. In these situations computer malfunction is far more than inconvenient or economically debilitating. In these cases, computers and their programs must be designed with reliability as a first priority.

■ Complexity and the Computer

Over time computer software has become more and more complex. Programs are more powerful and therefore longer and more complicated. This trend has come about naturally as the demands on computers increase: users want software to perform more sophisticated tasks, requiring more sophisticated programs. However, complexity can create problems.

■ *Complex programs involve many hands.*

Complex computer programs are necessarily the result of the work of many individual programmers. Each person, responsible for only a small piece of the finished product, may not fully understand how the parts fit into the whole. If the program is large, its intricate interactions may not be fully understood by any one person. Usually, large programs are carefully planned before they are written so that all programmers understand what is expected of their piece of the program. Careful design and supervision can reduce the chances of misunderstandings but cannot eliminate them altogether. A poorly managed design effort involves even greater difficulties; it may be difficult to determine who contributed which piece of a program, and accountability may be lost.

■ *Loss of accountability may encourage lack of responsibility.*

When a large program is found to have bugs, it may be difficult to assign responsibility for them. It is common for individuals who are not held accountable to pay less attention to their work and to feel less responsibility. This tendency can have serious consequences in computer programming, particularly in programs relied on by many people. It is important that programmers take pride in their portions of a group project and take their participation in the project seriously. If programmers do not take full responsibility for their sections, there is a greater probability that the program will contain errors. We have all seen the consequences of errors in administrative computer systems such as those used by banks, billing companies, schools, and government agencies. Administrative errors are annoying. However, errors in certain on-line systems can be fatal.

■ *Complex computer systems have a high probability of containing errors.*

Even the most responsible programmers are human, and humans are error-prone. We make typing errors; more seriously, we overlook or fail to anticipate certain situations the program may encounter. Large programs are almost certain to contain errors. Many of these errors can be found through careful testing that involves running the program on many different sets of data and in many different circumstances. No amount of testing, however, can prove that a program is without errors. A program that has run successfully for many years may suddenly encounter an unexpected situation and behave erratically.

■ *Errors in computer programs can have very serious consequences.*

When programs behave unexpectedly, the consequences can be deadly. For example, during the Falklands War between England and Argentina, the British ship *Sheffield* was sunk by a French-made Exocet missile because air-defense computer programmers had not expected the Argentineans to use Exocet missiles and had programmed their air-defense computers to ignore them. A second example is offered by a U.S. fail-safe computer defense system that has mistakenly identified a flock of geese, a rising moon, and a shower of meteorites as fleets of Soviet missiles. A related event occurred when someone plugged a war-games tape into a fail-safe U.S. defense computer, and the computer mistakenly declared that Russia had launched a nuclear attack. The Western world was put on nuclear alert for 6 minutes. When the mistake was found, we were 14 minutes from the moment when nuclear weapons might have been launched.

As these examples indicate, the complexity of computers and their programs can create very real hazards. It is important that we all understand that the human intellect has limitations and that these limitations are reflected in the computer programs we write. We cannot anticipate all possible situations. We must be aware of this fact before we entrust our most crucial decisions to computers.

■ Human Relations and the Computer

Much has been written about the social impact of the computer. Clearly it is changing the way we work, play, do business, spend money, and communicate. The computer is also subtly changing the way we think, communicate, and view the world.

■ *Computers are changing the nature of interpersonal communication.*

Recent technology has provided two new means of communication: electronic mail and electronic messages. When people communicate electronically, they do not express themselves as they do in person or over the telephone or even on paper. Electronic mail tends to be more informal and to contain more colorful language. One explanation for this tendency is that the colorful language helps to compensate for the lack of voice inflection, eye contact, and body language. Another difference between conventional and computer communication is the lack of an established computer etiquette. People send electronic messages that they would never deliver in person. They respond impulsively, failing to entirely take into account the response of the person at the other end. Another difference is that people tend to communicate more democratically electronically; since each has equal opportunity to talk, no one can monopolize the conversation.

■   *Computers are changing the degree of human interaction.*

Some people question how human interaction will be affected by computers. Since we will be able to do more things by computer, we may lose some of the human contact we are used to. The ATM is one example of this: people who routinely use ATMs no longer come in contact with human bank tellers. This may seem a small loss, but what happens when it extends to more and more aspects of life? What of the college student who with her microcomputer and campus computer network can register for courses; use the card catalog; read library books and periodicals; receive, execute, and hand in assignments; communicate with friends and professors; and play games—all without leaving her room? What of the homemaker who can shop, read the newspaper, and bank without leaving her living room? What of the office worker with all the files, programs, and information he needs right at his fingertips? These people become more efficient, but how will they compensate for the lack of human contact?

On the other hand, many people with home computers speak of the friends they have made through electronic communication using telephone lines and electronic news/mail services. They praise electronic interchange because its lack of face-to-face contact permits people to get to know each other without the prejudgments that result from a person's physical appearance and manner.

■   *Computers may change our value systems.*

In his book *Technostress*, psychotherapist Craig Brod worries about the profound and disturbing effect computers have had on many of his clients. As they spent more time working with computers, these people grew to value the computer's virtues—speed, accuracy, and efficiency—and to expect these traits in the people around them. They grew impatient with the behavior of family and friends and often came to prefer the predictable behavior of the machine to the unpredictability of human beings. Brod fears that we may be adapting ourselves to the characteristics of computers rather than striving to make computers behave in more congenial ways. Instead we need to accept computers for the power they give us while continuing to recognize and appreciate our human qualities.

■   *Computers may alter the nature of work.*

The widespread introduction of computers in manufacturing could make human factory workers obsolete. Robots are able to handle many repetitive tasks more safely and efficiently than humans. What will become of the humans whose jobs are eliminated? What will happen to their families? Unless new jobs are created, displaced workers may suffer severe hardship.

If computer technology causes widespread unemployment, we may be forced to redefine our concept of work. Aside from the need for income, is work necessary for human fulfillment? Is a 40-hour work week necessary for this purpose? The industrial revolution eventually led to a shorter work week; the computer revolution might do the same. If we have additional leisure time, how we use it may have a profound effect on our society, creating new jobs, new values, and a very different lifestyle.

■ *Will computerization create a "global village"?*

Perhaps Marshall McLuhan's concept of a global village will become a reality. He imagined that television would bring people of different nations together by allowing them to observe each other's cultures and lifestyles. Broadcast television, however, is basically a passive medium observed by many and controlled by a few. The computer, on the other hand, can provide rapid and reasonably inexpensive discourse over large distances. It can also provide the capability to share knowledge and information that heretofore have been impossible to share. The primary limitation, of course, is that in order to participate, one must have access to a computer.

■ Conclusion

Simply put, the computer has the potential to do good or ill. Its ultimate worth depends on how we choose to use it. Like all technologies, computers are neutral. Computers can help educate as easily as they can facilitate crime. They can provide increases as well as decreases in productivity. We must choose how we are going to use the computer, or we will find that the choice has been made for us, and not necessarily in the way that we would have wanted.

We, the authors, are cautiously optimistic about the future. We have seen the computer used to perform beneficial tasks, trivial tasks, and inappropriate tasks. We believe that the future will be neither as rosy as some paint it nor as black as others see it. We welcome not only the computer revolution but the careful thought and planning that human beings must invest to make the computer revolution beneficial to the human race.

Glossary

abacus An ancient calculating device that uses beads strung on wires for addition, subtraction, multiplication, and division.

ability phone A special telephone designed to help some physically handicapped individuals live independently.

absolute pathname The pathname of a file in a hierarchical file system that begins with the name of the root directory.

access To retrieve or examine a piece of information.

accumulator A register in the CPU that contains the most recent result of a computation.

adder A circuit that adds two binary numbers.

address The physical location of a piece of information in the memory of a computer.

administrative systems Computer systems that record information about and possibly oversee the manufacturing process. See *computer-integrated manufacturing*.

AI See *artificial intelligence*.

algorithm A plan for solving a problem on a computer.

ALU See *arithmetic/logic unit*.

analog computer A computer that does its calculations using continuous rather than digital quantities. One example is the measurement of time: a sundial is an analog means of measurement, and a digital clock is a digital means of measurement. See *digital computer*.

analytical engine Charles Babbage's conception for a general-purpose computer.

anticipatory text selection A technique whereby a computer program anticipates the next letter or word in a phrase to help the handicapped communicate.

antilog The inverse of a logarithm; the antilog of a number z is the number x such that $z = \log x$.

arithmetic/logic unit (ALU)   The part of a CPU that performs arithmetic and logic operations.

array   A collection of related items that are accessed by a common name and an integer subscript indicating the position of each item in the array.

array element   A single item in an array.

artificial intelligence   The branch of computer science whose goal is to program computers to act intelligently.

assembler   A program that translates assembly language into machine language. See *assembly language, machine language*.

assembly language   A symbolic representation of machine language with some additional features that are easier for humans to use and understand. Command names and addresses, for example, are mnemonic words instead of sets of binary digits.

assignment statement   A program instruction that assigns a value to a variable.

asynchronous communication   The transmission of data in spurts. Asynchronous communication is slower and cheaper than synchronous communication. See *synchronous communication*.

attribute   In a database, a heading for a particular column or field.

audit trail   A continuously generated history of all changes made to a database, enabling administrators to keep track of the persons using the database and of the changes that they have made.

authoring system   A computer program that assists educators writing CAI programs. See *computer-aided instruction*.

backup copy   A duplicate copy of a computer file. A backup copy can be retrieved and used if anything happens to the original file.

base   A set of digits used in a number system. See *base 10, base 2*.

base 10   The set of digits {0, 1, 2, 3, 4, 5, 6, 7, 8, 9}. Sequences of these digits are used to represent numbers in base 10 (e.g., 21976). See *decimal number system*.

base 2   The set of digits {0, 1}. Sequences of these two digits are used to represent numbers in base 2 (e.g., 10011). See *binary number system*.

BASIC   Beginner's All-Purpose Symbolic Instruction Code; an introductory procedure-oriented programming language designed for beginning programmers.

batch formatter   A computer program that formats a document all at once after the user has inserted formatting commands to specify the way the document should appear. See *interactive formatter*.

batch processing   A means of efficiently using the computer's resources by grouping together computer jobs and running them one right after the other. Programs that are batch processed cannot be run interactively but must have all of their data specified before the program is submitted to the computer.

binary digit   A digital quantity that can have one of two distinct values, such as 0 or 1 or True or False. See *bit*.

binary memory cell   A device that can store a binary digit.

binary number   A number represented by binary digits.

binary number system   A number system that represents all numbers by using binary digits.

binary string   A sequence of binary digits.

bit   An abbreviation for binary digit, a symbol that can have one of two values, typically 0 and 1 or True or False.

bitmap   A complete bit-by-bit representation of the display screen of a computer.

block comment   In a computer program, a multiline comment set off from the rest of a program and surrounded by special characters. See *comment*.

Boolean algebra   A type of logic concerned with statements that are either true or false. Boolean algebra provides rules to determine the truth or falsity of compound statements, which consist of simple statements combined by Boolean operations such as AND, OR, and NOT.

boot To turn on a computer system and initialize it.

bottom-up approach A method of problem solving that works toward a solution of a large problem by combining solutions to subproblems. See *top-down approach.*

brute force method An unstructured, spontaneous method of problem solving.

buffer An internal storage area where intermediate results of an operation can be temporarily stored.

bug An error in a computer program or computer circuit.

byte 8 bits.

CAD/CAM See *computer-aided design/ computer-aided manufacturing.*

CAE See *computer-aided engineering.*

CAI See *computer-aided instruction.*

carry bit In binary arithmetic, the bit that is carried over to the next column in an addition.

cathode ray tube (CRT) A tube with phosphor-coated screen containing an electron gun that illuminates points on the screen when the gun is on and is directed at the points. CRTs are used as television screens and as computer display screens.

cell A place in an electronic spreadsheet (referred to by specifying its row and column) where a label, a value, or the result of a computation can be entered.

central processing unit (CPU) The part of the computer that processes data by following the instructions of a computer program.

chief programmer The person responsible for the conceptual integrity of a program written by several people.

chip A small piece of silicon containing many miniature transistors made of semiconductor materials that are combined into logic circuits.

CIM See *computer-integrated manufacturing.*

circuit A collection of logic gates, such as AND, OR, and NOT gates, interconnected to

perform some task, such as the addition of two binary numbers. Gates can be implemented with electromagnetic relays, semiconductor materials, and many other technologies.

CMI See *computer-managed instruction.*

code A collection of programming language statements.

code generation The process of translating a program written in a programming language into machine language. See *machine language.*

collision-based network A type of computer network in which every user is connected to every other user. Messages are broadcast when a user does not hear another user transmitting and collisions can occur because of the delay in receipt of messages across the network.

Colossus The computer invented at Bletchley Park, England, during World War II for deciphering messages transmitted by the German military.

combinatorial explosion The exponential growth in a quantity by successive multiplications. It makes the search for some computer solutions impossible.

command processor In an operating system, a program that accepts commands from a user, interprets them, informs the user of illegal commands, and executes the valid commands.

comment A line in a program that helps a user understand what the program is supposed to do; comments are written for humans and are not executed by a computer.

compile To translate an entire program into machine language. See *machine language.*

compiled language A programming language that must be compiled before it can be run by the computer.

compiler A program that translates an entire program from a high-level language to machine language at one time. See *high-level language, machine language.*

complete adder A circuit composed of a series of full adders, used to add two multidigit binary numbers. See *full adder.*

computer A device that can take in, store, process, and return information and whose activities are controlled by a program.

computer-aided design/computer-aided manufacturing (CAD/CAM) The application of computers to all aspects of design as well as to the implementation of computer designs in the manufacturing process.

computer-aided instruction (CAI) The use of the computer as an aid or replacement for traditional instruction. See *dialog.*

computer graphics A field concerned with the generation by computer of graphs and pictures.

computer-integrated manufacturing (CIM) An approach to manufacturing that integrates CAD/CAM, factory automation, and administrative systems. See *computer-aided design/computer-aided manufacturing, factory automation, administrative systems.*

computer-managed instruction (CMI) The management of classroom instruction by a program on a computer. See *computer-aided instruction.*

computer-aided engineering (CAE) The use of computer-aided design in engineering analysis.

conceptual model A description of the way a particular computer system appears to operate from the user's point of view.

condition A program statement that is either true or false. The value of a condition can determine one of two courses of action. For example, it can determine whether or not a loop is to terminate, or it can select one of two branches in a program.

conditional branching A process of choosing one of two courses of action depending on whether a condition is true or false.

constant A fixed piece of information used by a computer program. Constants, unlike variables, cannot change values during the program's execution.

control character A character typed by holding down the CONTROL key while striking another key; often referred to with the symbol ^ and a character: ^P.

control paths Paths in a CPU along which messages are sent to and from a control unit as the control unit directs the activity of the CPU.

control unit A special circuit in the CPU that interprets and executes each instruction.

core memory An early type of primary memory consisting of small magnetizable donut-shaped pieces.

coupling A relationship between procedures. Two procedures are said to be coupled if they depend closely on each other. See *input/output (I/O) coupling.*

CPU See *central processing unit.*

crash A term commonly used to describe a computer breakdown.

CRT See *cathode ray tube.*

cryptography The enciphering and deciphering of messages in secret code.

cursor A blinking line, solid rectangle, arrow, or other marker used to indicate the user's current position on a computer display screen.

cursor movement key A special key on a computer's keyboard usually labeled with an arrow that causes the cursor to move in some direction when depressed.

cut To remove a block of material from a file, perhaps for pasting elsewhere in the file.

data definition language A programming language used to determine which information stored in a database specific users can look at and which information they can change.

data paths Paths along which data is sent within a CPU. Typically the data move between registers, a memory, and an ALU. See *arithmetic/logic unit, central processing unit, memory, register.*

data tablet and stylus See *stylus and data tablet.*

data type A type of data, such as a string, a real number, or an integer.

database A collection of data organized to be accessible to users of a computer. See *hierarchical database, network database, relational database.*

database administrator The person who has overall responsibility for a database management system.

database management system (DBMS) A computer system consisting of a database, software to operate it, and a language with which to retrieve or change items stored in the database.

DBMS See *database management system.*

debugger A program used to help locate the bugs, or errors, in a program. See *bug, debugging.*

debugging The discovery and correction of errors in a computer program.

decimal number system A number system that represents all numbers in base 10. See *base 10.*

declaration In some programming languages, the act of defining what type of data a particular variable will contain.

decoder A logic circuit that translates the address in the memory address register (MAR) into a command to the RAM to select the register whose address is in the MAR. See *memory address register, random access memory.*

decryption The process of taking an encoded message and reconstructing the original message.

default drive The disk drive that a computer uses by default if none is specified; usually drive A.

definite loop A loop that specifies in advance the number of times it will be used.

demodulator A device that receives analog information transmitted by a modulator and converts it into digital form. See *modulator, modem.*

dialog A sophisticated CAI program that tutors a student in a Socratic style, asking questions designed to lead the student through some material. See *computer-aided instruction.*

difference engine A mechanical computer built by Charles Babbage in the early nineteenth century to automatically compute and print large tables of numbers needed by astronomers.

digital An adjective that refers to quantities that assume a fixed number of values, such as 0 and 1 or True and False.

digital computer A computer in which all quantities that are received and computed are digital, that is, they assume one of a small set of values, such as 0 and 1 or True and False. See *analog computer.*

directory A classified list of names. A file directory consists of a classified list of filenames stored in a computer.

disk An object shaped like a disk used to store information, usually magnetically.

disk drive A device to store and retrieve information from a disk.

divide and conquer A method of problem solving in which the problem is broken down into a small number of easily managed subproblems.

dot command A formatting command used by some word processors. Placed in a textual file, the command starts with a period at the beginning of a line. (.pp is a dot command that indicates the start of a new paragraph.)

editor A computer program used to create and change documents electronically. Editors exist for use with text, graphics, and programs.

editor/formatter An editor that also formats a document on the screen to give some semblance of the printed document. See *editor.*

electromagnet A coil of wire wrapped around an iron bar that acts as a magnet when electrical current is passed through the wire.

electromagnetic relay A mechanical switch controlled by an electromagnet. Early computers were made out of electromagnetic relays.

electromechanical device A device that has electrical and mechanical components; a relay is an example of an electromechanical device.

electron gun The device in the back of a CRT that shoots electrons onto the screen, thereby producing a picture. See *cathode ray tube.*

electronic computer A computer constructed from electronic components, such as vacuum tubes and transistors. See *transistor, vacuum tube.*

electronic document The contents of an electronic file, such as a textual document, a graphics document, or a program.

electronic mail Messages sent electronically between computers.

electronic spreadsheet A computer program that displays on a screen a table that looks much like a conventional spreadsheet. The electronic spreadsheet simplifies the entry and computation of data and makes it possible for the computer to redo calculations immediately any time data are changed. See *spreadsheet.*

encryption The process of encoding a message so that it is incomprehensible to anyone who does not have the information necessary to decrypt it. See *cryptography, decryption.*

encrypted password A password that is encrypted so that the operating system can identify it but so that it is difficult or impossible for a human to do so. See *encryption, password.*

example value A means of requesting an operation from a relational database by showing by example the desired outcome.

experiential learning The process whereby a student learns through experimentation and discovery. Compare *structural learning.*

expert system A sophisticated computer program or system that incorporates knowledge from many experts in a given field.

external storage Any medium outside the computer that can store information so that it can be read by the computer; examples include magnetic tapes, magnetic disks, punched cards, and punched tape. See *internal storage.*

factory automation The use of computers and robots in the process of manufacturing products.

fetch-and-execute cycle A cycle of computation performed by a CPU when running a program that has been stored in the memory of a computer. An instruction is fetched from memory, executed, and then another cycle is begun.

field In a record, a storage place for a particular type of information. In a relational database, a particular column. See *record, relational database.*

file A storage area for an electronic document. Each file has a unique filename to identify it.

file system A set of commands and programs to manage files on a computer.

filename extension The portion of a filename that indicates what type of information the file contains. For instance, a filename extension might specify if the file is a program in a particular language, a word processing file, or a list of operating system commands. Also called a *secondary name.*

fill command A graphical editor command to fill in a region with a specific color or pattern.

flat directory A file directory in which all the filenames are listed under one heading. Compare *hierarchical directory.*

flip-flop A memory cell made of logic circuits each of which can store one binary digit.

floppy disk A secondary storage device consisting of a flexible piece of plastic with a magnetic coating on which data can be stored. Floppy disks are typically used with microcomputers and can store less information than hard disks. See *hard disk.*

flow of control The order in which instructions in a program are executed.

format To place certain information on a blank disk or tape so that an operating system can subsequently store files on it.

formatter A computer program that formats textual documents to be displayed on a screen or printed on paper. See *editor/formatter*.

full adder A circuit that can add two digits and a carry to produce a sum and a carry. See *adder*.

full-screen editor A type of editor that allows the user to examine a full screen of text at a time and to make changes at any point on that screen.

function A specific name for a series of steps in a program.

general-purpose computer A computer that can be programmed for a great variety of tasks. See *special-purpose computer*.

gigabyte A billion bytes. See *byte*.

glossary A collection of comments that explain or define the variables used in a computer program.

graphical editor A program to create and modify a picture or drawing on a computer screen. See *layout editor*.

graphics See *computer graphics*.

grid gravity A graphical editor that helps a designer align objects in a drawing by pulling the cursor to grid points on the screen.

hand simulation The process of manually working through a computer program to locate an error.

hard disk A secondary storage device consisting of an inflexible disk with a magnetic coating on which data can be stored. Hard disks can store much more information than floppy disks. See *floppy disk*.

hard copy A printed copy of a document stored in a computer. See *soft copy*.

hardware The physical components that make up a computer.

head The device in a disk or tape drive that reads and writes information to and from a disk or tape. See *disk, disk drive*.

header comment A comment at the beginning of a computer program explaining what the program does and how it works. See *comment*.

hierarchical database A type of database in which the data are organized as a collection of trees, resembling family trees, with information stored on various branches.

hierarchical directory A file directory in which files are contained in subdirectories, so that they can be organized by category for easy retrieval. Subdirectories can contain files and/or subdirectories. See *directory*.

high-level language A programming language that uses concepts more easily understood and used by humans than are concepts in machine languages. Programs in high-level languages must be translated into machine language before they can be run. See *low-level language, machine language*.

home directory A user's primary file directory, through which subdirectories are accessed. See *directory*.

I/O processor A CPU that takes some of the load away from a principal CPU by processing input and output (relatively slow operations), thereby freeing the more powerful CPU for actual computation. See *central processing unit*.

icon A user-friendly device in some computer programs by which commands are represented as small pictures on the computer screen. Icons are often used in menus to represent actions that the user can select.

indefinite loop A loop that doesn't specify in advance how many times it will be executed but that has some means of determining when to stop execution. See *loop, definite loop*.

initialize To assign an initial value to a variable.

in-line comment A comment contained in a line of a program with a program statement. See *comment*.

input Information entered into a computer; to enter information into a computer.

input statement A programming statement that instructs the computer to retrieve information (either from another file or from a user sitting at a terminal).

input/output (I/O) coupling The use of two procedures such that the output of one procedure is the input to the other. See *coupling.*

instruction A single command in a programming language.

instruction register A special register that contains the current instruction to be executed. See *register.*

integer variable A variable containing an integer, such as 1, 5, − 16. See *variable.*

integrated circuit A collection of very small logic gates on a chip. See *chip, large-scale integration/very-large-scale integration.*

interactive Allowing users to communicate with a computer system, program, or language while they are using it.

interactive formatter A computer program that formats the document as it is being created or edited. Compare *batch formatter.*

interactive language A computer language that permits the user to communicate with a program while it is being run.

internal storage Storage space or memory inside a computer that is actively used by the computer. See *external storage.*

interpreted language A programming language that is run through an interpreter before it is executed. See *interpreter.*

interpreter A program that translates statements one at a time from a high-level language to machine language.

invoke To request the execution of a program or command.

job control language A language that allows a user to specify which programs are needed to run a specific job.

join In a database management system, the process of combining portions of two tables to form a new table.

joystick A pointing device consisting of a stick held in a base for use with a computer terminal. To move the cursor on the computer screen, the user moves the stick in the appropriate direction. Joysticks are common pointing devices for video games. See *cursor.*

K See *kilobyte.*

keyboard A set of labeled switches that allow a user to communicate with a computer; generally it resembles a typewriter keyboard.

keyword A word in a language reserved for a specific purpose, such as LOAD, STORE, ADD, JUMP, GOTO, FOR, WHILE.

kilobyte 2^{10} bytes = 1,024 bytes. A kilobyte is a measure of the capacity of a storage device or computer and is abbreviated by the letter K (e.g., 32K = 32 kilobytes). See *byte.*

large-scale integration/very-large-scale integration (LSI/VLSI) An integrated circuit with a very large number of circuit elements in a very small space. See *integrated circuit.*

latency The time required to retrieve a piece of information from a disk.

layout editor A graphical editor for creating and manipulating drawings. An object in a drawing can be defined and moved around without losing the part of the picture obscured by the object before it is moved. See *graphical editor, paint system.*

lexical analysis A process in which the text of a program is scanned and its components are identified according to their type, such as a name, an operator, or a keyword.

lightpen A device used to draw on or point to a computer screen. The lightpen is placed on the surface of the screen and its position is sensed by a light detector in the pen itself.

line editor A text editor that can edit only one line of text at a time. Line editors have been largely replaced by full-screen editors but are used to edit programs on many home computers. See *full-screen editor.*

line number A number identifying the position of a line in a file.

listing A collection of the statements in a program.

literal A fixed string of characters that is

used by a program but that is not stored in a variable. Each time the program is run, the literal has the same value. A literal is printed exactly as it appears in the program.

logarithm A property of numbers; the logarithm or log to the base b of y ($\log_b y$) is defined as the power to which one must raise b to get y.

logging in/logging on The process by which a user enters a multi-user computer system by specifying a computer account number and password. See *password*.

logging out/logging off The process by which a user leaves a multi-user computer system by signing off.

logic circuit An electronic circuit consisting of logic gates and intended to perform logic operations such as AND, OR, and NOT.

logic gate The most basic element in any digital computer; typical logic gates are AND, OR, and NOT gates.

logic operation A Boolean function such as AND, OR, or NOT.

logic programming Computer programming in mathematical logic. PROLOG is a programming language for this purpose.

loop A set of commands to be repeated by a computer program again and again.

loop counter A variable that keeps track of the number of times a loop has been executed.

low-level language A language with instructions very similar in complexity to the instructions understood by the hardware of a computer. See *high-level language, machine language*.

LSI/VLSI See *large-scale integration/very-large-scale integration*.

M See *megabyte*.

machine language The program instructions read and executed by the hardware of a computer; machine language instructions consist of strings of ones and zeros. See *high-level language, low-level language*.

macro A single command that substitutes for a series of commands. In a formatting program, a macro command might replace a series of dot commands so that the same action could be performed with less typing.

macro language A collection of macros.

macro preprocessor The program that replaces each macro with the series of commands it represents.

magnetic domain A small region on a magnetic disk or tape that can be magnetized to represent either a one or a zero.

mail system A computer system whereby users can send, read, and respond to electronic mail. See *electronic mail*.

mainframe A multipurpose computer that can be accessed by many users simultaneously through terminals. Mainframes differ from minicomputers in that they are designed to handle more users and typically employ a special CPU (called an I/O processor) to handle input and output. They thus provide efficient service to a large number of users. See *I/O processor, minicomputer*.

mainline The main part of a computer program, which calls on procedures at the appropriate time.

MAR See *memory address register*.

mark character A special character in a word processing system used to designate a specific block of text so that it can be moved, copied, or deleted.

mask A stencil or pattern used in producing microchips; one mask is used for each layer of material applied to the chip.

MDR See *memory data register*.

means-ends analysis A method of problem solving used in artificial intelligence in which a program has a current state and a goal state and evaluates all possible successor states to see which is more likely to move it toward its goal. If the program discovers that it is moving away from its goal state, it will backtrack to a previous step and choose another path.

megabyte 2^{20} bytes = 1,048,576, or about one million, bytes. Abbreviated M: 3M = 3 megabytes. See *byte*.

memory A place in a computer where information is stored.

memory address register (MAR)   The register within a RAM that indicates where in memory data are coming from or going to. See *random access memory, register.*

memory data register (MDR)   The register within a RAM that holds a piece of information that is being stored or retrieved. See *random access memory, register.*

menu   A list of possible commands in a computer program. Often a choice can be selected from a menu by moving the cursor to the choice and pressing a key.

microcomputer   A small computer designed for a single user and widely used in homes and small businesses; also called a *micro.*

microprocessor   A miniature CPU on a chip. See *central processing unit.*

mill   Babbage's term to describe the part of the analytical engine where computations took place.

minicomputer   A multipurpose computer designed to be accessed by many users simultaneously through terminals. Minicomputers are not as powerful as mainframe computers and are designed to accommodate fewer users at a time. See *mainframe.*

mnemonic   Referring to a name or group of characters chosen to remind the user of its purpose. Variables are often given mnemonic names.

model   A simplified representation of reality designed to imitate or predict reality. See *simulation.*

modem   A modulator and demodulator combined into one device. Modems are used to communicate digital data over lines that accept only analog signals, such as telephone lines. See *demodulator, modulator.*

modulator   A device to convert digital data to analog form so that it can be transmitted over analog lines such as telephone lines. See *demodulator, modem.*

mouse   A handheld pointing device whose motion over a surface moves a cursor on a computer screen. Many such devices have a ball underneath that rolls as the mouse moves. A mouse typically has buttons on top to select actions.

multiprogramming   The ability of a computer to quickly switch from running one program to running another. This can be done to give the appearance to several users that they each have the computer entirely to themselves or simply to use the idle time on a CPU while it is waiting for input.

music compositional facility   A computer program or system typically consisting of a "piano" keyboard, a computer, a CRT to display musical notation, and an audio output device to produce sound.

natural language   Language that humans use to communicate.

nest   To place one programming statement within another; for instance, to place one loop within another or one IF statement within another.

network   A means of communication between computers.

network database   A database that is distributed over a network of computers. See *database.*

noise   Any disturbance that interferes with data transmission.

nonprocedural language   A programming language in which the programmer tells the computer what to do, not how to do it.

numeric variable   A variable containing a number. See *variable.*

object-oriented language   A programming language that views the world of the program as a set of communicating objects each having its own internal methods of operation on data.

off-line programming   A method of programming a robot with a CAD/CAM workstation in which the robot motion is simulated and displayed graphically on a computer screen. See *on-line programming.*

on-line programming   A method of programming a robot by manually taking the robot through each of its movements. See *off-line programming.*

one-way function   See *trap-door function.*

on-line testing Educational testing done at a computer or terminal.

operating system A set of programs to control a computer.

optimization In a compiler, the process of modifying a program to improve its efficiency without changing its meaning.

output Information produced by a computer. See *input*.

overstriking In a word processor, replacing old text by typing new text directly over it.

paint system A graphical editor that provides direct control over pixels. It views the screen as a collection of pixels and allows the user to alter pixels directly, with a pointing device such as a mouse or stylus and tablet. See *graphical editor, layout editor, pixel*.

parallel arrays Two or more arrays in which elements with the same subscript correspond to one another. See *array*.

parameter A variable whose value can be read by a procedure or function.

parsing The process of subdividing each program statement into its syntactical elements in a programming language.

Pascal A high-level procedure-oriented programming language designed to encourage structured programming.

pass Action occurring on only one part of a problem after the problem has been broken down into subproblems; an iteration.

password A secret code used to ensure that a user is authorized to use a particular computer account.

password file A file containing the account numbers and corresponding passwords of users on a computer system.

password verification A means of determining that a password given by a user is valid.

paste To place text cut from a file (and thus stored in a buffer) elsewhere in the file. See *cut*.

pathname A sequence of characters that describes where a particular file is located within a hierarchical file directory.

pattern recognition The recognition of patterns using computers.

peripheral memory External storage that can be physically separated from the computer, such as disks and tapes.

permutation A one-to-one translation from a set of characters to another.

personal workstation A small, self-contained computer with graphics capabilities and a pointing device that can be linked to other workstations through a computer network.

photolithography The technology used to imprint very small wires and transistors on a microchip. See *chip*.

pipeline An operating system facility that allows the output of one operation to be used as input to another operation without explicitly creating intermediate storage files.

pixel Picture element; a single dot in a computer display screen. A pixel is the unit used to measure the resolution of a computer screen.

pointillism A painting technique popular with Impressionist painters in which a painting is constructed out of many small dots. Computer graphics uses a similar technique to construct pictures out of pixels. See *computer graphics, pixel*.

pointing device A handheld device that allows a user to quickly move a cursor to a place on a display screen. Examples of pointing devices are a mouse, joystick, and stylus and tablet.

pop-up menu A menu that is not visible on the screen until it is called on.

predicate function A function that returns a value of true or false. See *function*.

prefix notation Notation for commands in which the name of the command precedes the information on which it operates.

preprocessor See *macro preprocessor*.

primary field One entry in each database record that is different for each record. The entry in a primary field is used to identify the record.

primary memory A fast memory directly accessible to the CPU in which each piece of information can be accessed in the same amount of time.

primary name The portion of a filename that distinguishes it from another filename; the name of the file. See *secondary name.*

procedural representation In expert systems, knowledge about how to solve a problem. See *expert system.*

procedure A method used to solve a problem; in computer programming, a block of programming code that can be executed by using the name of the procedure.

procedure-oriented language A language that conceptually views a program as an extended CPU that takes data from memory, operates on them, and returns the results to memory.

process planning The use of a CAD/CAM system for the planning of a manufacturing process such as the production of a new product. See *computer-aided design/ computer-aided manufacturing.*

production system In artificial intelligence, knowledge represented by conditions that trigger responses when satisfied.

profile An abstract picture of an individual formed by information stored in a database.

program A series of instructions that tells a computer what to do.

program counter The register within the CPU that holds the place currently running in a program.

program editor A computer program used for the creation and modification of other programs. Such editors may have knowledge of a particular programming language. See *syntax-directed editors.*

projection In a database management system, the process of selecting columns from one table to create another. See *database management system, selection.*

prompt A message from the computer to a user consisting of characters in a display. A prompt usually indicates to the user that the computer is ready to receive a command or data or that the user has made an error.

pseudocode An outline for a solution to a problem written in English but having the rough form of a computer program.

query language In a database, a language in which users specify information that is to be retrieved from or stored in the database.

RAM See *random access memory.*

random access memory (RAM) A type of storage in which each piece of information can be accessed quickly and in the same amount of time as any other.

raster graphics A type of computer display in which the picture is drawn by an electron gun that sweeps out rows from top to bottom of the display. Each row contains a sequence of dots or pixels. See *pixel, vector graphics.*

read To retrieve information from the memory of a computer or from an input device such as a keyboard or mouse.

read access Permission granted to a user to examine the contents of a file.

read-only privileges The ability of a user to examine but not change the contents of a file.

read-only memory (ROM) Storage in which information can be read but not altered in any way.

read/write access Ability of a user to both read and modify the contents of a file.

read/write privileges See *read/write access.*

real-number variable A variable containing a real number, such as 10, 0.65, −2.3.

real-time computation A computation in which a number of time-critical tasks are processed as they occur.

record One entry in a database consisting of one or more fields containing information. See *database, field.*

redirection In an operating system, the act of taking input from a nonstandard input source or sending output to a nonstandard destination or both.

redundancy A check against errors in storage or transmission of a message. One form of redundancy is the repetition of a message.

register A storage place for a piece of information in a CPU. See *central processing unit.*

relative pathname An abbreviation for a pathname consisting of the pathname of a file relative to the directory currently being used. See *pathname.*

relational database A type of database that organizes information into tables.

relay See *electromagnetic relay.*

reserved word In a programming language, a word that has a specific meaning in the language. For example, in Pascal the words BEGIN, END, IF, THEN, READ, and WRITE are reserved because they have a certain well-defined meaning in the language. Reserved words cannot be used as variable names.

resolution A measure of the quality of pictures that can be drawn on a computer display. Resolution is measured in the number of pixels per linear or square inch that can be drawn on the screen. High-quality graphics displays are said to have a high resolution; poorer-quality displays (such as television sets) are said to have a low resolution. See *pixel.*

ring network A type of computer network in which all the computers are connected in a ring and information passes from one computer to another until it reaches its destination.

ROM See *read-only memory.*

rule-based language A programming language in which a program consists of a set of rules that must be followed.

run To execute a program; the execution of a program.

scanner A communication device for people with poor motor control; the computer presents a menu of choices, highlighting them one at a time so that the individual can select a choice by making a motion when the desired choice is highlighted.

script In an operating system, a single name representing a collection of commands.

scroll The action of moving a viewing window up or down to see other parts of the file.

secondary memory Peripheral memory for long-term electronic storage of information. See *peripheral memory, primary memory.*

secondary name See *filename extension.*

sector A pie-shaped region on a disk.

selection In a database management system, the process of choosing specific rows from one table to create a new table. See *database management system, projection.*

semantic net A type of knowledge representation system consisting of nodes and links in which related elements are connected by links. Links are followed to locate related information.

shielding In a database, a method that restricts users to viewing only the portion of the database for which they are authorized.

simulation The use of a model to imitate or predict reality. See *model.*

slide rule An analog calculating device consisting of logarithmic scales plotted on two rulers that slide next to each other. The slide rule is used for multiplication and division.

soft copy The display on a computer screen of information stored in the computer. See *hard copy.*

soft-copy facsimile A formatted version of a textual document displayed on a computer screen rather than on paper.

software Computer programs.

solid modeling The drawing, coloring, shading, and lighting of three-dimensional objects on a computer screen. Solid modeling is used to provide realistic views of a design before it is actually constructed.

soroban A Japanese abacus.

special-purpose computer A computer built to serve one specific function, such as a video game or a calculator. See *general-purpose computer.*

spreadsheet A type of table used widely in

business, consisting of a sheet of paper ruled into rows and columns and used to analyze and display data. See *electronic spreadsheet.*

standard input   Input entered from a keyboard or pointing device.

standard output   Output displayed on a computer screen.

star network   A type of computer network in which several computers are connected directly to a single computer at the center of the network. Communication between computers is via the computer at the center.

state   The current condition of a computer represented by the information stored in its memories and registers.

stepwise refinement   The process of breaking a problem into subproblems one step at a time.

sticky menu   A menu that is always present on the screen. See *menu.*

store   A term used by Babbage to describe the storage space or memory in his analytical engine.

stored-program concept   The storage of a program in the memory of a computer alongside the data on which it operates. Stored programs are executed by fetching the next program statement and then executing it. See *fetch-and-execute cycle.*

stream   A continuous sequence of characters.

stream editor   An editor that treats a file as a continuous sequence of characters rather than as a series of disconnected lines.

string   A sequence of characters—letters, numbers, blank spaces, punctuation marks, and symbols.

string variable   A variable containing a sequence of characters (word). See *word.*

structured learning   Learning that is organized for the student. Compare *experiential learning.*

stylus and data tablet   A pointing device often used for freehand drawing with a graphics system. The stylus resembles a pen or pencil, and the tablet a piece of paper.

The movement of the stylus on the tablet produces a corresponding line on the computer screen.

subdirectory   A directory of files within a directory. See *directory.*

subroutine   A block of program statements that is logically distinct from the rest of the program.

subscript   The number of a specific element within an array, usually enclosed in parentheses or brackets.

sum bit   In a binary adder, a bit that, together with a carry bit, represents the result of the addition of two or three binary digits.

supercomputer   A very fast, powerful, and expensive computer reserved for jobs requiring very large amounts of computational power.

superuser   An administrator of a computer system who has complete control of the computer and complete access to all data on the system.

supervisor state   In an operating system, a condition in which the operating system executes instructions that should not be made available to user programs. It is entered when a user program needs to read or write data. See *read, write.*

switched network   A type of computer network in which a path is created by making connections between intermediate transmission stations. Telephone companies usually provide switched network communications.

symbol manipulation   The manipulation of symbols in an expression by operations such as insertion or deletion of the first symbol in a list or reversal of the symbols in a list.

symbolic expression   A list of symbols.

synchronous communication   The continuous transmission of data between a transmitter and receiver where the receiver tracks the beginning and end of each piece of data. See *asynchronous communication.*

synchronous parallel logic   Logic circuits in which many steps are executed in parallel. See *logic circuit.*

syntactic analysis   Synonymous with parsing. The step performed by a compiler after lexical analysis in which the compiler evaluates the program to check the syntax according to the syntactic rules of the language. See *compiler, lexical analysis, parsing.*

syntax-directed editor   An editor that provides a set of templates for each of the syntactic elements in a programming language. Syntax-directed editors prevent users from entering program statements that are syntactically incorrect.

system monitor   A computer program that supervises the use of the resources of a computer.

systems analyst   A person who defines a problem to be solved by computer and tentatively decides which types of hardware and software are needed. See *programmer, systems designer.*

systems designer   A person who takes the tentative solutions of a systems analyst and carries them to completion. See *programmer, systems analyst.*

tape   A storage medium, typically magnetic, for information. In the early days of the computer, punched paper tape was used for this purpose.

tape drive   A device to store and retrieve information from a magnetic tape.

teleconferencing   The two-way transmission of audio and video signals along with data, pictures, and computer graphics over long distances for the purpose of conducting meetings between groups of people in different places.

terminal   A communication device consisting of a keyboard, a CRT, and electronic circuitry and used to communicate with a computer. See *cathode ray tube, keyboard.*

text editor   A computer program specifically designed to create and modify textual documents.

textual document   Any piece of text.

time slice   A small amount of computer time.

time sharing   A form of multiprogramming in which a CPU is alternately allocated to each of several users to give each the impression that they have the entire machine at their disposal. See *multiprogramming.*

token   The one-word description a compiler assigns to a piece of a program during the process of lexical analysis. See *lexical analysis.* Also a special character that is passed from computer to computer in a ring network to tell computers when they may transmit information. See *ring network.*

top-down approach   A problem-solving method that starts with the problem and breaks it down into smaller problems. See *bottom-up approach.*

touch-sensitive screen   A CRT that is sensitive to pressure. On a touch-sensitive screen, a user can select an action by touching its place on the screen.

track   A circle on a disk, analogous to a groove in a phonograph record. A set of tracks consists of a set of concentric circles.

transistor   An electronic device that can serve as a switch. Several transistors can be combined to form a logic gate. Computer chips are made of microminiaturized transistors and wires. They are much more reliable, smaller, and less energy demanding than either electromagnetic relays or vacuum tubes. See *chip, logic gate.*

trap-door function   A special type of mathematical function that is easy to compute but difficult to invert, even for someone who knows the formula used to compute it. In computer security systems, trap-door functions play an important role by computing the internal representation of passwords. Also called a *one-way function.*

truth table   A list of the conditions under which logical statements (constructed of Boolean functions such as AND, OR, and NOT) are true and false.

Turing test   A test developed by Alan Turing to determine whether a computer could be considered "intelligent." A computer or program would pass the Turing test if a human being could not distinguish between its behavior and that of a human.

turtle　A drawing device used in LOGO, a simple and powerful programming language designed for children.

undo facility　A feature of some editors that permits one or more editing operations to be canceled, returning the text to its previous form.

user view　A part of a database available to a group of users. User views are created using data definition languages. See *data definition language.*

utility　An application program provided with an operating system to perform standard tasks, such as editing or language translation.

vacuum tube　An electronic device developed for radio communication that acts as a switch. It performs the same functions as electromagnetic relays but more quickly. Vacuum tubes were used in early electronic computers such as the Robinson series, Colossus, and ENIAC.

value　The contents of a variable.

variable　A storage place for a specific piece of information.

variable name　The name given to a variable by a programmer.

vector graphics　An early form of computer graphics, in which a picture is constructed out of a series of lines. The endpoints of lines are stored and an electron beam is made to sweep out the lines in sequence. Vector graphics require less storage space than modern raster graphics, but drawings are less realistic since shading cannot be provided. See *raster graphics.*

very-high-level language　A programming language in which the commands are much closer in complexity to natural language statements than to machine language statements. See *high-level language, natural language.*

viewing window　An area on a screen through which a portion of a file can be viewed. For many terminals and computers, this area consists of the entire screen of a CRT; for more sophisticated computers (such as workstations) more than one window may be available so that a user can view different files simultaneously.

wildcard　A special character (often *) that represents an arbitrary string of arbitrary length. When a wildcard is used, it is replaced by an appropriate string. For example, if the string is meant to be the name of a file, the only replacements used are those that will give a valid filename. See *string.*

window　See *viewing window.*

window manager　A program that permits work to be done at once in several different viewing windows on a computer. See *viewing window.*

word　A unit of storage measured in bits or bytes. See *bit, byte.*

word length　The number of bits in a word. Commonly used in reference to computer memories to describe the number of bits in each word of a memory.

word processor　A computer or computer program that facilitates editing and formatting of text.

wordwrapping　A feature of a text editor in which words that overlap the right boundary of a screen are written on the next line. Wordwrapping simplifies the entering of text since text is guaranteed to be split along word boundaries regardless of how it is entered.

work cell　A production station within a factory.

write　To store or place information into memory or on an output device; to communicate with another user at that user's terminal.

WYSIWYG　An acronym for "what you see is what you get," referring to editor/formatters that fully format a document on the screen as it is being edited.

Index

Plate 5
Like many other arts previously executed by human hand using raw materials, Oriental rug design and manufacture has been automated through use of computer graphics. The graphics display processor involved in this rug design allows selection of sixteen different color combinations. (Photo courtesy of Lexidata Corporation.)

Plate 6
In advertising, a growing field for computer artists, images such as this television station logo are the products of a computer program rather than pen, paint or pencil. (Art Director: Richard Taylor, Art Durinski, John Whitney Jr.; Technical Director: Gary Demos. Digital scene simulation by Information International, Inc. Copyright 1980. All rights reserved.)